Covenantal Imperatives

Essays by Walter S. Wurzburger
on Jewish Law, Thought and Community

COVENANTAL IMPERATIVES

ESSAYS BY WALTER S. WURZBURGER ON JEWISH LAW, THOUGHT AND COMMUNITY

EDITED BY

ELIEZER L. JACOBS AND SHALOM CARMY

URIM PUBLICATIONS

Jerusalem • New York

Covenantal Imperatives: Essays by Walter S. Wurzburger on Jewish Law, Thought and Community
Edited by Eliezer L. Jacobs and Shalom Carmy

Printed at Hemed Press, Israel. First Edition.
Layout design by Satya Levine

ISBN: 978-965-524-000-9

Urim Publications
P.O. Box 52287, Jerusalem 91521 Israel

Lambda Publishers Inc.
3709 13th Avenue Brooklyn, New York 11218 U.S.A.
Tel: 718-972-5449 Fax: 718-972-6307, mh@ejudaica.com

www.UrimPublications.com

"We do not begin with extolling the beauty,
goodness or utility of what we have proclaimed.
Our first and foremost concern is its truth.
All other considerations are secondary."

–Walter S. Wurzburger, *God Is Proof Enough*

This collection is dedicated to the memory of

Rabbi Dr. Walter S. Wurzburger (1920–2002)

מוהר״ר שמואל בן בנימין, זצ״ל

In him peace and truth,
wisdom and learning,
simplicity and sophistication
came together.

CONTENTS

PREFACE

BY DR. NORMAN LAMM
CHANCELLOR, YESHIVA UNIVERSITY
ROSH HA-YESHIVA, RABBI ISAAC ELCHANAN
THEOLOGICAL SEMINARY

THE DIFFERENCE BETWEEN thinking and acting, contemplation and action, is no more than common sense. Yet it has proven deserving of concentrated thought by no less a figure than Aristotle, and has since become a staple of philosophical and theological discussion. The Sages of the Talmud too were fully aware of the distinction and debated, at a critical juncture in Jewish history close to two millennia ago, which of the two is superior.

I mention this in introducing this excellent volume of the essays of my late and respected colleague and friend, Rabbi Dr. Walter Wurzburger, because he represented an amalgam of both. His career was conducted on two tracks: the rabbinic pulpit, with its emphasis on the practical, and his university teaching at Yeshiva College, where he had the opportunity to share with his students the fruit of his philosophic thinking.

What is remarkable about his life's work is not that he embraced both the intellectual and the practical, but that he was able to have one influence the other. The two interpenetrated, so that his sermons were serious discourses, though expressed in simple rather than technical terms. They were never frivolous or pedestrian, and his philosophizing was never detached from the real world of flesh-and-blood humans.

This work, conceived and carried out by his loyal disciple Eliezer L. Jacobs, represents a cross-section of the stimulating themes that inspired – one might say agitated – his intellect as a Jewish philosopher.

The twenty-seven essays by our author, for the first time collected in this thoughtful anthology, reveal much of his background. He was a favorite student of Rabbi Dr. Joseph B. Soloveitchik, admiringly called "The Rav," the preeminent thinker of Orthodox Judaism in the twentieth century and the master Talmudist whose lectures for more than four decades at Yeshiva University raised and inspired two or more generations of rabbis and religious thinkers. Dr. Wurzburger was very much at home in the German schools of philosophy, as was Rabbi Soloveitchik, who had studied at the University of Berlin. He received his ordination from the Rav at Yeshiva University's affiliated Rabbi Isaac Elchanan Theological Seminary and his doctorate in philosophy from Harvard. During the years that Rabbi Wurzburger served as a rabbi in the Boston area, he became even closer to the Rav, who made his home in that New England city. Hence a significant number of these essays bear the imprint of his master's thought not only when directly quoting him, but as well in the general tone of so many of his writings. The very issues that engaged Wurzburger's attention are those that concerned the Rav.

Yet it would be a mistake to conclude that our author simply repeated what he had learned at the feet of the Rav with perhaps a change of nuance here and there. In this case, the teacher demanded critical thinking of his students, and this student was too original and creative merely to mouth what was spoon-fed to him.

Rabbi Wurzburger was blessed with a subtle sense of humor and he was always very much alive, never dull. Yet, having lived through the terrible twentieth century with its gory legacy of genocide and the almost successful extermination plans by the evil geniuses of Nazism, he carried with him an underlying sadness that was part an existentialist *Weltschmerz*, part a personality trait which leaned towards a genuine *gravitas* in contemplating human frailty and fate, and part the philosophic pessimism that often afflicts people who take ideas seriously. His intellectual pain and suffering vindicated for me the words of Koheleth (1:18), "He who increases knowledge increases pain." Indeed, there was something of Koheleth (whom Jewish tradition identifies as King Solomon) about my friend Walter Wurzburger: sad, brooding, and wise, as he looked deep into the human condition and, out of profound sympathy and love, gave it his greatest and most precious gift of the sacrifice of his soul's peace of mind.

Rabbi Wurzburger was an important thinker who thought, as it were, with his heart as well as his brain, and this collection is the least that can be done to honor his memory and his achievements.

Norman Lamm
October 10, 2007
28 Tishrei 5768

ACKNOWLEDGEMENTS

BY ELIEZER L. JACOBS

NEARLY EIGHT YEARS AGO, while I was working on a paper for his class at Rutgers University, Professor Chaim Waxman suggested that I get in touch with Rabbi Dr. Walter S. Wurzburger. What began as a simple e-mail exchange evolved into this book.

Throughout those early discussions, one quality I found most striking about Rabbi Wurzburger was his realistic view of the world. By "realistic" I mean his sense of religion as an organic part of a broader ethical and intellectual fabric. To Rabbi Wurzburger, engagement with the world was a Jewish imperative. Nothing was more anathema to him than the thought of using Torah to isolate oneself from interaction with general society. Rabbi Wurzburger's intrepid stances on social engagement were many: he fervently believed in the necessity of secular studies and professional participation in the secular sphere, and he participated in dialogues between Orthodoxy and other denominations of Judaism as well as with other religions. Yet all his positions stemmed directly from his understanding of Halakhah and ethics. He conceived of Torah as communicating essential values of personal and communal responsibility, if only Jewish law were understood in its proper light. I find this statement by Rabbi Wurzburger particularly instructive:

> Religion is neither politics nor business. In the spiritual sphere one cannot settle issues by making concessions. Total commitment is the very essence of a religious attitude. But what is needed is the ability to transcend institutional or denominational concerns in the quest for solutions that will enhance the welfare of the entire Jewish people.... History shows that in various areas of endeavor,

important breakthroughs were achieved once the proper questions were asked.[1]

Rabbi Wurzburger sought to pose questions that would reveal Judaism in all its social, spiritual, and intellectual richness. His essays also suggest the emphasis his philosophy placed on the principle of moderation, a personal leitmotif confirmed in conversations with him and learning about him from others. To be sure, Rabbi Wurzburger's notion of moderation does not take the form of compromise. Rather, he subscribes to the religious approach espoused by his teacher Rabbi Dr. Joseph B. Soloveitchik, who sought to describe "the predicament of the moderate individual." Quoting the Rav, Rabbi Wurzburger explains, "Because [the moderate] perceives the complexities and intricacies of issues, he must forgo the satisfaction of dogmatic certainty that the extremist obtains."[2] Rabbi Wurzburger's idea of moderation represents the most demanding and vibrant form of religious engagement possible.

Rabbi Wurzburger explores this difficult position in several of the essays included in this volume. In the essay "Alienation and Exile," he eloquently states:

> Being Jewish – or better, "not being a Goy" – becomes equated with the ideal of an authentic human life: not to feel at home in the universe because one deliberately elects to remain a foreigner, refusing to become completely naturalized into a full-fledged citizen of the world. In the phrase of Ben Halpern, Jewishness becomes "a ticket of admission to the community of alienated intellectuals."[3]

Rabbi Wurzburger's comprehensive approach addresses both participation in the world and the sense of not fully belonging to it. That complex metaphysic of simultaneous engagement and alienation is what drove me to read more of his essays and to pursue additional discussions

---

[1] Reuven P. Bulka. *The Coming Cataclysm: The Orthodox-Reform Rift and the Future of the Jewish People.* Skokie, Illinois: Hebrew Theological College Press, 1986, 11.

[2] Walter S. Wurzburger. "*Imitatio Dei* in the Philosophy of Rabbi Joseph B. Soloveitchik." In *Hazon Nahum: Studies in Jewish Law, Thought, and History Presented to Dr. Norman Lamm on the Occasion of His Seventieth Birthday,* edited by Yaakov Elman and Jeffrey Gurock, 557–576. New York: Yeshiva University Press, 1998.

[3] Ben Halpern, "A Theological Jew." *Jewish Frontier* (February 1964): 13.

with him. Our exchange ultimately led me to advocate publishing more of his writings, which solidified as the volume you are now holding.

The seven years I have been working on this collection of essays have been both humbling and awe-inspiring. Many people aided me and I would be remiss in not mentioning several. I am deeply grateful to the Wurzburger family for entrusting me with continuing this project after Rabbi Wurzburger's passing. Rabbi Shalom Carmy's guidance, help and expert editorial hand have been indispensable. It was a privilege to work with him. Without Rabbi Carmy, the project would have been impossible to complete. Professor Chaim Waxman, who graciously introduced me to Rabbi Wurzburger, steadily guided me through the editing process and pushed me to bring the book to fruition.

I have been lucky to learn from many outstanding teachers. I would like to give special recognition to a few who have made the deepest impact on me: Rabbis Azarya Berzon; Dr. Emanuel Feldman; Yamin Goldsmith; Naftali Harcsztark and Dr. Michael A. Shmidman – all of whom, perhaps unknowingly, continue to influence my Jewish identity profoundly. I also owe a debt of gratitude to Messrs. Bart Cannon and Joshua Gotlieb.

A special word of gratitude is due to two close family friends, Michael Bierman, editor of *Memories of a Giant: Eulogies in Memory of Rabbi Dr. Joseph B. Soloveitchik*, who directed me to Tzvi Mauer of Urim Publications, and to Janet Shafner, for allowing me to use a portion of her painting "Adam and Eve: The Sparks" on the cover. I appreciate the remarkable foresight that Tzvi has displayed throughout the process. I also appreciate both his patience and his enthusiasm.

To my many friends with whom I have discussed and argued all facets of life: you continue to challenge, entertain and motivate me. I would not be the person I am now without each and every one of you.

I owe the greatest debt to my family. My grandparents, The Honorable Oscar, o.b.m., and Betty Isaacson; Dr. Robert, o.b.m., and Shirley Jacobs; my brother Avi and our parents, Drs. Carl and Anita Jacobs. There is no way to express it other than to simply say, "Thank you."

Elie Jacobs
November 11, 2007
Rosh Chodesh Kislev 5768

INTRODUCTION

BY RABBI SHALOM CARMY

NEAR THE END of Marilynne Robinson's great novel *Gilead,* the narrator, an elderly Iowan clergyman who knows his days are numbered, has considered what he wants done with the thousands of sermons he has laboriously written out in the course of his career. He finally decides that he doesn't want them preserved: "They mattered or they didn't and that's the end of it."

Among the major figures of American Orthodoxy, Rabbi Dr. Walter Wurzburger would have been among the first to sympathize with the Reverend Ames's judgment. His view of the pulpit rabbinate, to which he devoted the bulk of his energies for half a century, allowed little room for self-aggrandizement and self-projection. "They mattered or they didn't," and if they did matter, if the cumulative impact of his preaching and many of his individual sermons was sufficient to alter human lives for the better, it is partly because the author's eye was on the job at hand, the Sabbath and holiday, the wedding and the commemoration, rather than on his literary immortality.

Yet side by side with his rabbinical work, Rabbi Wurzburger conducted parallel careers as a rabbinical leader on the national and international scene. He was the most prominent Orthodox thinker active in discussion with various Christian organizations and with non-Orthodox Jewish groups. He edited *Tradition* during its most prestigious years. More importantly, he wrote some of the most intelligent and influential papers of modern Orthodox thought. In these writings, he combined the incomparably balanced insight and lucidity that characterized his rabbinical communications with his Harvard training in philosophy and, above all, with the scholarship and theological orientation he had learned from his great teacher, Rabbi Dr. Joseph Soloveitchik.

With several decades of publication behind him, Rabbi Wurzburger summed up the essence of his mature thought on Jewish ethics in his *Ethics of Responsibility* (1994), to which he later added *God Is Proof Enough* (2000) on other topics of Jewish theology. These concise books appeared largely because many of his best students persuaded him that his thinking mattered not only to his immediate academic and congregational audiences, but also to the ongoing discussion of the subjects close to his heart and mind.

For many of us who had been affected by Rabbi Wurzburger's major essays, the reception of his two volumes was further evidence that his essays must be made available between the covers of a book. Before his death Rabbi Wurzburger began working on a selection. We are indebted to Elie Jacobs, who discovered Rabbi Wurzburger's work under the tutelage of Professor Chaim Waxman at Rutgers University and who, though not officially his student, made Rabbi Wurzburger his teacher, and assisted him in this undertaking.

Rabbi Wurzburger did not choose to include any of his sermons. In 1942, at the beginning of his career, he had published one Kol Nidre sermon, remarkable for the command of English exhibited by a German refugee who had arrived in the United States as a nineteen-year-old and found himself leading a congregation a few short years later and no less for the maturity of his thinking, which foreshadowed so many of his lifelong themes.[1] Rabbi Soloveitchik subsequently made a humorous remark about publishing sermons and, loyal talmid that he was, Rabbi Wurzburger never did it again. Many of them survive in shul bulletins and some cherished addresses were collected informally by congregants. He was also quite selective with the numerous papers presented to non-Jewish audiences on a variety of topics. Though his sense of perfect theological pitch, concision and clarity make these efforts worthy of emulation for those following in his footsteps, he did not choose to preserve them in this collection.

What made the cut? Primarily the essays on ethics and Halakhah and the studies on major figures in Jewish thought from the great medieval philosophers, most prominently Maimonides, down through Rabbi Hayyim of Volozhin and Rabbi Samson Raphael Hirsch in the eighteenth and nineteenth centuries, ending with his master Rabbi Soloveitchik. While some

---

[1] It appeared in the RCA Sermon Manual 1943, was unearthed by Rabbi Wurzburger's student Yoel Oz and reprinted at his initiative in the Yeshiva College Commentator following Rabbi Wurzburger's death. See my discussion in "Where the Tree Falls: Remembering Rabbi Walter Wurzburger" in *Jewish Action* 63:3 (Spring 2003 [5763]).

of the historical papers, such as the one on Rabbi Hayyim of Volozhin, range over a wide range of subjects, here too, Rabbi Wurzburger concentrates on ethics.

This concentration reflects the reality of Jewish life and Torah study, where performance of mitzvot and their understanding occupy pride of place. We know God by discerning His will for us and by realizing it in the world. Rabbi Hayyim Volozhin presented a model of Lithuanian piety, with theurgic overtones, that stressed the power of human engagement in Torah study and fulfillment. Rabbi Hirsch contributed a less mystical account of religion as obedience to the divine command. Rabbi Soloveitchik developed these themes in a twentieth-century context. Rabbi Wurzburger devoted himself to exploring some important implications of this outlook.

It may be useful to note three motives in Rabbi Wurzburger's writing on ethics and Halakhah. One derives from the need, in the mid-twentieth century, to distinguish Orthodoxy from other contemporary versions of Judaism. Both Conservative Judaism and Orthodoxy proclaimed loyalty to Halakhah; both affirmed belief in the Torah as divine revelation. Yet Conservatism arrogated to itself a latitude in halakhic decision-making that was alien to Orthodoxy even though Orthodoxy also recognized the place of human interpretation in deliberation. Rabbi Wurzburger's review essays on the work of Conservative jurists is devoted to clarifying these issues. It is an aspect of his work that probably strikes twenty–first-century readers as time-bound mainly because the ideas he is responding to are no longer well known or attractive. While the alternatives to Orthodoxy of philosophers like Buber and Rosenzweig still arouse interest, the current legal debate between mainstream Orthodoxy and more liberal or post-modern views is anchored in theories about the rabbinic literature and its interpretation in a way that is both more historically and hermeneutically sophisticated and more academic than it was forty to fifty years ago.[2]

A second strand in Rabbi Wurzburger's engagement is practical. Both opponents and upholders of halakhic Judaism often cast it in a legalistic mold. Ethics, from this point of view, is exhausted in the performance of halakhically mandated acts. Even supererogation (going beyond the law) has value only to the extent that such behavior is explicitly recommended by the

---

[2] Alan Brill's critical study of Rabbi Wurzburger, forthcoming in *Tradition*'s memorial volume to him, is particularly useful in attempting to excavate this phase of his work.

Halakhah. All sensitivity to general ethical values, any perception of duty not imposed by overt divine legislation, is beside the point. Here Rabbi Wurzburger was a champion of the aphorism he cites in the name of Rabbi Soloveitchik: "Halakhah is a floor, not a ceiling." In other words, what Halakhah requires of the Jew by way of ethical behavior (and likewise by way of devotion to God) is not all that God requires of us: Halakhah is the beginning, but each individual and each community, standing on the floor of Halakhah, so to speak, reaches out for the good by building on that foundation.

In the present volume Rabbi Wurzburger's approach to these problems is represented at two levels. In his studies of *darkhei shalom,* for example, he investigates a specific halakhic formulation that calls upon Jews to respond to general values. He demonstrates that the law of *darkhei shalom,* according to which many ethical commitments inherent to Jewish communal life must be extended to our relations with non-Jews as well, is not a concession to practical exigencies, but is integral to the Jewish religious ideal.

On a more general plane, Rabbi Wurzburger, following Rabbi Soloveitchik, among others, promoted general principles underlying Halakhah. It was he who popularized the term "meta-Halakhah" in this connection. Several essays describe the central role of *imitatio Dei* (והלכת בדרכיו) in Jewish law for Maimonides and for Rabbi Soloveitchik.

These concerns link up with the third motive driving Rabbi Wurzburger's philosophical ethics. The following is a short account of recent philosophical ethics. Utilitarianism, which maintains that whether actions are right or wrong depends on their consequences, whether they promote the greatest preponderance of pleasure over pain, has been the dominant philosophy for most of the twentieth century. While it can be dressed up in a form compatible with halakhic behavior (if one believes that obeying its dictates leads to the greatest happiness), the general tenor of this doctrine undermines a life predicated on man's response to the divine imperative and dedicated to His worship. The Kantian alternative is superficially more encouraging to Jewish ethics because it treats duty as primary and absolute, not always dependent on the outcome. Yet Kantian adaptations of Judaism intensify the image of halakhic Judaism as mechanical legalism; Kantianism, especially in its influential Rawlsian form, has no room for the relationship of obedience, imitation and passion of the human being towards the personal God.

"Virtue ethics" arose in part as a counterweight to these theories. Going back to Aristotle, and often cultivated by twentieth-century analytic philosophers who were theists, this approach defined ethics in terms of character excellence. It accorded well with Jewish orientations that emphasized character traits and personal relations to other human beings and to God. "Covenantal imperatives," to use the phrase of Rabbi Wurzburger that we chose as the title for this collection, articulate the relationship between God and Israel. Such a philosophy would likely be pluralistic, in the sense of denying any monolithic formula (like pleasure or Kantian rationality) for the good life and rejecting any attempt to regard some human value, however valuable, as good without qualification.

Though some aspects of this way of thinking are evident in some of the then unpublished writings of Rabbi Soloveitchik, it was his student Rabbi Wurzburger, who followed the debate about virtue ethics in the philosophical literature of the 1970s and 1980s. The pluralistic position set forth in *Ethics and the Limits of Philosophy* (1985) by Bernard Williams was the last element he needed to present his mature views in *The Ethics of Responsibility*. The reader of this volume will be able to trace the path followed by Rabbi Wurzburger in discovering and working out his contribution to Jewish thought.

ON ETHICS

FOUNDATIONS OF JEWISH ETHICS[1]

ALTHOUGH CLASSICAL JEWISH LITERATURE considers moral conduct one of the essential components of piety, one may question whether such a subject as Jewish ethics exists at all. It is difficult to resist the temptation to declare that there is no such thing as Jewish ethics. For if it is Jewish, it is not ethics; and if it is ethics it is not Jewish.

There is an impressive array of serious scholars who contend that Judaism is so radically theocentric and legalistic in orientation that only divine imperatives possess normative validly. Within such a setting, various autonomous moral perceptions cannot be treated as an independent source of moral obligation. For all their divergent approaches, such eminent thinkers or religious authorities as the Chazon Ish,[2] Yeshayahu Leibowitz,[3] and Marvin Fox[4] agree that, according to traditional conceptions, the Jewish normative system is based exclusively upon Halakhah, which is acknowledged as a body of law which, directly or indirectly derives its authority from divine revelation. As long as the will of God represents the only legitimate normative standard. The term "Jewish ethics" is really a misnomer. For what we designate as ethics is simply Halakhah, which

---

1 From the Solomon Goldman Lectures, vol. 5, 119–127. Chicago: Spertus College of Judaica Press, 1990.

2 *Sefer Chazon Ish*, ed. S. Greineman (Jerusalem, 1954), 21–43.

3 Yeshayahu Leibowitz, *Torah u-mitzvot ba-zeman ha-zeh* (Tel Aviv, 1954).

4 Marvin Fox, "Reflections on the Foundations of Jewish Ethics and their Relation to Public Policy." In *Selected Papers*, Society of Christian Ethics, Twenty-first Annual Meeting, 1980, 23–62.

derives its authority exclusively from our obligation to submit to the will of God as revealed in his commandments.

But our difficulties with the term "Jewish ethics" would by no means disappear were we to abandon the halakhic stance and adopt the position of a number of liberal Jewish thinkers, who, in the attempt to cast Judaism in the mold of Kantian categories stripped it of all features that could not be fitted into the Procrustean bed of ethical monotheism. In their view, the promptings of the autonomous human conscience constitute the ultimate court of appeals for all normative issues. As is well known, Kant went so far as to brand as immoral Abraham's readiness to obey God's command to sacrifice his son as a burnt offering. He should have realized, so Kant argues, that a benevolent God could not possibly have commanded the killing of an innocent person. It was inconceivable that a perfectly moral being such as God would issue commandments which violate the categorical imperative. In the Kantian view, murder would remain murder even if mandated by God. The fact that it would have been explicitly commanded by God would have no bearing upon its morality, since all rational agents, including God, are subject to universally applicable criteria of ethical propriety. Hence, whatever is perceived as immoral by human reason could not possibly have been commanded by God.

It follows from these premises that we can accept as revealed commands of God only what conforms to our own ethical standards. This explains classical Reform Judaism's rejection of all sundry ritual practices which cannot be shown to contribute to the enhancement of our moral life. Mere submission to a divine command without subjecting it to the scrutiny of the autonomous human conscience was stigmatized by a leading Reform thinker as *Kadavergehorseim* (the obedience of a dead animal), unworthy of a rational being.

But even the adoption of a Kantian approach, which essentially reduces religion to a handmaiden of ethics, would not enable us to speak of a Jewish ethics. If ethics is totally grounded in rationality and so dependent upon its ability to be made universal that it must be divested of all empirical elements, then a Jewish ethics is no more possible than a Jewish mathematics. In the Kantian scheme, particular historic factors cannot have any bearing upon moral considerations. Hence Jewishness must be totally irrelevant to the validity of an ethical approach.

It is highly revealing that Hermann Cohen, one of the foremost exponents of Kant, entitled his exposition of Judaism *The Religion of Reason – Out of the Sources of Judaism*. For Cohen, Judaism is merely the source of concepts, ideas and ideals, which enjoy universal applicability and validity. Within the framework of Cohen's pan-ethicism, there is no place for the unique and particular reflecting historic contingencies. In the final analysis, the Jewishness of an ideal or norm does not affect its validity. In other words, there is no Jewish ethics; only a universal ethics out of the sources of Judaism.

Yet despite all our difficulties with the concept of a distinct Jewish ethics, there is a widely and persistently held belief that there is something uniquely Jewish about Jewish ethics. Although Ahad ha-Am was unable to realize his ambition to demonstrate how the Jewish ethical system differed from those of other cultures or nations, he tenaciously clung to his conviction that the national Jewish spirit manifested itself in a unique approach to ethics. Similarly, Nietzsche was so obsessed with what he considered the debilitating impact of Jewish moral conceptions that he unleashed tirades against what he dubbed "Jewish slave morality," which allegedly had corrupted Western civilization by sapping its vigor and vitality.

While it may not be possible to reconcile the conception of a Jewish ethics with a radical Kantian approach that treats autonomy as the hallmark of morality, it still may be feasible to formulate Jewish conceptions of ethics which are compatible with the acknowledgment of the primacy of a divinely revealed legal system (Halakhah) as the ultimate normative authority. The fact that numerous moral prescriptions are perceived as divine imperatives by no means prevents us from acknowledging them also as moral norms. In this regard, G.E. Moore has pointed out that even for the theist the meaning of the term "good" is not identical with "being commanded by God."[5] It should be borne in mind that numerous medieval Jewish thinkers distinguished between commandments whose moral goodness was recognizable and those that were obeyed solely because they were divine imperatives. Were the property "goodness" translatable into "being commanded by God," one could obviously no longer make this distinction, since the *hukim* (ritual laws for which there was no obvious rational

---

[5] G.E. Moore, *Principia Ethica*. Cambridge: 1966.

justification) derive their very authority from their being commanded by God.[6]

To be sure, since God is not merely the supreme power but also a morally perfect being his commandments must be moral. Hence, obedience to his commands is a moral requirement. This being the case we need not invoke the Kierkegaardian "suspension of the ethical" as justification for Abraham's response to the divine command to offer Isaac as sacrifice to God. We have every right to claim that Abraham was not merely a "knight of faith" but a knight of morality as well, inasmuch as he was prepared to set aside all considerations of natural sentiments and inclinations in order to fulfill his supreme moral duty – i.e., to obey the highest-possible moral authority. As long he was certain that the command to sacrifice his son truly emanated from God, he was morally and not merely religiously obligated to abide by this divine imperative.[7] It is only because Kierkegaard weighed Abraham's conduct on the scales of Kantian notions of morality that he was unable to provide any kind of ethical justification for the actions of an Abraham. This left him no alternative but to base his defense of Abraham upon the claim that the "suspension of the ethical" represents the highest level of religious loyalty.

It is one thing to assert that all divine imperatives are moral and another to claim that only what is commanded by a divine imperative can be morally good. Since we do not equate the property "goodness" with the property "commanded by God," the fact that we may regard a certain action as morally desirable in itself constitutes a normative consideration. There is nothing to prevent a theist who regards the will of God as the supreme normative criterion from maintaining that in the absence of conflict with a revealed divine norm, we ought to do or strive to be whatever is perceived to be morally desirable. There is no need to deprive purely moral rules of normative significance. As Yehezkel Kaufmann[8] has pointed out, covenantal

---

[6] See Aharon Lichtenstein's invaluable discussion of this and other related issues, in his essay, "Does Jewish Tradition Recognize an Ethic Independent of Halakhah?" In *Modern Jewish Ethics*, edited by Marvin Fox, 62–88. Columbus, Ohio: 1975.

[7] See Philip I. Quinn, *Divine Commandments and Moral Requirements* (Oxford, 1978), 96–105. Especially significant is the treatment of this issue in Emil L. Fackenheim, *Encounters between Judaism and Modern Philosophy* (New York: 1973), 33–37.

[8] Yehezkel Kaufmann, *The Religion of Israel*, translated and abridged by Moshe Greenberg (New York, 1960), 233–234 and 327–329.

morality does not abolish natural morality, but supplements it and supplies it with religious motives and sanctions. Numerous traditional Jewish thinkers dwelt upon the importance of *derekh eretz*, which they defined as commonly accepted notions of morality reflecting utilitarian considerations. In keeping with this interpretation, the rabbinic adage *"derekh eretz* precedes Torah" amounts to an endorsement of a utilitarian morality, which is deemed indispensable to the proper functioning of society.[9]

To be sure, this does not imply that the ethical domain must be acknowledged as an independent normative authority. One could plausibly maintain that a moral imperative automatically becomes also a religious imperative. This is as a matter of fact the position of Nahmanides, who noted that the Torah commands, "Thou shalt do what is right and good" in addition to numerous specific moral prescriptions and norms. In his view, the latter general principle is needed to insure that whatever is perceived as falling within the category of the right and the good is automatically accorded the status of a religious imperative.[10]

Be that as it may, there is absolutely no justification for the canard that Jewish ethics is so legalistic and focuses so exclusively upon narrow, formal requirements that it becomes completely blind to considerations of ethical sensitivity. Jewish ethics, while grounded in law, is not merely an ethics of obedience to specific moral rules but also an ethics of responsibility,[11] which mandates a pattern of conduct reflecting the awareness that all human beings bear the image of God. According to Ben Azzai, the verse "This is the book of the generations of man: when God created man, he created him in his image" constitutes the most fundamental passage of the entire Torah.[12] That such a preeminent position is assigned to this particular verse demonstrates that the belief in the irreducible dignity and sanctity of creatures bearing the divine image plays a pivotal role in the Jewish religio-ethical system.

---

[9] See Judah Loew, *Netivot Olam*, "*Netiv Derekh Eretz.*"

[10] Nahmanides, *Commentary to the Torah* to Deuteronomy 6:18.

[11] For a more thorough treatment of this subject, refer to my article, "Covenantal Imperatives," in *Samuel K. Mirsky Memorial Volume* (New York: 1970), 3–12 (page 46 in this volume). See also my essay, "Law as the Basis of a Moral Society," in *Tradition* 19, no. 1 (Spring 1981): 42–54 (page 61 in this volume).

[12] JT *Nedarim* 9:4.

A cogent argument is advanced by the fifteenth-century Jewish philosopher Joseph Albo[13] in support of the thesis that the area of what is religiously prescribed or recommended must extend beyond the domain of what is the subject of specific legislation of the Torah. After all, the finite number of specific regulations contained in the Torah could not possibly cover all the contingencies arising from ever-changing socio-political and economic conditions. Hence in matters not concretely spelled out in the Torah, we must rely on our own moral perceptions for guidance as to how we can best obey the divine imperative of doing what is right and good. To be sure, these moral perceptions, in turn, should reflect the value system underlying the various particular norms of the Torah. It is expected that as the result of exposure to specific ethical norms, we gradually develop the capacity to intuit theonomous moral requirements that extend beyond the range of the explicitly stated specific norms of the Torah.[14]

It must, however, be realized that the acceptance of the authority and validity of moral intuitions which extend beyond the confines of heteronomous laws in no way entails the acknowledgment of the basic premises of autonomous morality, which looks upon the human self as the ultimate source of moral obligation. In the words of the prophet Micah, "to do justice and to love mercy" is a response to "what God demands of thee" – not a self-imposed duty. Anyone familiar with the history of Jewish ideas is aware that, though apprehended by the human intellect, Bahya's "duties of the heart" or Saadiah's "rational commandments" derive their authority not from the autonomous human self but from their status as divine imperatives disclosed by reason. In the telling formation of Menachem Meiri,[15] human beings must be treated with the reverence due to a Torah scroll because they are endowed with the capacity for discerning with their own minds obligations that are not explicitly stated in the Torah. In a similar vein, Samson Raphael Hirsch[16] refers to an "inner revelation" of God which supplements the "outer revelation" of Sinai. It is through this "inner

---

[13] Joseph Albo, *Sefer ha-Ikkarim* 3:23.

[14] That the enactment of new ordinances in response to newly emerging conditions was a corollary of the commandment "to do what is right and good" was pointed out by Vidal Yom Tov of Tolosa, *Maggid Mishnah* to Maimonides' *Mishneh Torah*, "Hilkhot Shekhenim," 14:4.

[15] Meiri *ad Shabbat* 105b.

[16] Samson Raphael Hirsch, *Horeb*, trans. Dayan Dr. I. Grunfeld, "Introduction," 91.

revelation" – the voice of conscience and reason – that God speaks to us and provides us with moral instruction in the course of the historic process. When moral imperatives are regarded as divine imperatives, it becomes readily understandable why the feature of overridingness distinguishes moral values as opposed to aesthetic or intellectual values. In point of fact, what is perceived as an obligation to our fellow human beings automatically points to an obligation to God. As Emil Fackenheim put it so succinctly, Jewish morality is a three-term morality.[17] Ethics is not an independent sphere but an integral part of the quest for holiness. Hence, ideally, ethical conduct should be inspired by the desire to serve God and to imitate his ways.

Since God represents the supreme moral authority, his imperatives must not be subjected to moral scrutiny. To be sure, we are supposed to interpret his commands in the light of our rational understanding. But obedience to divine imperatives must not be made contingent upon their conformity to our notions of moral propriety. The explicitly revealed will of God must reign supreme. Moral considerations are invoked only in case of doubt concerning the meaning of a divinely revealed norm. It was taken for granted that divine norms must be interpreted in accordance with the principle that Torah reflects the "ways of pleasantness," and the "ways of peace."[18]

It is one thing to adopt this approach as a hermeneutic device for the purpose of determining the meaning of Torah, and another to treat moral perceptions as an independent source of authority. It must be realized that Jewish morality, is theocentric not only because divine imperatives, whether obtained through reason or revelation, constitute the ultimate source of authority for its norms, but also because Jewish moral notions originate in specific divine laws governing interpersonal relations such as prohibitions against murder, incest, theft, etc. As Nahmanides pointed out, the meaning of a general principle such as "to do what is right and good," can be grasped only through inductive intuition from a fairly large number of particular instances exemplifying the general principle. Obviously, there is considerably less risk of reading our own subjective preferences into specific laws – e.g.,

---

[17] See Emil Fackenheim, op. cit., and his essay, "The Revealed Morality of Judaism and Modern Thought," in his *Quest for Past and Future* (Bloomington, Indiana: 1968), 204–228.

[18] An excellent collection of the source material can be found in *Encyclopedia Talmudit*, 7:712–723.

the obligation to place a fence around the roof – than into such broad and general principles as doing the right and the good.

The primacy assigned to specific legal norms also accounts for the unabashedly pluralistic orientation of Jewish ethics. This differs sharply from the bias towards monism that characterizes the bulk of contemporary ethical systems, which seek to justify all moral rules in terms of single principles such as rationality, utility or conformity to human nature. But Judaism eschews all such reductionist efforts. It is prepared to accommodate the requirements of a host of diverse divine imperatives, irrespective of whether or not they are perceived as being compatible with other general principles.

Given the pluralistic nature of Jewish ethics and its potential for clashes between conflicting norms and rules, casuistry – the analysis of the range of applicability of specific moral rules – emerges as one of the key concerns of Jewish ethical thought. In dealing with ethical dilemmas, the specific features of a given existential situation must be examined before informed judgments can be made. This is, of course, the very antithesis of the Kantian approach to ethics, which because of its preoccupation with universalizability insisted upon the utter irrelevance of the unique empirical factors characterizing a given situation. For Kant morality was categorical. History played no role. All that mattered was conformity to an abstract, formal principle. But Jewish morality takes seriously the moral requirements arising from the contingencies of the particular historic situation, be they obligations incurred to a benefactor, to one's family or, for that matter, duties to respond to the special needs of individuals, such as when Hillel offered his services as a footman to an individual who could no longer afford to live in the style to which he was accustomed. From a Jewish perspective, members of our own community have a far greater claim to our benevolence than individuals with whom we have no contact. In rabbinic parlance, the poor of your own city take precedence over the poor of another city.[19] It therefore follows that when competing demands are made upon our resources, we cannot simply determine priorities by computing the maximal utility to mankind. A thousand dollars sent to Africa to provide relief from famine would probably do more good than a thousand dollars spent on the education of my child. But a father must not ignore his specific parental responsibilities. Concern

---

[19] BT *Bava Metzia* 71b.

for the good of humanity must be balanced against the institutional responsibilities incurred by becoming a father.

Ahad ha-Am completely misunderstood the basic thrust of Jewish ethics when he adduced Hillel's negative formulation of the Golden Rule as evidence that Jewish ethics was such a purely formal system that it was concerned only with abstract justice and totally indifferent to considerations involving sentiments such as love, compassion, etc.[20] He conveniently ignored that the performance of acts of benevolence as well as the cultivation of various sentiments such as compassion, sympathy and charity are mandated by Jewish tradition.

Since Jewish morality is responsive to the requirements arising from the unique features of a given existential situation, it is a far cry from the kind of ethics which was denounced by Nietzsche as *Fernstenliebe* (love of the distant). While some Christian moralists may contend that "Love thy neighbor as thyself" implies that, ideally, in matters involving concern for others one should not discriminate between total strangers and members of ones own family. Jewish morality emphasizes that the nature and scope of our moral obligations is affected by historic factors. We cannot love everyone equally. As a matter of fact, according to Judaism, our own life takes precedence over the lives of others. But it is our duty to show every individual the kind of love which is appropriate in the light of the conditions characterizing a particular relationship. To be sure, Judaism rejects the Aristotelian notion that altruism is mandated only vis-à-vis friends. But Jewish morality would agree that bonds of friendship give rise to special obligations which go beyond those due to total strangers.

Inasmuch as a host of cultural and historic elements go into the formation of ethical situations, moral judgments cannot be reduced to simple formal rules. Moreover, moral dilemmas frequently are due to the fact that we do not have at our disposal any formal rule enabling us to assign relative weights to conflicting and competing values. In such cases we have no alternative to reliance upon intuitive perceptions in order to determine the moral requirements of a given existential situation. But there always remains a serious question as to the reliability of such intuitions, which are purely subjective and utterly devoid of any objective validity.

---

[20] Ahad ha-Am, "Judaism and the Gospels," in *Nationalism and Jewish Ethics: Basic Writings of Ahad ha-Am*, edited and introduced by Hans Kohn (New York: 1962), 301–302.

It is for this reason that traditional Jewish conceptions of ethics emphasize the need for guidance obtained through exposure to concrete models of ethical propriety. Since ethical ambiguities cannot be resolved through recourse to canons of formal reasoning, it is essential that we develop our capabilities for ethical judgment by imitation of appropriate role models. This may account for the fact that the Talmud ranks personal contact with scholars above formal study.[21] It is highly revealing that Maimonides, in the section of his Code dealing with the cultivation of virtues,[22] reinterprets in accordance with Jewish needs the Aristotelian doctrine that only the expert in practical wisdom is equipped to provide guidance on matters of ethics. In the Maimonidean scheme, it is only through close association with the *talmid hakham* (Torah scholar) and the careful observation of his conduct that one can obtain an grasp of what constitutes desirable traits of character – i.e., the proper balance between the extremes that ought to be eschewed.[23] That ethical conduct ultimately presupposes concrete exemplars was also stressed by Rabbi Naftali Tzvi Yehudah Berlin, who contended that the Book of Genesis was included in the Torah because the stories describing the conduct of the Patriarchs were intended to provide ethical role models.[24] Implicit in this view is the belief that the legal part of the Torah would not have sufficed for proper moral guidance. Despite the fact that the Law constitutes the very foundation of Jewish ethics, these "stories" were indispensable, if the Torah was to provide adequate direction for ethical decision-making, especially with respect to intricate and complex moral issues.

However important the role intuitions play in the realm of act-morality, they assume an even more pivotal role in the sphere of agent-morality contrary, to the stereotypes associated with Jewish legalism, "agent morality" or "virtue-ethics" is unquestionably a vital component of Jewish ethics. *Sifrei* (Deuteronomy, *Ekev*, 49) interprets the commandment "Thou shalt walk in his ways" as an imperative to cultivate moral dispositions. Maimonides adopts this approach and devotes an entire section of his Code to virtue-

---

[21] BT *Berakhot* 7b.

[22] *Hilkhot Deot.*

[23] *ibid.*, 6:2.

[24] Naftali Zvi Yehudah Berlin, *Haamek Davar*, Introduction to Genesis.

ethics.[25] For that matter, his *Guide of the Perplexed* reaches its grand finale in the kind of *imitatio Dei* which is attained through cultivation of moral dispositions. Moreover, already in one of his earliest works, the *Commentary on the Mishnah*,[26] Maimonides points out that in the ethical sphere, performance of the right action alone is totally inadequate. Unless moral actions are the external manifestations of a truly moral personality, one falls considerably short of the moral ideal. Our goal should be the performance of moral actions which are not merely motivated by a sense of duty, but also express the sentiments, inclinations or the very nature of the moral agent.

The centrality of virtue-ethics in the Maimonidean scheme can also be discerned in his treatment of supererogatory conduct. Whereas Nahmanides viewed supererogatory conduct as a para-legal requirement, Maimonides assigned it to the sphere of the "ethics of the pious," which in his scheme presupposes the cultivation of the higher levels of ethical sensitivity through both moral conditioning and intellectual perfection.[27]

It therefore can readily be seen that conformity to the law is treated within Judaism as merely a necessary but not a sufficient condition of morality. The creation of a truly moral personality represents a never-ending task. It is through study and observance of the Law, exposure to the Jewish ethos through living models as well as through the "stories" of the aggadah that we are expected to gradually develop ever higher levels of ethico-religious sensitivity.

But while we must strive for ever loftier rungs of ethical perfection, we must be wary of the pitfalls of a utopian, Messianic ethics. We live in an unredeemed world. It is the height of absurdity to apply to such a world the kind of rules and standards which would be appropriate for a society in which all degradation and violence has been overcome. With all our love of peace, we must categorically reject pacifism. Non-resistance to evil is an unconscionable moral wrong. Perpetration of violence cannot be condoned. We are not merely obligated to resist aggression by force whenever necessary

---

[25] See my discussion of this issue in my "Law as the Basis of a Moral Society," op. cit., 49–51.

[26] *Commentary on the Mishnah*, Introduction to *Avot*, chapter 6.

[27] I have dealt more extensively with the implications of the differences between Maimonides' and Nahmanides's conceptions of supererogation in my previously cited essay, "Law as the Basis of a Moral Society."

to assist other innocent victims, but we are duty-bound to resist aggression even for the protection of our own lives. Here Judaism parts company with the pacifistic streak of Christianity. Judaism rejects the notion that a saint will refuse to resort to force for the sake of self-protection. Judaism is more realistic. It maintains that in our unredeemed world, we must choose the lesser evil (i.e., the killing of an aggressor) over the greater evil (i.e., permitting ourselves to be killed by an aggressor). There are no perfect solutions for an imperfect world. Although we abhor violence, it is our task to conduct ourselves in the here and now, not in accordance with standards appropriate for an ideal Messianic society, but rather in accordance with the requirements of the real world, while hoping that our moral actions may help pave the way for the arrival of the Messiah.[28]

In grappling with the numerous ethical ambiguities and dilemmas we encounter, we must reconcile ourselves to the fact that the moral enterprise is too complex to operate by simplistic rules. The fact that we acknowledge absolute principles in no way dispenses with the need to fall back upon intuition to determine the moral requirements of a given situation. There is constant need for re-assessment and re-evaluation in the light of evolving historic realities and changing ethical sensitivities. In other words, Jewish ethics is dynamic rather than static. As Hillel expressed it to the prospective candidate for conversion, the ongoing quest for the ethical life demands that one "Go forth and study."

---

[28] See also my discussion of Messianism in "The Maimonidean Matrix of Rabbi Joseph B. Soloveitchik's Two-Tiered Ethics." In *Through the Sound of Many Voices*, edited by Jonathan V. Plaut, 181–182. Toronto: 1982 (page 161 in this volume).

WHAT IS UNIQUE ABOUT JEWISH ETHICS?[1]

JEWISH ETHICS DOES NOT only transcend the minimal legalistic requirements of Halakhah, but it also engenders a distinctly Jewish ethical perspective that may differ from those prevailing in different cultures. This position presupposes that the human mind cannot discern a universally valid ethics (e.g. natural law) and that, as opposed to Spinoza, Yeshayahu Leibowitz and Marvin Fox, Judaism recognizes ethical demands that are not grounded in Halakhah. This article demonstrates that Jewish ethics includes not only a unique act-morality but also a distinctive agent-morality.

Not very long ago, before multi-culturalism came into style, the claim that Judaism possess a unique ethics would have evoked an outburst of ridicule. Ethics was generally regarded as a completely objective branch of knowledge, universally applicable and completely impervious to the vicissitudes of historic contingency. It was taken for granted that just as there were only Jewish scientists or mathematicians but no Jewish science or mathematics, there could be no Jewish ethics. To paraphrase Hermann Cohen's well-known *Religion of Reason: Out of the Sources of Judaism*, Jewish ethical teachings are merely the source of universally valid ethical truth.

But developments in anthropology, sociology and ethical theory have wrought a sea of change in the intellectual climate. The belief in an objective ethics has been replaced by ethical relativism. Positivists, emotivists and some prescriptivists have reduced the status of moral beliefs to the level of mere personal preference. This being the case, cultural differences are bound

[1] *Le'ela* 49, London School of Jewish Studies (June 2000): 27–34.

to affect the formation of ethical attitudes. It therefore should be expected that those influenced by Judaism display uniquely Jewish ethical attitudes, which differ from those encountered in other ethical systems.

To be sure, the rejection of an objective basis of our value-system exacts a heavy price, especially in pluralistic societies. It has resulted in the growth of unbridled permissiveness and utter disdain for traditional values. In reaction to the value-crisis generated by this "moral nihilism," we are witnessing increasing interest in exploring whether and to what extent Jewish ethics could provide a solid foundation for moral objectivity.

But before we can address this question, we must first inquire whether we can speak at all of an entity called Jewish ethics. There are representative Jewish and non-Jewish thinkers such as Baruch Spinoza, Moses Mendelssohn, Immanuel Kant and Yeshayahu Leibowitz, who, for all their differences, agree that Judaism constitutes merely a legal system designed for regulation of the conduct of the Jewish people. In their view, even prohibitions against murder or theft which coincide with what are regarded as moral or ethical norms cannot be subsumed under the category of the ethical, because their authority stems, not from their being perceived as ethical requirements, but solely from their being acknowledged as parts of a divinely ordained legal system. Since in Judaism ethical and ritual laws form a seamless whole, the fact that we experience a feeling of ethical obligation with respect to some laws and not to others is totally irrelevant. Regardless of whether we are dealing with imperatives governing our relationships to our fellow human beings or with those to God, they are only obeyed because they constitute divine commandments. The requirements to practice justice, to engage in benevolent actions and to walk with humility are not perceived as autonomous, self-imposed duties but, as the prophet Micah (6:8) states, demands made upon us by God.

But when the area of Jewish ethics is viewed as completely co-extensive with that of Halakhah, it would follow that in situations for which Jewish law contains no clear-cut halakhic instructions, there could be no ethical requirements. Bahya ibn Pakuda apparently was troubled by what also strikes us as a serious shortcoming of Jewish ethics, when he stressed the domain of the "duties of the heart." In addition to the "duties of the limbs" which are spelled out in the divine legislation of the Torah, so Bahya contends, there are moral requirements implanted in the hearts of human beings which can apprehended by human reason and require no sanction by Revelation.[2] Saadiah Gaon recognized the authority of reason as a source of ethical laws when he described them as "rational commandments," which unlike purely "revelational commandments," may be discovered by human reason.[3]

The position of these two classical thinkers, however, must not be confused with that of the exponents of "natural law." Unlike the latter, the former do not maintain that the authority of the moral law is based upon the dictates of reason or human conscience. On the contrary, they fully subscribe to a "divine command" theory. But they claim that human reason is an instrument capable of disclosing to us the various duties governing our conduct and attitudes towards our fellow human beings, which God imposes upon us. In other words, reason becomes an instrument of divine Revelation.

But while the views of Bahya ibn Pakuda or Saadiah Gaon would enlarge the domain of Jewish ethics far beyond the narrow bounds of Halakhah, they still would not enable us to speak of a distinctly Jewish ethics. Both of these thinkers operate on what by now is the widely rejected premise that the human mind of conscience can supply us with objective, universally valid ethical knowledge.

A more promising road leading to a uniquely Jewish ethics is offered by Maimonides and Nahmanides. The former emphasizes that ethical imperatives cannot be provided by reason alone but depend upon divine commandments for their binding character. In the absence of a divine imperative, we would be left only with "commonly accepted notions" (conventions), which, however prudent they might be, would lack authority. But with commandments as the basis of ethics, Maimonides nonetheless succeeded in developing a Jewish ethics which goes far beyond legalism.

Maimonides accomplishes this by interpreting the biblical phrase "and you shall walk in His ways" as mandating the emulation of the divine moral attributes such as compassion, graciousness, truthfulness, and so on. According to Maimonides, Jewish ethics, in addition to regulating actions, also contains a virtue-ethics that demands the cultivation of moral virtues.[4]

---

[2] Bahya ibn Pakuda, *Duties of the Heart*, Preface.

[3] Saadiah Gaon, *Doctrines and Beliefs*, Part III.

[4] Maimonides, *Guide of the Perplexed*, I:2. See also the excellent treatment of Maimonides's rejection of natural law in Marvin Fox, *Understanding Maimonides* (Chicago University Press: 1990) Chapter 6.

Nahmanides extends the range of Jewish ethics by a different method. In his interpretation, the general commandments, "You shall do what is right and good in the eyes of God," governs the requirements of ethical conduct even in situations for which the Torah provides no explicit norms. He believes that in such cases we must rely on our own intuitive judgments to ascertain the meaning of "what is right and good in the eyes of God." Thus by a process of extrapolation from the various specific norms contained in the Torah we are expected to obtain a sense of our ethical requirements. He also points out that the concept of *lifnim mi-shurat ha-din* (going beyond minimal legal requirements) is based upon the same biblical verse.[5]

I have coined the term "Covenantal Imperatives" to denote Jewish religious imperatives for which no specific halakhic source can be invoked.[6] Whereas Nahmanides limits ethical requirements to what can be extrapolated from halakhic sources or can be justified by purely rational consideration, I propose that we follow in the footsteps of Rabbi Naftali Tzvi Yehudah Berlin, who in *Haamek Davar* maintained that the biblical narratives in Genesis provide us with models for ethical conduct,[7] and that we mine the treasures of both Halakhah and Aggadah to extract guidelines for a Jewish ethics which addresses itself to all areas of life. Exposure to Jewish teachings and practices will lead to the formation of authentically Jewish intuitive ethical responses, which are bound to differ from those which are bound to differ from those which were influenced by different cultural milieus.

In a sense, my notion of "Covenantal Imperatives" resembles that of *Da'at Torah*, according to which the views of eminent Torah scholars provide authoritative guidance even for matters which are not subject to halakhic legislation. But my conception differs in one important respect. I fully recognize that what is perceived as a religious requirement possesses merely subjective validity in the absence of explicit halakhic norms. Because of its lack of objectivity, it merely constitutes a legitimate Jewish ethical opinion but does not deny the Jewish legitimacy of alternate responses. Hence my

---

[5] Nahmanides, *Commentary to the Torah*, Deuteronomy 6:16.

[6] Walter S. Wurzburger, *Ethics of Responsibility: Pluralistic Approaches to Covenantal Ethics* (Philadelphia: Jewish Publication Society, 1994), 31–39. See also my article "Covenantal Imperatives," in *Samuel K. Mirsky Memorial Volume,* edited by Gersion Appel, 3–12. New York: Yeshiva University, 1970 (page 46 in this volume).

[7] Preface to *Sefer Bereshit*.

position allows for the advocacy of pluralistic approaches in all areas which are not subject to halakhic regulation. Evidence for my view can be adduced from the fact that Jewish tradition accommodates both rationalists and mystics, quietistic pietists as well as passionate advocates of intervention in worldly affairs, Neturei Karta as well as Religious Zionists.

For all their differences, the above-mentioned traditional approaches to Jewish ethics have one common denominator. Without necessarily defining Good in terms of divine commands, they represent variations of divine command theories of ethics, because whatever is good is commanded by God. Compared with secular theories, they have the advantage of being able to account for the characteristic of overridingness which we attach to ethical beliefs. Some modern philosophers question why moral considerations deserve priority over competing intellectual or aesthetic considerations. But viewed from the vantage point of Jewish ethics, the question hardly makes sense. Since moral imperatives are perceived as commands emanating from the most perfect Being, they enjoy absolute authority. Every other consideration must be subordinated to them.

The theocentricity of Jewish ethics also explains why provisions of Jewish ethics at times conflict with our own ethical intuitions. In these instances Jewish ethical requirements diverge from what would be the most beneficial rules of conduct to be adopted by society on the basis of purely utilitarian or pragmatic considerations.

The ultimate objective of Jewish ethics is not the collective well-being of human society but to make human individuals as God-like as possible. As Rabbi Joseph B. Soloveitchik repeatedly pointed out, the imitation of God is the pivot around which all Jewish ethics revolves.

One might, of course, argue that imitation of God is such an all-encompassing religious ideal that it transcends the realm of ethics. In contrast to Kant, Rudolph Otto maintained that the category of the holy is by no means reducible to that of the ethical. Otto's phenomenological analysis is in keeping with the thrust of Chapter 19 of Leviticus, which is introduced with the admonition, "Be holy because I the Lord am holy," in spite of the fact that it includes both ethical and ritual legislation. Moreover, the Torah also invokes the imitation of God as rationale for a ritual commandment, when the Torah mandates the observance of the Sabbath, "because in six days God made heaven and earth and rested on the seventh."[8] Since Sabbath observance is mandated exclusively for Jews, it can hardly qualify as an ethical commandment.

That imitation of God and holiness need not necessarily refer to ethical requirements can also be inferred from the different interpretations of the commandment "you shall walk after God."[9] rabbinic literature cites this as a proof text for the obligation to perform benevolent actions. Yet the Talmud also uses it as the scriptural source for purely ritual regulations designed to insure proper reverence for Torah scrolls.[10] It should be borne in mind that there are Jewish authorities who disagree with Maimonides and interpret the Torah's mandate to "walk in the ways of God" not as a specific reference to morality but more broadly to the observance of all ways prescribed by God, regardless of whether they are of ethical or ritual nature.

But while the notions of holiness and imitation of God are by no means exclusively associated with ethical requirements, ethical conduct, nevertheless, is an indispensable ingredient of Jewish piety. It represents the "way of God." The purpose of the special relationship between God and Abraham, according to Genesis 18:18, was to insure that his progeny "may keep the way of God to practice charity and justice." Insofar as the Tannaim were concerned, terms such as "following God" or "walking in all His ways" referred not merely to obeying God's explicit instructions but also to the emulation of divine attributes. Our own conduct should be patterned after the model of divine actions recorded in the Torah. Thus imitating God, we should clothe the naked, heal the sick, comfort the mourners, and so on.[11]

The halakhic Midrash, *Sifrei*, extends the notion of imitating God beyond the sphere of actions to the cultivation of His ethical attributes. "To walk in all His ways" (Deuteronomy 11:22) is invoked as a proof text for the requirement to cultivate an ethical personality and to become compassionate, gracious, righteous, and so on, in imitation of God's ways.[12] Maimonides paraphrases this *Sifrei* in his discussion of what he views as the source of an outright specific commandment to imitate God's moral attributes. Although the phrase "you shall walk in His ways" (Deuteronomy 28:9) could easily be

---

[8] Exodus 20:10–11.
[9] Deuteronomy 13:5.
[10] BT *Sotah* 39b.
[11] BT *Sotah* 14a.
[12] *Sifrei* Ekev, 49.

taken as a general reference to leading a life approved by God. Maimonides assigns to it a specific ethical meaning. As we noted previously, he interprets this verse in a highly original approach as the proof text of the religious duty to cultivate an ethical personality. We are mandated to imitate as much as possible God's ethical perfections, which He manifests by the ways in which He acts in the world.

In the opinion of Rabbi Joseph B. Soloveitchik, Jewish ethics does not merely prescribe the imitation of only what are defined as the moral attributes of God, but all of God's actions provide models after which we should pattern our conduct. He points out that the Torah describes the process of Creation not in order to provide us with cosmological information, but to challenge us to imitate in some way God's creativity. To this end, we should draw on all our scientific and technological resources and exercise our creativity in the attempt to reduce poverty, disease and suffering.[13]

Since Jewish ethics revolved around *imitatio Dei*, it is not surprising that altruism is assigned a pivotal role. Rabbi Akiva went so far as to declare that "Love thy neighbor as thyself; I am God" represents the very essence of the Torah.[14] In enumerating the ethical perfections of God, the Torah places special emphasis upon His *hesed* (loving concern for others). While characterizing God as compassionate, gracious, truthful, and so on, the Torah adds the adjective *rav* (abundant) only to His attribute of *hesed*. Jewish ethics accords priority to the latter. One is therefore advised to tell a lie if necessary in order to prevent harm to another individual.

Similarly, Jewish law prohibits spreading derogatory information about individuals. Contrary to current journalistic usage, not all newsworthy items are fit to be reported, let alone to be printed. Much of today's "investigative reporting," which aims to expose the folly or moral flaws of prominent figures, would fall under this halakhic prohibition. Even in private conversation it is strictly forbidden to make disparaging statements about people. While secular law only prohibits slander (making false statements), Jewish law forbids all derogatory statements unless others would be harmed

---

[13] See my essay, *"Imitatio Dei* in the Philosophy of Rav Joseph B. Soloveitchik," in *Hazon Nahum,* edited by Yaacov Elman and Jeffrey S. Gurock, 557–575. New York: Yeshiva University Press (page 172 in this volume).

[14] JT *Nedarim* 9:4.

if the information were withheld. Similarly, while Jewish law prohibits disclosure of confidential information, an exception is made when breach of confidentiality is necessary to prevent danger to human life.

Further evidence of the centrality of altruism is found in the Talmud. It reserves the term "trait of a Sodomite" to designate persons whose selfishness prevents them from granting benefits to someone else at no cost to themselves. Jewish law went so far as to actually outlaw such selfishness, limiting the property rights of landowners the right of pre-emption of adjoining property when it is offered for sale (*dina debar mitzra*).[15]

The concern for *hesed* comes to the fore when Isaiah castigates those who seek closeness to God without showing solicitude for the well-being of others. So deeply convinced were the rabbis that charity was an indispensable ingredient of piety that they looked upon failure to respond to human needs as being equivalent to practicing idolatry. It should be noted that the obligation to practice charity applies even when considerations of societal welfare do not warrant it. The Talmud reports that Hillel served as a footman to someone who due to financial reverses, could no longer afford the lifestyle to which he was accustomed. He did it because in the Jewish view, what is essential to the welfare of a person depends upon individual circumstances. This kind of concern for the welfare of individuals rather than of societal well-being makes sense only when it is motivated not merely by the requirements of a just society to meet the needs of the underprivileged but by the religious imperative to engage in altruistic pursuits designed to imitate the "ways of God."

Similarly, utilitarian or pragmatic values are completely disregarded when the sanctity of life is at stake. All of life is equally sacred. Under no circumstances may one take one life in order to save the lives of many others. In the frequently discussed "Trolley Problem" one would not be permitted to pull a switch to save many lives at the cost of killing an individual whose life would have been spared, had the path of the trolley not been diverted. Since a life has infinite value, quantitative factors are irrelevant. The Talmud prohibits handing over an innocent individual for execution by unscrupulous enemies even if failure to comply with the demand would result in the death of all the inhabitants of a town.

---

[15] BT *Bava Kamma* 108a; Maimonides, *Hilkhot Shekhenim* 12:5.

Yet while Jewish law would brook no qualitative or quantitative distinctions of life with respect to the taking of lives, the emphasis upon the absolute sanctity of life does not preclude taking such considerations into account when it comes to deciding on priorities for interventions to save lives. Thus there would be no objection to triage when there is no possibility of saving the lives of all injured.

Although it emphasizes the absolute sanctity of life, Judaism makes a radical distinction between the prohibition against killing and that against allowing one to die. The prohibition against killing is more stringent than the commandment "You shall not stand idly by the blood of your neighbor" (Leviticus 18:16). For this reason active euthanasia is always forbidden, but there are situations when passive euthanasia may be practiced out of concern for the quality of life of the patient. However, financial considerations must never be permitted to play a role in determining when treatment is to be discontinued. Thus Judaism would strenuously object to proposals to limit health care for the aged out of considerations of cost-benefit ratios.

The previously cited rabbinic texts mandating the cultivation of virtues clearly show that Judaism no less then Christianity stresses the cultivation of love and charity. To show that the alleged contrast between a Jewish ethics of law and a Christian ethics of virtue is nothing but a figment of the imagination, we need but recall that Scripture explicitly mandates that we "open our hands to our needy brethren" (Deuteronomy 15:8). Thus the attitude motivating the benefactor to engage in the practice of charity is deemed to be of crucial importance. Similarly, the Torah does not merely forbid the expression of hatred in actions, but contains the explicit prohibition "you shall not hate your brother in your heart."[16]

To be sure, many Jewish writers, following the lead of Ahad ha-Am, dismiss the religious importance of emotions. They adduce as evidence that Hillel found it necessary to reformulate the commandment "Love thy neighbor as thyself" in purely negative terms: "What is hateful to you, do not do to your fellow human being."

But the commandment to love cannot be reduced merely to concern for fairness and justice and avoidance of hateful behavior. An analysis of Maimonides' writings leaves no doubt that the commandment stipulates that

---

[16] Leviticus 19:17.

we experience the same kind of love for our fellow man as we do for ourselves.[17]

It appears that for Maimonides, as it was for Aristotle and many other Greek ethicists, the performance of morally desirable actions was considered a necessary means to the acquisition of virtuous dispositions. In other words, the cultivation of virtuous states of character, as the concluding chapter of the *Guide* indicates, possesses intrinsic rather than merely instrumental value. For this reason, according to Maimonides's Mishnah commentary, the performance of an ethical action involving a struggle against one's inclination is less meritorious than one motivated by a person's own disposition to act in this manner.[18]

The theocentric orientation of Jewish ethics also affects the type of sentiments or personality traits which are praised as virtues or condemned as vices. They differ sharply from the classical list of virtues. Most blatant is the radical divergence of the respective attitudes towards humility. Secular ethics from Plato to Spinoza disdained self-abasing humility, viewing it as being utterly incompatible with the sense of self-worth essential to human dignity.

Judaism, on the other hand, approaches humility from an altogether different perspective. It constitutes a pre-condition of all piety. How can a finite human being experience pride, let alone be arrogant, in the face of the majesty and grandeur of an infinite God? That is why haughtiness and arrogance are telltale signs of obliviousness of God's existence. As the Torah says, "When your heart becomes haughty, you will forget that there is a God."[19] This explains why the Talmud so strongly denounces all pride and haughtiness. One Amora, Rabbi Yohanan, regarded arrogance as an equivalent of idolatry,[20] while another Amora, Rabbi Hisda, went so far as to declare that "the *Shekhinah* (Divine Presence) cannot co-exist with an arrogant person."[21] According to the Talmud, a young man proud of his good looks heard himself addressed by a voice reprimanding him: "How can you boast about a world that is not yours?"[22]

---

[17] *Hilkhot Deot* 6:4.

[18] Maimonides, *Commentary on the Mishnah,* Introduction to *Avot*, Eight Chapters, 6.

[19] Deuteronomy 8:14.

[20] BT *Sotah* 4b.

[21] *ibid.*, 5a.

[22] BT *Nedarim* 9b.

Maimonides maintains that there can be no excessive humility; because the more removed we are from haughtiness or arrogance, the better. His advocacy of the most extreme humility represents a glaring exception of his general agreement with the Aristotelian notion of the "middle road," which defines virtue as the midpoint between opposite extreme dispositions. The virtue of generosity, for example, calls for equidistance from extremes of miserliness and wastefulness. But humility is different. One should stay away from haughtiness or arrogance as much as possible.

The theocentricity of Jewish ethics also manifests itself in the pivotal role assigned to the virtue of gratitude. Bereft of a sense of gratitude to benefactors, we would be unable to recognize our enormous indebtedness to God for granting us our very existence as well as abilities and opportunities. Since our parents are partners with God in bestowing upon us the gift of existence, failure to demonstrate gratitude to them is equated with lack of reverence for God.

But this is by no means the only case where events that transpired in the past engender special obligations arising from considerations of special status. There is, for example, a wide consensus that having brought children into the world gives rise to unique responsibilities towards them. Similarly, since we are the products of particular families and share a common past with other members of the family, we have responsibilities to them that go beyond those owed to others. That is why Jewish law stipulates that the needs of poor relatives should be accorded priority.

Similarly, the common history and fate we share with all fellow Jews imposes upon us the obligation to feel a special sense of kinship and solidarity with them and so Jewish ethics dictates that priority be accorded to Jewish needs. This, of course, has invited the charge that Judaism is so particularistic that it leaves no room for universalism. But this criticism is totally unfounded. A good case can be made for the proposition that special obligations arising from special relationships should be universally acknowledged. Thus it makes perfect sense to contend that every person owes a special debt of gratitude to his or her parents. By the same token, it is eminently proper for every ethnic or national group to accord priority to the needs of its membership. There is nothing ethically wrong with a healthy patriotism as long as it avoids the pitfalls of the kind of chauvinism which declares simply, "My country, right or wrong." Thus the alleged conflict between universalism and particularism has no basis in the facts. They can co-exist peacefully.

It was his failure to understand that special obligations arise from historic contingencies that prompted Hermann Cohen to oppose the establishment of a Jewish state. He contended that no state could possibly operate on an ethical level because national self-interest dictated that its own welfare be accorded priority over the interests of other states. In keeping with their mission to become a holy people, Cohen felt that Jews must sacrifice aspirations for political independence on the altar of ethical propriety. Obviously, this point of view differs sharply from the healthy realism reflected in Jewish ethics that seeks to sanctify, not to suppress, natural human sentiments and endows love of family, community and patriotism with religious significance.

The importance which the Jewish tradition attaches to the sense of solidarity with other Jews can be gauged by the fact that non-Jews cannot simply convert to Judaism through acceptance of the tenets of the Jewish faith and the commitment to abide by all halakhic regulations. To acquire the status of *kedushat Yisrael* it is also necessary to express one's readiness to become a member of the Jewish people and to identify with its fate. Converts to Judaism do not merely adopt another religion but become persons of a radically different identity. Their "rebirth" is celebrated with their receiving a new name in order to demonstrate that as a result of their new status, their links to biological ancestors are completely severed. They are no longer regarded as sons or daughters of their biological parents, but are treated as descendants of the Patriarch Abraham, "the father of all converts." Thus it can be seen that Jewish ethics mandates that Jews relate to each other as members of one extended family. Rabbi Soloveitchik repeatedly emphasized that Judaism is based not merely upon the Sinaitic Covenant, which demands obedience to divine commandments, but also upon the Abrahamitic Covenant which requires acquiring a sense of identification with Jews everywhere.[23]

This, however, does not imply that Jewish ethics is so preoccupied with obligations to other Jews as to ignore those involving the treatment of non-Jews. It should be pointed out that many American Jews did not want to protest against the Vietnam War, feeling that this might weaken support for

---

[23] See *Ethics of Responsibility* (note 5), 14–15.

the State of Israel, but Rabbi Aharon Soloveitchik inveighed against this policy. He called attention to the fact that the prophet Jonah was severely rebuked for refusing to preach to the people of Nineveh for fear that the success of his mission would result in embarrassing the Jewish people. Similarly, he felt that those who considered the Vietnam War to be unjust had an obligation to speak out, even at the risk of antagonizing the American administration.

Significantly, the Talmud employs the concept *mi-pnei darkhei shalom* (for the sake of peaceful relations) to mandate ethical conduct towards non-Jews even in situations when the formal Torah law does not cover obligations to non-Jews. While many authorities maintain that the additional requirements deriving from *darkhei shalom* are dictated by considerations of Jewish self-interest (such as forestalling antagonism towards Jews), according to Maimonides, they represent a profoundly ethical requirement based upon imitation of the ways of God who shows compassion to all creatures.[24] Latter-day authorities contend that even in cases where Halakhah seemingly discriminates against non-Jews, it is imperative that Jews refrain from taking advantage of various technical loopholes, but act in scrupulously ethical fashion towards Jews and non-Jews alike.[25] It thus can be seen that Jewish ethics reflects a dialectical tension between particularistic and universal elements.

---

[24] For a more extensive discussion of this issue, see *Ethics of Responsibility* (note 5), 47–52, and "Darkhei Shalom," (page 55 in this volume).
[25] See Mosheh Rivkes, *Beer Hagolah, Choshen Mishpat,* 248:5 and Israel Lipschutz, *Tiferet Yisrael, Bava Kamma,* 4:3.

COVENANTAL IMPERATIVES[1]

THE FAILURE TO PROVIDE specific solutions to the agonizing ethical dilemmas one encounters in such areas as American Vietnam policy, the urban crisis and racial strife, has exposed most forms of contemporary religion to the charge of irrelevance. Halakhic Judaism is especially vulnerable on this score because Jewish piety is largely conceived in terms of obedience to formal rules of law. But if one equates piety with adherence to halakhic standards, one automatically limits the domain of religious behavior to the relatively small area which is governed by explicit halakhic rules. Since the most sensitive issues confronting us today do not fall under this category, it would follow that religious values play no role whatsoever in the arenas which are of the greatest contemporary relevance. As long as one insists that in the final analysis piety consists of obedience to God's revealed law,[2] one cannot possibly endow a particular act with religious significance unless one would be able to point to a general law which applies to the particular situation in question.

But in the absence of a general law regulating our response to a specific situation (i.e., when no halakhic ruling is obtainable) we would find ourselves

---

[1] From *Samuel K. Mirsky Memorial Volume,* edited by Gersion Appel, 3–12. New York: Yeshiva University, 1970.
[2] For purposes of this essay we ignore those commandments that are specifically addressed to a particular event. Obviously, obedience to the revealed Divine Will may also manifest itself in carrying out instructions that relate to a specific historic situation.

in a religious no man's land, completely outside of the territory where religious imperatives can hold sway.

Actually there are two distinct components that can be distinguished in the charge of narrowness that is hurled against so called Jewish legalism. On the one hand, it is maintained that the imposition of specific, rigid, halakhic norms deprives individuals of their capacity to respond as free and creative human beings to moral challenges. Blind submission to legal rules, so it is claimed, leaves no room for the development and functioning of a truly sensitive conscience. To employ Erich Fromm's terminology,[3] Judaism is seen only as a system of duties, not of responsibilities. On the other hand, it is charged that Judaism is too limited in its claims upon the individual, inasmuch as compliance with legalistic standards is regarded not only as a necessary but also as a sufficient condition of an adequate religious response.

Much of the antipathy of modern existentialist thought to classical Judaism derives from the identification of Jewish piety with mechanical submission to formal rules of law. Viewed from the perspective of the existentialist, this is tantamount to the negation of the authenticity of the individual who, instead of making his own decisions, falls back upon ready-made rules which are supplied from without.[4]

Typical of the widespread notion that halakhic Judaism simply leaves no room for the creative response of the individual, because allegedly nothing matters but conformity to specific rules of conduct, is the statement of one of the most influential theologians of our time. Thus Bultmann notes is a revealing passage that the ideal religious Jew knows how to find "through ingenious interpretations of the law, the necessary rules of conduct for each situation of life and every relationship."[5] This purely formal obedience to the authority of the law is contrasted by Bultmann with the allegedly higher Christian ideal of "radical obedience"[6] which involves man's whole being.

---

[3] Erich Fromm, *You Shall Be As Gods: A Radical Interpretation of the Old Testament and Its Tradition.* New York: Holt, Rinehart and Winston, 1966, 56.

[4] This antipathy is, of course, largely reinforced by the misconception that Judaism, because of its stress upon the centrality of the Jewish people, is totally indifferent to individualistic values. For a discussion of this view, see my contribution to the symposium "Judaism and Modern Man," in the *Reconstruction of European Jewish Life and the Conference of European Rabbis*, edited by Rabbi Maurice Rose, 34–39, London: 1967.

[5] Rudolf Bultmann, *Jesus and the Word.* New York: Scribner, 1962, 69.

[6] *ibid.*, 75–77.

Insofar as Judaism is concerned, so Bultmann maintains, "man is only accidentally or occasionally claimed by God."[7] Unless "a rule in the Scripture, a formal authority"[8] can be applied to a particular given situation, we cannot, according to Bultmann, meaningfully speak in Jewish terms of obedience to God's commandment. Whereas, so Bultmann continues, Christianity teaches that "the whole man is under the necessity of decision,"[9] Judaism, because it defines obedience to God in purely legal terms, allegedly is less demanding and recognizes the existence of religiously "neutral situations."[10]

Among Jewish thinkers one also encounters disdain for a form of piety that is reducible to conformity with a formal system of general rules. Martin Buber, for example, goes as far as to regard the interposition of a law as a threat to the immediacy between God and man. He has nothing but contempt for those who barricade themselves behind "the ramparts of the law"[11] and thus forfeit the "holy insecurity"[12] which is experienced by those truly open to God. While "transcendence speaks to man in the essential moments of life,"[13] man's response to the divine address cannot be cast into the mold of obedience to a general law. Instead, according to Buber, man must hold himself "ready for the immediate word of God as directed to a specific hour of like."[14] For Buber, revelation cannot ever be "the formulation of a law."[15] It is always in terms of concreteness, singularity and individuality that in the life of the dialogue man must respond to God who "speaks to man through the life which he gives him again and again."[16] And man's decision must be made not on the basis of reliance upon fixed norms but in complete freedom. Thus man's response to the confrontation by the

---

[7] *ibid.*, 77.

[8] *ibid.*, 78.

[9] *ibid.*

[10] *ibid.*

[11] Martin Buber, quoted by Will Herberg, *The Writings of Martin Buber*, 19.

[12] *ibid.*

[13] Martin Buber, "The Dialogue between Heaven and Earth." In *Four Existential Philosophers*, edited by Will Herberg, 95.

[14] *On Jewish Learning*, Franz Rosenzweig, edited by N.N. Glatzer, 111.

[15] *ibid.*

[16] Martin Buber, "The Two Foci of the Jewish Soul." In *Israel and the World*, 33.

Divine is expressed not through adherence to His Law but "through the language of our answers is not what we call an answering for ourselves."[17]

Although Franz Rosenzweig in his famous exchange with Buber pleads for a far more sympathetic attitude towards the Law, it must be borne in mind that in principle he shares many of Buber's basic premises. Reliance upon the Law as such would, according to Rosenzweig, constitute a religiously worthless stance. But he does not go along with Buber in maintaining that the acceptance of legal norms automatically disqualifies one from openness to God. Instead he holds that it is possible for the individual to experience law not merely as law (and hence religiously worthless) but as a commandment through which he finds himself personally addressed by God. Yet it is the individual who must determine for himself whether or not a given law really speaks to him as a commandment. This explains Rosenzweig's insistence that only those parts of the Law which are regarded as "doable" be considered as binding by us. Moreover, Rosenzweig objects to the traditional conception of the Law inasmuch as it does not confront the individual with Divine imperatives in the vast domain of the "permissible." He abhors the resulting religious vacuum where the individual does not consider himself commanded by God in precisely those areas which are of greatest relevance and concern to him in a given historic situation.[18]

Thus it can be readily seen that Rosenzweig's position, apart from advocating for purely pedagogical considerations the provisional acceptance of Jewish practices and the tentative observance of the Law in the absence of proper motivation, is basically akin to the earlier stages in Buber's thinking where he still defined his stand as prenomian, since obedience to legal norms simply was not regarded as a decisive factor in man's confrontation with the Divine. It must be admitted, however, that some of Buber's later formulations went far beyond – as Buber averred[19] – the purely prenomian or metranomian stage. As a matter of fact, we encounter a pronounced antinomian position inasmuch as obedience to the Law is

---

[17] "The Dialogue between Heaven and Earth," *op. cit.*, 195–196.
[18] Franz Rosenzweig, *op. cit.*; 72–92 and 109–118.
[19] "The Two Foci of the Jewish Soul," *op. cit.*; 28–29.

portrayed as the very antithesis of a free and open response to the Divine address.[20]

Understandably, Buber's position has evoked the ire of those who regard the Law as a vital ingredient in the structure of Jewish piety. It is unfortunate, through, that this justifiable reaction has blinded many achievements to break the vicious stranglehold of the Kantian categories of thought which has blocked for such a long time the emergence of vital, authentic Jewish theological thought. The grotesque distortions to which Jewish religious and ethical values were at time subjected in the systems of Moritz Lazarus, Hermann Cohen and Ahad ha-Am are evidence of the pitfalls inherent in a approach that seeks to force Judaism into a straitjacket of Kantian categories which limit the scope of moral significance and ethical worth to the domain of the categorical imperative with its one-sided stress upon universalizability. It could hardly be expected that such a conceptual scheme could do justice to a religion which reveals in the individual, particular and concrete.

halakhic Judaism, it should be borne in mind, never viewed man's commitment to the service of God merely in terms of sheer conformity to legal norms. The overriding religious ideal of Judaism is not theonomy, the acknowledgment of laws deriving their authority and sanction from God, but rather – to adopt Dr. Belkin's usage of the term[21] theocracy – the rule of God. One need not be a follower of Paul of Tarsus, or for that matter of Martin Buber, in order to recognize that the covenant of Abraham did not entail the acceptance of a legal code. Yet, according to the Talmud, Abraham pioneered a spiritual revolution, not so much by emphasizing the oneness of God, but rather by stressing that God was to be served as the Master.[22] To perform an act "for the sake of Heaven"[23] does not necessarily imply that the act in question represents an instance of a religiously ordained general norm or precept. It should be remembered that Judaism parts company with the Kantian notion of autonomy not only because theonomy displaces autonomy not only because of the undue emphasis upon the first term – the "auto" (the stress upon the self) but also because of "nomy" aspect – the

---

[20] Letter to Franz Rosenzweig in *On Jewish Learning*, 111, and Martin Buber, *Two Types of Faith*, 57.

[21] See Samuel Belkin, *In His Image*. New York: Abelard, 1960, 16.

[22] BT *Berakhot*, 7b.

[23] *Avot* 2:19; *Betzah* 16.

complete identification of the moral good with that which prescribed by law (whatever it source may be). Notwithstanding the protestations of neo-Kantians, Judaism cannot be reduced to a "religion of law"[24]

For Judaism, sheer compliance with the Law as such was never regarded as the ultimate value. It rather represented a means to the fulfillment of the Divine Will. This is evidenced by the fact that provisions of the Law may be suspended for the purpose of achieving other general religious objectives (*hora'at sha'ah*).[25] And while it may be argued that in this eventuality we merely encounter a situation where certain specific laws are suspended in order to enable us to comply with other laws, we must not forget that there are occasions when in the absence of such considerations, suspension of the Law is still condoned. There is definite recognition of the principle of *averah lishmah*, that a transgression may be considered meritorious if it is motivated by the desire to serve God.[26] Although the application of the principle is discouraged except under extraordinary circumstances,[27] it nonetheless is for theoretical purposes extremely important to know that the religious significance of an act is not necessarily grounded in its relation to a general law but can arise solely from the fact it is performed for "the sake of Heaven." It thus follows that even outside the relatively small area which is subject to regulation by specific legal laws on principles; there may be ample room for the notion of religious obligation and significance. I propose the term "Covenantal Imperative" to denote its sanction from a general norm or law. The covenantal imperative does not have to be apprehended through a process of reflection as constituting an instance, capable of being subsumed under a general rule, but can be immediately intuited as an individual's religious obligation arising out of his covenantal encounter with God.[28]

---

[24] For a criticism of the view that identifies ethical propriety with universal obligation, see Nicolai Berdyaev, *Slavery and Freedom*, 43.

[25] BT *Berakhot*, 54a and 63a; BT *Yoma* 69b; BT *Yevamot* 90b; BT *Horayot* 6a.

[26] BT *Nazir*, 23b; BT *Horayot* 10b.

[27] Cf. *Nefesh ha-Hayyim* by Rabbi Hayyim of Volozhin, Chapter VII, and also *Orhot Hayyim*, Sec. 132. See also my treatment of the subject in "Rabbi Hayyim of Volozhin," in *Guardians of Our Heritage*, edited by Leo Jung, 201 (page 105 in this volume).

[28] Compare however, J.S. Mill, *Utilitarianism*, 5. "The Morality of an individual action is not a question of direct perception but of the application of law to the individual case."

It is precisely the very individuality and particularity of the concrete situation that elicits a specific covenantal imperative.[29] Under such conditions the individual cannot fall back on some prefabricated rules to guide him in a given existential situation. Instead, it is the personal element which must largely determine what an individual believes to be the covenantal imperative addressing him at specific moment. Thus the covenantal imperative possesses, to make use of the existentialist term, the authenticity of a personal decision, which cannot be avoided by recourse to pre-established rules and ready-made principle.

It is, of course, relatively easy to demonstrate that mere compliance with legal standards does not exhaust the meaning of Jewish piety. Numerous authorities[30] have balked at narrowly conceived definitions of Jewish religious obligations and have invoked the Talmudic statement[31] which looks upon the verse "In all thy ways thou shalt know Him"[32] as the most inclusive and adequate characterization of the range over which piety should hold sway. But we are still left with the formidable task of correlating the realm of covenantal imperatives with that of the Halakhah. Would we not in essence revert to a basically Gnostic world view if the entire structure of the law would be deemed irrelevant to the domain of covenantal imperatives? Are we prepared to follow the footsteps of the Gnosis of old and postulate some special faculty which enables us to grasp covenantal imperatives directly and independently without any relationship to Torah or halakhic reasoning. Should not the intuition of the covenantal imperative in some measure be related to the world of the law which plays such a dominant part in Judaism and is regarded as the link par excellence between man and God?

Nahmanides, in a famous comment,[33] suggests an approach that may be useful for our purposes. Addressing himself to the question of why the Torah should find it necessary to provide, in addition to such general rules as "to do what is good and right in the eyes of God,"[34] a number of specific

---

[29] Compare Rabbi Naftali Zvi Berlin, *Haamek Davar* on Exodus 19:5.

[30] Maimonides *Hilkhot Deot*, 3:3, see also his introduction to *Avot* Chapter V, see also Tur *Shulhan Arukh, Orah Hayim*, ch. 231, and *Shulhan Arukh, Orah Hayim*, ch. 231.

[31] BT *Berakhot* 63a.

[32] Proverbs 3:6.

[33] Nahmanides, *Commentary to the Torah,* Deuteronomy 7:18.

[34] Deuteronomy 7:18.

instances exemplifying the rule in question, advanced the view that it is through understanding of particular instances that we learn to grasp intuitively the range of situation to which a vague general rule may be applicable. By the same token, it may be said analogically, that as we become exposed to the halakhic categories, out understanding of covenantal imperatives will reflect somewhat out understanding of the law. In a sense, this characterization of covenantal imperatives resembles in one respect the widely abused notion of *Da'at Torah*, which accords special weight to the view of eminent halakhic scholars even in areas where no formal halakhic decision (*pesak*) is feasible. Implicit in this doctrine is the notion that the residual influence of halakhic categories of thought can make itself felt outside the relatively limited area to which the law per se is applicable. What differentiates our approach to covenantal imperatives from the doctrine of *Da'at Torah* is the emphasis on the personal responsibility of the individual to make his own decisions in areas not subject to halakhic legislation or authority. One cannot abdicate one's religious responsibility by claiming that halakhic authorities provide authoritative guidance in areas which ultimately have to be reserved for the individual's exercise of his personal freedom.

We are, however, still left with a formidable problem. We have yet to show how the Law can be expected to enhance our understanding of covenantal imperatives, which by definition do not come within the purview of legal rules and precepts. For this purpose it would be most helpful to sketch briefly the theological assumptions underlying out approach. Basic to our position is the thesis that the Sinaitic revelation first and foremost was a revelation of the Divine Presence and only secondarily the communication of specific content.[35]

Maimonides goes as far as to claim[36] that at Sinai, with the single exception of Moses, the people were unable to grasp the content of what they had heard. In his opinion, the event at Sinai represented, insofar as the experience of all but Moses was concerned, a Revelation of the Divine Presence but not the communication of content. Moreover, even those authorities who maintain that Sinai yielded content to the rest of the people

---

[35] Compare the famous statement of the Pesach Haggadah: "Even if he had met us at Mt. Sinai and not given us the Torah, that would have been enough." This clearly shows that the exposure to the Divine Presence at Sinai, apart from receiving the content of Revelation, is regarded as an intrinsic value.

[36] Maimonides, *Guide of the Perplexed*, II:35.

will not deny the importance of the Divine Presence which is stressed so much in the Biblical account.[37] But while at Sinai, Presence preceded content, after Sinai the situation is reversed. True, every Jew throughout history is regarded as having stood at Mt. Sinai. It must, however, be borne, in mind that since Sinai the mode of the address is different. After Sinai the Jew is addressed first by the content of Divine Revelation. The experience of the Divine Presence comes not before, but after hearing the Divine Word. As Franz Rosenzweig saw so clearly, the Mitzvah is not merely content as such but a revelation link to God as the *metzaveh*, the Commander. After Sinai, it is through exposure to the content of the Divine Revelation that we come near the Divine Presence. The more one's thinking becomes conditioned by halakhic categories, the better one can extrapolate halakhic categories of thought and perceive covenantal imperatives which arise out of the awareness of one's covenantal encounter with God. The more we allow ourselves to be addressed by God's Torah and mitzvot, the better our chance for refinement and enhancement of our spiritual faculties enabling is to become more open to the covenantal imperatives which confront us with God's demands upon us in the here now in all their uniqueness and particularity.

Thus, true to its name, the Halakhah does not serve as the final goal of the Jew, but rather as the way, guiding him in his individuality towards authentic personal decisions in the domain of covenantal imperatives. After all, Jerusalem, so the Sages have told us, was destroyed because our forebears merely abided by the letter of the law.[38] In the final analysis we can properly fulfill our covenantal obligations only when, reaching out beyond the minimum requirements of the law, we respond as free individuals to the summons to an all encompassing service which is issued to us as individuals in our existential subjectivity, uniqueness and particularity by a God who is One and Unique.

---

[37] Deuteronomy, 5:19–25, 4:10–14, Exodus 19:15–19.
[38] BT *Bava Metzia* 30b.

DARKHEI SHALOM[1]

DARKHEI SHALOM (on account of the ways of peace) represents a maxim which is frequently invoked in Talmudic literature as justification for a variety of rabbinic ordinances designed to supplement or modify biblical legislation. The range of subjects where the application of this rule has exerted a pronounced impact is rather extensive. But for fairly obvious reasons, it was primarily in areas where the utilization of this principle has affected relationships to the non-Jewish world that the analysis of its meaning and significance has evoked the greatest interest.

The basic question that must be faced is whether the enactments prompted by concern for *darkhei shalom* should be regarded as expediency measures dictated by the enlightened self-interest of the Jewish community or whether we are dealing in these cases with a supreme ethical principle which transcends purely pragmatic considerations.

Historically, divergent views have been presented on this question. On the one hand, Christian writers, bent as they are on demonstrating the alleged superiority of Christian universalism over Jewish particularism, tend to relegate *darkhei shalom* to the level of a purely prudential device aiming at facilitating coexistence with the non-Jewish world.

In what appears to be an overreaction precipitated by apologetic fervor, an array of prominent scholars such as Professors Hoffman, Lazarus, and Lauterbach categorically reject any suggestion that *darkhei shalom* was intended solely as a device to protect the stability and security of the Jewish

---

[1] *Gesher* 6, RIETS, (1978): 80–86.

community. The ordinances promulgated to advance the "ways of peace," they argue, were inspired not by purely pragmatic considerations of enlightened self-interest, but rather by lofty ethical principles.

One of the most crucial arguments advanced in support of the thesis that the "ways of peace" represent an overriding ethical principle, and do not merely reflect considerations of expediency, is based upon a Talmudic passage.[2] The Babylonian Talmud states that the entire Torah reflects "the ways of peace," as it is written, "Its ways are the ways of pleasantness and all its paths are peace."[3] It has been argued, that if, "the ways of peace" represent an all pervasive distinguishing feature of the entire Torah, how could such a prominent characteristic be relegated to the purely pragmatic level. What is overlooked in this argument is a rather significant point. There is no indication whatsoever in the Talmudic passage cited, that "the ways of peace" represent the ultimate aim and overall objective of the Torah. The texts in question really emphasize that "the ways of peace" represent one of the numerous features characterizing the precepts of the Torah. There is no evidence whatsoever that these characteristics constitute any more than merely pragmatically useful consequences which ensue in the wake of living in accordance with the precepts of the Torah. The text, however, does not provide any support for the contention that the very purpose of the Torah is to bring about conditions of peace and pleasantness.[4]

Another frequently advanced argument in support of the ethical thesis is equally unconvincing. It has been maintained that the term *darkhei shalom* conveys much more than merely the intent to prevent animosity between individuals. If *darkhei shalom* merely amounted to an effort to reduce or prevent friction or strife, then, so it is claimed, the appropriate term would have been *devar ha-shalom*[5] or *mi-pnei evah* (prevention of animosity). The very usage of the term *darkhei shalom* (the ways of peace) is construed as evidence that what the Talmudic sages had in mind was a far more general and sublime ethical goal than merely the attainment of a stable social order.

---

[2] BT *Gittin* 59b.

[3] Proverbs 3:17.

[4] We need but recall the well-known comment of the Tur in *Choshen Mishpat* 1. Accordingly, truth, war, and peace are treated as necessary conditions for the existence of the world, but not as the *raison d'être* or ultimate purpose.

[5] This term is employed in BT *Yevamot* 67b.

The only trouble with this kind of argument is that it is not borne out by the facts. Many Tannaitic ordinances that are similar to the type of enactments justified in the Mishnah on the grounds that they are vital because of *darkhei shalom* are in the Gemara explained on the grounds they were prompted by the attempt to prevent *evah* (hatred). This clearly shows that insofar as the Talmud is concerned, there is really no conceptual difference between the positive formulation ("the ways of peace") and the negative formulation *mi-pnei evah* (prevention of hatred).

As a matter of fact, it seems that, disregarding one or possibly two exceptions, the term *evah is* not at all employed by the Tannaim either in the Mishnah or in the Tosefta.[6] On the other hand, when the Amoraim explained the reasons for certain enactments previously decreed by the Tannaim, they have recourse to the term *evah*. But since the Amoraim employ the term *evah* to explain Tannaitic enactments that are similar to those justified in the Mishnah explicitly by reference to *darkhei shalom,* it follows that insofar as the Amoraim were concerned, "the ways of peace" were the equivalent of the prevention of *evah*.

To be sure, nothing we have established so far can be construed as evidence against the "moral" thesis. There is no reason whatsoever that the prevention of *evah* should be regarded as a purely pragmatic objective. After all, in the Jewish religious code, the mandate to pursue peace plays a very important role. Among the religious acts that qualify for reward, both in this world and in the World to Come, are included the measures designed to promote peace between man and his fellow man.

But even if we recognize that efforts to eliminate friction are endowed with enormous religious and ethical significance, we are still left with a major question. We have not yet resolved whether *darkhei shalom* or *evah,* when applied to relationships with the non-Jewish community, represent an intrinsic or an instrumental value. It might well be argued that ultimately our concern for "the ways of peace" in our relationship with the non-Jewish world stems ultimately from Jewish self-interest. Obviously, the well-being of the Jewish community would be adversely affected by inviting friction with the non-Jewish community. Thus, it would be only the moral and religious imperative to insure the stability and security of the Jewish

---

[6] There are, of course, two exceptions to this rule. The Mishnah in *Kiddushin* 63a, and according to some versions, the Tosefta in *Betzah* 4:10 also employ this term.

community that would serve as the matrix for the enactment of regulations aiming to remove grounds for friction with the non-Jewish community. With such an approach to *darkhei shalom* there would be totally absent from the Jewish value structure any intrinsic concern for the well-being of those outside of the Jewish covenantal community. We would be left only with counsels for enlightened self-interest.

In contrast with this ethnocentric conception one might with the same degree of plausibility advance the thesis that "the ways of peace" and, for that matter, considerations of *evah* reflect an overriding universal moral principle. Accordingly, *darkhei shalom* would provide the matrix for binding moral obligations extending the range and scope of legalistic requirements. In this conception, *darkhei shalom* supplements legalistic formulations and adds a moral dimension of universal significance.

Upon closer examination, it becomes evident that the two respective interpretations of the rabbinic maxim are perfectly compatible with the source material. Significantly, rabbinic authorities in the Middle Ages already held divergent views with respect to the nature and scope of the concept. On the one hand, some scholars operated within a purely ethnocentric framework and maintained that regulations rooted in "the ways of peace" or *evah* were in effect only when the Jewish society in some sense depended upon the goodwill of the non-Jewish world. But in situations where Jews had no ground to fear the reaction of the non-Jewish world, no allowances had to me made for "the ways of peace."[7]

Other scholars categorically rejected this position and insisted upon the unconditional applicability of the precept, irrespective of any considerations as to whether or not an action in question would enhance the welfare of the Jewish community *per se*. Maimonides, for example, makes it abundantly clear that concern for the welfare of a non-Jew transcends consideration of enlightened self-interest and reflects the religious mandate to imitate the ethical attitudes of God. It is for this reason, that when Maimonides[8] discusses the obligation to give alms to non-Jews, he cites the verse "God is good to everyone and His mercy encompasses all His creatures,"[9] before quoting the passage from Proverbs which the Talmud invokes as justification for "the ways of peace." Apparently, Maimonides went out of

---

[7] *Tosafot Yeshanim* on BT *Shabbat* 19b; Rashba on BT *Bava Metzia* 32b.

[8] *Hilchot Melakhim* 10:12.

[9] Psalms 119:9.

his way to guard against any attempt to look upon moral actions towards non-Jews as grounded exclusively in purely pragmatic considerations calculated to secure the peace of the Jewish community. By linking the pursuit of "the ways of peace" with the divine attribute of compassion, Maimonides suggests that what is involved in "the ways of peace" is an overriding religious imperative. Significantly, the verse "God's mercy extends to all His creatures" is also cited by Maimonides[10] as evidence that the cultivation of compassion constitutes one of the ways in which we comply with the mandate to emulate divine attributes of ethical perfection.

What emerges from the Maimonidean formulation of "the ways of peace" is an emphasis of what might be termed "agent-morality." Accordingly, even in situations where for a variety of reasons certain provisions of "act-morality" may not be applicable, considerations of agent-morality form the matrix of additional obligations. To give a specific example, the Biblical commandment prescribing alms-giving does not include an obligation to support non-Jewish poor. Yet considerations of agent-morality (the precept mandating the cultivation of moral disposition patterning itself after the divine model) dictate that we display compassion to all individuals regardless of their religious or ethnic background. Thus, while Jewish act-morality might contain features that differentiate between obligations toward Jews and those who are outside of the covenantal community, agent-morality, relating as it does to the dispositions of the agent, eliminates all such differences. Insensitivity to the needs of others is no less reprehensible a trait when it is exhibited in behavior toward non-Jews than it would be towards fellow Jews. It should also be noted that in the context of Maimonides's philosophy, the expression "the ways of peace" is especially appropriate to convey a moral thrust. Characteristically, for Maimonides, the entire system of law governing interpersonal relationships can be subsumed under the overall principle of altruism. And it is through altruistic behavior that, in the Maimonidean view, one helps create the kind of social order which is conducive both to general welfare and personal happiness. As a matter of fact, it is precisely because ethical acts have such beneficial consequences, that they create their own reward, in this world, apart from the spiritual reward that can be expected in the World to Come.

---

[10] *Avadim* 9:8.

To be sure, Maimonides is by no means alone in the contention that concern for peace is integrally related to various other ethical norms. According to an opinion expressed by Tosafot, "the ways of peace" are so broadly defined as to include features which not even by the widest stretch of the imagination could possibly be regarded as constituent elements of domestic peace. Tosafot contends that the proviso that one may deviate from the truth on account of considerations of humility or modesty is part and parcel of the general rule that considerations of "the ways of peace" warrant the telling of white lies.[11] It is noteworthy that Tosafot does not adopt the approach of many other commentators who regard concern for various moral virtues as a completely independent category justifying deviation from the truth, without, in any way, being reducible to the right to deviate from the truth on account of the interests of peace. Tosafot's broad definition of "the ways of peace" is obviously totally incompatible with the thesis that the notion amounts merely to a counsel of prudence devoid of any intrinsic moral significance.

It might, of course, be argued that the expression *darkhei shalom* possesses a variety of meanings ranging from mere consideration of expediency to the loftiest moral maxims. There certainly is no conclusive proof that the expression must have the same meaning in the various contexts in which it has been employed. One, therefore, might contend that while for Tosafot, *darkhei shalom* in certain cases represents an ultimate religious moral ideal, in other cases, for example, in the relationship to the non-Jewish community, it amounts merely to the counsel of enlightened self-interest.

While such a position is indeed logically tenable, it appears that the burden of proof rests upon those who insist that "the ways of peace" hold an entirely different meaning when applied to relationships with the non-Jewish world. At any rate, it can be seen from our preceding analysis that at least for Maimonides and possibly for many other Jewish authorities, "the ways of peace" are treated as the ethical religious norm and not merely as a pragmatic device to safeguard Jewish self-interest.

---

[11] Tosafot, *Bava Metzia* 23b. It should be observed that Tosafot, unlike Maimonides, does not differentiate between *darkhei shalom* and *devar ha-shalom*.

LAW AS THE BASIS OF A MORAL SOCIETY[1]

BY ERECTING A WALL of separation between law and morality, modern legal theory has helped precipitate the authority crisis that afflicts contemporary institutions. In the long run, without recourse to some transcendent authority, no legal system can command respect. Law and order cannot be maintained simply through reliance on the power of sanctions. However important the feature of enforceability may be for the effectiveness of legal institutions, ultimately their legitimacy hinges not upon power but authority. Since under contemporary conditions the legal system is perceived as utterly lacking in transcendent support, it is difficult to see how the erosion of its authority can be halted.

In contrast with prevailing conceptions that divorce law from morality, Judaism provides an extremely close link between the two spheres. Unlike philosophical doctrines such as natural law theories or utilitarianism that ground law upon morality, in the Jewish scheme the reverse holds true. Morality ultimately derives its normative significance from the transcendent authority of the law which, in turn, serves as the matrix for the development of moral conceptions.

It must, however, be emphasized that by treating the law as the basis of morality we do not wish to align ourselves with the legalistic position according to which all ethical or moral questions are ultimately reducible to purely legal issues. To treat the law as the basis of morality is a far cry from regarding it as its very quintessence. There is no need to overreact to the

[1] *Tradition* 19:1 (Fall 1981): 42–54.

charges of legalism by claiming that in every single instance of ethical decision-making we can be adequately guided by formal halakhic rules. As against several prominent contemporary Jewish ethicists, we shall attempt to show that Jewish morality contains features which go beyond the scope of any "law-ethics."[2]

The accent we place upon the extra-legal dimension, however, by no means detracts from the centrality and primacy of the law in the ethico-religious sphere. That already the *Septuagint* rendered such a basic term as "Torah" with the Greek "*nomoi*" (laws) provides conclusive evidence that already in antiquity the legal components of the Pentateuch were widely regarded as its most salient feature. Typically, throughout history, the Jewish religious community was relatively indifferent to purely theoretical theological concerns involving matters of dogma. What primarily agitated the community were questions pertaining to matters of practice. By the same token, traditionally the function of a rabbi was not to serve as a theological expert, but to provide authoritative guidance of legal questions. It is revealing that in reaction to the challenge of the Reform movement, the traditional Jewish community did not define itself as "Orthodox" – a term of derision that was foisted upon it by its antagonists. It chose the designation "*gesetzes-treu*" (loyal to the law) in order to make it clear that the basic issue dividing the two opposing camps was their respective position vis-à-vis the binding authority of the law.

The traditionalists assigned the law such a dominant position because they perceived it as the explicit command of the Divine Sovereign. Hence, the overriding authority of the law was deemed to be a function not of its content but of its transcendent source. Such an approach to the normative character of the law must, however, not be confused with John Austin's "Command Theory of the Law," where the authority of legal institutions derives exclusively from the power vested in the sovereign. In Austin's scheme, the law possesses only power but not authority, because of its power to command is exclusively a function of the enforceability through sanctions at the disposal of the sovereign. In Jewish law an entirely different situation prevails. The law possesses moral authority because God, unlike pagan gods, represents not merely supreme power but the highest moral

---

[2] Stanley Hauerwas, "Obligation and Virtue Once More," *Journal of Religious Ethics* 3 (Spring 1975): 27–44. Frederick S. Carney, "The Virtue-Obligation Controversy," *Journal of Religious Ethics* 1 (Fall 1973): 5–20.

authority conceivable. God is not only omniscient and omnipotent but also omni-benevolent. Hence, submission to His will is not simply surrender to absolute power but obedience to the supreme moral authority.

Jacques Elul[3] and Harold Berman[4] have called attention to the religious dimension which in primitive societies provided the law with the authority derived from a transcendent source which could command respect and reverence. To be sure, some philosophers, notably Kant, insist that the categorical authority of a moral law cannot depend upon theological support. It is, however, extremely dubious whether, in point of fact, autonomy can endow a law with the same kind of authority it possessed when it enjoyed the support of theological props. With the benefit of hindsight, we can convincingly argue that the Kantian doctrine that the law qua law commands respects is really a "survival" of a primitive era. As Mrs. Anscombe has shown,[5] any kind of "law-ethics" patterned after the Kantian model fails to reckon with a fundamental problem. Once the element of a Divine legislator is eliminated, law can hardly be expected to command the kind of respect it bore when it was endowed with the authority of a Divine imperative.

Because of its theocentric nature, Jewish ethics attributes the "imperativeness" of the moral law to the property of being commanded by God. Thus, the foundation of morality is provided by specific legal norms, e.g., prohibitions against murder, incest, theft, not by overall principles from which various specific norms are deducible. As Nahmanides put it, the very meaning of a general ethical principle such as "Thou shalt do what is good and right in the eyes of God"[6] can be properly understood only if we have at our disposal sufficiently large numbers of concrete, specific rules exemplifying the underlying principle as to enable us eventually to acquire an intuitive grasp of the principle itself.

It must be admitted that such an approach to morality runs counter to the philosophical bias towards monism. As a general rule, philosophers gravitate towards systems where specific moral norms and rules are deduced

---

[3] Jaques Elul, *The Theological Foundation of Law* (New York: Doubleday & Company 1960).

[4] Harold J. Berman, *The Interaction of Law and Religion* (Nashville: Abington Press, 1974).

[5] C.E.M. Anscombe, "Modern Moral Philosophy." *Journal of Philosophical Studies* 33 (1958): 13–14.

[6] Nahmanides, *Commentary to the Torah*, Deuteronomy 7:18.

from or at least justified by reference to a single overall principle e.g. greatest utility, rationality, etc. But as Stuart Hampshire[7] has pointed out, the moral data available hardly warrant such an approach. The formation of our moral conscience usually begins with specific moral rules such as prohibitions against violence, theft, murder, etc. Overall basic moral principles such as the sanctity of life or the obligation to consider the welfare of others are only secondary. Such a pluralistic stance which emphasizes the primacy of particular ethical norms hardly will satisfy the philosopher's quest for neatness. But it far more accurately describes the actual psychological processes that govern the evolution of conscience as external norms gradually become internalized. It should also be borne in mind that we have no assurance whatsoever that our various independent moral judgments are really compatible with one another. It is quite likely that some of our criteria for evaluation of public morality may contradict some of our moral standards governing private morality. But be that as it may, we are unable to demonstrate the consistency of our various moral principles, let alone support the claim that they form a coherent system that can be deduced from a small set of postulates.

The doctrine that law functions as the source of morality obtains additional plausibility in the light of the close linkage between moral and legal concepts. Aristotle already discusses the view that justice represents a legal conception. But while he personally rejects this position, Walter Kaufmann in his *Without Guilt and Justice* goes so far as to discard justice as a moral value since, in his opinion, justice involves a legal rather than a moral frame of reference.[8] But we wonder whether, instead of dismissing altogether a moral value that has been regarded as well as one of the most essential characteristics of all morality, it would not have been preferable to accept the proposition that legal notions serve as the matrix of moral conceptions.

A good case can be made for the thesis that the very notion of a moral "ought" derives from a sense of obligation evoked by a law which is rooted in a transcendent realm. The very meaning of an absolute unconditional demand addressed to man, as opposed to a purely prudential requirement

---

[7] Stuart Hampshire, "Morality and Pessimism." In *Public and Private Morality,* edited by Stuart Hampshire, 9–11. Cambridge University Press: 1978.
[8] Walter Kaufmann, *Without Guilt and Justice.* New York: Delta Publishing Co., 1973, 97–100.

seems, as Martin Buber suggests, to point to a religious dimension. Contrary to the claims of the utilitarians, the notion of "ought" is not reducible to value terms since, as Prichard has shown,[9] it is by no means self-evident that we ought to strive for the greatest possible good. Viewed from the perspective of Jewish ethics, the notion of ought can be traced back to the imperativeness associated with the mitzvah, the transcendent command which underlies the legal system.

To avoid any misunderstanding, it should be emphasized that our analysis by no means implies the proposition that moral *values* are based upon law. Nothing we have asserted rules out the possibility of an ethic that is independent of, or transcends Halakhah.[10] We have merely claimed that; from a Jewish perspective, the obligation to promote moral values rests upon a legal foundation i.e. "to do what is good and right" (Deuteronomy 7:18). The actual determination of what in effect are the requirements of the good and the right may be left to the perceptions of the human conscience.

It should also be borne in mind that the relationship between law and morality is by no means one-sided. Considerable interaction occurs between the two respective domains. Moral perceptions engendered by the law, become, in turn, an important factor in legislation.

Numerous Talmudic and post-Talmudic enactments have been prompted by the concern for the improvement of social welfare (*tikkun olam*)[11] or "the ways of peace."[12] Whenever the meaning of a biblical ordinance or the range of its applicability is in question, the Talmud employs as a hermeneutical device, for the purpose of eliciting the "real" meaning of the biblical text, the doctrine that "the ways of pleasantness" and "the ways of peace" are the hallmark of the entire Torah.[13] It must, however, be realized that the Jewish doctrine of the primacy of the law, which, in turn,

---

[9] H.A. Prichard, "Does Moral Philosophy Rest upon a Mistake?" *Mind, N.S.,* 4 (1912): 20–37.

[10] Aharon Lichtenstein, *"Mussar ve-Halakhah be-Masoret ha-Yahadut."* *Deot* (46): 57–97, and "Does Jewish Tradition Recognize Ethic Independent of Halakhah?" in *Modern Jewish Ethics,* edited by Marvin Fox, Ohio State University Press: 1975. (See also Marvin Fox, "Maimonides and Aquinas on Natural Law." *Dinei Yisrael* 3 (1972): 5–36.)

[11] Mishnah *Gittin,* Chapter 5.

[12] "Darkhei Shalom," *Encyclopedia Talmudit* 7, 715–724. See also my essay, "Darkhei Shalom," *Gesher* (1977–1978): 80–86 (page 55 in this volume).

[13] *ibid.,* 711–715.

becomes the matrix of morality, operates with an entirely different set of premises than conceptions (such as advocated by utilitarian or "natural law" schools of thought) which ground the law not upon its own intrinsic transcendent authority, but upon that provided by underlying moral values, such as utility or justice.

The belief that the authority of the law is a function of its transcendent source rather than of its intrinsic or instrumental value is by no means incompatible with the proposition that adherence to the law produces highly desirable consequences. According to the Talmud, all the provisions of the Torah result in the attainment of peace.[14] But, it is especially in the moral sphere, that the social utility of the law becomes most evident. In the words of Maimonides, morality promotes "civilized life and social intercourse."[15]

Din (administration of law) is portrayed by a well-known Mishnah,[16] as one of the pillars required for the preservation of human society. In the words of a Babylonian Amora, "He who renders a true judgment becomes a partner with God in the process of Creation."[17] Conversely, *chamas* (violence) poses the ultimate threat to social stability. Because of its debilitating effect upon the social fabric, its harmful consequences surpass the havoc wrought by other offenses[18] (including even idolatry, the cardinal sin in a monotheistic religion). Since society cannot function without a system of law, *mishpatim* (civil laws) are characterized by the Tannaim as the type of laws that ultimately would have been enacted by human society, even if they had not been the subject of Divine legislation.[19]

Dinim, the establishment of the judicial system, is included among the seven Noahide laws which, unlike the provisions of the Siniaitic Covenant, are regarded as directed not only to the people of the Covenant, but to all segments of humanity.[20] According to a well known Talmudic principle, Jews owe allegiance not only to their own religious code, but are also duty-

---

[14] BT *Gittin* 59b.

[15] Maimonides, *Hilkhot Deot,* 7:8.

[16] *Avot* 1:18. See also the treatment of this mishnah with respect to the treatment of the centrality of Law in Tur, *Choshen Mishpat.*

[17] BT *Shabbat* 10a.

[18] BT *Sanhedrin* 105a.

[19] BT *Yoma* 67a. With respect to the special importance of civil law, also see Nahmanides, *Commentary to the Torah,* Deuteronomy 7:12.

[20] BT *Sanhedrin 566.*

bound to respect the authority of the "law of the land."[21] Some traditional scholars derive this principle from the provision of the Noahide code which mandates non-Jewish societies to establish juridical systems. Others justify the principle on the grounds that the violation of the law of the land will be tantamount to infringement of the property rights of the sovereign. Another explanation invokes the notion of implicit consent. By residing in a given territory, one implicitly obligates oneself to accept the social contract governing the inhabitants of the territory in question.[22]

Apart from these purely legal grounds, there are also pragmatic reasons dictating obedience to the "law of the land." Disintegration of the social order would result in utter chaos. "Human beings would devour each other alive."[23] Hence, one should do everything in one's capacity to strengthen the social fabric of society.

However, with all deference to the "law of the land," there are limits to its authority. Noncompliance or outright civil disobedience is warranted or mandated in a variety of situations. To begin with, obedience to the law of the land is enjoined by Jewish law only when the laws in question conform to the basic standards of fairness. No sanction is given to governmental procedures which in defiance of fairness and justice amount merely to "legalized violence."[24] Moreover, even if a particular law cannot be faulted on the grounds of fairness, in case of conflict with Jewish law the latter must take precedence (with the obvious exception of instances where, e.g., in monetary matters, Jewish law itself contains clauses stipulating that the "law of the land" should govern certain transactions).[25] But it is one thing to attribute to Divine law overriding authority in the face of all competing claims whether emanating from different systems of law or from the magisterial commands of the human conscience, and another to assign to law a total monopoly in the moral economy. Treating the law as the matrix of moral perceptions is not equivalent to making the latter logically dependent upon the former. At the very most, we affirm a causal but not a logical dependence between law and morality. It must also be noted that

---

[21] For an extensive discussion, see Shmuel Shilo, *Dina de-malkhuta dina.* Jerusalem: 1974.

[22] *"Dina de-malkhuta dina," Encyclopedia Talmudit, vol.* 7, 295–308.

[23] Mishnah, *Avot* 3:2. See also BT *Avodah Zarah* 4a.

[24] *Encyclopedia Talmudit, ibid.*

[25] *ibid.*

obedience to the law is regarded merely as a necessary but not a sufficient condition of morality. A foundation is not a finished structure. The law constitutes merely the foundation of a multi-tiered morality that, beginning with fundamental moral obligations, rises to the loftiest heights of elitist ethical ideals. To be sure, even the legal system does not present us with a monolithic structure. There are legal obligations giving rise to correlative rights which can be claimed by recourse to juridical procedures. But other legal obligations, though giving rise to correlative rights, cannot be claimed through juridical procedures. In addition, there are various types of legal obligations such as the requirement to make restitution to satisfy "heavenly demands" *(latzet yedei Shamayim)*, which do not give rise to any kind of correlative rights at all.[26] Roughly speaking, a parallel structure can be noticed in the ethical sphere which consists of different levels. The lowest tier contains moral obligations (perfect duties) which create correlative rights on the part of others. Above it, are moral obligations that do give rise to correlative rights (imperfect duties). From there, we proceed to various levels of higher ethical ideals which are deemed valuable but not as morally obligatory.

That a rigid formal legalism cannot possibly do justice to the Jewish religious ideal becomes evident in a Talmudic statement which at first blush strikes us as if it could have been part of a Christian polemic against Jewish legalism. In blatant contradiction to all the stereotypes associated with Pharisaic mentality, the Talmudic sages blamed the destruction of Jerusalem on the prevalence of a legal formalism which totally ignored extra-legal requirements.[27] It must be admitted, that, in the opinion of a number of contemporary scholars, the Talmudic statement itself makes no reference whatsoever to the realm of moral obligation that extends beyond the letter of the law.[28] It has been claimed that the import of the statement is restricted to the juridical setting, enjoining judges to concern themselves not only with formal legal principles, but also with considerations of equity.[29] Be that as it may, post-Talmudic authorities attach considerable weight to the performance of supererogatory acts as a halakhic demand. In other words,

---

[26] See Menachem Allon, *Mishpat Ivri*. Jerusalem: 1973, 171–180.

[27] BT *Bava Metzia* 30b.

[28] See Ephraim E. Urbach, *Chazal*. Magnes Press, Jerusalem: 1969, 248ff.

[29] *Ibid.*

the Halakhah itself stipulates that "legalism" be transcended in the quest for more advanced levels of piety.

One could, of course, argue that supererogatory acts, inasmuch as they reflect a halakhic demand, still come within the purview and scope of the law, just as concern for equity can be treated as an aspect of the juridical processes. Whether, in point of fact, supererogatory acts really can be regarded in a purely para-juridical or paralegal sense is a widely debated issue among contemporary ethicists.[30] Proponents of "law-ethics" insist that the authority of the moral "ought" derives from the respect and reverence due to law. Aretistic (virtue-ethics) conceptions of morality, however, are under no constraint to subsume all and sundry types of moral requirements or ethical ideals under the rubric of law. Hence they need not ascribe to supererogatory requirements a paralegal character.

In discussing the Jewish position, it should be noted that we encounter two different approaches. Nahmanides, for example, operates with the premise that the performance of supererogatory acts is mandated by legal provisions. The verse "to walk in His ways" is cited as the biblical source of this religious duty. Maimonides, however, finds himself unable to operate with the notion of a law that makes no unconditional claim to obedience. It is for this reason that Maimonides rejects the notion of a law that mandates the performance of supererogatory acts. For Maimonides to "walk in His ways" remains a strictly legal obligation, but not of act-morality. Instead, it emerges as a universally applicable binding provision of agent-morality, mandating the cultivation of virtuous states of character.[31] It is through *imitatio Dei* – compliance with the commandment to cultivate virtuous dispositions – that one reaches the higher levels of ethical sensitivity, which, in turn prompt an agent to perform supererogatory acts. But while Maimonides's supererogatory requirements, as such, transcend the realm of the law, they are, however, directly related to it, inasmuch as his entire

---

[30] Joel Feinberg, "Supererogation and Rules," *Ethics* 71 (1961): 276–288.

[31] It may be revealing that in his earlier *Sefer ha-mitzvot,* Maimonides still included the performance of specific acts (such as visiting the sick, comforting the mourner, etc.) among the obligations deriving from the commandment "Ye shall walk in His ways." But in his magnum opus, which represents his mature outlook, the commandment applies only to the cultivation of moral states of character.

system revolves around the paradeutic function of the law.[32] Accordingly, it is obedience to the law which engenders desirable moral and intellectual attitudes. Obviously, Maimonides utilized the Aristotelian conception, according to which virtue is acquired by conduct that is in accordance with the requirements of virtue. Moral conduct is seen as a process of conditioning that aims at the cultivation of the virtuous states of character which distinguish the truly moral person. Maimonides adapts the Aristotelian approach to his own Jewish purposes. In his view, it is through obedience to the law, which includes provisions for the imitation of the conduct of appropriate role models, (i.e., scholars of the law) that one cultivates intellectual and moral values and thus advances on the road towards the "knowledge of the Lord." The concluding chapter of the *Guide* explicitly states that this "knowledge" largely refers to the attainment of moral virtues which, in turn, manifest themselves in ethical conduct.[33] That such a goal is by no means an exclusive prerogative of an intellectual elite is underscored by the concluding statement of his *Code*.[34] This monumental *magnum opus*, which is intended for all segments of the community, reaches its grand finale with the quotation from Isaiah, "The world shall be full of the knowledge of the Lord even as the waters cover the sea."[35]

Without subscribing to all the salient features of the Maimonidean system, numerous medieval thinkers share his convictions with respect to the paradeutic function of the law. With remarkable eisegetical ingenuity, they manage to read their own conviction into the midrashic statement that "the mitzvot were given solely for the purpose of ennobling creatures[36] and invoke this dictum as evidence supporting the thesis that in the final analysis the law is deed as a pedagogical device for the refinement of the human personality.

The pronounced emphasis upon agent-morality that we derive from the classical halakhic tradition runs counter to contemporary trends in Jewish thought. A considerable number of leading thinkers, such as Yeshayahu

---

[32] For a thorough treatment see Isadore Twersky, *Introduction to the Code of Maimonides (Mishneh Torah)* (New Haven: Yale University Press, 1980), 356–507.

[33] Maimonides, *Guide of the Perplexed,* Part 3, Chapter 54.

[34] Maimonides, *Mishneh Torah, Hilkhot Melakhim,* Chapter 12.

[35] 54:10.

[36] Vayikra Rabbah 13:3. Shemot Rabbah, 44:1, Midrash Tanchuma, Shemini 12. See also Nahmanides, *Commentary to the Torah,* Deuteronomy 22:6.

Leibowitz[37] and Marvin Fox,[38] claim that the area of Jewish ethics is coextensive with the requirements of Jewish law. In their view, it is impossible to speak of Jewish ethical positions with respect to issues where legally binding halakhic rules cannot be invoked as justification. In our opinion, such a one-sided "pan-halakhic" approach – to borrow A. J. Heschel's[39] felicitous term – represents a totally unwarranted concession to a narrow formalism, which clashes head-on with the Jewish ideal of seeking to relate the totality of human existence to the service of God. Although unavoidably tainted by subjectivity, moral perceptions cannot be dismissed as utterly irrelevant simply because they cannot be buttressed by explicit, formal rules of religious law. After all, the Torah mandates "to do what is right and good in the eyes of the Lord,"[40] which, according, to rabbinic interpretation,[41] mandates consideration of prevailing notions of moral propriety. For that matter, the law itself, as pointed out by the author of *Maggid Mishneh*,[42] must accommodate itself to the inevitable evolution of the notions of moral propriety in the wake of ever changing social, economic and cultural conditions. As Nahmanides pointed out,[43] no finite set of specific regulations could possibly cover the requirements of all future contingencies. Pursuing a similar train of thought, Rabbi Naftali Zvi Yehuda Berlin[44] observes that it was necessary for the Sinaitic Covenant not only to include specific legal rules, but also an overall elastic clause, "you shall become a holy people."[45]

In light of the foregoing analysis, it can readily be seen that one simply cannot do justice to the requirements of the Jewish religious code, without

---

[37] Yeshayahu Leibowitz, *Torah u-Mitzvot ba-Zeman ha-Zeh*. Tel Aviv: Massada Press, 5714.

[38] Marvin Fox, "Reflections on the Foundations of Jewish Ethics and their Relation to Public Policy." In *Selected Papers*, Society of Christian Ethics, Twenty-first Annual Meeting, 1980, 23–62.

[39] Abraham Joshua Heschel, *God in Search of Man: A Philosophy of Judaism*. New York: Farrar, Strauss, and Giroux, 1955, 328.

[40] Deuteronomy 7:18.

[41] *Sifri*, Deuteronomy 72.

[42] Vidal Yom Tov of Tolosa, Maggid Mishneh, Hilkhot Shekhenim 14:4.

[43] Nahmanides, *Commentary to the Torah,* Deuteronomy 7:18.

[44] Naftali Zvi Yehudah Berlin, *Haamek Davar, Shemot,* (Jerusalem: *Vaad ha-yeshivot be-eretz Yisroel* 725), 161.

[45] Exodus 19:6.

making room for the operation of an intuitive moral faculty. But it is one thing to recognize the important function of conscience as a supplement to purely legal elements, and another to treat it as an overriding authority. Nowhere in Jewish law is there any suggestion that the objection provisions of the law may be subordinated to the dictates of the subjective conscience. The law itself is the ultimate court of appeals.[46] As we stressed previously, in a theocentric system, moral requirements ultimately must be regarded as possessing the property of being willed by God. This being the case, conscience can never supersede the law, which, because of its transcendent source, is regarded as the Will of God. All that conscience can do is to supplement the law by 1) discerning Divine requirements which are not explicitly formulated in the law and 2) helping to determine the meaning and range of applicability of laws when their formulation contains an element of ambiguity. According to Bahya ibn Pakuda, the function of conscience is to ascertain "the duties of the heart" which should supplement "the duty of the limbs" which are specified in the legal code.[47] In the striking formulation of Meiri, "The commandments apprehended by the human heart are like the letters of the Torah Scroll."[48] In other words, the authority of the human conscience derives from the fact that its promptings are regarded as a disclosure of God's will. To be sure, such an analysis of the authority of conscience radically differs from the notion that conscience imposes its own laws because it is endowed with autonomous authority. Jewish morality rejects autonomy because of its theocratic (rule of God) orientation. I employ the term "theocratic" rather than the more common term "theonomous" because I find it necessary to make room for elements of existentialist ethics that cannot be accommodated within the framework of law-ethics.[49]

In view of the fact that moral intuitions play such a prominent part in Jewish religious life, we reject the contention that Judaism revolves

---

[46] David Weiss Halivni, "Can a Religious Law Be Immoral?" *Perspectives on Jews and Judaism Essays in Honor of Wolfe Kelman,* edited by Arthur A. Chiel. Rabbinical Assembly, New York: 1978, 165–170.

[47] Bahya ibn Pakudah, *Hovot ha-levavot,* Introduction.

[48] Meiri, BT *Shabbat* 105b.

[49] See my essay, "Covenantal Imperatives." *Samuel K. Mirsky Memorial Volume,* edited by Gersion Appel, 3–12. Jerusalem: Sura Institute for Research, 1970 (page 46 in this volume).

exclusively around obedience to formal rules. Contrary to Bultman, who alleges that Judaism recognizes no religious requirement unless one can find "through ingenious interpretation of the law the necessary rules of conduct,[50] we contend that Judaism mandates an ethics of responsibility[51] as well as an ethics of obedience. That the Jewish ideal of piety is all – encompassing becomes evident in the Talmudic comment that the verse "in all thy ways thou shalt acknowledge Him" represents the most adequate formulation of the ultimate goal of religious life.[52] There are no religiously neutral zones. In the words of Hillel, "All thy actions are to be performed for the sake of Heaven."[53] Obviously, performing an act for the sake of Heaven does not imply that the act in question constitutes an instance of a specific religious norm. In another paper,[54] I have coined the term "covenantal imperative" to designate what are intuitively perceived religiously mandated responses to particular existential situations. The fact that these religious imperatives possess purely subjective validity in no way detracts from their significance. Objective standards of the law represent only the minimal requirements of piety. There is ample room for the exercise of individuality in the pursuit of religious excellence.

As opposed to objective moral norms which must be grounded in the law, subjective ideals reflect a continuous interaction between the various components that go into the makings of an individual's ethos. To be sure, the law itself, because of its paradeutic function, functions as a matrix of religiously valid ideals. But the Aggadah (non-legal religious literature) can also play a major role in shaping an ethos which engenders religiously significant ideals. It was already noted by Rabbi Naftali Zvi Yehuda Berlin that biblical narratives are intended as a source not so much of historical information but of paradigmatic role models.[55] From the "stories" of the Bible, there emerges a world view which profoundly affects our ethical

---

[50] Rudolph Bultman, *Jesus and the Word*. New York: Charles Scribner's Sons, 1958, 69.

[51] Richard H. Neibuhr, *The Responsible Self*. New York: Harper & Row, 1963. See also Albert Rabbi Jensen, *Responsibility in Modern Religious Ethics*. Washington: Corpus Books, 1968.

[52] BT *Berakhot* 63a.

[53] *Avot* 2:19. BT *Betzah* 16a.

[54] Walter S. Wurzburger, *loc. cit.*

[55] Naftali Zvi Yehudah Berlin, *op. cit.*, Bereshit, p. 1.

perspectives. Obviously a *Weltanschauung* revolving around Creation, Revelation and Redemption contains beliefs and attitudes that are likely to produce a value system which sharply differs from a purely secular ethics. It must also be realized that moral questions call for the exercise of judgment in the effort to balance the competing claims issuing from a variety of *prima facie* obligations as well as conflicting values. There are no formal rules available to resolve moral dilemmas. This being the case, purely theoretical guidance hardly suffices; it is through the imitation of proper role models that one cultivates the capacity for making proper moral judgments. "Personal contact with the masters of the law is of greater value than their teachings."[56] Maimonides does not even attempt to define the nature of the various moral states of character one ought to cultivate. Instead, exposure to and imitation of the paradigmatic individuals is the only method through which the meaning of the commandment "to walk in His ways" can be clarified. Just as in the *Nichomachean Ethics,* Aristotle provides only an ostensive definition of virtue by pointing to the standards of virtuous persons who are renowned for their expertise in the conduct of life, so for Maimonides, the standards of "the ways of the wise" or "the ways of the pious" can be formulated only by reference to the standards exemplified in the conduct of the scholars of the law. This conclusively shows that for Maimonides the demands of agent-morality necessitate reliance upon purely intuitive factors which cannot be accommodated within the framework of a formal "law-ethics."

---

[56] BT *Berakhot* 6b.

RELIGION AND MORALITY[1]

THE RELATIONSHIP BETWEEN religion and morality cannot be discussed in abstraction. There are many varieties of ethical and religious systems that radically diverge from each other with respect to the values, norms, and ideals that they advocate. Therefore, one can examine their interrelationship only after specifying what particular religions or ethical systems one has in mind.

Although this may surprise us, there are religions (for example, paganism and Shintoism) that are purely cultic and make no ethical demands on their adherents. Yet contrary to the claims of many religionists, the absence of religious sanctions need not adversely affect the standards of morality prevailing within a given society.

Some religionists argue that commitment to ethical values on the part of secularists attests to the residual impact of religion, the root of our ethical beliefs. Just as cut flowers can retain their beauty for a short period of time after they are severed from their roots so, they claim, commitment to ethical values in a secular society is a "survival" of a religious age. They are convinced that sooner or later, an ethical system that has been uprooted from its religious roots is bound to wither.

However, it is simply not the case that ethical systems must originate within a religious setting or can flourish only on religious soil. Although there is little doubt that many of our own moral beliefs derive from religious

---

[1] From *Towards Greater Understanding: Essays in Honor of John Cardinal O'Connor,* edited by Anthony J. Cernera, Sacred Heart Press, Fairfield, 1995.

cultures, it does not follow that their ongoing viability depends upon the continued existence of the factors and conditions that originally brought them into being. After all, a house can outlive its builder. We would be guilty of committing the "genetic fallacy" were we to maintain that in order to function properly our moral beliefs must continue to be buttressed by religious underpinnings.

That ethics can be completely independent from religion was driven home to me several years ago during a visit to Japan. I discovered to my amazement that, although most Japanese professed a religious faith which revolved exclusively around cultic acts and was completely lacking in moral requirements, there was far less crime in Japan than in the United States, where most religions mandate ethical conduct. Comparison between the incidence of crime in the two countries clearly shows that strong societal pressures to conform to an ethical code can at times be more effective than religious sanctions as incentives for ethical conduct.

Be that as it may, it is certain that monotheistic religions demand moral conduct. As opposed to polytheistic cults which worshipped their gods as sources of power, the monotheistic God figures not only as the omnipotent Source of Being but is worshipped as the supremely moral Being, Who demands righteousness and justice. In the words of Micah (6:8), "It hath been told thee, O man, what is good and what the Lord demands of thee: to do justice, love kindness and walk humbly with thy God."

A monotheistic perspective makes it possible to subscribe to a divine command theory of ethics. Accordingly, what renders an action, state of mind, or intention good is the fact that it is commanded by God. But it is equally plausible to hold that goodness is by no means synonymous with the property of being commanded by God. Instead God, as the supreme moral authority, commands whatever is good. It is not His command that makes actions or states of mind good; on the contrary, He commands them because they are good.

This issue has been debated ever since the time of Plato. Because of his polytheistic premises, he could not define goodness in terms of divine approval, especially since the Greek gods were conceived as powers rather than exemplars of morality. Since different gods may possess divergent desires, they are likely to issue conflicting commandments or be pleased by mutually exclusive forms of conduct. Therefore, Plato had no choice but to insist in his *Euthyphro* that goodness is a property which is independent of divine command or approbation.

In recent history, G.E. Moore contended that when we define goodness in terms of being commanded by God, we commit the "naturalistic fallacy." To be sure, many critics observed that it was only on the basis of his highly controversial views on the nature of analysis that Moore could charge those who define goodness in terms of non-ethical properties with committing a fallacy.

While religious believers have every right to disagree with Moore's thesis and contend that goodness actually means pleasing to or commanded by God, there is really no reason why they should do so. Were they to define goodness in terms of divine approval, they would no longer have a common universe of discourse with atheists or agnostics. Were religionists to insist that the very meaning of the term "good" amounts simply to "it is commanded by God," they could not engage in moral arguments with individuals who do not share their theistic beliefs. It is only when it is granted that the meaning of goodness is independent of divine approval or command that it makes sense to debate moral issues with non-believers.

Although religious believers can agree that the meaning of the term "good" is not directly connected with divine approval, they may assert that the proposition "it is good," without being synonymous with the proposition "it is commanded or approved by God," is its equivalent nonetheless. While the term "good" does not actually mean "it is commanded by God," it is, nevertheless, logically necessary that whatever is commanded by an all-benevolent God be good. This, however, need not lead to the Kantian position that the fact that something is commanded by God is totally irrelevant to morality. We may well argue that a divine commandment is bound to be moral even if human intelligence is unable to discern its goodness.

The most blatant illustration of a conflict between what is commanded by God and what human intelligence perceives as moral is the biblical account of Abraham's readiness to sacrifice his son Isaac. Kant argued that Abraham should have refused to obey a command that ran counter to the dictates of his autonomous conscience, since it is inconceivable that God would have issued a command that contravenes moral requirements. Kierkegaard also agreed with Kant that Abraham's conduct was unethical. But it was precisely because his "suspension of the ethical" demonstrated his readiness to subordinate all ethical concerns to the demands of faith that he became the "knight of faith" par excellence.

However, Kierkegaard's approach leaves us with serious difficulties. It hardly makes sense to claim that God, the supremely moral being, would command an immoral act. Thomas Aquinas's approach is far more palatable. In his view, there is an ethical requirement that we obey the dictates of a higher moral authority. In view of the fact that Aquinas adopted a consequentialist ethical perspective, he had no problem with God's ordering an act that strikes us as immoral. As the omniscient moral authority, He obviously knows best what would lead to the most beneficial results. Murder, as a general rule, will result in evil consequences to society. But when it is directly ordered by God, the supreme expert on goodness, an act of killing is bound to result in the best possible consequences.

Professor Emil Fackenheim[2] has shown that even on the basis of a purely deontological ethics, one can contend that it is one's supreme duty to obey the dictates of the highest conceivable moral authority. Killing a person as a divinely-ordained sacrifice does not constitute murder. It seems puzzling that Kant, who regards the execution of a murderer as a moral imperative, cannot find it acceptable to kill a person at the specific command of God. Hence, there is no need to justify Abraham's conduct by invoking the "suspension of the ethical," a notion that strikes us as absurd when applied to a religious faith that extols God as the perfectly good Being.

In sharp contrast with modern ethical theories, biblical moralities treat ethical imperatives as objectively valid norms or values. Unlike emotivism or prescriptivism, which ultimately ground ethical imperatives on subjective factors, biblical moralities emphasize that they represent the Will of God. It is this responsibility to God which distinguishes biblical from Greek moralities. The latter, while also claiming objective validity because they reflect the requirements of human nature, are essentially prescriptions for personal well being. In the felicitous formulation of Professor Nazick, they constitute "push moralities."[3] They are designed to help the individual attain the best possible life, which is evaluated solely in terms of his/her happiness. Because of this self-centered conception of morality, Aristotle, who regards

---

[2] See the chapter "Abraham and the Kantians" in Emil Fackenheim, *Encounters between Judaism and Modern Philosophy*. New York: Basic Books, 1973, 33–77.

[3] Robert Nozick, *Philosophical Explanations*. Cambridge: Harvard University Press. 1981, 40 ff.

friendship as an integral part of a good life, recognizes the obligations deriving from the needs of a friend but has no concept of charity. For him, there were no requirements to concern oneself with the needs of strangers. This is why charity was classified as a "theological virtue" during the Middle Ages.

Biblical morality, on the other hand, is not egocentric but is responsive to the claim of "the other." Its basic premise is that human beings are responsible to God, Who demands that we concern ourselves not only with our own individual good (be it happiness, self-realization, pleasure, and so on) but acknowledge the claims of the other. As Leviticus[4] puts it, "Love thy fellow human being as thyself; I am the Lord."

Our moral obligations to our fellow human beings arise not simply from nature or from rationality, but derive their obligatory character from their being apprehended as divine imperatives. Even the most rationalistic classical Jewish philosophers do not treat moral duties simply as rational requirements or dictates of nature but as "rational commandments." The concept of autonomy does not figure at all in Jewish ethics. The human self does not create or impose moral obligations; human conscience or reason merely discover divine imperatives. Even those Jewish thinkers who subscribe to the view of natural law that can be discovered unaided by supernatural revelation still maintain that they amount not merely to rational or natural duties but to divine commandments that our rational faculties apprehend.

Alasdair MacIntyre[5] has called attention to the difficulties encountered by secular ethics. Ever since Descartes rejected the notion of final causes, science has become value-free. With the delegitimization of teleology, it is no longer possible to adopt the Aristotelian approach and base upon the foundations of immanent purposes within nature. Kant's attempt to provide a secure foundation for morality by grounding it on rationality was also doomed to failure. As Anscombe has pointed out,[6] reverence for the moral law hardly makes sense without a divine lawgiver. It therefore is not surprising that we have arrived at a point where ethics, as in the emotive and

---

[4] Leviticus 19:19

[5] Alasdair MacIntyre, *After Virtue*. Notre Dame: University of Notre Dame Press, 1981.

[6] G.E.M. Anscombe. "Modern Moral Philosophy." *Journal of Philosophical Studies* 33 (1958): 13–14.

prescriptive theories currently in vogue, ceases to posses any objective validity.

I have shown elsewhere[7] that the characteristic of "over-ridingness" which distinguishes the ethical norm from other prescriptions or evaluations can also best be explained by reference to a divine commander. This option is available to all adherents of monotheistic religions. Jews, Christians and Muslims alike accord their moral beliefs the statues of an absolute norm that is due to a divine imperative, the highest possible source of authority.

Kant contended that with the exception of providing sanctions or incentives to abide by the moral law through the prospect of eternal bliss in the hereafter, religion had nothing to contribute to morality. We see now that Kant was completely wrong when he claimed that the only contributions that religion could make to morality was the ability to provide sanctions and incentives for moral conduct by promising reward in the hereafter. In light of our preceding discussion it becomes clear that theistic belief affects the very nature of the authority of a moral norm. After hearing "performing X is irrational," one may ask "So what?" But one cannot reply in the same fashion to the statement, "Performing X is a transgression of a divine imperative."

Kant's claim may have had some plausibility in his time when it was taken for granted that there could be only one universally valid ethics, especially since he managed to incorporate within his ethical system all the ethical beliefs of the dominant religion of his society. One could well claim that his entire approach was an attempt to hide a liberal Christian approach under the cloak of pure rationality. But with the sharp disagreements on moral issues that divide various segments of society, we can no longer appeal to a moral consensus. The controversies raging about abortion, assisted suicide, or euthanasia provide telling examples of the wide gulf between the various camps, each defending their respective positions on the basis of mutually irreconcilable moral beliefs.

In a pluralistic and democratic society, these issues must be resolved by recourse to democratic processes. But it is the height of absurdity to allow fear of the breakdown of the separation of church and state to disqualify from public debate any moral opinion engendered by religious faith. Since

---

[7] See my *Ethics of Responsibility: Pluralistic Approaches to Convenental Ethics*. Philadelphia: Jewish Publication Society of America, 1994, 24.

the validity of moral opinions cannot be demonstrated either on scientific or rational grounds, it simply does not make sense to recognize moral opinions of atheists or agnostics while discriminating against the opinions of those whose moral outlook has been molded by religious faith.

One of the most basic features of biblical morality is the emphasis upon the sanctity of human life. Human beings must not be treated in the same fashion as other members of the animal kingdom, because "He made man in the image of God."[8] The Palestinian Talmud[9] goes as far as to assert that the verse "On the day when God made man, He created him in the image of God" represents the most fundamental principle of the entire Torah. Whereas the Bible, in describing the creation of various organic creatures, states that they were formed "in accordance with their species," no mention whatsoever is made of the species with respect to human beings. The Mishnah already notes, "Man was created as a single creature to teach us that the destruction of one person is the equivalent of destruction of the entire universe."[10] Every human being is irreplaceable. After all, so the Mishnah continues, "Each human being bears the image of God in a unique way… and each human being is required to say 'For my sake was the world created.'" Since each individual possesses infinite value, no individual may be sacrificed on the altar of the collective welfare. Quantitative or qualitative factors are irrelevant. Euthanasia and suicide are categorically forbidden. Moreover, there is an overriding obligation to save life. According to Jewish law, one is duty-bound to make efforts to preserve one's own life.

To be sure, Jewish law recognizes the distinction between killing and allowing to die. In the latter case, priorities must be assigned when it is not feasible to save everyone. Similarly, when prolongation of life would only result in severe suffering for the patient, some medical interventions designed to keep the patient alive may be discontinued. Under no circumstances, however, would Jewish morality sanction any form of active euthanasia.

Jewish law operates with the principle that no human life may be displaced for the sake of another or, for that matter, any number of lives. There is only one exception to this rule: One is required to take the life of a

---

[8] Genesis 5:1.

[9] JT *Nedarim* 9:4.

[10] JT *Sanhedrin* 2:5.

pursuer, whenever necessary, in order to save the life of an individual, regardless of whether one's own life or that of a third party is endangered. When threatened by a pursuer, one is mandated to protect one's own life even by taking the life of the aggressor if that should be necessary. Non-resistance to evil is not a hallmark of a saint but a grievous offense against God, Who has conferred upon us the precious gift of life and human dignity. This is why Jewish law permits abortions in life-threatening situations. If the embryo imperils the mother's life, it is regarded as the pursuer. We must perform all actions deemed necessary to save the life of the mother.

The implications of the biblical doctrine that man bears the image of God are by no means limited to considerations involving the sanctity of life. As Rabbi Joseph B. Soloveitchik has pointed out,[11] the rabbinic doctrine of *kevod ha-briyot* (human dignity), which stipulates that at times various religious requirements are set aside when their observances would entail the violation of a person's sense of dignity, is a corollary of the unique status which, according to Genesis, is assigned to human beings. Every individual matters because every person bears the image of God in a unique manner and is entrusted with a unique mission that no one else can duplicate. So sensitive was the Talmudic sages' concern for human dignity that they compared causing embarrassment to human beings to shedding their blood.[12] Jewish law not only prohibits libel but also frowns upon disclosing unfavorable information about an individual unless the disclosure of such information is necessary to protect another individual from harm.

Moralities that have developed within the matrix of religion tend to praise as virtues traits of character that would not be acceptable to secular moralities. We need but recall Nietzsche's strictures against "slave morality" that extols pity, compassion, humility, etc., in order to realize the enormity of the chasm gaping between biblical and non-biblical moralities. Similarly, Aristotle's and Spinoza's disdain for humility are poignant examples showing how strongly the absence of religious foundations impinges upon the formation of value-systems.

---

[11] Joseph Soloveitchik, *Yeme zikkaron* (edited by Moshe Kroneh). Jerusalem: World Zionist Organization, Department of Torah Education and Culture in the Diaspora, 1986, 9–11.

[12] BT *Bava Metzia* 58b.

The central role that benevolence plays in modern secular systems such as Humean ethics or utilitarianism also attests to the residual impact of biblical influences even upon agnostic philosophers. Social hedonism owes much more to the biblical imperative "Love thy neighbor as thyself," which precludes exclusive concern for one's own welfare, than to Greek ethical thought, which revolved around the ideal of self-sufficiency and fostered an essentially egotistical outlook that runs counter to the basic thrust of biblical religion.

Although according to numerous Jewish thinkers, ethical laws[13] are geared toward promoting the well-being of society, in some instances they clearly transcend considerations of social utility. Thus the obligation to assist the needy is defined in individualistic rather than general terms. Basing themselves upon the biblical verse which mandates helping others "in accordance with [their] needs,"[14] the Rabbis maintained that one should help individuals to enjoy luxuries to which they have been accustomed even if they are beyond the reach of ordinary individuals.

It must be emphasized that, as the Talmud observes,[15] performing acts of lovingkindness constitutes *imitatio Dei*. Hence even if Ayn Rand and Adam Smith were correct and the pursuit of our own self-interest guided by the "invisible hand" would in the long run maximize social utility, we still would be required to perform acts of lovingkindness.

Since the divine ethical attributes as enumerated in Exodus[16] are supposed to function as exemplars of the virtues to be cultivated by human beings,[17] it is especially significant that the term "abundant" is employed only in connection with God's lovingkindness and not with respect to other ethical properties such as graciousness, compassion, patience, or truthfulness. This is another illustration of the primacy of chesed (lovingkindness) in the hierarchy of values of a theocentric ethics. For all its concern for justice, biblical morality treats justice not just as a formal property but views it as the proper distribution of love.[18]

---

[13] See my *Ethics of Responsibility*, 40–66.

[14] Deuteronomy 15:8.

[15] BT *Ketubbot* 67b.

[16] Exodus 24:6.

[17] BT *Sotah* 14a.

[18] Paul Tillich, *Love, Power and Justice*. London: Oxford University Press, 1954.

Under the influence of Kabbalistic categories, many Jewish thinkers point to the linkage between chesed and humility. In this view, it was out of God's concern for beings other than Himself that He created all creatures. In order to make space for the world, it was necessary for God to engage in *tzimtzum*. It is this self-limitation that constitutes the very essence of humility. According to the Talmud, God's power is always associated with His humility.

Some Kabbalistic thinkers such as Cordovero treat humility as the very core of virtues. Without going so far, even a rationalist such as Maimonides attaches such importance to humility that he treats it as one of the few exceptions to the general rule that moral virtues are supposed to strike a balance between extremes. In the case of humility, Maimonides unequivocally advocates extremism rather then the "golden mean" or the "middle road."[19] In his brief but seminal essay, "Majesty and Humility,"[20] Rabbi Joseph B. Soloveitchik contended that Jewish ethics reflects the dialectical tension involved in imitating both the majesty as well as the humility of the divine Creator.

The impact of religious norms upon ethical attitudes can be gauged when we compare the prevailing sexual ethics with that of the beginning of the Enlightenment, when, as MacIntyre has demonstrated,[21] secular moralities basically reflected the prevailing moral standards of Christian Europe. Thus Kant, for all his rejection of theological ethics and his insistence upon autonomy, nonetheless found it possible to condemn masturbation (self-abuse), extra-marital sex, and homosexuality, and even advised women to choose death rather than submit to rape. But with the decline of religious influences and the growing secularization of the modern ethos, nowadays very few secular moralists would be prepared to endorse these recommendations. Incidentally, most Jewish religious authorities would permit women to endure rape if necessary to save their lives.

Another feature distinguishing biblical from secular moralities is the emphasis upon obligations arising from concrete historic situations rather than from general principles. When Nietzsche ridiculed the love-ideal as *Fernsten-Liebe*, he was unfair to many religious traditions. Judaism, for example, clearly mandates that when dispensing charity, members of our

---

[19] *Hilkhot Deot* 2:6.
[20] Joseph Soloveitchik, "Majesty and Humility." *Tradition* 17:2 (1978): 25–37.
[21] MacIntyre, *After Virtue*.

own families should be given priority, and the Talmud operates with the principle that "The poor of one's own city take precedence over the poor of another city."[22] Moreover, as we noted previously, the extent to which we are supposed to render assistance to the needy is not a function of "average" or minimal standards of living but is based upon the specific requirements of the particular individual concerned.

It has been argued that the biblical preoccupation with the requirements of humans has bred utter insensitivity and indifference to the welfare of all other organic and inorganic creatures. There is a widespread feeling that man's alienation from nature resulted from the biblical doctrine which granted human beings the right to exercise dominion and manipulative attitudes towards nature, which now imperil our very survival, are in large measure due to the radical dichotomy between man who was created in this image of God and the rest of nature which was completely desacralized.

To be sure, as some theologians have noted,[23] the Bible can hardly be accused of licensing irresponsible exploitation of nature, since the Torah's charge to humanity "to fill the earth and subdue it"[24] does not stand in isolation but is counterbalanced by the observation of the second chapter of Genesis that Adam was placed in the Garden of Eden "to work it and to guard it."[25] The latter statement unequivocally affirms human responsibility for proper stewardship of the resources placed at our disposal.

Upon closer analysis it can be readily seen that the ontological as well as axiological primacy that the Bible assigns to humankind cannot be blamed for the ecological crisis. On the contrary, awareness of our responsibility to God for the preservation of the world acts as a much-needed curb on human arrogance, which is frequently engendered by technological triumphs. There is a tendency to treat technology and science as ends in themselves, to be pursued for their own sakes irrespective of the ecological and human cost. Judaism teaches that the world does not belong to man but to God, the Creator and, therefore, the Owner and Master of the universe.[26] Interference with natural processes is regarded as legitimate only to the extent that it contributes to the fulfillment of divine purposes. Conservation of non-

---

[22] BT *Bava Metzia* 71a.

[23] Theodore Hiebert, "Ecology and the Bible." *Harvard Divinity Bulletin* (Fall 1989): 7.

[24] Genesis 1:28

[25] *ibid.*, 2:15

[26] Psalms 24:1

replenishable resources and protection of the environment are not merely matters of prudence but ethico-religious imperatives. Disregard of the limits to man's right to harness the forces of nature adversely affects human welfare. When scientists ignore the potential damage that genetic research may cause, their hubris could cause unimaginable suffering to future generations. Similar considerations dictate that we exercise caution and restraint with respect to any technological progress, lest it contribute to the pollution of the environment. Before embarking upon further expansion, we must carefully determine whether the benefits will outweigh the negative effects upon the ecology. We cannot make these decisions based upon the operation of the open market, since the laws of supply and demand are much more responsive to humanity's short-term selfish considerations than to its long range requirements. As stewards of resources placed at our disposal by the Creator, we are duty-bound to expand our concern beyond instant gratification and economic benefits and assign much greater weight to our policies' effect upon posterity.

While it is questionable whether secular ethics can sustain the notion of ethical obligations towards future generations, for Jewish ethics it is axiomatic that we bear responsibility for survival of the human species. In addition to the specific commandment to "be fruitful and multiply,"[27] the verse "He created it not a waste, He formed it to be inhabited[28] is interpreted in the Talmud as the source of the duty to procreate.[29] This commandment's paramount importance is also highlighted by Rabbi Eliezer's statement that "He who does not engage in the propagation of the human species is regarded as though he had shed blood."[30]

Since for Jewish ethics preservation of the environment is mandated to ensure that the earth will be able to serve as a suitable habitat for humanity, it follows that population control for the purpose of reducing the strain on

---

[27] Genesis 1:28.

[28] Isaiah 45:18.

[29] BT *Gittin* 41b and Tosafot ad loc. s.v., *"Lo tohu be-ra'ah lashevet yetzarah."* Especially significant is the statement of Tosafot, BT *Pesachim* 88b s.v., *"Kofin et raabb"* which emphasizes that the obligation is so strong that, although as a general rule one does not recommend to an individual to commit a sin in order to save another from another more serious sin, an exception is made in this case because the transgression of a prohibition is necessary to enable another individual to fulfill the commandment to procreate. See also BT *Hagigah* 2b, Tosafot s.v., *"Lo tohu be-ra'ah."*

[30] BT *Yevamot* 63b.

natural resources is unacceptable. Because of the sanctity of life, not only is it forbidden to take life, but procreation takes precedence over maintaining a high quality of life. Although the Talmud forbids procreation during a famine,[31] as long as minimal requirements for sustenance can be met, Jewish law demands that we lower our standard of living rather than limit population growth.

Although biblical morality primarily revolves around concern for people, it is also solicitous of the well-being of other creatures. Provision for the preservation of the various species in nature is one of the salient features of biblical morality.[32] The first chapter of Genesis records the divine blessing bestowed upon the various species compromising the animal kingdom. In a moral system based upon *imitatio Dei*, we are mandated not only to ensure the survival of the species but also to be solicitous for the well being of all sentient creatures. Since "God is good to all and His Mercy is over all His creatures,"[33] we, too, must display compassion towards the animal world. This is why the Jewish tradition strictly prohibits inflicting unnecessary pain upon animals.

It must, however, be reiterated that Judaism assigns preeminent status to human beings because they alone bear the image of God. Jewish morality rejects the extremism of the advocates of animal rights, who equate the suffering of animals with that of human beings. As long as all necessary steps are taken to reduce the suffering of animals as much as possible, Jewish morality would unquestionably allow the performance of painful experiments on animals whenever necessary for medical research. Concern for the sanctity of human life overrides solicitude for the well-being of other creatures.

---

[31] BT *Taanit* 11a. See C.H. Medini, *Sedei Chemed*, vol. 5, 331.

[32] It is noteworthy that according to Maimonides, God's special Providence extends only to human beings. The rest of creation is subject only to the exercise of the general Providence governing the species.

[33] Psalms 145:9.

ON JEWISH THOUGHT

THE CENTRALITY OF VIRTUE-ETHICS
IN MAIMONIDES[1]

ONE OF THE MOST STRIKING FEATURES of Maimonidean ethics is the pivotal role assigned to agent-morality, which focuses on the ethical quality of the state of mind of the agent rather than the propriety of particular actions. In contradistinction to many other halakhic authorities who, while recognizing virtue-ethics as a sublime religious idea, either do not include it at all among religious obligations or relegate it to a mere means to virtuous conduct. Maimonides both in his legal and philosophical writings treats the cultivation of moral virtues as an intrinsic value, which is explicitly mandated as an indispensable aspect of Jewish piety.

Although one may be tempted to attribute this predilection for virtue to Aristotelian influences, it must be borne in mind that for Maimonides, ethics represents not a quest for personal happiness or self-realization but a response to the religious imperative of *imitatio Dei*.[2] In his scheme, even the

---

[1] From *Studies in Jewish Religious and Intellectual History: Presented to Alexander Altmann on the Occasion of His Seventieth Birthday*. Edited by Siegfried Stein and Raphael Lowe. Published in association with the Institute of Jewish Studies, London, by the University of Alabama Press, 1979.

[2] See the important study of Marvin Fox, "The Doctrine of the Mean in Aristotle and Maimonides," in *Studies in Jewish Religious and Intellectual History*, edited by Stein and Loewy, 93–129. 1979. Cf. Steven Schwarzchild, "Moral Radicalism and 'Middlingness' in the Ethics of Maimonides." *Studies in Medieval Culture* 11 (1977): 65–94.

cultivation of the "middle road" which Hermann Cohen[3] characterized as an outright concession to Aristotle, was viewed not merely as a dictate of prudential ethics but as the fulfillment of the Biblical commandment "Thou shalt walk in His ways."[4]

In view of Maimonides's penchant for systematic arrangement, it is highly revealing that the section dealing with the cultivation of virtues is located in *Sefer Mada*, The Book of Knowledge, the first of the fourteen books comprising the *Mishneh Torah*, rather than in parts of the Code which treat interpersonal or social obligations. This in itself indicates that Maimonides looked upon virtue not simply as an instrumental value conducive to ethical conduct, but as an independent and intrinsic value to be pursued for its own sake. Even more noteworthy is the fact that, although Maimonides considered the commandment "Love thy neighbor as thyself" as the underlying principle of all norms governing relations "between man and his fellow man,"[5] there is no mention at all of this commandment until the sixth of the seven chapters that comprise his *Hilkhot Deot* is reached. The first five chapters revolve exclusively around the commandment "thou shalt walk in His ways," which is defined as the obligation to cultivate the divine moral attributes (the ways of God) according to one's ability.

The commandment "Love thy neighbor" is introduced only in that section of *Hilkhot Deot* which deals with various factors which impact upon the formation of dispositions and character traits. After describing the power of environmental influences, Chapter 7 addresses itself to the requirement to select proper role models. It is only at this point that reference is made to various commandments, starting with "Love thy neighbor as thyself," which mandate rules of conduct in the realm of interpersonal relationships. Special attention should be focused on the fact that Maimonides' interpretation here sharply diverges from that offered in *Hilkhot Avot* [6] where "Love thy

---

[3] Hermann Cohen, *"Charakteristik der Ethik Maimunis,"* Jüdische Schriften 3 (1924): 221–229. See also Shimon Ravidowicz, *"Perek be-torat ha-mussar la-rambam,"* in *Sefer ha-yovel li-khvod Mordechai Menachem Kaplan*, 1953, 236. See also my article "The Maimonidean Matrix of Rabbi Joseph B. Soloveitchik's Two-Tiered Ethics," in *Through the Sound of Many Voices*, edited by Jonathan V. Plaut, 178–180, 1982 (page 161 in this volume).

[4] Deuteronomy 28:9.

[5] *Commentary to the Mishnah*, Peah 1:1.

[6] *Hilkhot Avel* 14:1. While I disagree with many of the conclusions, I have benefited from Shalom Rosenberg's *"Ve-halakhta bi-Derachav"* in *Mivhar Ma'amarim be-*

neighbor as thyself" is cited as the source of the obligation to perform acts of benevolence. In *Hilkhot Deot*, on the other hand, the commandment is interpreted as an aspect of virtue-ethics, i.e., the obligation to experience love towards fellow Israelites and to manifest this disposition in our conduct.

This formulation as well as the placement of "Love thy neighbor as thyself" together with the other commandments listed in chapters 7 and 8 of *Hilkhot Deot* suggests that, merely as a secondary consideration. *Hilkhot Deot* is a treatise on personal morality rather than social ethics. It addresses itself primarily to the ethico-religious task of striving to emulate divine moral attributes. The commandments included in this section of the Code are viewed not as ordinances useful to society but as instrumentalities helpful in engendering virtuous dispositions within agents. The commandments discussed here can fulfill this paradeutic function because human conduct, even more than surroundings or role models, exert a profound impact upon the formation of character.

The belief that conduct molds attitudes and dispositions is a cornerstone of the Maimonidean ethics. It comes to the fore already in many of his earliest writings. In his *Commentary on the Mishnah* there is considerable emphasis upon the notion that as the result of frequent repetition in the performance of a mitzvah, our character is refined and ennobled.[7] He similarly points in the first chapter of *Hilkhot Deot*[8] that morally desirable dispositions can only be acquired by practice. It is through disciplining oneself to act in the proper manner that one ultimately becomes conditioned to appropriate moral virtues, rendering moral conduct completely natural and effortless. Obviously, this opinion echoes the Aristotelian doctrine that virtue is acquired by acting in accordance with the requirements of virtue.

To be sure, Maimonides is by no means unique among Jewish thinkers in attributing such efficacy to the performance of a mitzvah. A considerable number of medieval Jewish thinkers refer to the Midrashic statement that the mitzvot were given *letzaref et ha-beriot*[9] and interpret it in a manner that it

---

Filosophiah Kelalit vi-Yehudit, edited by Halamish and Kascher, 72–91. Some of his solutions were anticipated in my article *"Darkhei Shalom," Gesher* (1977–1978): 80–86 (page 55 in this volume).

[7] *Commentary to the Mishnah*, Avot 3:17.

[8] *Hilkhot Deot*, 1:11.

[9] Lev. Rabbah, 13:3 and Genesis Rabbah, 44:1.

is construed as evidence for the proposition that the refinement of human character was the ultimate purpose of the mitzvot.[10]

But this by no means detracts from the originality of the Maimonidean approach which regards the imitation of God through the cultivation of moral dispositions as a specific religious imperative. That the Maimonidean view was far from commonplace is attested by the fact that in *Hilkhot Teshuvah* (7:3) he finds it necessary to engage in sharp polemics against the opinion that repentance is necessary only for sins involving conduct and to insist that sins involving evil traits of character pose a far greater threat to one's spiritual well-being than wrong actions. It should also be noted that the Scriptural proof text (Isaiah 55:7) adduced by Maimonides hardly constitutes conclusive evidence for his case, since it could easily be argued that when the prophet pleaded for reformation of "the way" and "the thoughts" of the wicked, he was concerned with the elimination of the *causes* of sin rather than mere repentance from sin.

Although Maimonides ostensibly bases his virtue-ethics on a rabbinic text, it must be realized that the passage of the *Sifre*, which is cited in support of his thesis, actually is not offered as a comment on the Biblical verse involved as proof text for the obligation to cultivate moral virtues. Whereas Maimonides refers to the verse, Deuteronomy 28:9, he actually adduces a rabbinic comment offered to a similar but different verse. It is with respect to Deuteronomy 11:22 (not 28:9) that *Sifre* notes that "to walk in all the ways of God" refers to the ways of God. As God is called compassionate, you shall also be compassionate, as God is called gracious, you shall also be gracious.

At first blush it appears rather strange that Maimonides resorts to the *Sifre's* explanation of the meaning of *imitatio Dei* and completely ignores the Talmudic definition (BT *Sotah* 14a) which is formulated in terms of the emulation of divine *middot* (traits) such as clothing the naked, visiting the sick, comforting the mourners and burying the dead. As I have pointed out elsewhere,[11] Maimonides quoted the latter text in combination with the *Sifre* in the earlier formulation of the mitzvah in *Sefer ha-Mitzvot*. But as agent-

---

[10] Nahmanides, *Commentary to the Torah*, Deuteronomy 22:6. See also Asher Crescas to *Guide of the Perplexed*, III:26.

[11] See also my essay, "*Imitatio Dei* in Maimonides's *Sefer Hamitzvot* and the *Mishneh Torah*." In *Tradition and Transition*, edited by Jonathan Sacks, 321–324, 1986 (page 100 in this volume).

morality or virtue-ethics became more dominant in his orientation, he restricted the scope of *imitatio Dei* to the cultivation of dispositions and deliberately excluded from it any facet of act-morality.[12]

The increasing prominence of virtue-ethics in the Maimonidean system can also be gauged by the fact that in his earliest major work, the *Commentary on the Mishnah,* no mention is made of *imitatio Dei* in his exposition of various aspects of virtue-ethics. Even his extensive introduction to *Pirkei Avot,* the *Shemoneh Perakim,* which revolves around moral virtues, is totally devoid of any reference to *imitatio Dei.* It therefore seems plausible to conclude that in the progressive development of Maimonides' thought, cultivation of moral virtues was transformed from a religious desideratum into an outright religious obligation. But even in the earliest stage of his development, when, in contrast with his more mature writing, he sanctioned deviation from the middle road only as a corrective measure but refused to recommend any form of excess as a moral ideal, nonetheless, even in the absence of a formal link between the quest for moral perfection and *imitatio Dei,* he regarded the obligation to cultivate virtuous dispositions as an essential feature of Jewish piety and as a prerequisite to the attainment of prophecy.

---

[12] It should be noted that the phrase "the way in which you walk" (Exodus 18:20) is interpreted in BT *Bava Kamma* 100a and BT *Bava Metzia* 30b as a reference *not* to dispositions but to *acts* of benevolence, especially visiting the sick and burying the dead.

It is highly significant that Maimonides does not quote an obvious Talmudic source that could be cited in support of virtue-ethics. Abba Shaul (BT *Shabbat* 133b) interprets the verse in Exodus 15:2 as mandating the imitation of the divine attributes of grace and compassion. The most likely explanation for his reluctance to cite this source relates to his doctrine of attributes of action. For Maimonides it would be the height of absurdity to treat the imitation of God Himself as a religious norm, since His utter uniqueness and unity renders this impossible. Only the imitation of His ways is within the ken of human capacities. It is for similar reasons that Maimonides does not utilize the *Sifra* on Leviticus 19:2, which cites Abba Shaul's interpretation of the Biblical commandment "Be holy because God is holy." Although this particular verse in Leviticus is the most obvious source of *imitatio Dei,* Maimonides prefers to base himself upon the commandment to walk in the ways of God lest the radical distinction between God and His creatures be blurred. He categorically rules out any attempt to go beyond the imitation of the *ways* of God. The *Sifre* cited by Maimonides is eminently suited for Maimonides' purposes, because there is no assertion that God actually possesses various moral attributes, only that he is *called* by these terms.

It is therefore readily understandable that in Chapter 8 of *Shemonah Perakim* he finds it necessary to make a basic distinction between the ideal motivation for ritual acts and that for moral conduct. Whereas in the ritual sphere, he operates with the principle that "the reward is proportionate to the effort," he emphasized that, in the realm of moral conduct, those who perform moral actions after an inner struggle between inclination and obligation are inferior to those who are motivated by virtuous dispositions and hence need no battle against conflicting inclinations. Professor Eliezer Schweid claims[13] that the distinctions reflect the assimilation of Greek categories of thought on the part of Maimonides. But in the light of our preceding analysis it appears that even before he formally linked cultivation of virtues with *imitatio Dei*, Maimonides regarded virtue-ethics not simply as a matter of mental health indispensable to the proper functioning of the human personality but as an integral part of Jewish piety. Greek ethics hardly holds a monopoly on the notion of virtue. There are numerous Biblical and rabbinic passages which could be adduced in support of the thesis that a religiously developed personality is characterized by truly moral dispositions.

The emphasis upon virtue is by no means incompatible with the statement in *Hilkhot Teshuvah* (7:4) which extols the repentant person, who experiences great difficulties in overcoming his proclivity for sin. According to Maimonides, he is spiritually superior to an individual who was never subject to temptation and, therefore, required no effort to curb sinful tendencies. Although Professor Isadore Twersky[14] observes in his brilliant analysis that this passage implies that moral conduct involving struggle against inclinations should be assigned a higher spiritual status than effortless moral conduct that is motivated by virtue, it must, however, be realized that for Maimonides an undesirable ethical disposition, even when repressed to such an extent that it does not manifest itself in overt conduct, still calls for repentance. Hence, an individual who can perform moral actions only after inner struggle, while deserving great praise for his conduct, is, nevertheless, inferior to an individual who possesses desirable traits of character. To be sure, Maimonides, in the spirit of Chapter 7:4 would still contend that an individual who had to struggle to overcome his undesirable dispositions

---

[13] *Iyyunim bi-shemonah perakim le-Rambam*, 1969, Chapter 6.
[14] Isidore Twerksy, *Introduction to the Code of Maimonides*, 1980, 453–459.

before acquiring virtue is spiritually superior to an individual whose virtuous dispositions was attained without any effort on his part.

Maimonides's concern for virtue-ethics also accounts for his ability to dispense with the need for an outright religious commandment to engage in supererogatory conduct. Unlike Nahmanides,[15] who bases the obligation to go beyond the minimal religious obligation and to perform acts of supererogation on the Biblical verse "thou shalt do the good and the right," Maimonides contends that supererogatory conduct is an outgrowth of the development of virtuous dispositions. It is for this reason that instead of prescribing supererogatory conduct, he simply refers to the one "who acts in keeping with the standards of the pious."[16] It is only the virtuous person who is able to perceive the need to go beyond explicit legal commandments in the attempt to imitate the ways of God.

In a similar vein we can also explain why Maimonides, in seeming conflict with the biblical view that the mitzvot were intended for the good of man, places such extraordinary emphasis upon the selfless service of God that he parts company with numerous other Jewish thinkers by including the desire for spiritual satisfaction in the hereafter among the ulterior motives which are incompatible with the religious ideal of serving God out of pure love.[17] But once we recognize the centrality of *imitatio Dei* in the Maimonidean scheme, it becomes obvious why the desire for spiritual satisfaction is bound to interfere with the attainment of the highest rungs of piety. Any type of self-regarding motivation, however noble and sublime, betrays the lack of an essential component of the higher levels of *imitatio Dei*, since the love that God manifests to His creatures is totally other-regarding and completely untainted by selfish motives.

---

[15] *Commentary to the Torah*, Deuteronomy 6:18.

I have dealt with the differences between Maimonides and Nahmanides in their respective treatments of supererogatory conduct in my essay, "Law as the Basis of Moral Society," *Tradition* 19:1 (Spring 1981): 48–49 (page 61 in this volume). See also my "Law, Philosophy and *Imitatio Dei* in Maimonides," *Aquinas* 30 (1987): 27–34.

In my article "Darkhei Shalom," *op. cit.*, I have shown how the focus on agent-morality and virtue-ethics is reflected in Maimonidean attitude towards the treatment of non-Jews. Cf. also my "Law, Philosophy and *Imitatio Dei* in Maimonides," *op. cit.*, especially 33.

[16] *Hilkhot Gezelah va-avedah*, 11:17, and *Hilkhot Rotzeah* 13:4.

[17] *Hilkhot Teshuva*, 10:2.

While *imitatio Dei* constitutes a universally applicable religious norm, it allows for a variety of responses dependant upon individual psychological and intellectual capacities. Hence, the nature and scope of the obligation varies from individual to individual. Significantly, Maimonides, in defining the commandment, stipulates that the cultivation of the dispositions is mandated "in accordance with the capacity of the individual."[18] As he already made it clear in his *Commentary to the Mishnah*,[19] whereas the lower levels of ethical perfection can be acquired as the result of conditioning through moral conduct, the attainment of the higher levels (the ethics of the pious) presupposes intellectual achievements. This reflected his basic conviction that the intellectual apprehension of God is a necessary condition of the cultivation of the moral vision and selfless motivation without which the highest rungs of moral perfection cannot be reached. It is for this reason that the concluding chapter of the *Guide of the Perplexed* extols moral perfection which is grounded on the intellectual apprehension of God as the highest manifestation of piety.

It has been argued by a number of scholars that the ideal of *imitatio Dei* as described by Maimonides in the *Guide* refers exclusively to the political function of the prophet, who, like Plato's philosopher-king, must forego purely contemplative activity and assume the burdens of a statesman. Thus L.V. Berman maintains that "the imitation of God which comes after the acquisition of theoretical knowledge refers to political activity in founding and governing a state."[20] Following this approach Professor Pines maintains that the obligation "to apprehend divine justice, righteousness and charity and to acquire a similarity to them… is not laid upon all men endowed with a moral sense, but only upon the philosophers who also have a social and political activity."[21] Especially puzzling is the latter's assertion that "the legislator and the statesman should in his imitation of God be… either beneficent or cruel, not because he has the corresponding sentiments, but

---

[18] *Hilkhot Deot* 1:6.

[19] *Avot* 2:5.

[20] L.V. Berman, "The Political Interpretation of the Maxim: The Purpose of Philosophy is the Imitation of God." *Studia Islamica* 15 (1961): 60.

[21] Shlomo Pines, "Spinoza, Maimonides and Kant." *Scripta Hierosolymitana* 20 (1968): 28. For a similar approach, see also Eliezer Goldman, "Ha-avodah ha-meyuhedet be-masigei ha-amitot," *Bar Ilan Yearbook*, 1968, 23ff.

because these modes of action are necessary for... the creation and preservation of the highest possible type of community."[22]

Since the cultivation of virtue is defined by Maimonides as the fulfillment of the commandment "thou shalt walk in His ways" it would hardly make sense to demand less moral perfection from an ideal statesman, who is supposed to pattern himself after the prophet, then from ordinary individuals. It seems far more plausible to adopt Professor Twersky's approach[23] and maintain that the *imitatio Dei* described in the concluding chapter of the *Guide*, far from being the exclusive prerogative of the statesman, represents the highest possible level of responding to the divine imperative of "thou shalt walk in His ways," which however can be attained only by the philosopher, irrespective of whether or not he functions as a statesman. To be sure, *some* (but by no means all) divine moral attributes – as is made clear in Part I Chapter 54 – have relevance only as models for the statesman, but not for individuals without political responsibilities. But this in no way supports the thesis that the other divine moral attributes especially those enumerated in Chapter 1 of *Hilkhot Deot*, are irrelevant to the quest for *imitatio Dei* on the part of ordinary individuals. It must be realized that in the Maimonidean system "thou shalt walk in His ways" represents a continuous challenge, beginning with the attempt to cultivate moral virtues through moral conduct and pointing to the ever-higher dimensions of *imitatio Dei* which can be engendered only by intellectual perfection.

---

[22] Shlomo Pines, "Translator's Introduction to the Guide of the Perplexed." In Moses Maimonides, *The Guide of the Perplexed*, 1963, 122.

[23] Isadore Twersky, *op. cit.*, p. 511m note 390. Compare also with the thesis of David Hartman, "Maimonides: Torah and Philosophic Quest," 1976. See also Alexander Altmann, "Maimonides' Four Perfections," *Essays in Jewish Intellectual History*, 1981, 73; Yitzchak Engelard, "Equity in Maimonides," *Israel Law Review*, 21, 3–4, note 102, p. 329 and Daniel H. Frank, "The End of the Guide: Maimonides on the Best Life for Man," *Judaism* 34:4 (1985): 485–495.

IMITATIO DEI IN MAIMONIDES'S *SEFER HA-MITZVOT* AND THE *MISHNEH TORAH*[1]

IMITATION OF DIVINE moral attributes plays a key role in the Maimonidean system. *Da'at Hashem* (the knowledge of God) encompasses not merely intellectual perfection, but also the acquisition of moral *de'ot* (traits of character or disposition), as evidenced by the concluding chapter of the guide. As a matter of fact, it could be argued that Maimonides deliberately chose the term *da'at* instead of *middot* in order to emphasize that the cultivation of desirable traits of character constitutes an integral feature of the overriding religious goal of *da'at Hashem*.

There is, however, a striking contrast in the treatment of the Commandment "Thou shalt walk in His ways"[2] as presented in the *Sefer ha-Mitzvot* (Positive Commandment #8) and in his later, more authoritative *magnum opus Hilkhot De'ot* in *Mishneh Torah*. Significantly, in both sources Maimonides completely omits any reference to Abba Shaul's classic dictum "Be like him – as He is gracious and compassionate, you shall be gracious and compassionate" (BT *Shabbat* 133b). In view of the fact that the Maimonidean doctrine of negative attributes rules out the feasibility of emulating Divine properties, *imitatio Dei,* in the Maimonidean scheme, can

---

[1] From *Tradition and Transition: Essays Presented to Chief Rabbi Sir Immanuel Jakobovits to Celebrate Twenty Years in Office,* edited by Jonathan Sacks, 321–324. London: Jews' College Publications, 1986.

[2] Deuteronomy 28:10.

refer only to the emulation of Divine attributes of action, not to the quest for Godlike properties.

Both *Sefer ha-Mitzvot* and *Mishneh Torah* interpret "Thou shalt walk in His ways" in keeping with the text of the *Sifei* to Deuteronomy 11:22 "as it says 'kindness' you shall be kind; as it says 'generous' you shall be generous" as a requirement to emulate Divine moral attributes. There is, however, an important difference between the two Maimonidean versions. In the earlier work, Maimonides lumps together (a) The cultivation of moral attributes and (b) (basing himself on the exposition of Deuteronomy 13:5 in BT *Sotah* 14a), the performance of benevolent actions such as clothing the naked, visiting the sick, comforting mourners and burying the dead. In his later work, however, the commandment "Thou shalt walk in his ways" no longer contains any references to the performance of the type of actions as stipulated in (b). As a matter of fact, Maimonides expounds the obligation to perform benevolent actions not in *Hilkhot De'ot* but in *Hilkhot Avelut* of the *Mishneh Torah*. Moreover, there is no mention made at all of "Thou shalt walk in His ways" in conjunction with the religious obligations mandating altruistic conduct. The only Biblical source cited for the obligation to perform acts of loving kindness is the verse "Thou shalt love thy neighbor as thyself (Leviticus 19:19)."[3]

At first blush it seems rather strange that Maimonides failed to codify in his *Mishneh Torah* the mandate to perform acts of loving kindness as an aspect of the Biblical commandment "Thou shalt walk in His ways" in the same manner as he conceived it originally in the *Sefer ha-Mitzvot*, which was designed as a preliminary work to the *Mishneh Torah*. But upon considering the centrality of the cultivation of the intellectual and moral virtues in the Maimonidean system, we can appreciate why, as his views matured, he felt constrained to limit the scope of the commandment "Thou shalt walk in His ways" exclusively to the cultivation of virtues. The definition of the mitzvah as provided in the *Sefer ha-Mitzvot* is prone to give rise to the misconception that the cultivation of moral virtues is not really an intrinsic but merely an instrumental value – as a means to the performance of moral actions. Actually, such an interpretation would completely distort Maimonides's position. Following in the footsteps of Aristotle who maintained that virtue

---

[3] For an interesting contrast, however, see *Sefer Mitzvot Gadol Mitzvot Aseh* 7 for a definition of the mitzvah of "Thou shalt walk in His ways" exclusively in terms of actions such as clothing the naked, etc.

is attained by performing acts in accordance with the requirements of virtue, Maimonides maintains that the performance of acts of lovingkindness is a stepping stone towards the attainment of moral virtue.

It must be borne in mind that in the Maimonidean ethical system, moral virtue is not reducible to the disposition to obey moral rules. For exponents of law-ethics such as Hume and Kant,[4] virtue matters only as a means to an end. Its sole function is to promote obedience to moral laws. Obviously, a virtuous individual is less likely to succumb to the temptation to transgress moral rules than an individual for whom obedience to morality precepts has not yet become second nature. But for Maimonides, such an account of virtue will not do. For him, virtue literally is its own reward. It is *the* reward of the mitzvah (see his *Commentary to Avot* 1:2). Viewed from this perspective, the performance of moral actions represents merely a means to the religious goal of striving for moral perfection. It is only in this light that the concluding chapter of the *Guide* can be understood. Julius Guttman charged that when Maimonides extols the cultivation of lovingkindness, justice, etc. as the ultimate religious goal, he in effect breaks with the basic thrust of his philosophy which revolves around the knowledge of God rather than the performance of religious deeds. However, upon closer analysis it becomes evident that this objection is unfounded. For the last chapter of the *Guide* the grand finale of the Maimonidean system, does not revert to act-morality. Maimonides deals with the impact of the attainment of *da'at Hashem*. Insofar as the Maimonidean agent-morality is concerned, we reach the peak of our development, when, the attainment of *da'at Hashem* – intellectual *and* moral perfection – constantly manifests itself in moral actions which are inspired by virtue.

The realization that cultivation of virtue constitutes an intrinsic religious goal that transcends considerations of act-morality enables us to grasp why for Maimonides it is so essential that moral actions, in contradistinction to ritual observance, should ideally be motivated by virtuous dispositions rather than be performed after an inner struggle, where religious duty ultimately prevails over inclination. Eliezer Schweid[5] claims that the Maimonidean insistence upon the distinction between the appropriate motivations for moral as against ritual mitzvot respectively has no basis in Jewish sources

---

[4] See A. MacIntyre, *After Virtue: A Study in Moral Theory.* Notre Dame, IN: University of Notre Dame, 1981, 216–217.

[5] *Iyyunim bi-shemoneh perakim le-Rambam,* Chapter 6.

and is a concession to Greek categories of thought. Actually, there is really no basis for this stricture. The requirement to cultivate moral virtues is rooted in his interpretation of the commandment "Thou shalt walk in His ways," which following the above-cited *Sifrei*, adds the dimensions of virtue-ethics to the provisions of law-ethics.

The emphasis upon agent-morality and virtue-ethics in the Maimonidean system also sheds light on his treatment of supererogation. Whereas Nahmanides[6] argues that the commandment, "Thou shalt do what is good and right" entails the obligation to go beyond minimal standards and to engage in supererogatory acts, Maimonides never recognizes *"Lifnim mi-shurat ha-din"* as a para-legal obligation. Instead, he defines it exclusively in terms of agent-morality.[7] Insofar as act-morality is concerned, there is no place at all for the notion of superogatory conduct, are always couched in terms of *"ha-oseh lifnim mi-shurat ha-din."*

In the Maimonidean scheme, the practice and study of the law is expected to lead to ever higher standards of religious and moral sensitivity. Formal rules cannot do justice to the religious ideal. It is precisely because they are mandated not only to perform moral actions, but to strive to imitate God as the exemplar of moral perfection that we cannot remain content with merely meeting the requirements of law-ethics but that we must supplement them with moral intuitions grounded in virtue-ethics. The law, insofar as agent-morality is concerned, merely mandates the cultivation of the "middle way" between the extremes. The higher level – "the way of the pious" – cannot be demanded. It is adopted, not out of sense of obligation, but inspired by the ongoing quest for perfection, which enables us to perceive ever higher ethico-religious requirements.[8]

The recognition of the pivotal role of virtue-ethics in the Maimonidean system also enables us to understand what otherwise would strike us as a totally superfluous complication. As is well known, Maimonides frowns

---

[6] *Commentary to the Torah,* Deuteronomy 6:18.

[7] *Hilkhot Deot,* 1:5.

[8] See my discussion of the subject in my article "The Maimonidean Matrix of Rabbi Joseph B. Soloveitchik's, Two-Tiered Ethics." In *Through the Sound of Many Voices,* edited by Jonathan V. Plaut, 172–183 (page 161 in this volume). See especially note 20. See also Marvin Fox, *The Intellectual History – Presented to Alexander Altman,* edited by Stein and Lowey, 93–120, and David S. Shapiro's "The Doctrine of the Image of God and *Imitatio Dei*" in *Studies in Jewish Thought* 1: 15–43.

upon the predication of attributes of God, since in his view, the ascription of properties to God is incompatible with the absolute unity of God. If for this reason, he introduces two distinct forms of analysis. Essential properties of God are construed as "negative attributes." On the other hand, moral properties are rendered as "attributes of action," which do not characterize God but the manner of his actions in the world. But why was it necessary for Maimonides to have recourse to "attributes of action?" Why could he not have simplified his system by treating moral attributes also as "negations"? In the light of our preceding analysis, it, however, becomes clear that in view of the fact that the divine moral attributes are supposed to function as guides towards *imitatio Dei,* we cannot dispense with the notion of "attributes of action." Had Maimonides provided a purely negative definition of moral attributes, God could not serve as the exemplar of moral perfection. If, on the other hand, Maimonides would have been willing to settle for the interpretation of "walking after God" which was provided in BT *Sotah* 14a and defined the commandment, as *Sefer Mitzvot Gadol* did, as exclusively referring to the performance of benevolent acts, he could have eliminated the entire category of "attributes of action" and relied exclusively upon the doctrine of "negative attributes."

RABBI HAYYIM OF VOLOZHIN[1]

IT WAS DURING a very turbulent period in Jewish history that Rabbi Hayyim of Volozhin made his significant contribution towards the preservation of classic Judaism, which accords the Halakhah (religious law) a pre-eminent position in the life of the Jew.

The emergence of the Hassidic movement hurled a formidable challenge against the rabbinic doctrine, which regarded strict observance of the Halakhah as the cornerstone of Judaism. Hassidism stressed the *subjective* religious experience of the individual. Weighed in the Hassidic scale of values, it seemed to be of relatively only minor importance whether or not a given religious act fully conformed to the rigid standards circumscribed by *objective* halakhic norms. Especially during the early stages of Hassidism, there loomed the danger that the new movement might completely succumb to antinomian trends and, perhaps, break with the Halakhah altogether.

The gravity with which the leading rabbinic authorities of the time viewed the anti-legalistic orientation of Hassidism is attested by the fact that the Gaon of Vilna, who always scrupulously avoided any type of involvement in communal activity, temporarily abandoned his isolation and plunged into the forefront of the battle against the new sect. But in spite of the determined opposition of the Mitnaggedim, Hassidism made tremendous inroads into the rank and file of the Jewish masses. The tide could not be stopped by pronouncements or declarations charging Hasidism with

---

[1] From *Guardians of Our Heritage,* edited by Leo Jung, New York: Bloch Publishing Co., 1958.

deviations from accepted traditional forms. What was necessary was a vindication of the halakhic approach to Judaism. It had to be established that meticulous adherence to the objective norms of Jewish law was not a matter of dry and barren legalism, but that it constituted the repository of a dynamic religious way of life.

The task of formulating a constructive program aiming at a renaissance of halakhic Judaism fell upon the shoulders of Rabbi Hayyim of Volozhin, who possessed in abundant measure the qualities of leadership called for in such a crisis. He was endowed with an unusual array of talents, combining intellectual brilliance and profound erudition with a remarkable genius for practical affairs. He was as much at home in the intricacies of the Talmudic law, the veiled regions of mystical speculation, as he was in the world, where his intuitive understanding of people and his skill in the solution of communal problems brought him great fame. Unlike his spiritual mentor, the renowned Gaon of Vilna, who withdrew from society and devoted himself to intellectual pursuits, Rabbi Hayyim eagerly accepted the burdens of communal responsibility. It was his passionate concern for the welfare of his fellow-man that impelled him to assert leadership in the Jewish community. Altruism was the keynote of his philosophy of life. As recorded by his son, Rabbi Hayyim's credo could be summed up in the words that "man was created not for his own sake, but to help others to the limit of his capacities."[2] A study of his life will show that it was due to his extraordinary sensitivity to the spiritual plight of his people that he emerged as the predominant figure of halakhic Judaism of his time.

Rabbi Hayyim was born in 1749 in Volozhin and brought up in a prosperous, pious home, his father serving as *parnas* (lay leader) of the Jewish community. Hayyim received the traditional training, which emphasized the Bible, Talmud, and Codes. The extent of his brilliance can be gauged by the fact that at the age of twelve he was already studying under the illustrious Rabbi Rafael Hamburger. At the age of fifteen, he sat at the feet of Rabbi Aryeh Leib, the author of *Shaagat Aryeh* and one of the leading Talmudists of his time, distinguished for his independence of mind and self-reliance in the pursuit of truth.

---

[2] *Nefesh ha-Hayyim*, Preface.

But the decisive influence exerted upon his intellectual development was the Gaon of Vilna, the association with whom began when Rabbi Hayyim was nineteen years old. Three or four times a year, Hayyim would come to Vilna for a month at a time in order to submit questions and problems to the Gaon; from him he acquired his basic philosophy of life as well as the methodology for the study of the Torah.

The close relationship between them, which lasted throughout the latter's lifetime, molded Rabbi Hayyim's pattern of thought and activity to such an extent that one may be inclined to view him as the executor of the spiritual legacy which the Gaon bequeathed to his people. Rabbi Hayyim popularized and promoted his teacher's philosophy of life, because he was advocated by the methods of the Gaon held the answer to the spiritual crisis which confronted the Jewish people.

By his approach to the discovery of the original meaning of the classical sources of Judaism, such as Bible, Talmud, Midrash and Zohar, the Gaon had wrought a major intellectual revolution in Jewish thought. He was strongly averse to the method of *pilpul* (a form of casuistry) which solved Talmudic difficulties by ingenious, though sometimes far-fetched, modes of analysis. Instead, he substituted scientifically sound methods of elucidations and other forms of literary criticism. The student of the Talmud is often fascinated to observe how the Gaon of Vilna with one brief note or comment disposes of difficulties which had given rise to a vast body of literature.

The Gaon's methodology was inspired by the determination to discover authentic Judaism formulated in the classic texts. He firmly believed that a religious practice or observance could be regarded as genuinely Jewish only if it could be validated by some reference either in the Bible or the literature of the Talmudic period. In his search for authentic Judaism, he was willing to disregard or even set aside the opinions and rulings of well-established authorities, if he held that their views were incompatible with those of the Talmud. By the same token, he was most vehement in his opposition to the religious reformation advocated by the Hassidic movement, which emphasized the subjective religious experience at the expense of strict adherence to Talmudic law. Any departure from the norms of Talmudic Judaism was in the eyes of the Gaon an inexcusable defiance of the supreme religious authority of Israel.

The religious philosophy which the Gaon imparted to a circle of select disciples became the guide of large segments of the Jewish people, primarily because Rabbi Hayyim dedicated his almost unlimited energy to the dissemination of his master's teachings. He was so self-effacing that he looked upon himself primarily as a pupil and follower of the Gaon. But he protested vigorously when others referred to him as a "disciple" of his illustrious teacher. In his humility, he felt that the intellectual superiority of his teacher over him was so pronounced as to constitute a difference not of degree but of kind. Hence it would be a reflection upon the Gaon's greatness if he permitted himself to be called his disciple.[3]

But his humility must not mislead us into a false appraisal of his historic importance. He was too much of a creative personality in his own right to be relegated to the role of a blind follower of his revered mentor. His independence of mind is attested to by his divergence from the Gaon's position on a number of important issues ranging from such practical matters as the determination of the policy toward Hassidism to such metaphysical problems as the interpretation of the Kabbalistic notion of *tzimtzum* (divine self-limitation to make room for the universe). He possessed a remarkably systematic mind, which enabled him to cull from the vast Talmudic and Kabbalistic literature a succinctly formulated philosophy of halakhic Judaism, which he presented in his *Nefesh Hayyim*. Because of his genius for practical affairs, he succeeded in creating the instrumentalities for the implementation of a philosophy of life which, though it had sprung from the matrix of the Gaon, still bore the stamp of his own individuality.

At an early age Rabbi Hayyim was thrust into a position of leadership in the Jewish community. He was only twenty-five years old when he became Rabbi of Volozhin, a community which he served almost continuously until his death.

Financially independent, he refused to accept any remuneration for his services. His fortunate economic situation later on enabled him to start his own yeshiva and, at the beginning, to finance it exclusively from his personal funds.

At the age of forty he was called to Vilkomir, staying on as rabbi of this community for only a year. Certain influential Vilkomir businessmen were resentful of their rabbi's policy of supporting himself from income derived

---

[3] Rabbi Hayyim's introduction to the *Sifra de-tzeniuta* by the Gaon of Vilna.

from his business enterprises and refusing to accept a salary from the community. As a result of strained relations with them, he returned to his native city and resumed the spiritual leadership of Volozhin.

Jewish folklore attributes his departure from Vilkomir to a trivial incident. Rabbi Hayyim is supposed to have been asked by one of the more prominent members of the Vilkomir community to give him the time of the *molad* (the exact time when the new moon becomes visible). Since the rabbi did not have a Jewish calendar with him at the moment, he was unable to furnish the requested information, whereupon a whispering campaign, charging the rabbi with gross ignorance for not knowing such an elementary thing as the time of the *molad*, swept through Vilkomir!

His bitter experience in Vilkomir prompted him years later to offer a unique admonition whenever he conferred *semikhah* (traditional ordination) upon one of his disciples. He would invariably tell the young rabbi that in addition to mastering Jewish religious and civil law, it would also be necessary for him to know the time of the *molad*. As this down-to-earth advice to his students would indicate, Rabbi Hayyim, notwithstanding his intellectual brilliance and profound scholarship, never became alienated from the needs of the common man. It may appear paradoxical that the advocate of a way of life that concentrated on an intellectual approach to God should nevertheless find the key to the hearts of the people.

While he labored to create an intellectual and spiritual elite that would be committed to the study and analysis of Halakhah, his personality would not allow him to become estranged from the rank and file. A glimpse into his daily working routine furnishes a typical illustration. Nothing was permitted to interfere with the popular lectures that he delivered every evening in the *bet midrash* (the local study hall), where he spoke to the worshippers on the portion of the week. Here was a pre-eminent Talmudic authority whom rabbis from all over Lithuania constantly consulted on important decisions, who did not begrudge his time and energy to the community at large on matters that others might have been inclined to view as of no great consequence.

His concern for the spiritual welfare of his fellow Jew is revealed by the order of priority which he assigned to the publication of his books. Rabbi Hayyim, in the course of the years, wrote numerous responses on intricate problems of Talmudic law. He was surely aware that in order for his reputation as one of the outstanding contributors to halakhic thought to be perpetuated, it was desirable that his contributions in this field be printed. Yet he never requested this of his son, although he did urge him to make every possible effort to have the *Nefesh ha-Hayyim* published after his death.[4] It is not difficult to find the reason for his preference for the latter book. He felt that it could prove to be of tremendous practical value to the Jewish community because it would promote a better understanding of what he regarded as authentic Judaism. He was convinced that at a time when the vagaries of an unbridled emotionalism were rampant, an urgent need existed for a work that would emphasize the primacy of Torah study and would stress the importance of strict adherence to halakhic norms even though at times this might appear to curb spontaneous religious expression.

But Rabbi Hayyim's concern was not limited to the spiritual well-being of his people. He was especially perturbed by the plight of the unfortunate *agunot* (Jewish women who cannot remarry because they cannot furnish convincing evidence of their husband's death). He brought his vast Talmudic erudition to bear upon the solution of numerous cases of *agunot*. Many of his responses dealing with the *agunah* problem reveal the tormenting inner conflicts and the tensions he had to endure whenever he had to make a bold decision permitting the remarriage of an *agunah* under conditions where other authorities would take exception to his ruling. But he felt that he had no moral right to shirk responsibility for rendering decisions on acute problems. His intellectual honesty outweighed all other considerations. He repeatedly emphasizes that he was admonished by the Gaon of Vilna that, when it came to the realm of Torah, "where truth is the sole criterion,"[5] never to bow to any other authority.

He was too multi-dimensional a personality to have his service to his fellow man confined to the sphere of intellectual labors. He was one of the moving spirits of the assembly of Jewish notables that met in Minsk in 1806 and decreed that a Jewish family that could afford more than two *challot* Friday night had to contribute a certain amount of money for the relief of the struggling Jewish farmers in one of the impoverished districts of Lithuania. He undertook to become one of the two administrators of this relief fund. He was instrumental in reorganizing the *Kupat Rambam*, an old, established charity for the support of scholars in Israel. Thanks largely to his

---

[4] Introduction to *Nefesh ha-Hayyim.*
[5] *Hut ha-Meshulash*, responsae 8 and 9.

efforts, that institution was able to regain its prestige and influence among all segments of Jewry, who submerged their internal divisions in order to forge a common link with Zion.

In his diverse philanthropic efforts Rabbi Hayyim was immeasurably aided by his reputation for practical wisdom. To the common people, he epitomized common sense at its best. Numerous folk tales and legends sprang up extolling his brilliant handling of such situations. Whether it was advising a French general on the outcome of the Napoleonic wars or persuading a reluctant yeshiva supporter not to withdraw his subsidy, popular fancy always wove a halo of infallibility around him.

His intuitive grasp and keen psychological insights are best illustrated by an incident which made a tremendous impression upon his contemporaries. With a great deal of pomp and fanfare there came to Vilna a very impressive person, dressed in Oriental attire. Upon arrival, he was received by officials of the Russian Government. The story was circulated that he was an emissary of a Jewish king in Africa who had sent him to bring the good tidings that the beginning of the redemption was at hand.

The man referred to himself merely as the "Crimean Jew." While praying, he displayed extraordinary fervor and his entire bearing was one of extreme religious devotion. He accepted an invitation to one of the most pious and prominent homes in Vilna only under the condition that he could personally slaughter the chicken, which had to be cooked in new utensils. Moreover, he requested that he have a private minyan (quorum for public worship) arranged at his home so that he could personally lead the services. All these requests were gladly granted by his host, who was overjoyed to have as his guest a man about whom it was rumored that if he was not the Messiah himself, he was at any rate, his representative.

Thus the "Crimean Jew" obtained access to the most influential homes and was taken into the confidence of practically all the leaders of the Jewish community. Only Rabbi Hayyim of Volozhin was suspicious. Sensing that some fraud was being perpetrated, he advised extreme caution. His judgment was soon vindicated when, within a very short time, it was discovered that the "Crimean Jew," far from being a representative of the Messiah, was actually a secret agent of the czarist government who wanted to check on tax evasions by the Jewish population!

The rabbi's deft handling of affairs, his sound approach, as well as his reputation, paved the way for success in the crowning achievement of his life, the founding of the Yeshivah of Volozhin. It was a most difficult venture upon which he embarked with a great deal of reluctance. He was fully convinced of the desperate need for the establishment of an institution that would spearhead the drive to win back the Jewish community to the ideal of Torah study. But Rabbi Hayyim was too modest to believe that he was the man for such a gigantic undertaking. The leading rabbis of Lithuania, however, regarded him as the logical choice to lead this all-important effort, and he eventually succumbed to their persistent pleas and agreed to start a yeshiva in Volozhin.

Its beginnings were extremely humble. In 1803, he gathered ten disciples who were supported from his own private means and instructed by him personally. Although Rabbi Hayyim approached his task in a spirit, to use his own words, comparable to the "insignificant sexton who summons people for worship in the synagogue,"[6] the yeshiva from the very beginning reflected the personality of its founder. He made certain that its atmosphere would be conducive to the development of a spiritual elite. Nothing was allowed to detract from the dignity of the yeshiva student, who was never permitted to forget that the study of the Torah outranks all other occupations and activities. For this reason Rabbi Hayyim could not tolerate the practice employed at other yeshivot, where needy students received their stipends in the form of free meals provided on a rotating basis in the homes of public-minded individuals. He realized that this form of subsidy was fraught with serious psychological hazards since handouts received at private homes were apt to induce feelings of inferiority. He undertook the onerous burden of organizing ambitious campaigns for the support of his yeshiva when, owing to its phenomenal growth, he found it no longer possible to maintain it out of his personal funds.

It is difficult to present an adequate appraisal of the revolutionary impact which the Yeshiva of Volozhin made upon the intellectual and spiritual life of Lithuanian Jewry. Prior to the founding of the yeshiva, the intensive study of Torah had fallen into neglect. This was due in some measure to the severe economic pressure to which Lithuanian Jewry was subjected. But the chief responsibility for the decline of Jewish learning must be pinned upon the inroads of the Hassidic movement, which accorded to scholarship only a secondary place in the Jewish scale of values. Since, as Hassidism holds, the

---

[6] His open letter, quoted by M.S. Schmuckler, *Toldot Rabbenu Hayyim mi-Volozhin*, 38.

presence of God is revealed everywhere, knowledge of the Torah is not necessary to achieve close communication with Him. The Hassidic ideal is personified by the *Tzaddik* (the Saint) who need not be a *talmid hakham* (a scholar). Hassidism had shifted the center of gravity of Judaism from the study of the Torah to the cultivation of religious experience, which reaches its climax in prayer. Knowledge of the Torah ceased to be an intrinsic value.

This revolutionary conception dealt a devastating blow to the status of Jewish learning. Instead of occupying a pivotal place in the hierarchy of Jewish values, learning was relegated to the role of a handmaiden of sentimentalism. The ultimate objective of learning was not producing a deeper insight into the Torah, but to induce intense feelings of reverence and piety.

The immediate consequence of this upheaval was the neglect of Talmudic studies. Instead of concentrating upon the analysis of its intricate legal problems, people turned to the study of devotional literature, which seemed to offer a far richer return in the cultivation of religious emotions. Talmudic studies were abandoned to such an extent that in many synagogues one could not even find copies of the book that previously had occupied a commanding position in Jewish life.[7]

When Rabbi Hayyim founded the Yeshivah of Volozhin, he provided a base of operations from which a counter-attack could be launched against the inroads of excessive emotionalism. Lithuania did not posses any other academy of learning which could sustain an organized effort at restoring the primacy of Torah study. If that country subsequently gained renown for its network of yeshivot, it was due to Volozhin, "the mother of yeshivot." Its pioneering efforts inspired the establishment of numerous other yeshivot throughout Lithuania.

Therefore, the founding of the Yeshivah of Volozhin must be regarded as the birth not merely of an institution but of a movement that changed the entire complexion of Lithuanian Jewry and brought about a renaissance of learning. The resurgence of intellectualism was a triumph of Rabbi Hayyim's philosophy of life, which saw in the study of Torah the most exalted form of divine worship. He utterly objected to the Hassidic contention that the study of Torah possesses religious significance only to the extent that it is motivated by the intention of achieving communion with God.

---

[7] *Nefesh ha-Hayyim* IV:1.

Drawing upon his mastery of rabbinic thought, he demonstrated that the proper motivation for the study of the Torah was *li-shmah* (for the sake of gaining a better insight into the Torah) and not for the purpose of intensifying religious emotions.[8] For Rabbi Hayyim, the cultivation of awe and reverence for God was only the *beginning* of all wisdom. Without the fear of God, a human being could not serve as a receptacle for God's Torah. But a receptacle is only a means to an end. It does not make sense to concentrate all one's time and energies upon the building of a perfect container. One must acquire the treasures that are to be stored away in it. The perusal of devotional literature, therefore, must not be allowed to become the predominant intellectual concern of the Jew, for nothing can replace the real treasure, i.e., the intensive study of the Halakhah.[9]

Since in his hierarchy of supreme values, intellectual virtues rank above practical ones, the study of the Halakhah must not be geared exclusively to the needs of religious observance. He emphatically objected to any attempt to by-pass the research of the original Talmudic sources by concentrating Jewish learning upon the mastering of the various codes of Jewish law (e.g. the *Shulhan Arukh*) extracted from the Talmud.

According to a popular saying, to study the codes of the law without their original Talmudic sources is like "eating fish without spice." But Rabbi Hayyim went one step further and charged that it was like "eating spice without fish."[10]

Searching analysis of the classical halakhic sources represented to him the highest form of divine service. Although he was so scrupulous about his daily prayers that he went at times to extreme efforts in order to worship with a *minyan* (quorum for public worship), he nevertheless told his disciples that he would be willing to trade the value of all his prayers for the discovery of a single novel law that would derive from his Talmudic research.[11]

He constantly admonished his students to be mindful of the hegemony of learning in the Jewish religious life. He warned them to be on guard lest exaggerated concern over their spiritual growth interfere with their pursuit of halakhic studies. Even the Mishnah's recommendation to ponder "the proper way that man should choose for himself" does not apply to precious

---

[8] *Nefesh ha-Hayyim* IV:3.
[9] *ibid.*, IV: 6–9.
[10] *Keter Rosh, Orchat Hayyim*, Sec. 49.
[11] *ibid.*, Sec 48.

time which one could possibly devote to the study of the Torah. According to our rabbi, it is intended only for those periods which could not be used for the acquisition of halakhic knowledge.[12]

He gave dramatic expression to his conviction that Torah study had to provide the spiritual justification for the very existence of the universe. Since "the world might collapse if at any given moment it would be totally deprived of the spiritual support furnished by the pillar of Torah learning,"[13] Rabbi Hayyim took steps to ensure that in his yeshivah there would be at all times, day and night, at least one individual engaged in the study of Torah. At the conclusion of the fast on Yom Kippur, while the students went home to break the fast, he remained in the yeshivah, engaged in study, until one of the disciples finished his meal and was able to relieve him.

It was on the issue of the primacy of halakhic studies that the vast theoretical differences between Rabbi Hayyim's philosophy and that of Hassidism revealed themselves. Because the latter assigned a secondary place to the study of Torah, Rabbi Hayyim was convinced that it represented a major departure from classic Judaism. But he nevertheless maintained cordial personal relations with the Hassidim, since he felt that they had no *intention* of making a radical break with the Halakhah.

His conciliatory attitude towards the new sect stands in striking contrast to the position of the Gaon of Vilna, who excommunicated them and even refused to enter into discussions with the leaders of the movement, who were anxious to convince him of their loyalty to halakhic Judaism. The Gaon's unbending opposition was due to his suspicion that the new movement was another manifestation of the pseudo-Messianic tendencies which had played such havoc with traditional religion. Since Hassidism followed so closely upon the heels of the Frankist movement, there were ample grounds to fear that relatively minor changes it had introduced into the order and timing of prayers foreshadowed the outbreak of a major antinomian revolt and the beginning of a new sect which ultimately would openly challenge the validity of the Halakhah. Hassidism's accent upon religious sentiment and its disparagement of learning represented to the Gaon further danger signals, warning that a complete break with the Halakhah might be in the offing.

---

[12] *Ruach Hayyim*, II, 9.
[13] *Nefesh ha-Hayyim*, IV:25.

Rabbi Hayyim did not share the apprehensions of his mentor. He was satisfied that the Hassidism had no desire of seceding from halakhic Judaism. But while he conceded the nobility of their motives, he was convinced that the methods advocated by them reflected a misunderstanding of the unique nature of Judaism.

He felt that, while the movement did not abrogate the authority of the Halakhah, it reduced Halakhah to a secondary place in the realm of religious values. What really mattered in the Hassidic scheme was not adherence to the Halakhah but rather the quality and intensity of the sentiments accompanying the performance of a religious act. To them, the fulfillment of a mitzvah possessed genuine significance only to the degree that it was suffused with *kavanah* (the intention of achieving communion with God). By the same token, infringements on halakhic precepts could be justified, under special circumstances, on the grounds that the technical violation of the law was necessary for the attainment of a spiritual end.

We can thus recognize that Hassidism was walking a tightrope in attempting to adhere to the rigid pattern of the Halakhah while at the same time acknowledging the primacy of the individual's subjective intention.

Although Hassidism wished to remain loyal to halakhic Judaism, it nonetheless subordinated the specific halakhic values to spiritual values that can be based upon an appeal to universal religious sentiments. In the final analysis, its approach stressed the elements of natural religion that are common to all of mankind rather than the particular Jewish values that rest solely upon a specific divine revelation to Israel.

Rabbi Hayyim did not deny the validity of the universal religious values that the Hassidim espoused in their doctrine that God could be found everywhere and that every act can serve as the expression of man's desire to seek communion with God. But he demonstrated that insofar as Judaism is concerned, the subjective factor in religion (the *kavanah* of the individual) must be accommodated within the objective domain of the Halakhah.

A person may spend the entire night of Passover meditating upon the profound spiritual values expressed by the eating of the matzo. Yet all this will be of no avail if he fails to perform the prescribed physical act of eating the matzo. On the other hand, the individual who eats the matzo without being conscious of the *kavanot* that should be associated with this act still has satisfied the requirements of the law.[14]

According to Rabbi Hayyim, the subjective religious experience must never be allowed to overrule the objective Halakhah. He frowned upon any suggestions that under extraordinary circumstances, deviations from the Halakhah might serve a genuine spiritual purpose. Hence, transgressions of the Halakhah cannot be justified on the grounds that they are deemed necessary for the attainment of a sublime spiritual objective. Ever since the Torah was given, the Halakhah has remained the ultimate standard for the evaluation of any act performed by a Jew. Whatever favorable references to *averah li-shmah* (violation of the law committed with a holy intent) are found in the Talmudic literature, according to him they apply either to the period before the Torah was given on Mount Sinai or to the non-Jew, who even today is not bound by the content of Sinaitic revelation.[15]

Behind his ardent espousal of a strictly halakhic approach to religion was a metaphysical view concerning the relation of God to the world that differed radically from that of Hassidism. The latter doctrine stressed the nearness of God, whose glory fills the universe. Accordingly, reflections of the divine can be experienced everywhere. As Rabbi Schneur Zalman of Liady put it, in a classic passage:

> All that man sees – the heaven, the earth and all that fills it – all these things are the external garments of God, but by observing them, man recognizes the inner spirit, the divine vital force that permeates them.[16]

Rabbi Hayyim believed that the Hassidic position regarding God's immanence in the world was fraught with serious dangers to the integrity of Judaism. It was very likely that in the popular mind the doctrine might be confused with an outright pantheism. Moreover, if God's presence is equally revealed everywhere, then all the distinctions between the sacred and the profane would be obliterated. How then, he asks, could the Halakhah regard certain locations as disqualified for the act of prayer or for the study of the Torah?[17]

---

[14] *Nefesh ha-Hayyim*, IV.

[15] *ibid.*, Chapter 7, cf. also *Orchat Hayyim, Keter Rosh*, Sec. 132.

[16] *Tanya*, Chapter 42.

[17] *Nefesh ha-Hayyim*, III:6.

He rejects the notion that man can directly encounter God's immanence in the world. God's presence in the world is a mystery beyond the ken of all human understanding. Insofar as the Halakhah is concerned, we must treat the world *as if* God's relation to His creation would be confined to the exercise of Divine Providence. While God is immanent in the world, he is concealed in such a manner that we cannot apprehend Him directly. The halakhically prescribed way of life is based not upon the ultimate metaphysical *reality* but rather upon the *appearance* of the world to a finite human mind.

"Though, in truth, from His side, all of existence is equally filled with this Being without any separations, distinctions, or divisions, as if creation had not taken place at all, we are neither capable of contemplating nor permitted to contemplate this fact at all."[18]

However illusory the appearance of finite creatures may be, the halakhic approach disregards all questions regarding ultimate metaphysical realities. The Halakhah postulates individual finite beings existing in time and space. How the existence of a finite and composite world can be reconciled with the absolute infinity, simplicity, and unity of God, constitutes a serious metaphysical problem, which the Kabbalah attempted to solve by the notion of *tzimtzum* (God's self-limitation or contraction to make room for the world: "To make possible the existence of a finite world, God, as it were, withdrew, in some sense from the universe"). It was on the interpretation of *tzimtzum* that Hassidism clashed with the staunch advocates of the halakhic approach. Rabbi Schneur Zalman of Liady contended that the notion of *tzimtzum* had to be invoked in order to account for the problem of how a transcendent God became, through this self-limitation, the immanent God who is actually present in the universe.

This interpretation of God's relation to the world was extremely objectionable to the Gaon of Vilna since it certainly implied a blurring of the distinction between the Creator and His creatures. If, as Hassidism suggested, the verse "the entire universe is full of His glory" is to be taken literally, implying God's immanence in the universe, one might easily arrive at an outright pantheistic position. This is why the Gaon of Vilna insisted that the notion of *tzimtzum* be taken not as mere concealment but as actual

---

[18] *ibid.*

withdrawal: God limiting His presence in the universe to the exercise of Providence.

Rabbi Hayyim accepted in substance the position of the Gaon, although he adopted in certain details Rabbi Schneur Zalman's exposition of the term *tzimtzum*. Because of the superficial resemblance between the latter's interpretation and Rabbi Hayyim's, many writers have mistakenly assumed that the Gaon's favorite disciple forsook the metaphysical view of his own teacher to embrace that of Rabbi Schneur Zalman.[19] However, one fundamental difference has escaped their attention. Although both interpret *tzimtzum* not as withdrawal but as concealment, each one applies it to two entirely different aspects of God. For Rabbi Hayyim, it is the *immanent* God who has concealed himself to make possible the appearance of an independent world. *Tzimtzum* supplies the answer to the question: How can there be any room for individual finite beings if God's presence permeates all of reality? Accordingly, God's self-concealment makes it possible for the world to appear as if it possessed independent reality. While metaphysically speaking, God is immanent in the world. His presence is a mystery transcending the bounds of human cognition. Hence, insofar as our knowledge is concerned, we must treat the world as if it possessed independent reality, subject, of course, to Divine Providence.

For the author of the *Tanya, tzimtzum* relates not to the immanence but to the transcendence of God. He encounters the problem of God's relation to the world on a different level. The difficulty solved by *tzimtzum* is how the existence of a world can be reconciled with the transcendence of an infinite God. In Rabbi Schneur Zalman's scheme, *tzimtzum* is the self-concealment of the transcendent God that made it possible for Him to become the Creator of the Universe, in which He is immanent and in which He can be apprehended, since the entire universe is literally filled with His presence.

---

[19] Thus Mordechai Teitelbaum in *Harav mi-Liady* (Warsaw: 1941), vol. 2, 92 maintains that the differences between Rabbi Hayyim and Rabbi Schneur are merely a matter of terminology. Rabbi Charles Chavel incorporated Teitelbaum's conclusions in his essay "Schneyur Zalman of Liady" in *Jewish Library*, vol. 6, 75. The interpretation set forth in this study, which obviates the need for the rather implausible assumption made by Teitelbaum, is based largely upon extremely helpful suggestions that I received from my revered teacher, Rabbi Joseph B. Soloveitchik, to whom I am also indebted for having drawn my attention to the implications for natural religion that follow from the views of Rabbi Hayyim and Rabbi Schneur Zalman concerning *tzimtzum*.

Whether *tzimtzum* applies only to God's transcendence or to His immanence in the world is far from a purely theoretical, metaphysical issue. It is responsible for two completely divergent attitudes towards the entire domain of natural religion. Since Hassidism limited the self-concealment of God to His transcendence, God's presence can readily become manifest to the discerning mind that can penetrate beyond the outer surface to the inner essence of reality. Therefore, we need not rely on any special Divine revelation to find reflections of divinity. The human mind and heart can gain access to God without having recourse to the bridge established by His revelation in the Torah. Hence, natural religious impulses based upon universal human experience play a paramount role in the Hassidic structure of religious values.

In Rabbi Hayyim's system of thought, the situation is completely reversed. There prevails a rather negative attitude towards any form of natural religion. Since God's presence in the world is subject to His self-concealment, it is extremely difficult for the human intellect or emotion to encounter Him through any of His manifestations in reality. Instead, the revealed word of God becomes, for all practical purposes, the only means of reaching Him. Paradoxical though it may sound, according to Rabbi Hayyim, man finds it easier to establish contact with the transcendent God than with the immanent God. While God's immanence in reality is a mystery veiled from human understanding, the transcendent God has revealed Himself in the Torah, and it is through the study of the Torah that man can achieve communion with Him.

In Rabbi Hayyim's theology, the revealed word of God must bear the main burden of providing a link between man and God. Since God's presence in the world is completely concealed, our rational and emotional faculties are inadequate to the task of gaining any real insight into His nature or His relation to the universe. With natural religion shoved to the sidelines, there is little to be gained from employment of the philosophical method. Whatever knowledge can be obtained about fundamental metaphysical issues must be grounded upon God's Divine revelation to select geniuses in the realm of the spirit. Small wonder, then, that in a slighting reference to the Jewish rationalistic philosophers, Rabbi Hayyim declared, "The wisdom of the Kabbalah begins at the point where all the philosophy ends."[20]

---

[20] *Orhot Hayyim, Keter Rosh*, Sec. 61.

His own metaphysical views, which were intended to provide a rationale for meticulous adherence to every iota of Jewish law, were largely based upon kabbalistic notions. Man is given a key position in the universe. Since he represents within himself a cross-section of all reality, from the lowest to the highest regions of being, he alone is capable of serving as a bridge between the various realms. It is up to man to determine whether the cosmic chain of being will be brought closer to perfection or further away from it. The performance of a mitzvah, though it may seem a trivial physical act, therefore possesses cosmic significance because it sets into motion a series of events that have repercussions even in the most exalted realms of being.

In this anthropocentric universe, even God depends in some measure upon man. Just as food is necessary to enable the human body to be united with the soul, the world at large requires the spiritual sustenance of the mitzvot in order that God may be united with His creation.[21] Thus, God is present in the world to the degree that man brings Him into it. The human task consists in the consecration of our deeds to the service of our Creator so that we may succeed in expanding and enlarging God's presence in the universe. For Rabbi Hayyim, man's bearing the image of God implies that man partakes of God's creative powers in some measure. It is up to man to become a "builder" of the world by supplying the spiritual justification for its existence.[22]

Rabbi Hayyim carries the notion of man's spiritual efficacy to the extreme of maintaining that man's immortality is the result of his creativity. Man's part in the World to Come is not only the reward bestowed upon him but also the "natural" product of his own spiritual labors. Accordingly, our share in the World to Come is not something ready-made, merely waiting for us to qualify for it by dint of our meritorious conduct. On the contrary, we ourselves must create our own portion of the World to Come. It is through our loyalty to a God-given way of conduct that we build the spiritual worlds in which we remain even after our physical existence has come to an end.[23]

The dynamic role assigned to man in this world view provided an attractive setting for the thoroughly halakhic approach that Rabbi Hayyim advocated. The strict observance of all the minutiae of Jewish law was not a matter of conformity to a barren legalism; rather, it was dictated by the

---

[21] *Nefesh ha-Hayyim* II: 6.

[22] *ibid.*, I:3.

[23] *ibid.*, I:12 *Ruach Hayyim*, I:1.

cosmic significance of each mitzvah. Yet, relatively speaking, even the scope of the mitzvot is limited, since their influence is confined to certain aspects of reality. However, the study of the Torah, which links man directly with the word of God, is the one method through which the total spiritual needs of the human personality can be satisfied. That is why Rabbi Hayyim's metaphysics lent itself especially to the revitalization and revival of Jewish learning, which was the paramount objective of his life.

To the modern mind, his system may appear somewhat narrow and excessively intellectual, leaving little place for the spontaneous elements which we may consider desirable in the religious life. But there can be no doubt that, historically speaking; his efforts were largely responsible for the renaissance of Torah learning that became the hallmark of Lithuanian Jewry.

When Rabbi Hayyim died in 1821, he left an impressive array of disciples. Inspired by their master, they carried on his work, laboring for the preservation of halakhic Judaism, which regards "the four cubits of the Law as God's pre-eminent domain in the world."

Bibliography

Rabbi Hayyim of Volozhin. *Nefesh ha-Hayyim*. Vilna: 1874.
Idem. *Ruach Hayyim*. Vilna: 1874.
Maimon, S. *Sefer ha-Gra*. Jerusalem: 1954.
Idem. *Sha'arei ha-Meah*. Jerusalem: 1952.
Schmuckler, M.S. *Toldot Rabbenu Hayyim mi-Volozhin*. Vilna: 1909.
Ha-Kohen, Asher. *Orhot Hayyim: Sheiltot Keter Rosh*. Tel Aviv: 1955.

SAMSON RAPHAEL HIRSCH'S DOCTRINE OF INNER REVELATION[1]

IT IS WIDELY TAKEN for granted that Samson Raphael Hirsch's insistence upon the eternal validity of the Sinaitic Revelation clashes head-on with any doctrine that acknowledges the legitimacy of progress in the realm of religious truth. Hirsch categorically rejected the thesis of Reform theologians who adapted to their own needs the Hegelian conception that the "spirit of the time" represents the Revelation of the Absolute in the historic process. Therefore, he protested vigorously against the doctrine of "progressive revelation" that was fashionable at the time. This doctrine stipulated that the norms of the Torah be evaluated in terms of their compatibility with the ethos of a given age, which, according to Hegel, functions as the medium of divine revelation. As a champion of Orthodoxy, he ridiculed the suggestion that Judaism should accommodate itself to the value-system of a specific historic era. For Hirsch there was no doubt that the binding authority of the Torah derived from an eternally valid act of divine revelation. Hence, its norms were impervious to the vicissitudes that beset the world of time and change.

Polemics against those who regard "the spirit of the time" as a factor that should be taken into account when determining religious norms recur throughout his voluminous writings. He bitterly objects to the relativization

---

[1] *From Ancient Israel to Modern Judaism: Intellect in Quest of Understanding. Essays in Honor of Marvin Fox,* vol. 4, ed. Jacob Nuesner, Ernest S. Frerichs, Nahum M. Sarna, 3–11. Atlanta: Scholars Press, 1989.

of religious truth that results from the Reform thesis that the content and meaning of divine revelation is not static but is modified by historic developments. For Hirsch, such an extreme historicism represents the height of absurdity because it fails to take account of basic postulate of Judaism – the acceptance of the Sinaitic Revelation as a supernatural event *sui generis* that must be conceived as an incursion of eternity into the realm of time and space rather than a link in the causal nexus between historic phenomena.

Therefore, it is hardly surprising that Hirsch's repeated emphasis upon the immutable nature of the Torah as the very essence of Judaism led to the impression that he had divested the historic process of all intrinsic religious significance and meaning. As Professor Nathan Rotenstreich put it, the Hirschian approach "reflects a tendency to withdraw the essence of Judaism from the historic process, posing it as incontrovertibly as divinely revealed, eternal statute."[2] Rotenstreich equated the emphasis upon the centrality of an immutable and eternally valid divine law with the adoption of a radical ahistorical stance. He therefore alleges that, according to Hirsch, "the inner life of the Jew remains untouched by the historic process. An Orthodox Jew prays, as it were, outside the world in which he lives and returns to the world to which his prayers do not pertain."[3] Similarly, Isaac Breuer, Hirsch's grandson, constantly harped upon the ahistorical character of the Jewish people, whose arena is in meta-history rather than in history. He never tired of pointing out that Judaism relates to eternity rather than time because the Sinaitic Revelation constitutes an incursion of eternity into the spatio-temporal world.[4] That a great-grandson of Hirsch chose *Timeless Torah*[5] as the title of an anthology of Hirsch's writings is further evidence of the extent to which ahistoricism was perceived to be the hallmark of his ideology.

The wide acceptance[6] of this view both among devotees and critics of Hirsch appears, however, to be based upon a total misunderstanding of the

---

[2] Nathan Rotenstreich, *Ha-machshavah ha-yehudit ba-et ha-chadashah.* Tel Aviv: 1966, 115.

[3] *Tradition and Reality,* New York, 1972, 113.

[4] Isaac Breuer, *The Concepts of Judaism,* edited and selected by Jacob S. Levinger, 27–107. Jerusalem: 1974. Cf. Arthur Cohen's characterization of Hirsch's attitude to history in his work *The Natural and Supernatural Jew,* New York, 1962, 50–54.

[5] Timeless Torah, An Anthology of the Writings of Samson Raphael Hirsch, edited by Jacob Breuer, New York, 1957.

[6] I wish, however, to point to a notable exception to his tendency. In his invaluable study, *Juedische Orthodoxie im Deutschen Reich 1871–1918,* 81–83, Mordechai Breuer calls attention to this misinterpretation. But he does not support his thesis, as I have

Hirschian ideology, which in large measure can be attributed to the utter disregard of the doctrine of an "inner Revelation," which is interspersed in many of Hirsch's writings. To be sure, references to this doctrine occur only sporadically. But it must be remembered that Hirsch was essentially a man of affairs whose preoccupation with communal and educational activities made it impossible for him to find the time needed for a systematic and comprehensive formulation of his religious ideology. His literary activities, however extensive, essentially responded to pressing, practical concerns. They frequently were exercises in polemics designed to vindicate his controversial positions. His other writings consisted largely of sermons or addresses which, while attesting to the rhetorical prowess of a brilliant orator, were hardly suited for the thorough examination of theoretical issues. It must also be borne in mind that even his Bible Commentaries, which are widely read even in our time, were intended for the edification of the general public and were, therefore, more of a homiletical than scholarly nature. Since this type of writing does not lend itself to the balanced and systematic presentation of the various ingredients that went into the makings of his ideology, it is hardly surprising that he suffered the fate of so many other prominent religious leaders who have been far more adulated than understood, especially by their most ardent devotees.

It is quite possible that Hirsch's doctrine of an "inner Revelation" was widely ignored because of its popularity and lack of originality. As a matter of fact, the terminology "*innere* (internal)" and "*auessere* (external)" revelation was already employed by Hirsch's teacher, Isaac Bernays.[7] Moreover, in the age of Enlightenment statements such as "Truth and justice are the first revelation of God in your mind"[8] or "a general conception of Right, of what man owes to his fellow man is planted in the conscience of every uncorrupted human being and this general consciousness of Right is also the voice of God"[9] were so commonplace that they would hardly attract attention. He merely echoed the widely accepted ethos of his time when he declared in his inaugural sermon: "God teaches us: His voice is heard like a

---

attempted in this paper, by analyzing the doctrine of "inner Revelation." I have also greatly benefited from I. Grunfeld's discussion of "innner Revelation" in his Translator's Introduction, to *Horeb,* London, 1962, 81–118.

[7] Isaac Heinemann, *Taamei ha-mitzvot be-sifrut Yisrael.* Jerusalem: 1956, vol. 2, 95.

[8] Samson Raphael Hirsch, *Horeb,* paragraph 325.

[9] *Commentary on the Torah,* Leviticus 18:4.

trumpet in conscience, in nature, in history...."[10] He similarly described justice as "an expression of what man recognizes from his inner revelation to be the just claim of his fellow-man."[11] One can easily recognize in such statements the impact of Butler, Kant and, especially, Hegel, who, as Noah Rosenbloom[12] has shown, exerted such a powerful influence upon the formation of Hirsch's thought.

It must also be remembered that the doctrine of an "inner Revelation" was bound to be perceived by readers familiar with Jewish medieval philosophy as a restatement of views expressed by numerous scholastics, who acknowledged reason as an independent source of religious truth that supplemented the teachings obtained through supernatural communication. It was in this spirit that Saadiah argued that although the "rational commandments" theoretically could have been discovered by human reason unaided by Revelation, it was necessary for them to be included in the Sinaitic Revelation in order to make them available to the Jewish people even before they had reached the intellectual level required to apprehend these truths rationally. In other words, as far as the rational commandments were concerned, Revelation merely served as a shortcut to what properly qualified individuals could achieve in due time on the strength of their own intellectual resources.[13] Bahya ibn Pakuda went even further and insisted that the "duties of the heart," which are indispensable to the proper fulfillment of our religious responsibilities, are not reducible to explicit norms of the Torah and therefore can be apprehended only by the human conscience.[14] In a similar vein, Meiri treated the promptings of the human conscience as an authoritative source for ascertaining the will of God. To employ his own striking formulation, "The commandments apprehended by the human heart are like the letters of the Torah scroll."[15] Especially telling is the widely-quoted statement of the legist Vidal Yom Tov of Tolossa, who maintained that Jewish law must take account of the inevitable evolution of conceptions

---

[10] Samson Raphael Hirsch, *Jeshurun,* 1, 1914, 73ff. Quoted by Isaac Heinemann in "Samson Raphael Hirsch," *Historic Judaica,* 13, 1951, 33–34.

[11] Hirsch, *loc. cit.*

[12] Noah H. Rosenblooom, *Tradition in an Age of Reform.* Philadelphia: 1976.

[13] Saadiah Gaon, *Emunot ve-Deot,* Chapter 3.

[14] Bahya Ibn Pakuda, *Chovot ha-Levavot,* Introduction.

[15] Meiri ad BT *Shabbat* 105b.

of moral propriety caused by the transformation of socio-economic and cultural realities.[16]

There is no justification for the belief that, according to the above-mentioned classical Jewish thinkers, historic developments left no impact upon the capacity of human intelligence to intuit ethical insights. Seen against this background, it is highly implausible to impute to Hirsch the view that the historic process exerts no influence whatsoever upon the apprehension of religiously significant truth. Nothing in Hirsch's writings justifies the thesis that the "timelessness" that characterizes the Sinaitic revelation applies to the "inner revelation" as well. In this connection it is important to point out that Hirsch, rejecting Mendelssohn's rationalism with its accent upon "eternal verities," enthusiastically embraced Lessings's philosophy of history, which revolved around the belief in the intellectual and moral progress of humankind.[17]

The religious significance of the historic process is also implicit in the Hirschian thesis that the Commandments represent not merely statutory laws but function as divinely ordained instrumentalities for *Bildung* (the formation of a harmonious personality). Since the purpose of the Torah is not merely to provide an immutable normative system that must be obeyed for its own sake but also to direct man towards ever higher levels of moral consciousness, the very meaning of Torah involves the historic arena. Moreover, in the Hirschian scheme, it is only the content of the purely supernatural Revelation (the "external revelation" in his terminology) as contained in the Torah that is perceived as being totally independent of all cultural factors and as being hermetically insulated from the historic process. But the situation is entirely different regarding other facets of divine revelation such as nature, history and culture which, according to Hirsch, represent religious truth as long as they are compatible with the teachings of the external revelation contained in the Torah.

In this connection it should be mentioned that Hirsch vehemently opposed all mystic tendencies, which denigrated the participation in various socio-economic and cultural activities. Denouncing asceticism and, for that matter, all forms of withdrawal from worldly concerns, he appealed to his followers to plunge into "an active life that is always intended to progress

---

[16] Vida Yom Tov of Tolosa, *Maggid Mishnah, Hilkhot Shekhenim*, 14:4.
[17] Mordechai Breuer, *op. cit.,* 62.

and flourish." Time and again he proclaimed with all the impressive rhetorical skills at his command that the ultimate goal of Judaism was not to provide an escape mechanism from this-worldly realities, but to apply the norms and teachings of the Torah to the *Derekh Eretz* of the world, so that human progress in science, technology, the arts, and so on, would lead truly to the enhancement of mankind's spiritual and moral welfare.

It must be realized that Hirsch advocated *Torah im Derekh Eretz* not merely as an expedient way to find a *modus operandi* for Judaism during the Enlightenment and Emancipation but as the very essence of Judaism. In his opinion, *Torah im Derekh Eretz* was not an amalgam of two distinct elements but a corollary of the traditional notion that the Torah was a "Torah of life," which he interpreted as the demand that Torah address all facets of human culture and harness them towards the advancement of God's Kingdom. In the words of Yitzchak Breuer:

> *Torah im Derekh Eretz* is merely a slogan. Actually… a Judaism which does not separate itself from nature and history… but understands itself from its relationship to life. This is a Judaism which affirms culture and every creation of the human spirit. It looks upon them as values if they can stand the scrutiny of the Torah which is the divine instrument for our self-understanding in nature and history.[18]

To be sure, with the resurgence of fundamentalism in the Orthodox community there have come into vogue revisionist, rather far-fetched re-interpretations of Hirsch which argue that *Torah im Derekh Eretz* was offered by Hirsch merely as a temporary expedient (*hora'at sha'ah*) in an attempt to salvage as much as possible from the tidal waves of assimilation that had inundated German Jewry. It is important, however, to realize that Hirsch looked upon *Torah im Derekh Eretz* not as a legitimate option but as a form of piety superior to that of the "unenlightened" traditionalists who advocated isolation from the mainstream of modern culture. This is evidenced by the fact that in his polemics against Rabbi Seligmann Baer Bamberger regarding secession from the non-Orthodox community, he

---

[18] Isaac Breuer in *Jakob Rosenheim,* Frankfort: 1930, 206–211.

complains about his antagonist's failure to appreciate the religious merits of Hirsch's more enlightened approach.[19]

Within this context it is important to refer to Hirsch's attitude towards the Emancipation, which many leading exponents of Orthodoxy viewed as a threat to Judaism's survival. They were afraid that the removal of the ghetto walls and the ensuing dissolution of an autonomous Jewish community would ultimately lead to the erosion of Jewish observance and assimilation into the surrounding culture.

In opposition to this negative assessment of the historic developments of his time, Hirsch hailed the Emancipation as a boon not merely for Jews as individuals but for the cause of Judaism. He welcomed the opening of the gates to full participation in cultural and socio-economic activities because they afforded Jews the opportunity to demonstrate the relevance of Torah to life in areas which previously had been closed to them.

With the acceptance of *Torah im Derekh Eretz* as an authentic religious ideal, the historic process, which is responsible for the development of various cultural phenomena to which Torah must be applied, emerges as all-important factor in the determination of the meaning of Torah for a given era. Significantly, Hirsch compares the data contained in the Sinaitic Revelation of Torah to those comprising the Divine Revelation in the laws of nature. Just as a scientific theory must seek all explanation of the data obtained by observation of nature, so must any explanation of the meaning of Judaism be based upon the data – namely, the content of the supernatural Revelation. But it must be remembered that while the natural law remains constant, scientific conceptions undergo constant revision as additional data become available. By the same token, the interaction between Torah and the particular *derekh eretz* of a given era is bound to affect our understanding of the meaning of the data of the Torah insofar as it relates to their application to the culture of the time.

Hirsch's passionate endorsement of the religious import and significance of cultural advancements is eloquently expressed in his ringing declaration: "Judaism welcomes every advance in enlightenment and virtue wherever and through whatever medium it may be produced."[20] Similarly, Judaism is

---

[19] See Mordechai Breuer's discussion in *Torah im Derekh Eretz – Ha-Tenuah, Ishehah ve-Ra'ayonoteha*. Ramat Gan: 1987, 85ff. See also Jacob Katz's work "Samson Raphael Hirsch: *mi-yemin u-mi-smol.*" ibid., 16.

[20] *Collected Writings*, ed. by N. Hirsch, vol. 2, 454.

extolled as "the only religion the adherents of which are taught to see a revelation of the Divine in the presence of a man who is distinguished for knowledge and wisdom, no matter to what religion or nation he belongs."[21]

The religious significance of human history and progress is also implicit in the Hirschian ideal of *"Mensch-Jissroel"* [sic], which, in turn, rests upon the premise that proper observance and understanding of the divine Commandments result in the cultivation of attitudes and insights that lead to higher levels of human development.[22] It is only through submission to the discipline and guidance of the theonomous commandments that we can do justice to the requirements of human nature and make progress toward genuine self-realization. History could be dismissed as religiously irrelevant by a Mendelssohn, who maintained that observance of the divinely given law had no impact at all upon Jews' metaphysical and ethical beliefs since by virtue of the total absence of dogma in Judaism, these beliefs were identical with the postulates of natural religion that all rational human beings embraced. Yet for Hirsch, the situation was completely different. The degree to which the commandments can succeed in providing individuals the value system they need to meet their worldly responsibilities according to the ideal of *"Mensch-Jissroel"* hinges upon several factors involving historic contingencies. It is precisely because he places Judaism's center of gravity within the flux of temporal events that he so strenuously objects to Mendelssohn's rationalism, with its reliance on "eternal verities."

It thus becomes clear that for all his opposition to the "spirit of the time" as the sole determinant of religious truth, Hirsch nonetheless treats it as an important factor. It is one thing to assert the primacy of the Sinaitic Revelation not only as a guide to normative practice but also as a source of religious truth, and another to delegitimize the "inner Revelation" completely. For Hirsch, the latter, to the extent that it supplements the former, is a vital ingredient of a wholesome religious approach. In the words of Isidor Grunfeld, one of the outstanding expositors of the Hirschian ideology, "While we can and should rely on our moral conscience as an 'inner revelation,' we must, however, never undertake to deny our

---

21 *Judaism Eternal*, translated by I. Grunfeld. London: 1956, vol. 1, 207.

22 See Isaac Heinemann, *Ta'amei ha-Mitzvot, op. cit.,* 106–107. I also learned much from his discussion of Hirsch's conception of theonomy.

obligations to the Divine will as manifested in the 'outer revelation' – that is the Revelation at Sinai."[23]

However, we must part company with Isidor Grunfeld when he attributes to Hirsch the Kantian notion of autonomy and declares that for Hirsch, "the human will is autonomous only in so far as it does not contravene the Divine will."[24] The very term "inner revelation," which is contrasted with "external Revelation," possesses a theonomous rather than an autonomous connotation. The human conscience is seen not as an independent source of authority but as the instrument through which the Divine Will is disclosed. As Hirsch put it in the chapter on justice in *Horeb*, "Justice simply means allowing each creature all that it may expect as the portion allotted to it by God."[25] The theonomous nature of morality is also eloquently formulated in the statement: "God's will has been revealed to you.... He has implanted in your mind the general principles of truth and right... and you... carry within yourself a voice demanding... to discharge the task of justice."[26]

It must also be taken into consideration that, unlike Kant, Hirsch did not believe that it was possible to build a moral system on purely rational foundations of *a priori* propositions. While rationality may provide man with the general conception of right and justice, it cannot yield adequate moral rules. "To some extent one can carry out the Torah-conception of social Right even before one has studied the Laws which God has revealed to us... But the laws of social Right, on which alone the whole human social happiness can truly flourish and blossom... require study from the revealed word of God."[27] Even more pronounced is the emphasis upon the inadequacy of a morality that is grounded upon purely rational foundations. When commenting on Psalm 19:2 he declares: "By merely looking at the heavens and earth, man will never discover the Divine Law which governs his task in the world. Whatever answer he would derive from this kind of study would enmesh him in hopeless confusion."[28] There can be little doubt that this rejection of a purely rational foundation of morality points to the

---

[23] I. Grunfeld, "Introduction to Horeb," *op. cit.,* vol. 1, 91.

[24] *Ibid.*

[25] *Horeb*, vol. 1, 217.

[26] *ibid.,* 219.

[27] Commentary on Psalm 19:1.

[28] Commentary on Leviticus 18:5.

influence of Hegel, who, criticizing the ahistorical stance of the Kantian formalistic ethic, replaced it with the conception of *Sittlichkeit* to underscore the role of the historic dimension in the moral domain.

Rabbi Joseph B. Soloveitchik as a *Posek* of Postmodern Orthodoxy[1]

In the circles of what is labeled "Modern Orthodoxy" or "Centrist Orthodoxy," Rabbi Joseph B. Soloveitchik is referred to as "the Rav." This appellation is not merely a sign of respect and reverence accorded a charismatic luminary, the mentor of generations of rabbis, academicians and communal leaders, but it also attests to his role as *the* authority figure of those segments of the Orthodox community that see no conflict between commitment to Torah and full participation in scientific and cultural activities of modern society.

To the popular mind, unfortunately, "Modern Orthodoxy" represents a movement characterized by the willingness to make all sorts of concessions to modernity at the expense of genuine religious commitment. It is perceived as a "moderate" brand of halakhic Judaism that lacks the fervor and passion associated with the Haredi community.

In this misinterpretation of the ideology of "Modern Orthodoxy," the adjective "modern" is treated as a modifier rather than as an attribute. To illustrate this distinction, there are all kinds of presidents: popular or unpopular, dynamic or passive, honest or corrupt. In these cases, the adjective functions as an attribute, characterizing a president. But when we speak of a past president, an honorary president, or a dead president, we are no longer dealing with presidents; the adjective does not merely add a

[1] *Tradition* 29:1 (Fall 1994): 5–20.

qualification to the noun, but completely modifies the meaning of the noun. Similarly, it is widely taken for granted that "Modern Orthodoxy" is not really an authentic form of Orthodoxy, but a hybrid of an illicit union between modernity and Orthodoxy, a kind of oxymoron. Its opponents ridicule it as a compromise designed to facilitate entry into a modern lifestyle by offering less stringent interpretations of Halakhah and even condoning laxity in religious observance.

Because the term "Modern Orthodoxy" has acquired such a pejorative meaning, Rabbi Norman Lamm has proposed that we replace it with "Centrist Orthodoxy."[2] In my opinion, "Post-Modern Orthodoxy" would be the most appropriate designation for a movement that stands not for evasion or accommodation but for uncompromising confrontation of modernity.

It is this type of halakhic Judaism that can invoke the spiritual authority of the Rav, who never wavered in his demand for scrupulous adherence to Halakhah. His aim was not to make halakhic observance more convenient. On the contrary, in many areas such as *hilkhot avelut*, the construction of *eruvin* in cities, and refusal to grant a *shetar mekhirah* authorizing non-Jewish workers to operate Jewish factories or commercial establishments on Shabbat, the Rav consistently issued rulings that were more stringent than those of right-wing authorities. He was especially particular in observing all the Brisker stringencies pertaining to the writing of *shetarot*. I recall spending close to two hours with the Rav on writing a simple *shetar prozbol*. Unlike other *poskim*, he did not condone the signing of a *ketubbah* before *shekiah* when the actual *huppah* would take place *bein ha-shemashot*. Similarly, he did not permit the scheduling of weddings *bein ha-shemashot* even when this would have been more convenient. For that matter, he was opposed to the modernization of synagogue services. He even objected to announcements of pages during the repetition of the *Amidah*, the composition of prayers for special occasions, and the recital of invocations because they smacked of the attempt to dilute traditional Jewish approaches with prevailing American practices.

The Rav's traditionalism can also be discerned in his emphasis upon what he called *mesorah ma'asit* (established practice). Once a halakhic practice

---

[2] See my article "Centrist Orthodoxy," *Journal of Jewish Thought*, Rabbinical Council of America, 1985, 67–75 (page 212 in this volume).

was agreed upon, it could no longer be modified by reliance on opinions which had previously been rejected[3] This respect for established norms manifested itself in his aversion to utilizing even newly discovered manuscripts of Rishonim for halakhic purposes.[4]

Notwithstanding the Rav's traditionalism, I disagree with Moshe Sokol's and David Singer's[5] contention that the Rav, for all his philosophical brilliance and extensive scientific knowledge, really cannot be invoked as an authority figure for Modern Orthodoxy, since in his halakhic decision-making he operates exclusively with traditional methods and does not permit philosophical ideas or the findings of modern textual scholarship to impinge upon the formation of his halakhic rulings. They claim that his halakhic positions and methodologies do not differ basically from those of other *poskim*, who have insulated themselves against modernity. The traditional nature of his halakhic reasoning is also evidenced by the fact that his vast Talmudic erudition and the profundity and originality of his scholarship are widely admired even by many of the leading figures of the Haredi community ("right-wing" Orthodoxy), which demands total isolation from modern, secular culture.

What differentiates the approach of Rav Soloveitchik from that of Haredi poskim and makes him the authority figure of so-called "Modern Orthodoxy" is his endorsement of secular studies, including philosophy, his espousal of religious Zionism, and his pioneering of intensive Jewish education for women. Although these policies are not logically connected, they are closely related to each other because they arise from the conviction that a *Torat Hayyim* addresses the realities of the world rather than seeking an escape from them. It is this religious philosophy, which engenders a unique approach to Halakhah, that has made Rav Soloveitchik into the *posek par excellence* of Modern Orthodoxy.

The Rav's objection to the employment of modern historic and textual scholarship to ascertain the meaning of Halakhah reflects not naive

---

[3] Rabbi Joseph B. Soloveitchik, *Shiurim le-zekher Abba Mori z"l.*, (Jerusalem 1984), 220–239.

[4] Rav Soloveitchik's attitude resembles that of the Hazon Ish, whose views on this issue were discussed by Zvi A. Yehudah, "Hazon Ish on Textual Criticism and Halakhah," *Tradition*, 18:2 (Summer 1980): 172–180.

[5] David Singer and Moshe Sokol. "Joseph Soloveitchik: Lonely Man of Faith." *Modern Judaism* 2 (1982): 227–272.

traditionalism but highly sophisticated post-modern critical thought. He insists that Halakhah operate with its own unique canons of interpretation. According to Rav Soloveitchik, scientific methods are appropriate only for the explanation of natural phenomena but have no place in the quest for the understanding of the normative and cognitive concepts of Halakhah, which imposes its own *a priori* categories that differ from those appropriate in the realm of science. It is for this reason that the Rav completely ignores Biblical criticism and eschews the "positive historical" approach of the "Science of Judaism."

However, whole-hearted endorsement of traditional halakhic methodology and concomitant rejection of historicism are fully compatible with a positive attitude towards some values of modernity. The Rav always insisted that historic contingencies have no bearing upon the halakhic process. In his view, Halakhah represented an *a priori* system of ideas and concepts to be applied to empirical realities. When Rav Soloveitchik looks upon the study of sciences and the development of technology as religiously desirable, it cannot he said that he reads the value system of the Enlightenment[6] into the halakhic tradition. After all, he unequivocally opposes many of the Enlightenment's most fundamental tenets. He rejects its belief that religion lacks cognitive significance and that its function is to manifest itself in the realms of feeling and actions rather than to concern itself with dogmas or articles of faith pertaining to theoretical beliefs.[7] Similarly, he categorically rejects the Enlightenment conception of the superiority of natural religion over the various revealed religions.[8]

For the Rav, Halakhah represents not a human construct designed to relate to Transcendence, but a divinely revealed cognitive approach to God and the world. He denies the fundamental premises of liberal religion because on epistemological grounds he maintains that human efforts to search for God are doomed to failure[9] and that human beings can find Him only when they are overwhelmed by His Presence. He stresses the primacy

---

[6] See my article "The Enlightenment, the Emancipation and the Jewish Religion." *Judaism* (Fall 1989): 309–407.

[7] Ernst Cassirer, *The Philosophy of the Enlightenment*, Fritz B. Koellin and James A. Pettegrove, trans. (Princeton, NJ: Princeton University Press, 1951), 169.

[8] *ibid.*, 170–171.

[9] See Rabbi Joseph B. Soloveitchik, *Ish ha-halakhah: galui ve-nistar*, World Zionist Organization, Jerusalem: 1979, 122–134.

not of the religious experience but of Halakhah. While the Rav's rejection of natural theology is similar to Karl Barth's position, it arises from his conviction that Halakhah is not merely a normative discipline, but must provide the foundation for Jewish philosophy.[10] Such an orientation is diametrically opposed to the ethos of the Enlightenment, which, as Kant formulated it, constitutes "man's exodus from self-incurred tutelage."[11]

Since the Rav stresses heteronymous divine Revelation rather than the autonomy of human reason and conscience, his notion of Adam I, the "man of majesty," is not a concession to modernity but an authentic interpretation of the Jewish value system. Those who follow in the footsteps of Rambam need not expound the Jewish tradition in conformity with the quietistic and pietistic mindset of European Orthodoxy.

However, it must be emphasized that for the Rav the endorsement of scientific methods is strictly limited to the realm of Adam I, whose function it is to harness the world of nature for the benefit of humanity. But causal explanations are irrelevant in the domain of Adam II, who can overcome his existential loneliness only through the establishment of a "covenantal community," enabling him to relate to transcendence.

The Rav's approach is reminiscent of the Kantian dichotomy between science and ethics. According to Kant, while determinism is indispensable to the perception of phenomena, it renders impossible the moral "ought." He therefore regarded freedom as an indispensable postulate of ethics. Similarly, Rav Soloveitchik insists that it is totally illicit to "explain" (in reality, explain away) religious phenomena by the application of methods which are legitimate only with respect to the concerns of Adam I.

The dichotomy between Adam I and Adam II, which in the Rav's view arises from the very ontological nature of man, mirrors the conflict which the Rav personally experienced with his move to Berlin. Reminiscing about his student days, the Rav once remarked to me: "You have no idea how enormously difficult it was for me to move from the world of Rabbi Hayyim to that of Berlin University. Even my children cannot appreciate it, because they already found a paved road. But my generation was challenged to become pioneers."

---

[10] Joseph B. Soloveitchik, *The Halakhic Mind* (New York: Macmillan), 1986, 85–89.
[11] See Ernst Cassirer, *ibid.*, p. 163.

It was out of this tension that Rav Soloveitchik developed a formula that enabled him to encounter the value system of modernity while remaining fully committed to traditional halakhic methodology. To apply scientific methods or the tools of modern historic scholarship to Halakhah would do violence to the integrity of the system. Those who insist upon applying historic scholarship to the analysis of halakhah commit the "genetic fallacy." In the Rav's view, Halakhah must encounter reality by imposing upon it its own autonomous set of *a priori* categories, which are completely independent of scientific or historic factors.

However, it is one thing to affirm that halakhic concepts are *a priori* and another to maintain that subjective factors play no role in halakhic decision-making. As a matter of fact, Rav Soloveitchik always emphasized that halakhic decision-making is not purely mechanical but highly creative. A *posek* is not a computer. It is therefore inevitable that like everyone else's, the Rav's halakhic rulings, especially the perception and assessment of the realities to which halakhic *a priori* notions are to be applied, reflect to some extent his personal philosophical convictions. From his perspective, human creativity and initiative in science and technology are not merely legitimate but eminently desirable, because they reflect the dignity conferred upon creatures bearing the divine image.[12]

This stance is usually rejected by the so-called "yeshivah world," which assigns religious significance to creativity only as much as it is directly and immediately related to the field of Torah. Rabbi Hayyim of Volozhin makes the point that while human beings are mandated to imitate the creativity of the Creator, this emulation is possible only in the exercise of spiritual creativity. This is in keeping with kabbalistic doctrines which affirm that only Torah study and observance of the commandments create new spiritual worlds in the higher regions of being and are instrumental in helping bring about the reunification of God with the Shekhinah[13] In the view of the

---

[12] Joseph B. Soloveitchik, "The Lonely Man of Faith," *Tradition* 7:2 (Summer 1965): 5–67, especially 13–16. See also my article, "The Maimonidean Matrix of Rabbi Soloveitchik's Two-Tiered Ethics," in *Through the Sound of Many Voices,* edited by J.V. Plant, 172–183. Toronto: Lester and Orpen Dennys, 1982 (page 161 in this volume).

[13] See Rabbi Chaim of Volozhin, *Nefesh Hayyim.* See also my article "Confronting the Challenge of the Values of Modernity," *Torah U-Madda Journal* 1 (1989): 104–112 (page 202 in this volume).

classical yeshivah world, science and technology do not qualify as genuine creativity, since they rely exclusively on purely natural processes. The Rav objects to this denigration of "secular" activities and contends that scientific and technological creativity also constitutes an intrinsically valuable mode of imitating the divine Creator.

It is against this background that we can appreciate the Rav's enthusiasm for scientific and philosophical studies. While in the Yeshiva world secular studies are condoned only to the extent necessary for making a living, the Rav endowed them with intrinsic value because they enable human beings to realize the ideals of Adam I. This explains why he encouraged many of his disciples to pursue graduate studies in secular fields.

The Rav's endorsement of Religious Zionism is also closely related to his belief that taking the initiative in ameliorating natural, economic, social or political conditions, far from being a usurpation of divine prerogatives, represents a religiously mandated activity of becoming partners with God in the process of Creation.[14] This position is radically different from the one that prevails in the Haredi community. Although they may not be quite as extreme as the Neturei Karta who refuse to acknowledge the legitimacy of the State of Israel, nevertheless, the rest of the Haredi community is not prepared to ascribe any religious value to the existence of a sovereign Jewish state in the pre-Messianic era. While reconciling themselves to the recognition of Israel as a de facto reality, they cannot view as a religious desideratum a Jewish state that came into being as a result of political activity rather than through supernatural intervention. In their opinion, reliance on human initiatives to establish a "secular" Jewish state cannot be reconciled with belief in God the Redeemer, who will restore the Jewish people to its national homeland when the process of catharsis was completed and Israel would become worthy of the Redemption.

Significantly, so dominant was the quietistic streak in traditional circles that the devotees of the Hatam Sofer opposed any involvement in the political arena, even for the limited purpose of improving the socio-political conditions of Diaspora Jewry. It was argued that if God really wanted the Jewish people to enjoy more rights and more tolerable conditions, He did not need the assistance of the Jewish community to accomplish this and

---

[14] See Michael Rosenack, "Ha-adam ha-yehudi ve-ha-medinah," in *Sefer ha-yovel li-khvod ha-Rav ha-Gaon R.Y.D. Soloveitchik*, edited by Shaul Yisraeli, Nachum Lamm and Yitzchak Raphael, 152–169. Jerusalem: Mosad Ha-Rav Kook, 1984.

there was no point in petitioning the rulers of the various nations for better conditions. With religious faith being equated with such total dependence upon God that all human efforts were dismissed as inconsequential, one could hardly expect sympathy for the Zionist revolution which, instead of merely passively awaiting the arrival of the Messiah, insisted upon human initiatives leading eventually to the birth of a Jewish state.[15]

Although the Rav's advocacy of Religious Zionism is closely connected with his conception of Adam I, it would, of course, have been possible for him to follow in the footsteps of Rabbi Samson Raphael Hirsch and endorse human initiatives in general while insisting that the return to a national Jewish homeland had to await the Messianic Redemption. He could have chosen the course charted by the German Agudat Yisrael, which enthusiastically subscribed to the ideal of *Torah im Derekh Eretz* while maintaining all-out opposition to Zionism. As a matter of fact, it was only after his arrival in the United States that he left Agudah and identified with Mizrachi, of which he subsequently became the leading ideologist.

The Rav shared with Yitzchak Breuer the conviction that the time had arrived when Torah ideals (especially those relating to Adam I) could best be realized by building a Jewish society in Eretz Yisrael. As opposed to Breuer, who developed and transformed the Hirschian doctrine of *Torah im Derekh Eretz* into that of *Torah im derekh Eretz Yisrael*, the Rav's approach to the building of a Jewish state was completely devoid of Messianic overtones but focused upon the material and spiritual needs of the Jewish people and the obligation to do everything in one's power to ameliorate their conditions.[16] Similarly, the absence of Messianic motifs prevented the Rav from subscribing to the Gush Emunim philosophy, which of late has made such inroads into Mizrachi circles.

This realistic approach to the State of Israel was responsible for his reluctance to authorize the recital of Hallel on Yom ha-Atzmaut and Yom Yerushalayim. If the chapters of Tehillim which comprised Hallel were to be recited, he recommended saying them some time after *Kaddish Titkabel* rather

---

[15] See my essay, "Religious Zionism: Compromise or Ideal," in *Religious Zionism*, Jerusalem: Mesilot, 1989, 26–31 (page 220 in this volume).

[16] See Rabbi Joseph B. Soloveitchik, *Hamesh Derashot*. Translated by David Telzner. Jerusalem: Tal Orot, 1974 and *Kol Dodi Dofek* in *Be-sod ha-yahid ve-ha-yahad*, edited by Pinchas H. Peli, 333–400, Jerusalem: Orot, 1976.

than immediately following the *Shemoneh Esreh,* as is customary on Yom Tov or Rosh Hodesh.

The Rav's commitment to Religious Zionism was possible only because he opposed the secessionist tendencies which Yitzchak Breuer had inherited from his grandfather, Samson Raphael Hirsch. Breuer disapproved of membership in the Zionist movement and, for that matter, frowned upon any association with groups that were not totally committed to the ideals of halakhic Judaism. The Rav maintained that Halakhah demands a sense of identification with all Jews regardless of their religious convictions or practices.

Although the rise of Hitler may have strengthened the Rav's conviction that Jews formed a community of fate[17] and not merely one of faith, opposition to total separation from non-observant segments of the Jewish community was a long-standing family tradition, which can be traced back to the Netziv.[18] The Rav frequently referred to the example of his illustrious grandfather, Rabbi Hayyim of Brisk who, on a Yom Kippur evening before *Kol Nidrei,* asked the community to desecrate the holiness of Yom Kippur in order to gather the funds needed to save the life of a follower of the Bund from execution. The fact that this "Bundist" was an atheist and an opponent of halakhic Judaism had no bearing upon the requirement to concern oneself with the fate of every Jew.

In his insistence that failure to observe Halakhah does not affect one's status as a full-fledged member of the Jewish people, the Rav went so far as to urge kohanim who were not Sabbath observers to participate in *Birkat Kohanim.* According to his ruling, only transgressions of prohibitions specifically governing kohanim, but not violation of other halakhic norms (with the exception of homicide), disqualify a kohen from *dukhening.*

The emphasis upon the nationalistic dimension of Jewishness is also apparent in the Rav's frequent references to the halakhic opinion that anyone who loses his life because of his Jewishness is regarded as having died *al kiddush ha-Shem.* He regarded this as precedent for his belief that any one who gives up his life in the defense of the State of Israel should be viewed as having died *al kiddush ha-Shem.*[19]

---

[17] *Kol Dodi Dofek,* 368–377.

[18] Naftali Zvi Yehudah Berlin, *Meshiv Davar,* responsum 44.

[19] See *Hamesh Derashot,* 89–90.

It was because of his solicitude for the material and spiritual well-being of every Jew that despite his insistence that a *mehitzah* was an absolute halakhic requirement, the Rav occasionally permitted rabbis to accept pulpits in synagogues that did not have one. His leniency was due to his belief that the presence of a dedicated rabbi was likely to result in the raising of religious standards (e.g., establishment of day schools, *kashrut, taharat ha-mishpahah,* and so on). I vividly recall the Rav's address to a Rabbinical Council convention where he discussed the dilemma facing the *posek* who is torn between the prohibition against worshiping in a synagogue that violates halakhic standards and the responsibility to prevent the total assimilation of a Jewish community. The Rav cited this as an illustration of the difficulties inherent in the *derekh ha-benoni*, a philosophy of moderation, which, unlike extremist positions, must mediate between a plurality of conflicting values and obligations.

The emphasis placed upon the ethnic and nationalistic components of Jewish identity inspired the Rav's interpretation of the meaning and implications of the *Brit Avraham* and the *Brit Mitzrayim,* which established the Jewish community of fate.[20] These covenants mandate a sense of solidarity and kinship among all the members of the Jewish Covenantal community of fate and affirm the need to recognize the centrality of Eretz Yisrael in the destiny of the Jewish people. Since these covenants preceded the community of faith established by the Sinaitic Covenant and constitute integral and indispensable components of the Jewish faith, we must not limit our concern to the protection of the interests of the religious sector. We should aim not only to preserve isolated religious enclaves but also to create a society that will foster loyalty to Torah on the part of the entire Jewish people.[21] The Torah is not addressed to a religious elite but to the entire Jewish people.

The importance that the Rav attached to the *berit Avraham* also explains his refusal to concur with the famous *issur* (prohibition) banning participation in the Synagogue Council of America and the New York Board of Rabbis that was issued by a group of prominent roshei yeshivah.

To be sure, the Rav could not have harbored the slightest sympathy for Jewish religious movements that deviated from halakhic norms. His conception of Judaism was so Halakhah-centered that he denied that purely

---

[20] *Kol Dodi Dofek,* 368–380, and *Hamesh Derashot,* 87–92.
[21] See my essay, "Religious Zionism: Compromise or Ideal?" *op. cit.,* 26–31.

subjective attempts to reach out for transcendence had any Jewish religious significance. Moreover, his followers in Boston did not belong to the interdenominational Rabbinical Association or to the Associated Synagogues, a lay body consisting of some Orthodox and a large number of Conservative and Reform congregations. He went so far as to rule that one should not worship in a Conservative synagogue even when there was no other opportunity to listen to the sounding of the shofar.

What prevented the Rav from joining other roshei yeshivah in demanding withdrawal from interdenominational umbrella groups was his fear that leaving organizations in which Orthodoxy had participated for many years would be a divisive move at a time when Jewish unity was so essential. Although ideally he would have preferred that these umbrella groups had not come into existence, he subordinated his ideological considerations to his overriding concern for the welfare of the Jewish people and the security of the State of Israel. Therefore, he did not object to the participation of Orthodox organizations in the Synagogue Council of America as long its functions were limited to representing the total Jewish community to governmental agencies or non-Jewish denominations (*kelappei chutz*).

There are some revisionist accounts of the Rav's attitude toward the Synagogue Council. It has been reported that while the Rav opposed the continued membership of Orthodox groups, the Rabbinical Council refused to abide by his instructions. To realize the absurdity of this claim one need only remember the indisputable fact that as the chairman of its Halakhah commission, the Rav was the unchallenged halakhic authority of the Rabbinical Council of America.

I cannot help but be amused by fanciful accounts of the Rav's views on the issue. I vividly recall a session with the Rav and the late Rabbi Klavan when we mapped strategy to prevent the Union from seceding from the Synagogue Council.

The Rav's opposition to moves that threatened the unity of the Jewish community also manifested itself in his attitudes towards non-Orthodox groups. He counseled against denying Conservative or Reform rabbis the right to use communal *mikva'ot* for conversions. Moreover, he once instructed me that Reform conversions that were accompanied by circumcision and immersion in a mikveh had to be treated as a *safek goy*. (Accordingly, a *get* would be required to dissolve a marriage in which one of the partners had previously undergone a Conservative or Reform conversion that conformed to the requirements of *milah* and *tevilah*.)

Rav Soloveitchik's emphasis upon Jewish particularism, which prompted him to attach so much weight to the welfare and security of the State of Israel and of all Jews regardless of their religious orientation, stood in marked contrast to the universalism and outright hostility to Zionism of Hermann Cohen, whose philosophical doctrines he not only analyzed in his Ph.D. dissertation but which also influenced the development of his own thought. Cohen's influence is especially noticeable in *Ish ha-Halakhah* and in the conception of Adam I of "The Lonely Man of Faith," which extol intellectual, cultural, scientific, technological and political activities as religious desiderata. Yet despite his admiration for some aspects of neo-Kantianism, the Rav categorically rejected Cohen's uncompromising rationalism and radical universalism, which were utterly incompatible with belief in supernatural Revelation or the affirmation of Jewish particularism.

Despite these fundamental disagreements concerning the essence of Judaism, Rabbi Soloveitchik adopted Cohen's thesis that the Rambam's ethical views reflected a Platonic rather than an Aristotelian approach. According to Aristotle, human beings became most God-like through intellectual perfection. However, Plato maintained that ethical conduct and attainment of virtue constituted *imitatio Dei*. This accounts for the centrality of ethics in the Rav's religious philosophy. Throughout his writings he repeatedly makes the point that the Torah is not a metaphysical treatise but the source of normative guidance.

Professor Ravitzky[22] has advanced some cogent arguments against Cohen's interpretation of Maimonides's ethical views. Nevertheless, this controversy is irrelevant for our purposes since it is of interest only to the student of the history of ideas. What matters for us is that basing himself on the Rambam, the Rav unequivocally declared that striving for ever-higher rungs of moral perfection is the pre-eminent approach to *imitatio Dei*.

This emphasis upon ethics must be seen not as a concession to modern Jewish thinkers such as Mendelssohn, Luzzatto, Ahad ha-Am and Cohen, but it reflects his affinity for Maimonidean approaches. Unlike Yehudah Halevi, who relegated ethical norms to the domain of social necessities and

---

[22] Aviezer Ravitzky, *"Kinyan ha-da'at be-heguto: bein ha-Rambam le-neo-Kantianism."* In *Sefer ha-yovel li-khvod ha-rav ha-gaon R.Y.D. Soloveitchik,* op. tit., 141–151.

assigned to the performance of ritual laws the function of cultivating the religious faculty (*Inyan ha-Eloki*), Maimonides stresses the religious significance of ethics. The Rav frequently pointed out that all our ethical norms are grounded in *imitatio Dei*. I show elsewhere[23] that Rambam himself (in his more mature formulation in the *Mishneh Torah*, as opposed to his earlier conception in the *Sefer ha-Mitzvot*) did not go so far; he invoked *imitatio Dei* only as proof text for the cultivation of ethical character traits but not for the performance of ethical actions.

It should also be noted that the Rav had serious doubts as to whether a purely secular system of ethics is possible. In this he anticipated the critique of Alistair McIntyre of all post-Enlightenment attempts to posit ethics without reference to a divine source.[24] Moreover, Rabbi Soloveitchik maintained that at the very most a purely secular system of ethics can do justice only to those aspects of human nature that reflect Adam I. But since the ontological nature of human beings also involves Adam II, a purely secular ethical system is bound to be inadequate.

Since the Rav maintains that the entire ethical domain is founded upon *imitatio Dei*, he was extremely sensitive to ethical demands. Out of ethical principles, he refused to grant a *shetar mekhirah* to one of the most important benefactors of his day school in Boston, who wanted to be able to operate his plants on Shabbat. When questioned why another renowned halakhic authority had no difficulty in arranging a *shetar mekhirah* for the same plants, the Rav explained that his refusal was motivated by his concern that enabling industrialists to operate their business on Shabbat by transferring ownership to a non-Jew would make it much more difficult for *shomrei Shabbat* Jews to obtain employment in firms owned by Orthodox Jews.

Even more revealing of the Rav's emphasis upon ethical values is his conviction that in a democratic society that grants equal rights and opportunities to Jews, some of the halakhic provisions regarding *mesirah* do not apply. He therefore unequivocally stated that governmental employees

---

[23] "*Imitatio Dei* in Maimonides' Sefer ha-Mitzvot and the Mishneh Torah." *Tradition and Transition*, edited by Jonathan Sacks, 321–324. London: 1986 (page 100 in this volume). Sec also my essay, "The Centrality of Virtue-ethics in Maimonides." In *Of Scholars, Savants and their Texts*, edited by Ruth Link Salinger, 251–260. New York: Peter Lang, 1989 (page 91 in this volume). See also chapter 5 of my book, *Ethics of Responsibility* (Philadelphia: Jewish Publication Society, 1994).

[24] See Alistair McIntyre, *After Virtue*. Notre Dame University Press, 1981, 49–75.

must apply the law to Jew and non-Jew alike. His sense of gratitude to America for according Jews full equality is also evident in his positive attitude towards the observance of Thanksgiving as a national holiday.

Ethical considerations also played a major role in his revolutionary ruling that yeshivot had the right to institute a lottery for the chaplaincy,[25] compelling rabbis who were exempt from the draft to volunteer to serve in the armed forces as chaplains. The Rav endorsed this procedure in spite of the fact that it was likely that the chaplain might be forced to desecrate the Sabbath. In support of his opinion, Rabbi Soloveitchik cited halakhic precedents demonstrating that one may embark on religiously worthwhile projects even at the risk that they might lead to serious transgressions of halakhic norms. However, it is significant that the Rav's solicitude for the welfare of personnel serving in the armed forces prompted him even to endorse sanctions against rabbis who refused to serve in the chaplaincy. His conviction that it was a moral obligation not to abandon Jews in need of rabbinic guidance overrode his reluctance to put observant Jews in a position where they had no choice but to desecrate the Sabbath. He made this ruling in spite of the generally accepted halakhic norm that "one does not encourage an individual to commit a sin in order to benefit another individual."[26]

Because of his deep-rooted conviction that Jews have an ethico-religious responsibility to the world at large, the Rav found it necessary to devise a formula to enable Jewish participation in inter-religious consultations and activities without jeopardizing the integrity and uniqueness of the Jewish faith experience. Contrary to widespread misconceptions, his essay "Confrontation" and the guidelines for interfaith discussions were not intended to forestall meaningful exchanges between representatives of Judaism and of other religions.

Rabbi Isadore Twersky, the Rav's son-in-law, told me that at one time the Rav considered an invitation to deliver a lecture at the Christian-Jewish colloquium held at Harvard Divinity School. Moreover, the Rav's classic article "The Lonely Man of Faith" was first presented as an oral lecture at a Catholic seminary in Brighton, Massachusetts. While he looked upon interreligious discussions of purely theological issues as exercises in futility,

---

[25] Emanuel Rackman, "Secular Jurisprudence and Halakhah." *Jewish Law Annual* 8:57.
[26] BT *Kiddushin* 55b.

he approved of discussions devoted to sociopolitical issues even though, as he noted in a footnote to "Confrontation,"[27] for people of faith such issues are not secular concerns but are grounded in theological convictions.

The Rav's sensitivity to ethical concerns also led him to sponsor research to find more humane methods than hoisting and shackling to prepare animals for *shechitah*. As a general rule, the Orthodox establishment was concerned only with blocking legislation affecting *shechitah*. But the Rav felt that it was irresponsible to ignore the clamor for reducing the pain animals endured prior to *shechitah*.

The Rav's sharp reaction to the tragic massacres in Lebanon,[28] when large segments of the Jewish community wanted to sweep the problem under the rug, also attests to his extraordinary concern for ethical propriety. It was because of his threat that unless the National Religious Party pressed for the appointment of an independent commission of inquiry he would publicly resign his membership in the Mizrachi movement that its leadership had no choice but to comply with his request.

His extraordinary ethical sensitivity engendered what at first blush strikes us as non-traditional attitudes towards women. Although he never advocated egalitarianism or questioned the halakhic stipulations governing the respective roles of the genders, he emphasized that these distinctions by no means implied an inferior status. Significantly, he interpreted the verse that Eve was to function as Adam's *ezer ke-negdo* in the sense that Eve was not simply to function as Adam's helpmeet, but that she was supposed to help him by being *ke-negdo*, i.e., complementing Adam by offering opposing perspectives. In a similar vein, the Rav invoked the special dignity of women as an explanation for the halakhic rule disqualifying women from serving as witnesses. He compared their status to that of a king who, according to Jewish law, is disqualified from serving as a witness because it is incompatible with royal dignity to be subjected to cross-examination. By the same token, he took pains to point out that the reason why *kevod ha-tzibbur* was invoked as the ground for barring women from receiving an *aliyah* reflected not inferior status but the fear that men might have improper thoughts when they heard the Torah read by an attractive woman.

---

[27] "Confrontation," *Tradition* 6:2 (1964): 5.
[28] See Michael Rosenack, *op. cit.*, 169.

Ethical considerations also prompted the Rav's refusal to participate in granting a *heter me'ah rabbanim* to husbands whose wives were unwilling to accept a *get*. The Rav explained that his policy was based upon the realization that, if the shoe were on the other foot, corresponding procedures would not be available to the wife.

Especially revolutionary was his pioneering of intensive Gemara study by women. He was convinced that under contemporary conditions it was necessary to confront the challenge of modernity, and therefore Jewish women must be provided with the intellectual resources necessary to appreciate the meaning of halakhic Judaism. Mere familiarity with the dos and don'ts of religious observance would no longer be adequate, especially at a time when mothers rather than fathers exercise the strongest influence upon children. If Jewish mothers were to provide proper guidance to their children in an era when relatively few Jews abided by Halakhah, they had to possess a real understanding of the halakhic process, since without knowledge of Halakhah one could not possibly acquire a genuinely Jewish perspective. It was for this reason that the Rav insisted that girls receive thorough instruction in Gemara at his Maimonides Day School in Boston. Many years later, Stern College and some other institutions followed suit, and, despite the traditional aversion to instructing girls in Gemara, initiated programs for intensive study not merely of the practical aspects needed for proper observance, but also of the theoretical underpinnings of the Halakhah.

We have so far discussed several specific issues that show the uniqueness of the Rav as an authority figure for Modern Orthodoxy. But even more important is the Rav's general approach to the nature of rabbinic authority, which in his view was limited to the domain of *pesak Halakhah*. He respected the right of individuals to form their own opinions and attitudes regarding matters that are not subject to halakhic legislation. Because of his respect for human autonomy and individuality, he never wanted to impose his particular attitudes upon others or even offer his personal opinions as *da'at Torah*.[29] On

---

[29] I am of course aware that in his eulogy on Rabbi Hayyim Ozer Grodzinski ("*Nosei ha-tzitz ve-ha-hoshen*" in Joseph B. Soloveitchik, *Divrei hegut ve-ha'arakha* (Jerusalem: World Zionist Organization, 1991, 187–194), the Rav insists that the authority invested in rabbinic leadership must not be restricted to formal halakhic rulings, but also extends over public policy issues. However, it must be borne in mind that the Rav referred here to an official Rav of a community whose authority was formally

the contrary, when I turned to him for guidance on policy matters, which at times also involved halakhic considerations, he frequently replied that I should rely upon my own judgment. Similarly, whenever the Rav expounded on his philosophy of Halakhah, he stressed that these were merely his personal opinions, which he was prepared to share with others but which did not possess any kind of authoritative status.

This non-authoritarian approach runs counter to current trends in the Orthodox community which seeks authoritative guidance from halakhic luminaries on all policy matters. Nowadays, fundamentalism flourishes because, as Eric Fromm has pointed out, there are many who desperately seek an escape from personal responsibility. Although the Rav's approach does not satisfy the demand for dogmatic pronouncements, in the long run it holds the greatest promise for those seeking to combine commitment to Halakhah with a selective acceptance of the ethos of modernity, which emphasizes the preciousness of individual autonomy anti freedom. According to the Rav, these "modern" values are implicit in the biblical and rabbinic doctrine of *kevod ha-beriyot,* the dignity due to human beings by virtue of their bearing the *tzelem Elokim.*[30]

One might argue that such a stance, far from constituting a concession to modernity, represents a reaffirmation of classical teachings of Biblical and rabbinic Judaism, which frequently have been neglected. One therefore might conclude that Orthodoxy would be spiritually far healthier if the Rav were accepted as a role model not merely by Modern Orthodoxy but rather by all halakhically committed Jews of the modern era.

---

recognized by election or appointment to a position of leadership. This must not be confused with the *da'at Torah* dispensed by various roshei yeshivah who cannot claim a public mandate for guidance of a community.

It should also be noted that the priest's authority was based upon the supernatural guidance provided by the *Urim ve-Tummi*m and the possession of *ruah ha-kodesh*. See also Lawrence Kaplan's discussion of the issue in his study *Daas Torah: Rabbinic Authority and Personal Autonomy,* edited by Moshe Z. Sokol, 8–10, Northvale, New Jersey: Jason Aronson, 1992.

[30] See Rabbi Joseph B. Soloveitchik, *Yemei Zikaron,* translated by Moshe Kroneh. Jerusalem: World Zionist Organization, 1986, 9–28.

THE CENTRALITY OF CREATIVITY IN THE THOUGHT OF RABBI JOSEPH B. SOLOVEITCHIK[1]

> God wills man to be a creator – his first job is to create himself as a complete being.... Man comes into our world as a hylic, amorphous being. He is created in the image of God, but this image is a challenge to be met, not a gratuitous gift. It is up to man to objectify himself, to impress form upon a latent personality, and to move from the hylic, silent personality towards the center of objective reality. The highest norm in our moral code is to be, in a total sense... and to move toward... real true being.[2]

THIS EXISTENTIALIST EMPHASIS on self-creation is a central theme in Rav Soloveitchik's philosophy. While it may remind us of Jasper's dictum, "To be a man is to become a man," or of Heidegger's espousal of authenticity, the Rav derives the centrality of creativity from the Torah, not from existentialism, neo-Kantianism or any other secular philosophy.

Significantly, many of the Rav's major writings revolve around the theme of creation and, in a sense, are commentaries on the first three chapters of Genesis. This preoccupation with creation themes is especially pronounced

---

[1] From *Tradition* 30:2 (Summer 1996): 219–228.
[2] Joseph B. Soloveitchik, "Redemption, Prayer, Talmud Torah." *Tradition* 17/2 (Spring 1978): 64.

in his later essays such as "Confrontation," "The Lonely Man of Faith," and "Majesty and Humility." He treats the Biblical account of creation merely as a metaphysical or cosmological doctrine but as the matrix of normative teachings that provide guidance and direction for human conduct.

The Scriptural portion of the creation narrative is a legal portion that contains basic, everlasting halakhic principles. If the Torah then chose to recount the story of creation to humankind, we may clearly derive one law from this manner of procedure – that human beings are obliged to engage in creation and the renewal of the cosmos.[3]

According to the Rav, human beings, as bearers of the image of God, are mandated to imitate the Creator. Since the commandment *ve-halakhta bi-drakhav* (*imitatio Dei*) refers exclusively to the divine moral attributes, the Rav treats creation as a moral category.[4] As we shall note later, this has important implications for his analysis of the Maimonidean conception of the "middle road."

Although it may appear that his emphasis on human creativity is inspired by the Enlightenment, it is actually rooted in kabbalistic doctrines such as *tikkun ha-olam*, the *itaruta de-le-tata* (the stirring below), which must precede the *itaruta de-le-eila* (the stirring on high), and the human role in bringing about the reunification of the Holy One, Blessed Be He, with the *Shekhina*.

Rabbi Hayyim of Volozhin, a forebear of the Rav, already used these kabbalistic ideas to define the human task as the realization of one's potential for spiritual creativity. In his view, the fact that human beings bear the image of God implies that they are charged with imitating His creativity. It is through novel insights into the meaning of the Torah or through meticulous observance of the mitzvot that man becomes a builder of spiritual worlds, with enormous repercussions in the highest regions of being. In a daring reinterpretation of a classic rabbinic text, *da ma le-ma'ala mimekha*, which literally means that human beings should be aware of a higher power, he reads into it the following thesis: "Whatever exists on high

---

[3] Rabbi Joseph B. Soloveitchik, *Halakhic Man*, translated by Lawrence Kaplan. Philadelphia: Jewish Publication Society of America, 1983, 100–101.

[4] Rabbi Soloveitchik emphasizes that the biblical doctrine of Creation makes it possible to take freedom and individuality seriously. While for Aristotle, the world was based upon eternally valid laws, the Torah's conception of creation introduces radical novelty and freedom. See *Halakhic Man*, 116 and 134, and *U-vikashtem*, 223.

must come from you" – that the regions of spirituality on high come into being solely as the result of human agency.

He goes so far as to assert that the bliss of the hereafter can be enjoyed only by those who actually create their own immortality. The World to Come is not a pre-existing domain to which God dispenses visas of admission to meritorious individuals. Everyone must, by their own good deeds, create his own spiritual domain in the World to Come.

The Rav adopts Rabbi Hayyim's interpretation of the Biblical statement, "He created man in the image of God," as referring to the human capacity for creativity. He rejects Maimonides's interpretation that it is the possession of reason that endows man with the divine image. This may be partly due to the Rav's theory of knowledge, which emphasizes the creativity of the human mind. While Maimonides adopts the Aristotelian approach, which defines knowledge as noetic identification with the object known, the Rav, who was strongly influenced by the neo-Kantian theory of knowledge, viewed cognition as a construct of the human mind, not a copy of external reality. Since, according to Hermann Cohen's idealism, even sensation is merely a question posed to the human mind, it is readily understandable why the Rav was far more comfortable with Rabbi Hayyim's emphasis upon creativity rather than that of Maimonides, who stressed the capacity for rational contemplation.[5]

The Rav develops Rabbi Hayyim's conception of spiritual creativity, expanding it considerably in the process. Basing his ideas upon Maimonidean conceptions, he shows that such fundamental religious notions as *teshuvah*, prophecy, individual providence, personal immortality and freedom of choice represent forms of self-creations.[6]

> The task of creation... is a triple performance; it finds its expression in the capacity to perform *teshuvah*, to repent, continues to unfold in *hashgahah*, the unique providence which is bestowed upon the unique

---

[5] Because the Rav adopted Hermann Cohen's thesis that Maimonides's ethical system was basically Platonic rather than Aristotelian, he particularly emphasized those aspects of the Maimonidean system that characterize the concluding section of the *Guide*.

[6] *Halakhic Man, op. cit.*, 110.

individual, and achieves its final and ultimate realization in the reality of prophecy and the personality of the prophets.[7]

With respect to *teshuvah*, the Rav focuses upon the emergence of a new personality rather than the attempt to secure atonement or win forgiveness. "Man, through repentance, creates himself, his own I."[8] Insofar as the attainment of individual providence or of immortality is concerned, the Rav resorts to the Maimonidean conception that the sub-lunar world, with the exception of humankind, is only subject to general providence. According to the Rav's interpretation of the Maimonidean thesis, individual providence extends only to those human beings who by dint of their intellectual and spiritual development have become genuine individuals and are no longer merely members of the human species.

When a person creates himself, he ceases to be a mere species ("man"), and becomes a man of God. Then he has fulfilled that commandment which is implicit in the principle of providence.[9]

The Rav's explanation enables us to understand why, in striking contrast with the Torah's description of the creation of various organic creatures, where it is stated that they were created "according to their species," there is no reference to the species in the story of the creation of man.[10] As the Mishnah[11] points out, Adam was created as a single person in order to underscore the importance of the individual.

The highest possible level of individuality is reached when a person turns into a prophet. In the Rav's words:

> The prophet creates his own personality, fashions within himself a new "I" awareness and a different mode of spiritual existence, snaps the chains of self-identity that had linked him to the "I" of old – to

---

[7] *ibid.*, 130–131.

[8] *ibid.*, 113. See also Ha-Rav Yosef Dov ha-Levi Soloveitchik, *Al ha-Teshuvah*, written and edited by Pinchas Peli. Jerusalem: Torah Education Department of the World Zionist Organization, 1974, especially Chapter I.

[9] *ibid.*, p. 128, See also Zvi Kolitz's discussion in *The Teacher* (New York: Crossroad, 1982).

[10] See my discussion of this issue in my *Ethics of Responsibility – Pluralistic Approaches to Covenantal Ethics*, Jewish Publication Society of America, 1994, 60ff.

[11] BT *Sanhedrin* 4:1.

man who was just a random example of the species… and turns into a man of God.[12]

Although in his work, *Halakhic Man,* the Rav, following in the footsteps of Rabbi Hayyim, refers to creativity only in the spiritual realm, in many other writings he enthusiastically endorses cultural, scientific and technological creativity as well. For all his affinity to the approach of Rabbi Hayyim, the Rav diverges from his radical disparagement of all purely secular creativity.

Insisting that our fate is completely in the hands of God, Rabbi Hayyim proclaimed the futility of all human efforts to improve human welfare. From his perspective, human agency directed towards the improvement of socio-political conditions is totally worthless. Rabbi Hayyim quotes the Talmudic statement that the destruction of the Temple was not a triumph of Titus's military skill, but was brought about by the sins of the Jewish people. Titus merely "burnt a burnt Temple."[13] In other words, the plight of the Jewish people was merely an epiphenomenon of its spiritual failings. Since *galut* (exile) was not the disease but merely a symptom, it could be cured only by spiritual therapy, with Torah and mitzvot as the only remedy.

Rabbi Hayyim's disparagement of attempts to improve the human condition exemplifies the pietistic quietism which predominated in the Jewish ethos of the pre-Emancipation and pre-Enlightenment eras, when no effort was made to improve the collective socio-political or economic conditions of the Jewish people. To be sure, quietism and pietism play a significant role not only in Judaism but in most religions. William James went so far as to make the exaggerated claim that "the abandonment of human responsibility is the hallmark of religion."[14] But there were many historic reasons why Jews gravitated towards pietistic approaches, especially during the long periods during which they formed an underclass of European society and were denied the opportunity to participate in the cultural or political life of their host countries. Because of their lack of political power and the belief that with the Messiah's arrival they would be ultimately redeemed by supernatural intervention, Jews were particularly

---

[12] *Halakhic Man, op. cit.,* 130.

[13] BT *Sanhedrin* 96b.

[14] William James, *The Varieties of Religious Experience: A Study in Human Nature.* Charleston: 2007, 260.

prone to this disparagement of human initiatives. Professor Emil Fackenheim has shown that the reason why Spinoza heaped so much contempt upon Judaism but not upon Christianity was that he felt the religious faith of the Jews was responsible for their willingness to endure powerlessness and rendered them totally uninterested in making any efforts to shape their own destiny.[15]

With all his admiration for the Yeshiva world and its passionate love of Torah, the Rav did not subscribe to the quietistic pietism that Rabbi Hayyim espoused. He felt that if Torah values were perceived as incompatible with modernity's emphasis upon human responsibility for our socio-political and economic situation, most of Jewry would dismiss Torah as irrelevant. He feared that a religious ethos that disparaged all human effort to improve socio-political conditions and frowned upon any involvement with the trappings of modernity could result, at best, in halakhically committed Jews being marginalized and relegated to a ghettoized existence on the periphery of Jewish life.

It was his unshakable faith that the Torah is a Torah of life, not an escape from it, that inspired him to search for formulations that would not only grudgingly condone secular studies and scientific, technological, industrial, commercial and political activities but would also endorse them as intrinsically desirable and religiously valuable as long as they conformed to halakhic standards.

What enabled the Rav to formulate a religious philosophy that would enable observant Jews to participate in all facets of modern culture was a reinterpretation of the very text that Rabbi Hayyim had relied upon in extolling human creativity in the spiritual realm. From the context of the phrase, "He created man in the image of God," it is quite clear that the Rav's interpretation, which includes all forms of scientific or cultural creativity, is actually far closer to the meaning of the Biblical text, because the very next verse states, "God said to them: Be fruitful and multiply, and fill the earth and conquer it and rule over the fish of the sea and the fowl of the heaven...." This shows that human beings are supposed to imitate the Creator first and foremost through activities that enable them to harness the forces of nature and help perfect the world. They are charged with the mission to attain dignity (*kevod ha-beriot*) by imitating the Creator in Whose

---

[15] Emil L. Fackenheim, *Mending the World.* New York: Stockmen Books, 1982, 38ff.

image they were created. This is why the Rav links the halakhic concept of *kevod ha-beriot* (human dignity) with the *tzelem Elohim* (the image of God).[16]

One may argue that this conception betrays the influence of neo-Kantian categories as formulated by Hermann Cohen. There can be no doubt that in spite of the Rav's irreconcilable differences with Cohen's views concerning the very essence of Judaism, he adopted many of Cohen's ethical views, especially that Rambam's ethical system reflects a Platonic rather than an Aristotelian approach.[17] According to Aristotle, human beings become most God-like through intellectual perfection. Plato, however, maintained that ethical conduct and attainment of virtue constituted *imitatio Dei*. This, in large measure, accounts for the centrality of ethics in the Rav's religious philosophy.[18]

Professor Ravitzky[19] has advanced some cogent arguments against Cohen's interpretation of Maimonides's ethical views.[20] Yet this controversy is irrelevant for our purposes since it is of interest only to the student of the history of ideas. What matters for us is that basing himself on Rambam, the Rav declared unequivocally that striving for ever higher rungs of moral perfection and working in partnership with God to overcome the imperfections of the universe is the pre-eminent approach to *imitatio Dei*.

In opposition to doctrines that denounce reliance on science and technology to advance human welfare as a usurpation of divine prerogatives (e.g., the Promethean myth), Rav Soloveitchik developed the notion of Adam I, who is summoned to exercise creativity as a member of the "majestic community." He fulfills his divine mandate of becoming a co-

---

[16] Ha-Rav Yosef Dov ha-Levi Soloveitchik, *Yemei Zikaron*, translated by Moshe Kroneh, Jerusalem: Department of Torah Education and Culture in the Diaspora, World Zionist Organization, 1986, 9–11.

[17] See my "The Maimonidean Matrix of Rabbi Joseph B. Soloveitchik's Two-Tiered Ethics," in *Through the Sound of Many Voices*. Toronto: Lester and Orpen Dennys Limited, 1982, 178–179.

[18] *Yemei Zikaron, op. cit.,* 85–87. See also the Rav's explanation of the reason for the recital of *Pesukei de-Zimra* in his *Shiurim Ie-zekher Abba Mori z"l*. Jerusalem: 1985, vol. 1, 17–34.

[19] Aviezer Ravitzky, *"Kinyan ha-da'at bel-leguto: bein ha-Rambam le-neo-Kantianism."* In *Sefer yovel Ii-khvod Moreinu ha-Gaon Rabbi Yosef Dov ha-Levi Soloveitchik,* edited by Shaul Yisraeli, Nachum Lamest, and Yitzhak Raphael, 141–151. Jerusalem: Mossad HaRav Kook and Yeshiva University Press: 1984, 141–151.

[20] *ibid.*

creator with God by not submitting passively to the forces of nature but rather by transforming them through the employment of rational faculties. In the Rav's view, when human beings engage in efforts to harness the forces of nature in order to advance human welfare, they are carrying out the God-given task of becoming partners with Him in completing the work of creation. Scientific and technological activities are not manifestations of hubris but the response to divine directive to conquer the earth.[21]

The Rav remains consistent with this definition of the human task in his approach to the problem of evil. Although, in keeping with the Kantian disdain for theodicies, he shies away from any attempt to provide metaphysical explanations for the existence of evil, he maintains that human beings are challenged to respond to evil. The human assignment is to eliminate want, misery and suffering as much as possible. If there were no evil in the universe, human beings could not help perfect the world of creation. The Rav goes so far as to declare that God had to leave the world in a state of imperfection in order to provide human beings with a mission.[22]

According to the Rav, seeking dominion over nature and attaining a dignified existence is only one aspect of human creativity. There is another dimension, which is symbolized by Adam II. In his existential loneliness, man becomes aware of the need to enter into a "covenantal community" in which he totally surrenders himself, giving everything to God.

Man, who was told to create himself, objectify himself, and gain independence and freedom for himself, must return everything he owns to God.[23]

In striking contrast with his work, *Halakhic Man*, which largely revolves around human creativity, his *U-Vikkashtem* is devoted to the analysis of the features associated with Adam II, who remains unfulfilled until he creates a covenantal community with God through total self-surrender and submission.

For the Rav, however, this act of renunciation also represents imitation of the divine Creator. As he points out in his "Ethics of Majesty and Humility," the act of creation, as emphasized in the Lurianic Kabbalistic notion of *tzimtzum* (divine self-contraction), was possible only because God, in a sense, withdrew in order to create space for the existence of the world.

---

[21] "The Lonely Man of Faith." *Tradition* (Summer 1965): 13–15.

[22] *Halakhic Man*, 105–1 l0; *Yemei Zikaron*, 85–91.

[23] "Redemption, Prayer, Talmud Torah." *Tradition* (Spring 1978): 72.

It is precisely because the act of creation involved the utilization of polar values, an ethics of majesty as well as of humility, that the Rav interprets the Maimonidean notion of the "Middle Road" not as an adaptation of Aristotelian ethics, but as the imitation of the moral attributes which the Creator manifested in the creation of the universe. In this respect he sharply differs with Hermann Cohen, whose overall approach to Maimonidean ethics is mostly accepted by the Rav. While Hermann Cohen had contended that the ethical system of the middle road is a "survival" of the Aristotelian elements that do not really fit into the Maimonidean system, the Rav argues that, far from representing an ethics of compromise, the ethical system of the middle road reflects the synthesis of polar qualities that the Creator of the universe manifested and that go into an ethics of *yishuv ha-olam*. Hence, not only the "ethics of the pious" but also the "ethics of the middle road" reflect not a concession to Greek notions of balance, but rather an authentically Jewish ethical system that revolves around the imitation of the divine attributes of action. The Rav calls attention to the fact that the kabbalistic doctrine of the *sefirot* operates similarly, with polar values that in turn are synthesized. Thus *hesed* and *gevura* yield *tiferet,* whereas the blending of *netzah* and *hod* engenders *yesod.*[24]

Like Kabbalah, which uses differences in gender to symbolize activity and passivity, the Rav suggests that a truly fruitful life is possible only by the interaction of both the active and the passive roles that are suggested in the Biblical account of creation, according to which Adam was created as both male and female (Genesis 1:27). Just as the kabbalistic *sefirot* reflect male and female characteristics, the human personality functions properly only when neither of the two distinct components is repressed.[25]

Because the dialectical tension between the two components of human nature (Adam I and Adam II) mandates divergent approaches to concrete situations, the Rav always insisted one cannot simply resolve ethical dilemmas with formal rules. It therefore becomes imperative to rely on ethical intuitions, which can be cultivated by the imitation of Torah personalities who can serve as role models.

It was this emphasis upon the need to respond to divergent and even polar values that accounted for his espousal of moderation. In public

---

[24] I have dealt with this issue more extensively in my *Ethics of Responsibility,* 101.
[25] *Hamesh Derashot,* 46–47, and *Yemei Zikaron,* 32–36.

lectures he often referred to Rabbi Yohanan ben Zakkai's state of mind before his death. Why was he, of all people, so apprehensive? The Rav contended that since Rabbi Yohanan was not an extremist, he had ample reason to question his place in Jewish history. Perhaps Rabbi Akiva was right when he ridiculed him for his failure to plead for Jerusalem instead of merely requesting Yavneh and its scholars and when he denounced Rabbi Yohanan's moderation as *meshiv hakhamim ahor*. But it might have also been possible that Vespasian, who granted Yavneh, would not have been ready to accede to a request for Jerusalem, and all would have been lost.[26] According to Rav Soloveitchik, the extremist enjoys the advantage of being self-assured. But whoever has deeper insight and perceives different aspects of issues must forego the satisfaction of dogmatic certainty.

Rav Soloveitchik points to the dialectical tension within human beings as demanding the balancing of *hesed* and *emet*. In his interpretation,[27] *hesed* mandates involvement in the world to transform it and create conditions conducive to human welfare. On the other hand, *emet* refers to the eternal values of the covenantal community, which transcend the world of temporal flux and which alone can provide us with a sense of meaning and purpose and enable us to overcome our existential loneliness. Since, according to halakhic Judaism, it is our task to seek to encounter God's Presence primarily in the lower realms of being (*ikkar Shekhinah ba-tahtonim*), we must not try to escape from this world by a flight into transcendental spheres. The human task is to create an abode for God in this world.

The Rav's emphasis upon creativity explains what prompted him to overcome all kinds of social pressures, defy family traditions, and incur alienation from the so-called Torah world by affiliating with Religious Zionism. He thereby affirmed the religious significance of the State of Israel, where Jews enjoy the opportunity to employ their creativity in developing a society in keeping with the ideals of Halakhah.

The Rav categorically rejects the position of Neturei Karta, which claims that any attempt to create a pre-Messianic Jewish state violates the prohibition against "forcing the end." He maintains that the Messianic faith entails human participation in the process of Redemption rather than total reliance upon supernatural intervention. He also contends that the belief in

---

[26] *ibid.*, 33–35.
[27] *ibid.*, 80–81.

the ultimate arrival of the Messiah is not merely an eschatological doctrine, but mandates that human beings dedicate themselves to the pursuit of the ideals that will be fully realized only with the arrival of the Messiah. Nevertheless, the Rav also disagreed with those who were prepared to grant *de facto* recognition to the State of Israel while refusing to endow the existence of a sovereign Jewish stare with intrinsic religious value.

In his *Hamesh Derashot*, the Rav described in most moving terms the tremendous price he paid for identifying with Religious Zionism.[28] To be sure, he was never comfortable in any political role. He always referred to himself as a *melamed*. But for all his disdain for political activities, the Rav felt an obligation to formulate an ideology that would enable Jews to live in two worlds[29] so that they would not feel it necessary to choose between the lure of modernity and the eternal truths of Torah. He felt that those who seek to confine Torah to the "tents" in order to avoid the challenge of "field" – the public arena that calls for participation in the development of agriculture, industry, science, technology and commerce – are in no position to implement the ideals of the Torah as a *Torat Hayyim*, which is supposed to guide and mold all facets of human existence.[30]

We thus note that the Rav's affirmation of the value of human creativity manifests itself in the endorsement not only of secular studies and scientific research, but also of Religious Zionism.

---

[28] *ibid.*, 24–26.
[29] *ibid.*, 112–113.
[30] *ibid.*, 113–115.

THE MAIMONIDEAN MATRIX OF RABBI JOSEPH B. SOLOVEITCHIK'S TWO-TIERED ETHICS[1]

RABBI SOLOVEITCHIK'S PHILOSOPHY revolves around the primacy of Halakhah. Because Halakhah figures as the revealed will of God, all other considerations are subordinated to its dictates. This approach to Halakhah is typical of Orthodox thinkers. But for Rabbi Soloveitchik, Halakhah's role is not limited to providing evaluative standards; instead, it functions as the matrix of his entire philosophy.

Therefore, one may seriously question whether one is at all justified in employing the term "ethical" within the context of such a thoroughly theocentric system, where the property of being commanded by God is the only relevant criterion for determining the validity of any norm. After all, *chukim* – positive laws obeyed solely on the basis of their having been commanded by God – enjoy no less authority than so-called ethical laws which, apart from the authority deriving from their being commanded by God, can also be buttressed by appeals to reason, conscience, or moral sentiment. But since in such a monistic system the property of being commanded by God is both a necessary and sufficient condition of normative significance, one is hard-pressed to assign any real significance to the ethical qua ethical.

---

[1] From *Through the Sound of Many Voices: Writings Contributed on the Occasion of the Seventieth Birthday of W. Gunther Plaut.* Edited by Jonathan Plaut. Toronto: L. & O. Dennys, 1982.

To complicate matters even further Rabbi Soloveitchik displays a somewhat ambivalent attitude toward secular ethics. Occasionally, he points to the development of ethical norms as a legitimate manifestation of human creativity, which itself forms an integral part of the human quest to impose order upon the raw data of our experience, in keeping with the divine mandate "to conquer the universe."[2] At other times, however, he calls attention to our inability to ground ethics in reason.[3] In his view, any attempt to establish a purely secular ethics is doomed to failure. However, it is not quite clear whether, in his opinion, the failure of secular ethics stems from its inability to provide the kind of incentives and motives for ethical conduct that religion can supply; from the intrinsic limitations of secular ethics that preclude the construction of an adequate system; or from the one-sidedness of a success-oriented secular ethics that fails to account for the dimension of the "ethics of humility" which, according to Rabbi Soloveitchik, represents one of the indispensable components of morality.

Much of the ambivalence we encounter in Rabbi Soloveitchik's thought can be attributed to the fact that the various components of his "system" are not in a state of equilibrium but in constant dialectical tension. Because he is willing to reconcile himself to the irreducibility of this tension, he is under no pressure to force disparate experiential data into a Procrustean bed for the sake of forming a neat and coherent system. Instead, he unabashedly advocates a pluralistic, multi-tiered ethics, eschewing the pitfalls of a reductionist approach, which in the interests of neatness and economy glosses over the disparities and incongruities that abound in the human condition.

The emphasis upon the irreducibility of dialectical tensions, which are grounded not in socio-cultural factors but in the very nature of the human condition, permeates not only Rabbi Soloveitchik's ethics, but all facets of his philosophy. To resort to the typology of "The Lonely Man of Faith,"[4] Adam I and Adam II represent two disparate components of human nature that account for the dialectical tension within man. Reflecting the distinctive features assigned to them in the respective chapters of Genesis, Adam I, as

---

[2] Joseph B. Soloveitchik, "The Lonely Man of Faith." *Tradition* (Summer 1965): 15; idem, "Majesty and Humility," *Tradition* (Spring 1978): 34–35.

[3] Soloveitchik, "*U-vikashtem mi-sham.*" *Hadarom* (Tishri 5739): 25–26; Joseph Epstein, ed. *Shiurei ha-Rav,* 47–48, 60–63; Abraham R. Besdin, *Reflections of the Rav,* 104–105.

[4] Soloveitchik, "The Lonely Man of Faith," 11–20.

portrayed in the first chapter of Genesis, uses his reason and imagination creatively in order to subdue and harness the forces of nature. Adam I engages in the process of "filling the earth and conquering it" in order to realize his potential as a creature bearing the image of God, the Creator. By exercising dominion over the forces of nature, man not only asserts his dignity but responds to the mandate of becoming a co-creator with God, who entrusted to man the task of helping perfect the universe.

In striking contrast with the Promethean myth, which disparages human creativity as an arrogant intrusion upon the divine realm, the Bible encourages man to employ his rational faculties to mold his environment in accordance with his needs. In the biblical conception, man is not intended to be a passive victim of circumstances or conditions. The function assigned to him in the divine economy is to achieve majesty by dint of his skill, resourcefulness, and creativity. Hence, science and technology reflect not human hubris, the improper arrogation of powers reserved for a higher being, but the fulfillment of a divine imperative mandating conquest of the natural universe.

But there is another facet of human nature where scientific triumphs or technological accomplishments play no role whatsoever. Success in manipulating the universe cannot assuage the existential loneliness of Adam II, who even under the idyllic conditions of the Garden of Eden must come to grips with the fact that "it is not good for man to be alone" (Gen. 2:18). In the final analysis, it is only through the formation of a covenantal community with God that Adam II's sense of isolation can be overcome. Unlike Adam I, who seeks dignity through control over his environment, Adam II yearns for redemption through self-surrender and self-sacrifice.[5]

Halakhah, in Rabbi Soloveitchik's opinion, recognizes the legitimacy of the two separate domains.[6] Since the dialectical tension between Adam I and Adam II is inevitable, Halakhah makes no attempt to resolve it, but seeks to provide a normative framework designed to make man function as a citizen of two worlds – the majestic as well as the covenantal community.

Similar considerations rule out the construction of any homogeneous ethics that would accommodate the requirements of the disparate components of human nature. In Rabbi Soloveitchik's opinion, in order to

---

[5] *ibid.*, 23–25.
[6] *ibid.*, 50–51

be adequate, ethics must involve continuous oscillation between the ethics of victory and the ethics of defeat.[7] Purely rationalistic ethics as formulated by Kant or Hermann Cohen is marred by one-sidedness. While taking account of the human quest to impose rational structure upon the world of experience, it is totally oblivious of those dimensions of the human personality that strive not for autonomy, mastery, and control, but for redemption through self-sacrifice.

In the light of Rabbi Soloveitchik's ethical doctrines as set forth in his recently published "Majesty and Humility,"[8] we must reject Professor Lawrence Kaplan's thesis that, according to Rabbi Soloveitchik, only ritual mitzvot qualify as sacrificial acts which, because they are performed in humble submissiveness to an incomprehensible divine will, involve the covenantal community.[9] Ethical mitzvot, on the other hand, supposedly address themselves exclusively to man as a member of the majestic community, since ethical norms express the majestic human quest to impose rational order upon conduct. But such a sharp line of demarcation between the ethical and the ritual spheres can hardly be maintained on the basis of the opinions expressed by Rabbi Soloveitchik in his "Majesty and Humility." As the very term "ethics of defeat" suggests, the need for humble submission to an unfathomable divine will characterizes not only the ritual sphere, but applies to the ethical sphere as well.

However, in fairness to Professor Kaplan, it should be pointed out that he offered his interpretation of Rabbi Soloveitchik's doctrine long before the appearance of "Majesty and Humility," which in our opinion is crucial for an understanding of the latter's position. We must also concede to Professor Kaplan that the specific illustrations provided for his ethics of humility in the essay "Majesty and Humility" really involve *chukim* ritual laws, not ethical requirements. But Rabbi Soloveitchik's repeated emphasis upon the inadequacies of a one-sided, success-oriented ethics further confirms our opinion that for Rabbi Soloveitchik the ethical domain involves both the majestic and the covenantal communities.

It has been suggested that Rabbi Soloveitchik's conception of the dialectical tension arising from man's ontological status mirrors the tensions

[7] Soloveitchik, "Majesty and Humility," 36.
[8] *ibid.*, 26.
[9] Lawrence Kaplan "The Religious Philosophy of Rabbi Joseph B. Soloveitchik." *Tradition* 14:2 (Fall 1973): 43–64.

between the neo-Kantian (Adam I) and the existentialist strands (Adam II) of his thought. In Professor Kaplan's view, the emphasis upon human creativity which predominates in the *"Ish Halakhah"*[10] and which characterizes the typology of Adam I can be traced back to the impact of Hermann Cohen's neo-Kantianism.[11] On the other hand, the influence of existentialist thinkers supposedly makes itself felt in his Adam II, who, à la Kierkegaard, surrenders in a spirit of sacrificial submission to an unfathomable divine will. Professor Kaplan contends that a gradual shift can be detected in Rabbi Soloveitchik's thought, with existentialist elements becoming increasingly prominent.[12]

Actually, this is a misconception that has arisen largely because of historical accidents relating to the publication of Rabbi Soloveitchik's writings. For many years, *"Ish Halakhah"* was his only major contribution to religious philosophy that was accessible to the general public.[13] Moreover, without the balance provided by some of his later writings, the thrust of his thought lent itself to misunderstanding. Regrettably, some interpreters were not aware that an early draft of his existentialist *"U-viskashtem mi-sham"* was already completed by the time *"Ish Halakhah"* had made its first appearance.[14] Small wonder, then, that in many circles the impression prevailed that Rabbi Soloveitchik's description of Halakhah as a discipline calling for the exercise of activity, spontaneity, and innovativeness rather than blind submission to the divine will showed the influence of Hermann Cohen, to whom the "given" was merely a question posed to the human mind.

Similarly, Rabbi Soloveitchik's enthusiasm for science and technology was seen as evidence of Hermann Cohen's influence, especially since Rabbi Soloveitchik's views on this issue diverge so much from those prevailing in his early environment. To cite a telling example: from the premise that man is mandated to emulate his Creator, he draws conclusions that have little in common with those drawn by his ancestor, Rabbi Hayyim of Volozhin. The latter, employing kabbalistic categories, was concerned with an entirely different sort of creativity. For him, the study of the Torah and the

---

[10] Soloveitchik, *"Ish ha-halakhah." Talpiot* (1944): 651–735.

[11] Kaplan, "The Religious Philosophy," 44.

[12] *ibid.*, 59.

[13] Soloveitchik, *"U-vikashtem mi-sham,"* 1–83.

[14] *ibid.*

performance of mitzvot were deemed creative acts because, in keeping with the doctrine that "stirrings below precede stirrings above," they initiate a chain reaction extending to the highest reaches of being. Human creativity manifested itself in the creation of spiritual values which affect the relationship of God to His world and are instrumental in helping bring about the reunification of the Holy One, Blessed Be He, and His *Shekhinah*.[15] When human creativity is interpreted in such pietistic fashion, it obviously cannot provide religious justification for science and technology. What mattered to Rabbi Hayyim were not the empirically observable consequences of human actions, but their supernatural repercussions.

In contradistinction to this approach, which even now permeates the 'yeshiva world' and results in total indifference to scientific pursuits, Rabbi Soloveitchik extols the merits of whatever activities enlarge the human capacity to exercise control over the environment and to achieve the dignity due to man as the bearer of the image of God.[16] Science and technology no longer are dismissed as purely secular enterprises, but rather cherished as invaluable instruments that facilitate the religious quest of imitating the creative ways of the Creator.

There can be no doubt that this openness to science represents a major shift from the ethos and value system of Eastern European orthodoxy. But we must not jump to the conclusion that this transformation was due to the influence of Hermann Cohen. A perusal of *"U-vikashtem mi-sham"* clearly reveals that Maimonides (especially in relation to the apparent conflict between the first and second chapters of *Hilkhot Deot*), rather than Cohen, provided the matrix for the development of Rabbi Soloveitchik's philosophy. In this context, it should also be borne in mind that, as Aharon Lichtenstein has pointed out, Rabbi Soloveitchik had originally planned to submit a dissertation on Maimonides, not on Hermann Cohen.[17] Rabbi Soloveitchik was forced to abandon the project because no member of the philosophy department in Berlin possessed sufficient expertise to supervise such a thesis.

---

[15] Hayyim of Volozhin, *Nefesh Chaim* 1:4.

[16] Soloveitchik, "The Lonely Man of Faith," 15–16. See also David Hartman, *Joy and Responsibility* (1978), 198–231.

[17] Aharon Lichtenstein, "Rabbi Joseph Soloveitchik," in *Great Jewish Thinkers of the Twentieth Century*, ed. Simon Noveck (1963), 285.

It must, however, be admitted that some aspects of Rabbi Soloveitchik's own highly original approach to Maimonides – which, in turn, provides the basic foundation of his entire religious philosophy – can in some measure be traced back to Cohen's insistence upon the predominance of Platonic elements in Maimonidean ethics.[18] Rabbi Soloveitchik subscribes to Cohen's basic premise that, notwithstanding the prevalence of Aristotelian notions and categories in his ethics, Maimonides could not accept Aristotle's basic premises, which relegated ethics to an inferior branch of knowledge. In the Aristotelian scheme, ethics figured as a prelude to politics. As a low-grade science, its function was to provide practical guidelines that are useful for the attainment of personal or communal well-being but unworthy of the high status commanded by a theoretical science. But for Maimonides, ethics transcends teleological or eudaemonistic considerations. Acquisition of virtue is not merely a prudential requirement, but a religious obligation (in other words, *imitatio Dei*).[19] Moreover, the concluding chapter of Maimonides's *Guide of the Perplexed* treats moral virtue not merely as a means to an end – that is, knowledge of God – but as an integral part of the *summum bonum*.[20]

Although Rabbi Soloveitchik agrees with many features of Cohen's approach, there are vital differences. Of special importance are their divergent views concerning "middle-road" ethics. Cohen had contended that only the ethics of the pious really qualified as genuine religious ideals. Whatever features of the Aristotelian golden mean Maimonides had incorporated into his *Hilkhot Deot* were dismissed as totally incompatible with the ethico-religious ideals that reflect the ultimate thrust of Maimonides.

In Cohen's view, the standards contained in the ethics of the wise are merely counsels of prudence which fail to satisfy the higher requirements of a religious ethics based upon *imitatio Dei*. Hence according to Cohen, there are strata of Maimodean ethics which are mere "survivals" of a prudential ethics; they should be overcome and transcended in the quest for religious ideals.

---

[18] Hermann Cohen, "Charakteristik tier Ethic Maimunis." *Judische Schriften* III (1924): 22,1–89.

[19] Maimonides, *Mishneh Torah,* Hilkhot Deot 1:5, *Sefer ha-Mitzvot* Mitzvot Aseh 8.

[20] Maimonides, *Guide of the Perplexed,* III, p. 54.

Rabbi Soloveitchik categorically rejects this doctrine. He shares Shimon Rawidowicz's view that the middle road cannot be dismissed as the intrusion of Greek elements upon biblical morality,[21] especially since Maimonides explicitly mentions the middle road as one of the features included in "Walking in His Ways."[22]

The ethics of the wise, not merely the ethics of the pious, constitutes *imitatio Dei* because for Maimonides it is indispensable to *yishuv ha-olam*, the settlement of the world. The cultivation of character traits required for the proper functioning of society ceases to be merely a prudent dictate of social utility. It is transformed into a religious imperative based upon the obligation to pattern ourselves after the Creator. In keeping with this interpretation, Maimonides allows no dichotomy between religious and supposedly secular (Aristotelian) ethics. Rather, there are two separate strands of religious ethics in a state of dialectical tension. If my thesis is correct, it can be put schematically: the ethics of the wise represents *imitatio Dei* on the part of Adam I (the majestic community), whereas the ethics of the pious reflects the quest for redemption through self-sacrifice, which characterizes Adam II (the covenantal community). But, according to Rabbi Soloveitchik, both ethics seek to appropriate divine moral attributes. Adam I emulates divine creativity. Through his acts of renunciation and withdrawal, Adam II imitates the divine *tzimtzum*, self-contraction, which kabbalistic doctrine regards as the precondition of the act of Creation.[23] Significantly, in chapter 2 of *Hilkhot Deot*, Maimonides advocates extremism rather than the middle road precisely in those areas that come under the purview of the ethics of humility.

To be sure, it is no simple task to satisfy the claims of two distinct levels of ethics which at times confront us with conflicting demands. But it should be realized that without the superimposition of an ethics of the pious, the ethics of the wise would still be plagued with all sorts of moral ambiguities

---

[21] Shimon Rawidowicz, "A Chapter in Maimonidean Ethics," in *Sefer ha-yovel li-khvod Mordekhai Menachem Kaplan* (1953), 236. But there is a pronounced difference between Rabbi Soloveitchik's and Rawidowicz's views, since the latter regards the "middle road" as an inferior sort of religious ethics that serves merely as the gate to the higher ethics of the pious.

[22] See my essay "Alienation and Exile," *Tradition* 6:2 (Spring 1964): 93–103 (page 229 in this volume).

[23] Soloveitchik, "Majesty and Humility," 35–36; 48–50.

and dilemmas. There is no formal principle that can be invoked to determine the precise nature of the golden mean. Aristotle already noted that guidance on matters pertaining to virtue can be provided only by the experience of individuals who excel in practical wisdom.[24] What renders the task of determining the requirements of the middle road even more difficult in the Maimonidean system is the fact that for him, the conception of the middle road is dynamic rather than static. While for Aristotle the golden mean is patterned after the Greek ideal of balance attained in a state of equilibrium, the Maimonidean religious ideal of the middle road reflects creative tension arising from oscillation between polar values.[25] Like Aristotle, Maimonides was unable to furnish a satisfactory definition of the desirable traits of character. It is only through the imitation of the proper model, the Torah scholar, that we can develop the intuitive faculties necessary to make proper ethical judgments.[26]

To be sure, the addition of another tier (in other words, the ethics of the pious) to the structure of morality exacerbates the difficulties further. If decision-making at the level of the ethics of the wise is beset by problems, they become compounded when we must wrestle with the additional question whether, in a given existential situation, we should invoke the standards of the ethics of the wise or those of the ethics of the pious. But these added difficulties amount merely to differences of degree, not of kind. As we have noted previously, because it must accommodate numerous conflicting values, the entire ethical domain is replete with moral ambiguities and dilemmas. Unfortunate though this may be, there is no magic formula that can be applied to settle conflicting ethical claims.

Our analysis so far has proceeded on the assumption that Rabbi Soloveitchik's ethics of majesty (Adam I) is the equivalent of Maimonides's ethics of the wise, while the ethics of humility (Adam II) is the counterpart of the ethics of the pious. But it must be admitted that for all their plausibility, these assumptions are beset by serious difficulties, inasmuch as Rabbi Solovcitcik maintains that the dialectical tension between Adam I and Adam II is at least in principle capable of resolution. Extraordinary

---

[24] Aristotle, *Nicomachean Ethics*, Book III.

[25] I haves elsewhere discussed Rabbi Soloveitchik's view that for Maimonides, the "middle road emerges as the resultant of an ongoing creative tension." See Maimonides, *Guide of the Perplexed.*

[26] Maimonides, *Mishneh Torah, Hilkhot Deot* 6:2.

individuals, such as the Patriarchs, find it possible to live simultaneously in the majestic and redemptive communities.[27] But it is difficult to envisage even the theoretical possibility of acting simultaneously in accordance with the requirements of both the ethics of the pious and the ethics of the wise since, by definition, the ways of the pious deviate from the middle road.

Notwithstanding the seriousness of this problem, there is no question that Rabbi Soloveitchik totally disagrees with the thesis of Hermann Cohen and Steven Schwarzschild, who reduce the ethics of the wise to a second-class ethics that is intended merely as a stepping-stone to the higher plateau of the ethics of the pious.[28] According to Rabbi Soloveitchik, the dialectical tension between the two indispensable elements of religious ethics, both of which reflect polar phases of *imitatio Dei,* does not disappear even in the ideal situation.

To be sure, in any given situation we cannot be certain whether we should act in accordance with the standards of the ethics of the wise or those of the ethics of the pious. But uncertainty and ambiguity characterize the entire ethical domain. There are numerous instances when conflicting moral claims leave no alternative but to rely on our admittedly exceedingly fallible intuitions for guidance in ethical decision-making.

There is a corollary of our analysis with important ramifications for contemporary moral issues. Since, according to our interpretation of Rabbi Soloveitchik's ethics, the dialectical tension between the two types of ethics is inherent in the human condition itself, the ethics of the wise can never be totally transcended. Hence, Rabbi Soloveitchik is bound to reject the utopian, messianic ethics of Hermann Cohen, which contributed so much to the latter's utter disdain for Zionism. Professor Schwarzschild, following in the footsteps of Hermann Cohen, went so far as to identify Maimonides's ethics of the pious with messianic ethics which, in his opinion, should supersede the ethics of the middle road.[29] This messianic perspective accounts for Professor Schwarzschild's aversion to the "militarism" of the

---

[27] Soloveitchik, "The Lonely Man of Faith," 52.

[28] Cohen, "Charakteristik," Steven S. Schwarzschild, "Moral Radicalism and 'Middlingness' in the Ethics of Maimonides." *Studies in Medieval Culture*, 65–92. While not going quite as far as Schwitzschild, Rawidowicz also essentially adopts this approach; see Rawidowicz, *"Perek be-torat,"* 236.

[29] Schwarzschild, "Moral Radicalism," 81–83.

State of Israel, which obviously does not conform to his standards of a utopian, messianic ethics.

Fortunately, Rabbi Soloveitchik's ethics is far more realistic. He would oppose any form of pacifism that would deny the legitimacy of Israel's policies to secure survival, if necessary, through reliance on military means. In his view, it would hardly make sense to apply to an unredeemed world the kind of moral norms that are suited to a perfect, redeemed world. Nonresistance to evil, be it on the individual or the collective level, can hardly qualify as a moral desideratum. To invite the liquidation of the State of Israel through the advocacy of a radical utopian ethics would be utterly incompatible with the requirements of an ethics that mandates continuous oscillation between the claims of majesty and humility.

To be sure, even for Rabbi Soloveitchik, the messianic doctrine is not just an eschatological article of faith, but possesses ethical significance.[30] It is the matrix of the ethical postulate to strive for everything possible to help bring about the realization of the messianic goal. But this kind of messianism has nothing in common with utopian ethics. It rather reflects the realism of a Maimonides, according to whom the need for a state will not wither away completely even in the messianic era.[31] Not the abolition of power but its exercise in accordance with the ideals of the Torah is halakhic Judaism's ultimate objective.

---

[30] Soloveitchik, "*Ish Ha-halakhah*," 722–723; idem. *"U-vikashtem mi-sham,"* 39.
[31] Maimonides, *Mishneh Torah,* Hilkhot Melakhim, chapter 11.

IMITATIO DEI IN THE PHILOSOPHY OF RABBI JOSEPH B. SOLOVEITCHIK[1]

ONE OF THE MOST striking features of the religious philosophy of the Rav, Joseph B. Soloveitchik, is the pivotal role assigned to *imitatio Dei*. He went so far as to consider it the basic principle underlying all of Jewish ethics[2] and to elevate it into the penultimate ideal of halakhic Judaism.[3]

To appreciate the full significance of the Rav's originality, it must be borne in mind that this view stands in sharp contrast to opinions which relegate *imitatio Dei* to a marginal position. It has even been argued that the legalistic thrust of Judaism and its focus upon divine transcendence excludes *imitatio Dei* from the parameters of Jewish piety.[4]

---

[1] From *Hazon Nahum: Studies in Jewish Law, Thought, and History Presented to Dr. Norman Lamm on the Occasion of His Seventieth Birthday,* edited Yaakov Elman and Jeffrey Gurock, 557–576. New York: Yeshiva University Press, 1998.

[2] Joseph B. Soloveitchik, *Shi'urim le-zekher Abba Mori,* vol. 11, Jerusalem, 5745, 8–9. "*U-vikashtem mi-sham,*" *Ish ha-halakhah: galui ve nistar.* Jerusalem, Department of Torah Education and Culture in the Diaspora, World Zionist Organization, 5739, 223ff. For bibliographic references, consult Tzvi Schachter, *Nefesh ha-rav,* Jerusalem, 5754, 59–71.

[3] Joseph B. Soloveitchik, "*U-vikashtem mi-sham,*" 180ff.

[4] See Leon Roth, *Ha-dat ve-erkhei ha-hayyim.* Jerusalem: 5733, 20–30. For bibliographical references, see Shalom Rosenberg, "*Ve-halalakhta bi-derakhav.*" *Jewish Philosophy,* Assa Kasher and Mosheh Chalmish. Tel Aviv University: 1983, 84–85 (Hebrew).

However, there are many references to *imitatio Dei* in both Biblical and rabbinic literature.[5] Because God rested on the seventh day of creation, the observance of the Sabbath, the very cornerstone of Judaism, was mandated (Exodus 20:11). Chapter 19 of Leviticus, which, according to the Midrash,[6] contains all the commandments of the Decalogue and therefore, by implication, the entire corpus of Jewish law, is introduced by the admonition "You shall be holy because I the Lord your God am holy." In Deuteronomy we encounter phrases such as "After the Lord your God you shall walk,"[7] "to walk in all His ways,"[8] and "you shall walk in His ways."[9] To be sure, the last-mentioned Torah text does not necessarily express an imperative to imitate God's actions or characteristics. According to the *Sefer Yere'im* it constitutes a commandment to obey the various laws or rules ordained by God.[10]

Rabbinic literature is even more explicit than the Torah in mandating *imitatio Dei*. The Babylonian Talmud quotes a statement attributed to the Tanna, Abba Shaul: "Be like Him! Just as He is gracious and compassionate, so must you be gracious and compassionate!"[11] The *Sifra* quotes Abba Shaul's statement in a slightly different version. Commenting on Leviticus 19:2, he is reported to have stated, "It is becoming for the King's entourage to be like the King."[12]

In Tractate *Sotah*,[13] the Babylonian Talmud interprets *imitatio Dei* as mandating the performance of benevolent actions. The *middot* of God to be

---

[5] See Arthur Marmorstein, *Studies in Jewish Theology*, Oxford University Press: 1950,s 109–221; David S. Shapiro, "The Doctrine of the Image of God and *Imitatio Dei* in Studies in Jewish Thought," New York, Yeshiva University Press: 1975, volume 1, 15–43; and Norman Lamm, "Some Notes on the Concept of *Imitatio Dei*" in *Rabbi Joseph H. Lookstein Memorial Volume*, edited by Leo Landman, 217–229. Hoboken: Ktav, 1980.

[6] *Leviticus Rabbah* 24:5.

[7] Deuteronomy 13:5.

[8] *ibid.* 10:12.

[9] *ibid.* 28:10.

[10] In his *Sefer Yere'im*, paragraph 261, Rabbi Eliezer Ben Samuel of Metz treats this phrase as the source of a positive mitzvah to keep all the commandments. This interpretation reflects the view of *Sifra*, Leviticus, *Kedoshim* 3:2, *Piska* 3.

[11] BT *Shabbat* 113b.

[12] *Sifra*, loc. cit.

[13] BT *Sotah* 14a.

emulated are defined as clothing the naked, visiting the sick, comforting mourners, and burying the dead.

There are also other instances of the Babylonian Talmud's invoking the example of divine actions as a model for human conduct. "Great is peace because even the Holy One, blessed be He, altered [His report to Abraham of Sarah's words] for its sake."[14] This is cited as a precedent to demonstrate that, when uttered in the interest of promoting peace and harmony; white lies are not only condoned but also recommended. Similarly, God's bringing together of Adam and Eve[15] gives rise to the maxim that "an eminent person should act as best man for a person of inferior status."[16]

Another important proof text that relates specifically to the imitation not of divine actions but of divine attributes is found in *Sifrei*, with a slight but important variation from Abba Shaul's statement reported in the Talmud: "Just as God is called compassionate, you too shall be compassionate... as God is called gracious, you too shall be gracious... as God is called *pious, you* too shall be pious... as God is called righteous, you too shall be righteous."[17]

Nothing in the Biblical or rabbinic texts adduced so far suggests that *imitatio Dei* constitutes a central concern for Jewish thought. Until the emergence of Kabbalistic ethics, it hardly played a major role.[18] It is even questionable whether *imitatio Dei* rates as an outright mitzvah in classical rabbinic teachings. Before Maimonides no codifier listed *imitatio Dei* among the commandments. What is especially strange about Maimonides's pioneering position is that both in the *Sefer ha-Mitzvot* and in the *Mishneh Torah* he invokes as the Biblical proof text for this mitzvah a verse (Deuteronomy 28:10) that does not seem to be intended as a commandment. The phrase "you shall walk in His ways" occurs within the context not of prescriptions but of predictions. *Prima facie*, it refers to the conditions to be fulfilled if Israel is to be rewarded for faithful adherence to the provisions of its Covenant with God.

What is even more surprising is the fact that Maimonides does not refer to any of the Biblical verses that are cited in the Talmud. Although the Babylonian Talmud uses the verse "after the Lord your God you shall walk"

---

[14] BT *Bava Metzia* 87a.
[15] Genesis 2:22.
[16] BT *Berakhot* 61a.
[17] *Sifrei, Ekev* 49.
[18] See especially Moses Cordovero's *Tomer Devorah*.

(Deuteronomy 13:5) to mandate benevolent actions such as clothing the naked and visiting the sick, Maimonides totally ignores this verse in his more mature *magnum opus*, the *Mishneh Torah*. To be sure, he referred to it in his earlier *Sefer ha-Mitzvot*, but even there it only plays a secondary role.

I have dealt elsewhere more extensively with the reasons for the transformation of the Maimonidean conception of *imitatio Dei*.[19] I pointed out that in his later phase, Maimonides deliberately eliminated from *imitatio Dei* any reference to the imitation of divine actions and restricted the mitzvah to the requirement to cultivate virtuous dispositions.[20] As opposed to the Gemara in *Sotah*, Maimonides no longer accepted the verse "after the Lord your God you shall walk" as a proof-text for the performance of benevolent actions. (The only source cited in the *Mishneh Torah* for benevolent practices is "Love your neighbor as yourself."[21]) Undoubtedly, Maimonides was uncomfortable with any suggestion that human beings could actually presume to imitate God. In keeping with his views on divine attributes of action, Maimonides avoided recourse to any Talmudic source that seemed to suggest that it was possible for human beings to imitate God Himself rather than merely His *ways*. For the same reason, Maimonides could not use the statement of Abba Sha'ul in Tractate *Shabbat* because it, too, was couched in language that seemed to refer to the imitation of divine attributes rather than His "ways" – the attributes of action.

This left Maimonides no choice but to rely on the *Sifrei* on the Biblical verse "to walk in all His ways."[22] Although this verse is not even mentioned in the Talmud with reference to *imitatio Dei*, Maimonides prefers this *Sifrei* to the other available rabbinic sources. To begin with, the *Sifrei* clears up the ambiguity of the expression "to walk in all His ways" by showing that it means the imitation of the moral attributes of God. As Rabbi Naftali Tzvi Yehudah Berlin pointed out,[23] had the *Sifrei* not adduced the text from Joel (3:5), the phrase "to walk in all His ways" might be interpreted simply as the

---

[19] See my essay, *"Imitatio Dei* in Maimonides's Sefer ha-Mitzvot and the Mishneh Torah," in *Tradition and Transition: Essays Presented to Chief Rabbi Sir Immanuel Jakobovits to Celebrate Twenty Years in Office,* edited by Jonathan Sacks, 321–324. London: Jews' College Publication, 1986. See also my *Ethics of Responsibility,* Philadelphia: Jewish Publication Society, 1994, 72–73.

[20] *ibid.*

[21] *Mishneh Torah, Hilkhot Avel* 14:1.

[22] Deuteronomy 11:22.

[23] *Sifrei Emek ha-Netziv* to *Sifri Devarim*, Piska 13.

equivalent of "to obey God's laws." The *Sifrei's* analysis demonstrates that this Torah text prescribes the imitation of the divine moral attributes rather than the observance of His laws.

In addition, the formulation of the *Sifrei* holds another attraction for Maimonides. Since the *Sifrei* does not refer to God as being merciful, compassionate, etc. but merely to *His being called* by these attributes, it lends support to the Maimonidean doctrine of divine attributes *of* action. Rav Soloveitchik fully adopts the pioneering conception of Maimonides which, instead of viewing the cultivation of moral dispositions merely as a means to facilitate the performance of benevolent actions, raises the attainment of desirable traits of character to the level of an intrinsic religious objective.[24] But he builds upon Maimonidean foundations and extends the concept *of imitatio Dei* to a much wider sphere. Whereas Maimonides, in his most authoritative work, the *Mishneh Torah,* restricted[25] the range and scope of *imitatio Dei* to imitation of divine attributes of action through cultivation of moral character traits,[26] Rav Soloveitchik expanded *imitatio Dei* to encompass the entire gamut of human activities and personality formation. Especially significant is his insistence that *imitatio Dei* include the imitation of divine creativity, which the Rav viewed as the prototype of ethical activity.[27]

Although no authoritative halakhic sources support this position unequivocally, the Rav was actually developing a notion of his ancestor, Rabbi Hayyim of Volozhin, the founder of the Lithuanian Yeshiva movement.[28] According to Rabbi Hayyim, the verse "He created man in His image"[29] refers to the capacity for creativity granted to human beings. To be sure, as we point out later on, the Rav went far beyond Rabbi Hayyim's parameters of creativity. Notwithstanding their profound ideological differences on the issue of quietism and pietism, there were many reasons why the Rav adopted Rabbi Hayyim's interpretation of the "image of God"

---

[24] See my "Centrality of Virtue-Ethics in Maimonides in *Of Scholars, Savants and their Texts: Studies in Philosophy and Religious Thought-Essays in Honor of Arthur Hyman,* edited by Ruth Link-Salinger, 251–260. New York: Peter Lang, 1989.

[25] *Hilkhot Deot,* chapter 1.

[26] See *Hilkhot Deot* 1:10. *Guide of the Perplexed* 1:54 and 111:54.

[27] See his essay "*U-vikashtem,*" op. cit., 223.

[28] *Nefesh ha-Hayyim,* chapters 1–2.

[29] Genesis 1:27.

rather than that of Maimonides, who had insisted that it was exclusively because of their rationality that human beings were described as creatures bearing the image of God.[30]

Despite his admiration for Maimonides, Rabbi Soloveitchik rejected his thesis that the attainment of intellectual and moral virtues rather than the performance of creative actions represented the highest level of religious perfection. The primacy assigned to intellectual contemplation in the Maimonidean system reflected the Aristotelian doctrine that only through intellectual activity could human beings become God-like.

The Rav's objection to this basic Aristotelian tenet of Maimonidean philosophy was not affected by his acceptance of Hermann Cohen's thesis[31] that Maimonidean ethics owed more to Plato than to Aristotle. The mere fact that Maimonides in his *Hilkhot Deot* speaks of the imitation of divine moral attributes represents a radical departure from Aristotelian doctrines, which stressed the self-sufficiency of God to such an extent that he was utterly unconcerned with any being other than Himself and therefore could not possess any ethical attributes. On the other hand, Plato maintained that the attainment of ethical perfection constituted imitation of God.

But even if the Maimonidean ethics with its added Platonic elements had not included some objectionable Aristotelian elements, the Rav still could not be comfortable with a philosophy that maintained that the image of God is to be interpreted solely in terms of the possession of rationality. It was the Rav's theory of knowledge, which was strongly influenced by Hermann Cohen, that prevented him from subscribing to the Aristotelian-Maimonidean doctrine that knowledge amounted to noetic identification with an existing object. In the neo-Kantian position, cognition is a construct of the human mind rather than a copy of an extra-mental reality. Since, according to Hermann Cohen's idealism, even sensation is merely a question posed to the human mind, it is readily understandable why the Rav preferred

---

[30] *Guide of the Perplexed,* chapter 1.

[31] Aviezer Ravitzky in his *"Kinyan ha-da'at be-haguto: bein ha-Rambam le-neo-Kantianism"* objects to the Rav's adoption of Hermann Cohen's approach to the Maimonidean ethics. *Sefer ha-Yovel li-khvod Moreinu ha-Gaon Rabbi Yoseph Dov ha-Levi Soloveitchik,* edited by Sha'ul Yisra'eli, Nahum Lamm and Yitzchak Raphael, 125–151. Jerusalem: Mosad Ha-Rav Kook, 1984.

the focus upon creativity of Rabbi Hayyim to the emphasis placed upon rational contemplation by the *Guide*.[32]

There are; however, far more basic reasons why the Rav adopted Rabbi Hayyim's view that bearing the image of God demands that human beings exercise their capacity for creativity and become "builders" of spiritual worlds, and why he maintained that "the passive type who is derelict in fulfilling his task of creation cannot become holy."[33]

One of the most fundamental characteristics of the Rav's philosophy is his insistence that any authentic Jewish philosophy of religion must be developed within the matrix of the Halakhah.[34] For him, the Halakhah is the crystallization of a religious approach *sui generis*, it does not represent a flight from the limitations of finite existence into transcendental realms. Instead, it strives to create space for the incursion of the divine into existential realities and summons human beings to carry out their mission of becoming co-creators with God. "The peak of religious perfection to which Judaism aspires is man as creator."[35]

The Rav's philosophy synthesized the Halakhah's emphasis upon practice with some of the key elements of neo-Kantianism, especially the primacy of the practical over the theoretical reason. In his "*U-vikashtem*" he follows Kant in rejecting all the classical proofs for the existence of God.[36] He maintains that it is beyond the ken of human reason to obtain any theoretical truth in the realm of metaphysics. He even rejects the Kantian argument that the existence of God is a postulate of practical reason. Whatever knowledge we have of His existence or His attributes must be derived from some form of divine revelation.

The Rav cites the Maimonidean doctrine of divine attributes, especially the analysis of God's affective attributes into attributes of action, as evidence that statements about God's characteristics are intended to serve as models providing normative guidance.[37] He quotes Maimonides's ruling:

---

[32] The Rav placed special emphasis upon the concluding chapter of the *Guide,* in which the imitation of God's moral attributes represents the highest level of the Maimonidean religious ideal: the attainment of the knowledge of God.

[33] *Halakhic Man,* Rabbi Joseph B. Soloveitchik, translated from the Hebrew by Lawrence Kaplan. Philadelphia, Jewish Publication Society, 1983, 108.

[34] *The Halakhic Mind.* New York: The Free Press, 1986, 85–102.

[35] *Halakhic Man,* 101.

[36] "*U-vikashtem,*" 122–142.

[37] *Shi'urim le-zekher,* 167–173.

In this manner the prophets called God by such descriptive terms as long-suffering, abundant in mercy, just, righteous, perfect, mighty, strong, and the like, to teach us that they are the right and good ways, and that a human being is obligated to practice them and to imitate flier according to one's ability.[38]

The Rav maintains that although only silence is an appropriate response to God, the Torah nevertheless permitted the recital of prayers of praise and thanksgiving in order that human beings "learn the ways of God and His actions... in order to imitate Him."[39]

It is in this light that the Rav explains the meaning and purpose of the various books of *Tanakh* other than the Torah. To be sure, one of the functions of the prophets was to rebuke the people and inspire them to mend their ways. But why were their writings canonized and recorded for future generations? After all, Halakhah stipulates that prophets are not permitted to add, delete, modify, or make any innovation whatsoever in any matter pertaining to Halakhah. According to the Rav, the main purpose of the prophetic writings is to provide us with normative guidance on matters governing human conduct, the details of which are not regulated by clear-cut provisions of the Law.

> There is a whole Torah in the books of the Prophets and the other Scriptural writings – the Torah of the ways of God. [It contains] the Torah of the descriptive terms applied to God, which obligate man to imitate his Creator.... The purpose of prophecy is to teach man how to participate in the traits of God and to merit His appellations.[40]

From the Rav's perspective, which in many respects is Barthian rather than Kantian, prophetic teachings are indispensable to *imitatio Dei*. Since the Rav rejects natural theology,[41] human reason cannot be the source of knowledge of the divine attributes. We are totally dependent upon supernatural revelation to teach us the ethical characteristics of God so that we can emulate them.

---

[38] *Hilkhot Deot* 1:6.

[39] *Shiurim*, 19.

[40] *ibid.*, 173. See also 19.

[41] See "*U-vikashtem*," 148.

Since in the Rav's opinion all of the Torah possesses normative significance, the fact that the Torah begins with an account of the creation of the world has important practical ramifications for the Jewish value system. "If the Torah then chose to relate to man the tale of creation, we may clearly derive one law from this manner of procedure – viz., that man is obliged to engage in creation and the renewal of the cosmos."[42] Because creativity plays such a preeminent role in the Rav's thought, it is not surprising that the bulk of his English publications revolve around expositions of Biblical passages dealing with the theme of creation.

We have called attention to the fact that the religious significance of human creativity came to the fore already in the writings of Rabbi Hayyim. But it must be borne in mind that for Rabbi Hayyim, human creativity was limited to a far narrower domain than for the Rav. As a pietist and quietist, Rabbi Hayyim believed that human beings could be truly creative only in the realm of the spirit. In the physical world, human actions were merely epiphenomena which did not possess causal efficacy. In support of this position, he cited the Talmudic statement that the people's sins, rather than Titus's actions, were the real cause of the destruction of God's sanctuary.[43] On the other hand, embracing Kabbalistic doctrines, he stressed the enormous spiritual repercussions of human activities in the highest realms of Being. In a striking reinterpretation of the rabbinic maxim *Da mah le-maalah mimkha* ("Know what is higher than you"), he renders it as *Da mah lemaalah – mimkha* ("Know [that] what is in the higher world must come from you").

The only type of human creativity that Rabbi Hayyim is prepared to recognize is the discovery of novel insights into the Torah and the meticulous performance of the mitzvot. These activities alone make it possible for new spiritual worlds to come into being. He goes so far as to assert that the bliss of the Hereafter is available only to those who *create* their own immortality by fulfilling their spiritual mission. Immortality is not just a reward that could be gratuitously dispensed by a compassionate God upon the undeserving. One's portion in the World to Come is not a preexistent entity, admission to which can be earned by meritorious conduct, but comes into being only through human efforts to create a spiritual world.[44]

---

[42] *Halakhic Man,* 71.
[43] *Nefesh ha-hayyim,* 1:4.
[44] *ibid.,* 1:12.

Unlike Rabbi Hayyim, the Rav does not limit the efficacy of human creativity to the transcendental spheres. Human beings are summoned to become partners with God in the work of creation in the here and now rather than in the higher regions of Being. This task, though encompassing all facets of life, first of all applies to the *creation* of the individual personality. "The most fundamental principle of all is that man must create himself. It is this idea that Judaism introduced into the world."[45]

One can hear in Rav Soloveitchik's existentialist approach the echoes of Kierkegaard, Jaspers, Heidegger, and Sartre, who all stressed that the human self is never finished but forever a work in progress. But the Rav himself pointed out that the notion of self-creation was already anticipated by Maimonides when he extended the notion of freedom of the will beyond what is regarded as the ethical sphere to include the attainment of intellectual virtues.[46]

The far-reaching ramifications of the Rav's existentialist conception of self-creation are best expressed in his own words.

> God wills man to be a creator – his first job is to create himself as a complete being…. Man comes into our world as a hylic, amorphous being. He is created in the image of God, but this image is a challenge to be met, not a gratuitous gift. It is up to him to objectify himself, to impress form upon a latent personality, and to move from the hylic, silent personality towards the center of objective reality. The highest norm in our moral code is to be, in a total sense… and to move toward… real, true being.[47]

In his *Halakhic Man,* the Rav enumerates a number of areas that make it necessary to view self-creation as a halakhic postulate. "The Halakhah introduced the concept of creation… into both the commandment of repentance and the fundamental principles of providence, prophecy and choice."[48]

To the Rav, the Jewish view of repentance is not salvation-centered. Unlike non-Jewish conceptions, the focus is not upon forgiveness. The

---

[45] *Halakhic Man,* 62.

[46] *ibid.,* 136.

[47] Joseph B. Soloveitchik, "Redemption, Prayer, Talmud Torah." *Tradition* (Spring 1978): 64.

[48] *Halakhic Man,* 110.

primary objective is self-creation rather than atonement. "Man, through repentance, creates himself, his own I."[49] This concept of repentance, which presupposes freedom of choice, runs counter to the basic tenets of psychological determinism. The radical transformation of the human personality demands a "creative gesture... which cannot be reconciled with the scientific concept of causality."[50] As formulated by the Rav, repentance entails that "man is free to create himself as a man of God; he has the ability to shatter the iron bars of universality and strict causality that imprison him *qua* man as a random sample of the species."[51]

Maimonides's formulation of the belief in divine Providence is also invoked by the Rav in support of the centrality of creativity in the Jewish scale of values. According to Maimonides, most sub-lunar creatures are subject only to general Providence governing the species.[52] Human beings alone may become worthy of attaining the exalted status of authentic individuals, who merit becoming subject to the exercise of individual Providence.[53] It is completely up to human beings whether they actualize their potentiality of rising above the level of being merely members of the human species by achieving a truly individual existence, manifesting itself in the attainment of individual Providence and immortality.[54]

Man, in one respect, is a mere random example of the biological species... an image of the universal, a shadow of true existence. In another respect, he is the man of God, possessor of an individual existence.... The former is characterized by passivity, the latter by activity and creation.... Action and creation are the true distinguishing marks of authentic existence.[55]

Thus, for Rav Soloveitchik, belief in the exercise of individual Providence ceases to be a mere article of faith – a purely theoretical metaphysical tenet. In keeping with his Kantian orientation, the dogma is

---

49 *ibid.*, 113.
50 *ibid.*, 116.
51 *ibid.*, 134.
52 *Guide* 3:17.
53 *Halakhic Man*, 144.
54 *ibid.*, 124–125.
55 *ibid.*, 125.

converted into a spiritual obligation[56] which, in turn, is defined in existentialist terms. Man's task is to choose between two forms of existence.

He may, like individuals of all other species, exist in the realm of images and shadows, or he may exist as an individual who is not part of the universal and who proves worthy of a fixed, established existence.... Species man or man of God, this is the alternative which the Almighty placed before man.[57]

The emphasis upon creativity goes hand in hand with the Halakhah's affirmation of uniqueness, particularity, and individuality. This represents the very antithesis of the basic thrust of Greek philosophy, which "had no room for the creative act. In its stead it posited an ever-unfolding, necessary concatenation of events."[58] Their preference for necessity over spontaneity led the Greeks to extol universality (be it in the Platonic Idea or the Aristotelian Form), while relegating the realm of the particular to a lower ontological status (Matter). However, the Rav's existentialist approach ascribes the superior ontological status of man over all other creatures to the capacity for the imitation of God through the creation of a truly individual self. "The realm of the universal exists from the very beginning of creation, the realm of the particular is created by man himself."[59]

Rav Soloveitchik invokes Maimonides's views on prophecy as additional evidence for his thesis that Judaism regards the imitation of divine creativity as one of its highest ideals.

> When a person reaches the ultimate peak, prophecy, he has fulfilled his task as a creator.... He will understand that he is not the same as he had been... as is said of Saul, "And thou shalt prophesy with them, and shalt be turned into another man."[60]

It is important to point out that for Maimonides, prophecy is not a gratuitous gift conferred by divine grace upon some individuals but an intellectual-moral-spiritual achievement. Although God may withhold the gift of prophecy even from deserving individuals, to become *worthy* of prophecy through the attainment of the requisite moral and intellectual

---

[56] *ibid.*, 128.
[57] *ibid.*, 125.
[58] *ibid.*, 133.
[59] *ibid.*, 134.
[60] *ibid.*, 130.

perfection represents the highest ideal which every individual should pursue. This explains why the subject of prophecy is discussed in his "Eight Chapters," the introduction to Tractate *Avot,* which is devoted to an analysis of ethical issues.

Although the ancient Greeks also had a concept of prophecy (as a purely naturalistic phenomenon) that represented it as the highest level of human personality development, it could not function as an ethical ideal. Their aversion to the notion of the radical novelty underlying the conception of creation prevented them from accepting "the new principle which Judaism brought to light – namely, prophecy as a binding ethical ideal, prophecy as an act of self-creation and renewal."[61]

Because the Rav rejected quietism and pietism, he expanded the mandate of imitating the Creator far beyond the parameters established by Rabbi Hayyim. The latter, influenced by Kabbalistic categories, limited human creativity to the creation of spiritual values, which affect the relationship of God to his world and are instrumental in helping bring about the reunification of the Holy One, blessed be He and His Shekhinah. The Rav, however, derived from the verse "God created man in His image" the mandate that human beings use their creative talents for the conquest of nature. Incidentally, this interpretation does more justice to the context of the verse, which deals with the exercise of dominion over other creatures. In the Rav's view, human beings are charged with responsibility for the world. When human beings engage in efforts to harness the forces of nature to advance human welfare, they are not merely performing a purely secular activity. They are carrying out the God-given task of becoming partners with Him in completing the work of creation. The Rav emphasizes that the creation of the world on the part of God was not merely a manifestation of His power, but represented a moral activity that man is supposed to emulate.

This conception enabled the Rav to give his enthusiastic endorsement to various scientific and technological activities designed to improve the material conditions of humanity in the struggle against a hostile environment. For him, such activities are not manifestations of hubris but rather the fulfillment of a divine mandate to conquer the earth. There are no echoes of the Promethean myth in Judaism.[62] On the contrary, as bearers of

---

[61] *ibid.,* 134.

[62] See my book, *Ethics of Responsibility,* 105.

the image of God, human beings possess dignity and are supposed to imitate the divine Creator by subduing the earth and harnessing the forces of nature for the benefit of humanity. In support of this view he cites the verse "You have crowned him with glory and honor, You made him to have dominion over the works of your hands."[63] Dignity was equated by the Psalmist with man's capability of dominating his environment and exercising control over it. Man acquires dignity through glory, through his *majestic* posture vis-à-vis his environment. The brute's existence is an undignified one "because it is a helpless existence.... Dignity is unobtainable as long as man has not reclaimed himself from co-existence with nature and has not risen from a non-reflective, degradingly helpless instinctive life to an intelligent, planned and majestic one."[64]

In contrast with many modern existentialists who bemoan the dehumanizing effects of our technological culture, the Rav regards mastery over nature as an indispensable source of human dignity. The more control man exercises over nature, the more dignity he obtains. "Dignity of man expressing itself in the awareness of being responsible and of being capable of discharging his responsibility cannot be realized as long as he has not gained mastery over his environment."[65]

As bearers of the image of God, human beings are mandated to imitate God, who is described as *Melekh ha-kavod*[66] ("the King of dignity").[67] Hence, Halakhah stipulates that we respect *kevod ha-beriot in* our own person as well as in others. Self-debasement is frowned upon because each human being has a unique mission in helping perfect the work of creation.[68]

The importance that the Rav attached to *imitatio Dei* by creative activities in subduing nature can be gauged by the fact that he used this idea to account for the existence of suffering and evil. In his opinion, God left the world in an unfinished state because He wanted to entrust man with the

---

[63] Rabbi Joseph B. Soloveitchik, *Yemei Zikaron,* translated from Yiddish by Mosheh Kroneh, Jerusalem, Department of Torah Education and Culture in the Diaspora, 5746, 9.

[64] "The Lonely Man of Faith," *Tradition* 7/2 (Summer 1965): 13–14.

[65] *ibid.,* 14.

[66] Psalm 24:8–10.

[67] Psalm 24:8 and 9–10.

[68] *Yemei Zikaron,* 9–21.

mission of completing the task he had begun during the six days of Creation.[69]

An important caveat must be mentioned here. The Rav does not attempt to offer any kind of theodicy. Embracing the basic tenets of the Kantian epistemology, he maintains that human reason is not equipped to tackle metaphysical issues. The Rav's position must not be misconstrued as purporting to provide a theoretical explanation for the existence of evil in the world. His concern is *practical.* Evil must be confronted, not understood. Our mission is to *respond* to evil by seeking to overcome it through responsible human creative action, fighting disease, misery, injustice, oppression, etc.,[70] as well as using personal suffering as a prod to eliminate our personality defects and blemishes in order to attain spiritual regeneration.[71]

For all the importance assigned to human activity as a mode of *imitatio Dei,* there is another dimension as well. The ontological condition of human beings mandates that they operate within both the "majestic community," striving for victory over a hostile environment, and the "covenantal community," in which they humbly acknowledge the inadequacy of all their efforts to create a world of meaning and purpose. Unlike Adam I, who seeks dignity through control over his environment, Adam II yearns for redemption through self-surrender and self-sacrifice. The dialectical tension between the requirements of Adam I (man of majesty = dignity) and Adam II (the man of faith) is not due to the contingencies of historical developments but necessarily arises from the very nature of human beings.

It is this dialectical tension that mandates the balancing of *hesed* and *emet.* In the Rav's interpretation, *hesed* calls for involvement in the world to transform it and create conditions conducive to human welfare. *Emet,* on the other hand, refers to the eternal values of the covenantal community, which transcend the world of temporal flux, and which alone can provide us with a sense of meaning and purpose and enable to us to overcome the existential loneliness characterizing the human condition.[72] Since, according to halakhic

---

[69] *Halakhic Man,* 101–105; *Yemei Zikaron,* 86–88.

[70] *ibid.,* 90–95; *Halakhic Man,* 105–109.

[71] *"Kol Dodi Dofek": Divrei Hagut ve-Ha'arakhah.* Jerusalem: World Zionist Organization, 5742, 9–19; *Halakhic Man,* 99–107.

[72] Rabbi Joseph B. Soloveitchik, *Hamesh derashot,* translated by David Telmer, Jerusalem, Tal Orot, 5734, 80–81.

Judaism, it is our task to seek to encounter God's Presence primarily in the lower realms of being *(ikkar Shekhinah ba-tachtonim)*, we must not escape from this world by a flight into transcendental spheres. The human task is to create an abode for God in the here-and-now.

The dialectical role has been assigned to man by God... who wants the man of faith to oscillate between the faith community and the community of majesty, between being confronted by God in the cosmos and the intimate, immediate apprehension of God through the covenant.[73]

The schism within man gives rise to two distinct moralities: a morality of victory and a morality of defeat. On the one hand, in imitation of divine kingship "Man is summoned by God to be a ruler... to be victorious."[74] On the other hand, Judaism mandates an "ethic of retreat or withdrawal," demanding at times humble submission and acceptance of defeat precisely in areas that matter most to the individual.[75] But the Rav emphasizes that this ethics of humility[76] is no less grounded in *imitatio Dei* than the ethics of majesty. It, too, constitutes the imitation of the Creator, because, according to the Lurianic doctrine of *tzimtzum,* God, as it were, contracted Himself and retreated in order to make possible the existence of a finite world.[77]

The adoption of a two-tiered system of ethics,[78] which responds to the requirements of an irreducible dialectical tension between two aspects of the nature of man, also enables the Rav to shed new light on the Maimonidean conception of the middle road. Hermann Cohen had contended that the ethics of the middle road is a "survival" of the Aristotelian elements, which do not really fit into the Maimonidean ethical system. Although the Rav mostly accepted Cohen's overall approach concerning the Platonic influences upon Maimonidean ethics, he insisted that the middle road represents not a eudaemonistic ethics of compromise but rather a

---

[73] "The Lonely Man of Faith," 54–55. For an especially poignant description of the dialectical tension, see "Majesty and Humility," 25–28.

[74] "Majesty arid Humility," *Tradition* 17:2 (1978): 133.

[75] "Catharsis," *Tradition* 17:2 (1978): 43–44.

[76] In his work *Tomer Devorah*, Cordovero developed an ethics of humility based upon the imitation of divine attributes. See my *Ethics of Responsibility,* 84.

[77] "Majesty and Humility," 35.

[78] See my essay, "The Maimonidean Matrix of Rabbi Joseph B. Soloveitchik's Two-Tiered Ethics," in *Through the Sound of Many Voices: Writings Contributed on the Occasion of the Seventieth Birthday of W. Gunther Plaut,* edited by Jonathan V. Plaut, Toronto. Lester and Orpen Dennys, 1982, 172–183 (page 161 in this volume).

theocentric ethics of *imitatio Dei*. For the Rav, the ethics of the middle road is not at all a concession to the Greek ideal of reaching the balance required by human nature if we are to attain a state of equilibrium through the avoidance of extremes. Instead, it is based upon the mandate to synthesize the polar qualities that were manifested by the Creator of the universe.

The need to accommodate polar values explains why ethical ambiguities and dilemmas are inescapable. There are no formal criteria enabling us to determine whether a particular situation calls for all ethics of majesty or for an ethics of humility. This is one of the major reasons why the Rav insisted that ethical dilemmas cannot be resolved simply by recourse to formal rules, and that we, therefore, have no choice but to rely upon intuitions for ethical guidance.

It was the requirement to respond to divergent and even polar values that accounted for the Rav's espousal of moderation. In public lectures he often referred to Rabbi Yohanan ben Zakkai's state of mind before his death.[79] Why was he, of all people, so apprehensive? The Rav attributed Rabbi Yohanan's anxiety to his lack of the self-assurance that the extremist enjoys. Because of his moderation, he questioned his place in Jewish history. Perhaps Rabbi Akiva was right in ridiculing Rabbi Yohanan's minimalist approach. Should he not have seized the moment and pleaded for Jerusalem rather than merely requesting Yavneh and its scholars? But it might also been possible that a maximalist approach would have resulted in catastrophe. Vespasian, who readily granted the request for Yavneh, might have balked at ceding Jerusalem, and all would have been lost. This, according to Rav Soloveitchik, illustrates the predicament of the moderate individual. Because he perceives the complexities and intricacies of issues, he must forgo the satisfaction of dogmatic certainty that the extremist obtains.

The preeminence of *imitatio Dei* in the Rav's philosophy is not merely due to the wide-ranging implications of this norm for human conduct. A unique qualitative feature also distinguishes *imitatio Dei* from other mitzvot. Where most mitzvot presuppose only the willingness to submit to a divine command, *imitatio Dei* represents a higher level of religious progress.

---

[79] *Hamesh Derashot*, 33–34.

The Rav emphasizes that religious faith cannot originate in "man's creative cultural gesture… but as something given to man when… overpowered by God."[80]

The sense of compulsion that overtakes human beings in the initial phase of the faith encounter manifests itself in the unconditional obedience to halakhic norms. As the Rav depicts religious development in his "U-vikashtem," it is at this stage that, overcome by the Presence of God, human beings feel constrained to submit to His will. It is the fear of God that prompts individuals to surrender to the heteronymous command of God.

But from this stage of total surrender, one may proceed to a higher level in which a human being attains a measure of freedom through *imitatio Dei*. The performance of ethical duties represents no longer mere obedience to commandments imposed by God. Once commandments are internalized, they are no longer experienced as heteronymously imposed imperatives. Instead, at this level human beings become partners with God in the creation of the norm.[81] Notwithstanding the similarity of this conception to the Kantian doctrine of autonomy, it must be realized that, for the Rav, ethical norms are not autonomous but theonomous.[82] The ultimate source of the obligation is not the human self but reverence for the transcendent authority of God.

At this stage of religious development, man is still torn asunder, vacillating between attraction to and recoiling from God. The peak of religious perfection is only reached in *devekut* (attachment),[83] when total freedom is attained, because there is no longer any conflict between human inclinations and divine imperatives. Although the Rav's emphasis upon

---

[80] "The Lonely Man of Faith," 64.

[81] "U-vikashtem," 180–181. Cf. BT *Kiddushin* 326, *Avodah Zarah* 18b–19a.

[82] The distinction between autonomy and theonomy is adopted from Paul Tillich's *Systematic Theology*, Chicago, Chicago University Press, 1971, I:85. It is noteworthy that Judah ben Bezalel Loew also states that walking in the way of God involves not merely obedience to a divine imperative but the internalization of the norm. See *Netivot Olam, Netiv Gemilut Hasadim* and *Gur Aryeh* sub-commentary on Rashi, Exodus 20:22.

That ethical commandments should ideally not be performed simply out of obedience to God but should express our own preferences and inclinations was already maintained by Maimonides in his Mishnah Commentary, "Eight Chapters," chapter 6.

[83] "U-vikashtem," 187.

individuality is incompatible with the mystical ideal of self-obliteration in the quest for total union with God, he nonetheless maintains that at the level of *devekut* human beings become totally free because they are capable of total identification with God's will in thoughts, affections, and actions.[84]

---

[84] *ibid.,* 193–204 and 234.

ON JEWISH COMMUNITY

COOPERATION WITH NON-ORTHODOX JEWS[1]

FEW ISSUES HAVE SPLIT the Orthodox community as much as cooperation with non-Orthodox Jews. The battle lines do not necessarily follow those dividing the traditionalist and the modernist camps. All-out opposition to any kind of formal linkage with non-Orthodox religious bodies is by no means confined to circles that look askance at any incursions of modernity into the traditional value system.

Contrary to prevailing misimpressions, substantial segments of Centrist Orthodoxy, for all their receptivity and openness to modern cultural values, frown upon cooperation with "deviationist" religious movements. This should hardly be surprising. After all, Samson Raphael Hirsch, who pioneered the *Torah im Derekh Eretz* ideology in order to enable the Orthodox Jewish community to emerge from the ghetto and enter the mainstream of civilization, was by far the most ardent and articulate spokesman of Secessionist Orthodoxy. For all his progressive propensities and his enthusiasm for modern culture, science and technology, he was no less committed to a policy of total segregation from the non-Orthodox community than the arch-conservative Rabbi Moshe Sofer (the Hatam Sofer), who would not brook even the slightest deviation from the traditional lifestyle.

To be sure, cooperation with non-Orthodox religious groups is merely part of a much larger problem that in one form or another has confronted the Orthodox Jewish community ever since the Enlightenment and the

[1] *Tradition* 22:2 (Spring 1986): 33–40.

Emancipation ushered in an era of mass defections from halakhic observance, creating a situation where strict adherence to Halakhah became the exception rather than the rule within the Jewish community. Rabbi Yaakov Ettlinger, a teacher of Samson Raphael Hirsch, declared in a historic responsum that the Talmudic rulings according to which public desecrators of the Sabbath forfeit their Jewish status were longer applicable to conditions prevailing in the modern era.[2] At a time when many Jews who profess loyalty to the ideals of the Sabbath, as evidenced by their recital of the *Kiddush,* are guilty of the most serious infractions of the prohibitions against work on the Sabbath, it hardly makes sense to construe their conduct as disavowal of the belief in God as the Creator or as a deliberate act of disassociation from the Jewish community.

Other halakhic authorities went beyond this. They granted permission to non-observant Jews to help form the quorum necessary for a *minyan* and to function in the capacity of *sheliah tzibbur* leading the congregation in public worship.[3] In the trenchant formulation of Rav Kook,[4] non-observance of Halakhah in the modern era reflects not an act of separation from the Jewish community but rather uncritical conformity to the life-style prevalent in an age of assimilation.

Equally significant was the growing reliance upon a ruling of the Maharam mi-Lublin[5] who contended that unless an individual has spurned a properly administered rebuke, he must not be treated as a *rasha* (a wicked person, whom one is allowed to hate). Since nowadays it is generally taken for granted that we "are no longer qualified to rebuke sinners properly," no matter how serious their breaches of halakhic norms, individuals must be given the benefit of doubt and are entitled to the presumption that they violated Halakhah only because they were not aware of the full consequences of their conduct.[6]

---

[2] Rabbi Yaakov Ettlinger, *She'elot u-teshuvot binyan Zion. Yoreh De'ah* 23.
[3] See David Zvi Hoffman, *Melamed le-ho'il,* vol. I, 28–29. See also Rabbi Moshe Feinstein, *Iggerot Moshe,* Orah Hayyim 23.
[4] See Tzvi Yaron, *Mishnato shel ha-Rav Kook,* 340–341.
[5] *She'elot u-teshuvot Maharam mi-Lublin,* 13, See also Hafetz Hayyim, *Ahavat Hesed,* 17 and Joseph D. Epstein, *Mitzvat ha-shalom,* 330–335.
[6] For an extensive discussion of the subject see Joseph David Epstein *op. cit.,* 309–310.

While, according to some views, the obligation "to rebuke one's fellow man" applies only when our fellow man qualifies as religiously observant,[7] the more liberal opinion contends that efforts to correct the conduct of our fellow Jews are inundated even when they refuse to accept the authority of Halakhah[8] as a matter of principle, the Hazon Ish[9] extends this tolerant approach even to confirmed agnostics or atheists on the ground that various Talmudic dicta governing the treatment of heretics are not relevant to contemporary conditions. Laws geared to the requirements of an age of faith cannot be automatically applied to an era of rampant skepticism, agnosticism and atheism, where even observant Jews cannot completely extricate themselves from the secular thrust of modernity.

In view of the enormous divergence of halakhic opinions concerning relationships with non-observant individuals, it should not be surprising that there have been so many sharp disagreements within the Orthodox community on the proper approach to non-Orthodox Jewry. The followers of the Hatam Sofer and of Samson Raphael Hirsch invoked the Talmudic injunctions against "association with the wicked" in support of their advocacy of total withdrawal from any Jewish communal organization that fails to commit itself unequivocally to adherence to halakhic norms. Those who rejected total segregation relied upon Seligman Ber Bamberger's opinion that as long as a united Jewish community adequately provides for the needs of the Orthodox elements, there is no need for a total break, though communal funds are also used for the support of Reform institutions.

To be sure, we detect even with the Secessionist camp considerable disagreement on the extent to which association with non-Orthodox elements is prohibited. Samson Raphael Hirsch frowned upon any association with non-Orthodox elements, even in the pursuit of philanthropic or charitable activities. On the other hand, while Rabbi Azriel Hildesheimer, the founder of the Secessionist Orthodox community of Berlin, sided with Hirsch in his controversy with Bamberger, he participated in activities of B'nai B'rith and various other social organizations comprised

---

[7] *She'elot u-Teshuvot Maharam Schick, Orah Hayyim,* no. 303.

[8] Joseph David Epstein, *ibid.*

[9] Hazon Ish, *Yoreh De'ah* 2, 16, and 21. However, it should be noted that the Chafetz Chaim dissented from this opinion. For a critique of the latter's position see Tzvi Yehudah Kook, *Ha-Torah ha-go'elet,* vol. 2, 296–300.

largely of non-Orthodox Jews. Moreover, Hildesheimer did not sever relations with his disciple Marcus Horowitz even when the latter disregarded his teacher's advice and assumed the position of rabbi of the non-Secessionist Orthodox community of Frankfurt, which was established over Rabbi Hirsch's protests.

It is highly revealing that the Orthodox communities of Poland, Russia and the Baltic countries were so averse to the approaches of German and Hungarian Orthodoxy that even the establishment of secular schools maintained by the general Jewish community did not precipitate agitation for secession.[10] Apparently, most of the Eastern European Jewish community harbored no illusions that membership in the Jewish community could be equated with affiliation with a religious denomination. They recognized that Jewishness was not simply a matter of professing a particular creed, but contained national and ethnic components. The conflicting perceptions of the nature of Jewish identity are illustrated by a conversation related by Rabbi Joseph B. Soloveitchik in his *Hamesh Derashot*.[11] When a well-known German rabbi asked the Rav, "What do I have in common with non-religious Polish Jews?" the Rav pointedly replied, "Hitler!"

Judaism is not merely a community of faith, but one of fate. One cannot do justice to the nature of Jewish identity without taking into account the two-dimensional covenantal character of Judaism that includes the Covenant of Abraham as well as the Covenant of Sinai. Whereas the latter involves a theological commitment to Torah, the former is formed by the awareness of a common fate and destiny. It is the Covenant of Abraham that engenders a sense of solidarity and kinship with all Jews. No matter how far an individual may have strayed from the fold, he is still regarded as a Jew.[12]

An interesting paradigm of this approach is provided by an incident involving Hayyim of Brisk. As the Rav reports it, his grandfather once appealed before *Kol Nidrei* to the Jewish community to desecrate Yom Kippur and bring to the synagogue the money needed to save an atheist – a member of the Bund – from execution by the Russian authorities.

Although Russian, Polish and Lithuanian Jewry eschewed Secessionism, the emergence of the Hovevei Zion and subsequently of the Zionist movement made it necessary to come to grips with the problem of

---

[10] See Rabbi Naftali Tzvi Yehudah Berlin, *She'elot u-teshuvot Meshiv Davar*, 44.
[11] Rabbi Joseph B. Soloveitchik, *Hamesh Derashot*, 94.
[12] BT *Sanhedrin* 44a.

cooperation with the non-Orthodox. Was it permissible to participate with avowedly secular Jews even for the fulfillment of a mitzvah such as *yishuv Eretz Yisrael*? Might affiliation with the Zionist movement represent not only a breach of the prohibition against "association with the wicked," but also the legitimation of an ideology that conflicts with the basic tenets of halakhic Judaism? After all, a secular definition of Jewish nationalism was incompatible with the belief in the Covenantal character of Jewish peoplehood.[13]

Of course, there were other reasons why Zionism evoked opposition in the Orthodox community. Some circles were totally committed to a quietistic, pietistic ideology that frowned upon any attempt to bring out radical change in the socio-political conditions of the Jewish people. They looked upon any effort to ease the plight of the Jewish people through the establishment of a national homeland as a violation of the religious injunction against "forcing the end." In this view, it is improper for Jews to take matters into their own hands. Instead, they are supposed to wait passively until the unfolding of a totally supernatural process of redemption that can be hastened only through prayer, repentance, and the performance of mitzvot.

It should be borne in mind that certain segments of the Orthodox communities were so much under the spell of quietism that they even frowned upon intervention with governmental authorities for the purpose of securing political rights for Jews in the Diaspora. The leadership of the Orthodox community of Hungary was so ultra-conservative that it opposed all efforts aiming to improve the socio-political status of Hungarian Jewry by political means!

Much of the Orthodox community did not share this attitude and welcomed efforts intended to ease the plight of the Jewish community. Nevertheless, they refused to align themselves with Zionism lest they transgress the injunction against "association with the wicked."

However, Mizrachi circles disagreed, contending that it was perfectly legitimate to join secular elements in the pursuit of what were in effect religiously desirable objectives such as the settlement of Eretz Yisrael. Rav Kook went even farther. Refusing to dismiss secular Zionism as totally

---

[13] For an extremely useful historic survey, see Charles S. Liebman and Eliezer Dan Yehiya, *Religion and Politics in Israel*, 57–78.

devoid of religious significance, he regarded it as phase of an incipient process of *teshuva*. As far as he was concerned, for all its shortcomings, the inadequate and defective formulation of secular Zionism constituted an important advance over the assimilationist ideologies that were designed to strip Judaism of its nationalistic elements and reduce it to a mere religious denomination. We need only recall the *Judenrein* name adopted by one of the most prominent German Jewish organizations – the Central Association of Germans of the *Mosaic* Faith (author's italics)! – in order to realize the extent to which large segments of Jews desperately struggled to remove the last vestiges of Jewish ethnic self-identification and to define themselves purely in terms of a religious creed.

Since for more than a century the Orthodox camp has been split on the issue of cooperation with the non-Orthodox, it is hardly surprising that in recent years the upsurge of fundamentalism throughout the world has exacerbated the conflicts within American Jewish community. This is especially true in light of the influx of Orthodox elements from countries where refusal to cooperate with non-Orthodox elements has been regarded as the acid test of true loyalty to Judaism.[14]

The failure to perceive the radical difference between the socio-religious climate of the United States and that of pre-War Europe has resulted in a situation in which the issue has become so emotionally charged that it has ceased to be a subject of rational debate. Regrettably, slogans and epitaphs have replaced intelligent discourse and argument. Proponents of "separatism" are maligned for their alleged lack of concern and love for their fellow Jews, while advocates of cooperation are denounced for legitimizing deviations from Halakhah.

A more rational analysis would show that since the entire intramural dispute is conducted within parameters agreed upon by all Orthodox groups, the various charges and countercharges are totally unwarranted. On the one hand, no one challenges the irrevocability of Jewish identity. By now, Rashi's ruling that even an outright heretic retains his Jewish status is universally accepted. On the other hand, all segments of Orthodoxy refuse to legitimize "deviationist" (i.e., non-halakhic) approaches to Judaism. There is complete unanimity that all Jews are subject to the commanding authority of the

---

[14] See Abraham Weinfeld, *Sefer She'elot u-Teshuvot Lev Avraham*, 142. Those who disagree with his view are branded *ra banim* instead of *rabbanim*.

Halakhah. Hence, what divides the Orthodox camp are not so much matters of principle or ideology but conflicting perceptions of the requirements of the contemporary situation.

Those opposing participation in umbrella groups containing non-Orthodox religious representation contend that joint activity is bound to be misconstrued as tacit recognition of the validity of non-Orthodox approaches to Judaism (a concern, which, it must be admitted, ought to weigh especially heavily upon us at a time when "religious pluralism" is so much in vogue).

This policy of separatism is pursued with various degrees of stringency. Agudath Israel goes so far as to refuse to join even coordinating groups such as the President's Conference of Major Jewish Organizations even though it limits itself to representing the Jewish community on matters involving the State of Israel or the protection of Jewish interests in the international arena. Others are prepared to cooperate with secular bodies, but not with religious ones. It is for this reason that the famous *issur* issued by a number of leading Roshei Yeshiva concerned only membership in inter-denominational boards of rabbis or in the Synagogue Council of America, but did not include other groups where non-Orthodox rabbinic bodies or congregational groups were represented together with Jewish secular organizations.

Of course, one may wonder why the Armed Services Commission of the Jewish Welfare Board or various other agencies which assign both Orthodox and non-Orthodox rabbis as chaplains to various institutions should not also come within the scope of the *issur*. In all probability, the Synagogue Council of America and the various Boards of Rabbis have become the favorite targets because of their symbolic significance.

Contrary to this position, the advocates of continued membership in these umbrella organizations claim that cooperation on matters of common concern has nothing to do with legitimation of the non-halakhic ideologies. In a pluralistic society, we must build coalitions with all kinds of groups that espouse all types of belief in order to attain various objectives of common interest. Against the background of the "open society" which has exacted such a heavy toll in terms of loyalty and attachment to the Jewish people, the overriding concern of the Orthodox community should be the large segments of Jews who are on the verge of losing the last vestiges of Jewish self-identification. Under such emergency conditions, highest priority must be accorded to the preservation of the Jewish community and to an all-out effort to mobilize its combined resources in the battle against total assimilation. Moreover, since the economic and political support of American Jewry is so vital to the State of Israel, any split in the Jewish community is detrimental to Israel's interest.

It can also be demonstrated that in eschewing isolation, Orthodoxy has not only made important contributions to the total Jewish community but has advanced its own interests. There can be little doubt that in recent years, Orthodoxy has been able to exert considerable influence upon the policies of the Jewish community far in excess of its proportionate numerical strength. That some of the most prestigious Jewish organizations, in marked contrast to the past, now have relatively large numbers of Orthodox professionals on their staffs is evidence of the merits of the non-exclusive approach.

In light of these developments it can be plausibly argued – and this still seems to be the dominant view within circles close to the Rabbinical Council of America and the Union of Orthodox Jewish Congregations of America – that it would be counter-productive for Orthodoxy to retreat into a self-enclosed ghetto and to forego the many opportunities of bringing an Orthodox perspective to bear upon the formation of policies for the Jewish community. It must be realized that current conditions are completely different from what they were when Samson Raphael Hirsch found it necessary to establish "Secessionist Orthodoxy." At that time, Reform saw Orthodoxy as its arch-enemy: a benighted relic of the past that blocked the road to progress. Yet today, Orthodoxy's vitality and dynamism command respect throughout the Jewish world. Strategies suitable for times when Orthodoxy was the target of derision are not necessarily appropriate for our generation, when the basic problem confronting all of Jewry is how to maintain a viable community amidst the blandishments of the secular "open society." With the resurgence of Orthodoxy on the American scene, there is no longer any need for the siege mentality that was appropriate in the era when Orthodoxy was widely perceived as a moribund sect doomed to extinction.

Orthodoxy's renewed buoyancy and vigor warrant self-confidence and optimism, but not a spirit of triumphalism. The mass defections from Conservative and Reform Judaism should fill us with sadness. We must realize that the bulk of those who abandon Reform or Conservative Judaism do not become *ba'alei teshuvah,* but instead end up with no ties to the Jewish community at all. Therefore, we should cooperate with Jews of all persuasions in a massive effort to resist the tidal wave of assimilation. After all, it is easier to win back to halakhic observance Jews who retain awareness of the religious significance of Jewish self-identification than those to whom Judaism has become totally irrelevant. The risk that participation in interdenominational groups may be misconstrued as legitimation of non-halakhic Judaism is negligible when compared with the consequences of a move that would entail the loss of many opportunities to expose American Jewry to Torah perspectives.

Above all, Orthodoxy must rise above the current trends of polarization that have manifested themselves in such deep rifts within our own camp (especially in Israel, e.g., the tension between *datiim* and *Haredim*). It certainly is the height of absurdity to permit well-intentioned disagreements over matters of policy to cause such deep divisions as to preclude any form of intramural Orthodox cooperation. After all, all the branches of Orthodox share wholehearted commitment to the absolute sovereignty of Halakhah. Why should the right wing not be able to follow the example of one of the foremost leaders of German Secessionist Orthodoxy, Rabbi Azriel Hildesheimer, who continued to cooperate with his disciple even though the latter disregarded his mentor's objections and became the rabbi of the non-Secessionist Orthodox community of Frankfurt? Why cannot the right wing accept at face value the unequivocal declaration of the centrist elements who publicly insist that their participation in the Synagogue Council in no way constitutes legitimation of non-halakhic approaches?

By the same token, why should not centrist Orthodox groups recognize that right-wing ideologies in no way reflect lack of concern or love for *Kelal Yisrael*? Centrist and right wing elements have every right to disagree and to question the soundness of the judgment of their opponents, but no one has the right to question sincerity of motives. Neither side of the argument enjoys a monopoly on integrity, piety or, for that matter, on love for all Jews and commitment to *Kelal Yisrael*.

CONFRONTING THE CHALLENGE OF
THE VALUES OF MODERNITY[1]

A NUMBER OF YEARS AGO, a *ba'al teshuvah* came to my office suffering from culture shock. Hailing from a fairly affluent family and raised in a Conservative congregation, he found the transition from a Midwestern university to the atmosphere of a *ba'al teshuvah* yeshiva rather difficult. He sought my help because – so he was advised – I was "a more liberal exponent of Orthodoxy." We had a pleasant chat, I gave him some literature and invited him to come for future conversations. When he returned three weeks later, he informed me that he was terribly worried about me. He was convinced that, since I resorted to contemporary categories of thought in my conversation with him as well as in my writings, I could not possibly espouse an authentic version of traditional Judaism. In other words, the mere fact that I used contemporary terminology and embraced some of the values of modernity automatically disqualified me from offering an authentic version of Torah.

This incident reflects a widely-shared attitude that genuine commitment to Torah demands turning one's back on all values of modernity. Many years ago, Mordecai Kaplan contended that those who subscribe to the Hirschian ideology of *Torah im Derekh Eretz* deviate to such an extent from traditional Judaism that they should be dubbed "neo-Orthodox." Similarly, Professor Jacob Neusner claims in a recent book that, notwithstanding their profession

---

[1] *The Torah U-Madda Journal* 1 (1989): 104–112.

of loyalty to traditional Judaism, those elements of Orthodoxy that condone participation in modern culture practice a "selective piety" that differs radically from the kind of Judaism that held sway until the Enlightenment and the Emancipation.[2] In the opinion of these distinguished scholars, the only type of Orthodoxy which is truly authentic is that which one encounters in Meah She'arim, Williamsburg or Squaretown. For them, any form of involvement in modern culture runs counter to the insistence upon isolation from the rest of the world, which is supposedly the hallmark of traditional Judaism.

Of course, it is not surprising that this view is widely accepted. After all, it reflects the basic outlook of what is called "the yeshiva world," which insists that exposure to modernity and scientific methodology taints religious faith and interferes with the cultivation of a genuine Torah perspective. Right-wing publications such as *The Jewish Observer* repeatedly stress that the inability to guard ourselves completely against the intrusion of the corrupting influences of modernity represents one of the greatest threats to contemporary Orthodox Judaism.

One does not have to be part of the yeshiva world to take this position. Meir Kahane argued in a similar fashion that the mere fact that one subscribes to such modern values as democracy and the dignity of human beings is evidence that one has been corrupted by modernity. In his opinion, a proper Torah perspective mandates calling for the adoption of *ma'amarei Hazal*. He, of course, arrived at his extreme views, which purport to represent authentic Judaism, by a process – to borrow Walter Kaufmann's expression – of "theological gerrymandering," which conveniently ignores whatever rabbinic sources differ with his own position. But what matters for our purposes is that Kahane insists that to be considered an authentic Jew, one must totally reject the entire value system of modernity.

Significantly, the term "modernity" is no longer fashionable in religious circles. Years ago, we referred to ourselves as "modern Orthodox." Today, we prefer the label "centrist" because the term "modern" evokes negative reactions, while the term "centrist" is safer. In the political arena, every one wants to be in the center because that is the position with the greatest electoral appeal. But even "centrist" Orthodoxy has become suspect. In many circles, there is a great desire for the "Amishization" of Judaism.

---

[2] See J. Neusner, *Death and Birth of Judaism.* New York: 1987, Chapter 3.

To be sure, unlike the Amish, even the opponents of modern Orthodoxy are prepared to tolerate the use of cars, word-processors, and even microscopes. What differentiates us from right-wing Orthodoxy is our acceptance not only of technology but also the belief that we should adopt some important modern values as well. We are inclined to stress human responsibility and activity rather than the passive submission of fatalistic resignation to our condition. The secularization of modern culture has led to the emphasis upon the use of our rational faculties, human resources and energies to create instruments to improve humanity's condition. In contrast with the mentality that prevailed during the pre-modern "age of faith," which placed exclusive reliance upon God and denigrated the efficacy of human action since human fate was completely in His hands, the modern mind emphasizes man's capacity to change and improve the human condition. If you want to become healthy, you consult a doctor and do not merely recite Tehillim. To improve your standard of living, you go to work. By the same token, if you seek the improvement of the socio-economic or political condition of the Jewish people, you do not use only prayer. You engage in political action and attempt to build a Jewish state.

To be sure, the yeshiva world is so immersed in pietism that it cannot appreciate the intrinsic value of science and technology and the application of human resources towards the transformation of the world. In this world, the only thing that really counts toward achieving *tikkun ha-olam* is the study of Torah and meticulous observance of the mitzvot. Science hardly matters. As Rabbi Eliyahu Dessler expressed it so strikingly, scientific laws are irrelevant because everything depends solely upon the *rezon ha-bore*. Since God controls the laws of nature, in effect there are really no laws but only miracles.[3]

It must be realized that today, Orthodoxy contains two opposite approaches. At one extreme is the position of the Hatam Sofer that *hadash 'asur min ha-Torah* – any form of innovation, any concession to modernity, any deviation from the traditional life-style is the very antithesis of Torah. On the other extreme, we have the position of Rav Kook, who maintained that *he-hadash yitkadesh*. Embrace the new by all means, but do so selectively. Make sure that the *hadash* can be integrated within our religious perspective,

---

[3] Rabbi Eliyahu E. Dessler, *Mikhtav Eliyahu*. Bnei Brak: 1964. Vol. 1, 177–183.

not only without doing violence to that perspective but actually contributing to its enhancement.

It is not surprising that Rav Kook's teachings have been widely misrepresented because this was also the fate of many other seminal thinkers such as the Rambam, Rav Samson Raphael Hirsch and the Rav (Joseph B. Soloveitchik). The Rambam's views have been so distorted that it has been argued that his statement in the next-to-last chapter of the *Guide of the Perplexed,* in which he maintains that those who only study Halakhah but are ignorant of philosophy are like an individual who reaches only the gates of the palace but is unable to enter it, could not possibly represent the Rambam's views but must be a forgery. Moreover, in most yeshivot today, the first two chapters of the *Mishneh Torah* and all of the *Guide of the Perplexed* are totally ignored so that the real Rambam is totally forgotten in these circles.

A similar fate has befallen Rav Samson Raphael Hirsch. The absurd view is advanced that Hirsch himself did not believe that *Torah im Derekh Eretz* represented a religious ideal, but that he advocated it solely as an emergency measure (*hora'at sha'ah*) to prevent the total assimilation of German Jewry. This misrepresentation of Hirsch is largely due to the fact that several *gedolim* of Eastern Europe who were stringently opposed to any exposure to secular studies felt compelled to explain Hirsch's approach as being only a concession necessary in his time to save his German co-religionists. Yet anyone familiar with Hirsch's writings will recognize that Hirsch himself believed that his religious approach was not merely a necessary evil but rather a superior brand of piety, *le-chatchila,* not *be-diavad.* In his famous speech delivered at a celebration in honor of the German poet Schiller, he enthusiastically praised the poet for having enriched our Jewish religious consciousness by articulating the ideals of human progress, equality and dignity in such a splendid manner.[4]

Unfortunately, Rav Kook's actual views have also been completely distorted even at his own Yeshivat Merkaz HaRav. Moreover, some of the followers of Gush Emunim invoke Rav Kook's legacy to justify their chauvinistic policies in utter disregard of the universalistic and humanistic dimension of his thought.

---

[4] Rabbi Samson Raphael Hirsch, *Gesammelte Schriften* VI, 351.

Of late, Rav Soloveitchik's views have also been subjected to a similar treatment. Until a relatively short time ago, certain elements of the "yeshiva world" simply ignored the Rav because they could not condone his positive attitude towards science, technology and various other facets of modern culture. Nowadays, a different strategy is employed. It is claimed that the Rav, too, adopted a negative attitude towards modernity, but that his disciples misrepresented his views. The fact that the Rav's writings reveal an openness towards modern culture matters not at all to those who advocate this revisionist approach, which does violence to the Rav's basic *weltanschauung*.

It seems to me that these revisionist tendencies are in large measure attributed to an insistence upon a monolithic approach to Judaism and the refusal to legitimize any form of pluralism, even though throughout Jewish history the traditional Jewish community condoned a variety of divergent approaches. I for one maintain that Halakhah is capable of accommodating various approaches which represent equally valid versions of the tradition. Without seeking to delegitimize any expression of halakhic Judaism, I personally prefer those readings of our halakhic tradition that seek to confront modernity rather than dismiss it.

It is interesting to compare the Rav's stance towards involvement in the culture of the world and his attitude towards technological progress with that of his ancestor, Rav Hayyim of Volozhin. Significantly, both attach great significance to the fact that the Torah begins with *Bereshit*. Both emphasize that this points to the need for man to emulate divine creativity. But for Rabbi Hayyim the kind of human creativity that is required is confined to the development of spiritual realms through the study of Torah and the meticulous observance of mitzvot. In his Ruach Hayyim, Rabbi Hayyim resorts to purely Kabbalistic categories for his definition of creativity. The Rav, however, defines the human task of creativity in keeping with the modern emphasis upon the use of science and technology to carry out the Biblical mandate of *ve-khivshuhah*.[5]

We can thus note two different conceptions of the human task based upon different interpretations of the rabbinic statement, "Since the day of the destruction of the Holy Temple, The Holy One Blessed be He has

---

[5] See for example, Rabbi Joseph B. Soloveitchik, "The Lonely Man of Faith," *Tradition* 7 (1965): 5–67.

nowhere to reside other than the four cubits of Halakhah" (*Berakhot* 8a). One can adopt Rabbi Hayyim's view and maintain that the study of Halakhah in the narrow sense of the term is the only intrinsically valuable activity. As he explains in his Ruach Hayyim, even such a question as "What is the proper way that man should choose?" is really not to be pondered in the *bet ha-midrash*. It is only when one is outside the *bet ha-midrash* that such a question should be entertained. The Rambam, on the other hand, defines the "four cubits of Halakhah" in much broader terms. In his view, it refers to the entire range of human conduct and not merely to the relatively narrow area circumscribed by formal Halakhah.

I am inclined to think that Rabbi Hayyim's narrow definition was largely prompted by his anti-Hasidic polemic. It was in a sense an overreaction to the Hasidic denigration of the value of halakhic learning that resulted from its focus upon the subjective personal experience of communion with God and the ensuing relative indifference to formal halakhic study. It must be borne in mind that Rabbi Hayyim's mentor, the Vilna Gaon, did not share such a negative attitude towards non-halakhic subjects. After all, the Gaon is quoted by one of his students as having said, "To the extent that a person lacks knowledge in other wisdoms, he will lack one-hundredfold in his knowledge of Torah. *Hokhmah* – wisdom – is required in order to understand Torah, for the Torah and wisdom are intertwined and must be studied together."[6] It is therefore quite apparent that his student rejected this more open approach to *hokhmah* only as a response to the specific historical reality that he confronted – i.e., Hasidut.

The need for familiarity with science and technology becomes obvious when we realize the demands of a universally acknowledged mitzvah: medicine. A ben-Torah who is a doctor would not be allowed to say, "I only practice Talmudic medicine and reject the medical procedures developed in the modern era." It is commonly accepted that *nishtanu ha-dorot* and that therefore one may not use the Gemara's medical prescriptions under contemporary conditions. The mitzvah of "causing to be thoroughly healed" (Exodus 21:19) can only be fulfilled through acknowledging the advances of modern technology and medicine.

I would like to go one step further. One cannot confront any contemporary halakhic problem without an understanding of today's

---

[6] See Rabbi Barukh of Shklov, *Sefer Euclidus*. The Hague: 1780, introduction.

technology. After all, the Torah is supposed to be a *Torat hayyim* – a living Torah. The story is told that when the famous Rosh Yeshiva of Kamenetz, Rav Barukh Ber Liebowitz, was asked a question about the kashrut of a chicken, he first was unable to identify the organ in question. When told it was the *kurkevan* or the innards, he instantly recalled the numerous intricate *sugyot* dealing with the problem of *mahat bi-kurkevan*. He admiringly fingered the innards exclaiming, "Is this the holy *kurkevan*?" and then turned to the dayan and said, "You make the decision."

We cannot train a whole generation of modern Jews, especially rabbanim who have to rule on technical questions, by saying to them, "We insulate ourselves; we don't have to understand any of these matters." It doesn't make sense. How can you *pasken* a *she'elah* about the use of electricity when you don't understand how electricity works? The Rav always said that he had a problem *paskening she'elot* on electricity because he did not know whether electricity should be understood in accordance with the undular theory or the quantum theory. One cannot resolve halakhah without understanding the nature of the phenomena involved.

One might argue that this only means that one must be acquainted with modern technology, using a microscope for example, providing it has nothing to do with the modern value system. But both Rabbi Samson Raphael Hirsch and Rav Kook knew that there is a great deal of positive value contained in modern attitudes of dignity, human understanding, and rationality. Rabbi Samson Raphael Hirsch went so far as to coin the term "inner revelation."[7] Obviously, where the Torah does not legislate behavior, we cannot reinterpret it if it conflicts with our modern value system. But whenever the Torah is silent, we can embrace many modern values, because that is one of the ways in which God reveals Himself.

This is not a very novel doctrine. The Meiri makes a very beautiful statement in analyzing the requirement of those present at the death of an individual to rend their garments. The Gemara explains that this is necessary because the death of a person is comparable to the burning of a sefer Torah. Just as one has to perform *kri'ah* when witnessing the burning of a sefer Torah, so too must one do this act when in the presence of the death of a human being.[8] The Meiri explains that just as a sefer Torah teaches us many

---

[7] See I. Grunfeld's introduction to *Horeb* by Rabbi Samson Raphael Hirsch (London: 1968).

[8] BT *Shabbat* 105b.

laws, so too is the human heart capable of discerning and comprehending many obligations.[9] A startling statement – in a sense, a human being serves the same function as a sefer Torah? The human heart can discern a variety of obligations that are not explicitly contained in the Torah.

A corollary of this is that sensitivity to modern values enables us to reach a certain level of understanding wherein some obligations will be interpreted differently than they were before. One example of this can be found in a comment of the Maggid Mishneh on a statement in the Rambam regarding the laws of *bar mezra*. According to Halakhah, if a person has property to sell and there is someone whose property abuts his, the neighbor must be given preference. What is the source of this? The Maggid Mishneh explains: that the reason why the owner of abutting property must be given preference over other potential buyers is due to the fact that while the Torah cannot possibly contain specific rules for all possible contingencies, it includes the "elastic clause" that we do "what is right and proper." It was in response to this mandate that the Sages deemed it necessary to enact this particular law.[10]

The definition of "right and good" may change from generation to generation. In other words, religious behavior need not be totally stagnant; there can be an evolution here as well.

In commenting on the verse, "You shall be to Me a kingdom of priests and a holy nation" (Exodus 19:6), Rabbi Naftali Zevi Yehudah Berlin asks why we need such a prescription. After all, the Torah already has 613 commandments; what does this add? Why should the Torah have to command us explicitly to become a "holy nation?" He answers that it is impossible for the Torah to legislate the appropriate human relationships for all possible circumstances. Therefore, the Torah gives us a kind of "elastic clause"; in any particular situation, we must do that which is mandated by the general religious requirement of responding to the demand to form a "holy nation."[11]

Let us look at a practical example. The Torah recognizes polygamy, but it was abandoned in the Middle Ages because of the famous *takkanah* of Rabbenu Gershom Me'or ha-Golah in the tenth century. Apparently, he came to feel that under the then prevailing conditions, polygamy was no longer the proper way to treat women. Similarly, he abandoned the concept

---

[9] Meiri, ad loc.

[10] Rabbi Vidal de Tolosa, *Maggid Mishneh, Hilkhot Shekhenim* 14:5.

[11] Rabbi Naftali Zvi Yehudah Berlin, *Haamek Davar* on Exodus 19:6.

of *get be'al korhah*. The point is that new moral insights that have been developed in the world affect our Jewish religious practices.

In more recent times, when the Bais Yaakov movement started in Europe, there was tremendous opposition from the Hasidic community: how could one teach women Torah? But Bais Yaakov prevailed and today, at Stern College for Women, Gemara is already part of the curriculum. Why? Because tradition changed, and in our age it became accepted that women should be granted all kinds of cultural and educational opportunities. I would argue further that today it is wrong for a married man to say, "I'd like my wife to be totally ignorant. After all, the Gemara says the main function of the woman is to be attractive and produce a lot of children and to be weaving. I do not want her to involve herself in anything related to modernity; no books, no newspapers, and so on." Although this was acceptable five hundred years ago, women must not be treated this way in our times because they have different expectations today. And those expectations can affect *pesak* as to what constitutes appropriate behavior.

Many years ago, I gave a lecture in which I demonstrated that our attitude towards formal *pesak* cannot be completely insulated from our attitude toward the world at large. For example, if I were to ask a *she'elah* about certain halakhic issues, I would get completely different answers from Rav Aaron Lichtenstein then from the rosh yeshiva of Hevron or other right-wing yeshivot. If the issue related to returning Israeli territory for peace, Rav Lichtenstein would give a different answer from that of the chief rabbis of Israel. Why? Because exposure to various modern value systems obviously affects one's way of responding to halakhic matters.

In my opinion, exposure to modernity is also imperative in order to overcome the myopic attitude concerning the scope of Halakhah that characterizes many segments of Orthodoxy. There are many areas such as problems involving ecology, nuclear war and social justice where no clear halakhic guidelines are available. But are we supposed to be indifferent to such issues? Are we not responsible for *yishuv ha-olam*? A number of years ago, I discussed the need for religious responses in areas where no explicit halakhic guidelines are available. I described these purely subjective religious responses as "covenantal imperatives."[12] Since we regard Torah as a "living

---

[12] See my essay "Covenantal Imperatives." In G. Appel, ed., *Samuel K. Mirsky Memorial Volume* (Jerusalem, 1970), 3–12 (page 46 in this volume).

Torah," we must not pursue a policy of splendid isolation and abdicate our responsibility for the world. Rather we must respond to the entire range of human concerns in the spirit of "and all your intentions should be for the sake of heaven" and use the resources of our tradition as well as sensitivity to the needs of the age for the issues of our time.

For other formulations of this issue, see H. Soloveitchik, "Three Themes in the Sefer Hasidim," *AJS Review* I (1976), 311–25; A. Lichtenstein, "Does Jewish Tradition Recognize an Ethic Independent of Halakhah?" In *Contemporary Jewish Ethics,* edited by M.M. Kellner, 102–123. New York: 1978.

CENTRIST ORTHODOXY: IDEOLOGY OR ATMOSPHERE?[1]

Disenchantment with modernity has stimulated the resurgence of religious fundamentalism throughout the world. Its impact is felt in the tremendous political clout of the "moral majority" in the United States and the growing influence of Muslim fundamentalism not only in Iran but in most Arab countries. Defying all predictions, religious movements that until recently were relegated to marginal status or dismissed as relics of bygone eras are displaying extraordinary vigor.

In keeping with Heine's Law – "*Wie es christelt, so judelt es sich*" – (trends in the surrounding Christian culture are bound to dominate in the Jewish community), Orthodox Judaism has enormously benefited from the charge in the cultural situation. Whereas only a few decades ago "enlightened" circles considered the demise of Orthodoxy to be a foregone conclusion, today Orthodoxy commands respect as a vibrant and dynamic religious movement. Twenty years ago Milton Himmelfarb could refer to Orthodoxy as "an unknown Jewish sect." Nowadays even the pages of *Time* and *The New York Times* prominently recognize its remarkable vitality.

These developments, however, have been far from an unmixed blessing for what is nowadays dubbed "centrist Orthodoxy." The mere fact that the term "modern Orthodoxy" is no longer in vogue and has been replaced by

---

[1] *Journal of Jewish Thought*, vol. 1, Rabbinical Council of America Jubilee Issue, Jerusalem: 1981.

an expression that deliberately avoids reference to modernity speaks volumes. The older term reflected the needs of an era when the projection of an image of modernity was necessary to counter the allegation that Orthodoxy was rigid, parochial and insensitive to universal liberal values, making it irreconcilable with the march of progress. The recent shift towards conservatism has changed the picture radically. Current trends favor religious groups that hold out the promise of a safe haven offering protection against the corrosive acids of modernity.

Operating in such a climate of opinion, centrist Orthodoxy finds itself caught in the middle between two powerful opposing forces. On the one hand, its "fundamentalist" theology is scorned by those who contend that for all its façade of modernity, centrist Orthodoxy clings to pre-scientific modes of thought that do not conform to the canons of modernity. On the other hand, it does not appeal to those who – in the wake of the urban and the ecological crisis, the anxiety over the growing danger of nuclear war, and especially the impact of the Holocaust and the isolation of the State of Israel – have been turned off by modern civilization. In an understandable reaction (or perhaps overreaction) to these traumatic experiences, there is a tendency in our post-modern era to idealize approaches that eschew the blandishments of modernity and to question the authenticity of centrist Orthodoxy.

The extent to which accommodation with modernity has been discredited can be gauged by the fact that some erstwhile followers of centrist Orthodoxy have accepted a revisionist version of Samson Raphael Hirsch's views. However absurd it may strike those familiar with Hirsch's writings, it is argued that Hirsch did not envisage *Torah im Derekh Eretz* as an ideal but rather as a temporary stopgap to save German Jewry from total assimilation.

Since the encounter with modernity is viewed in many Orthodox circles as a concession rather than an intrinsic value, it is not surprising that the impression has been created that higher standards of religious commitment and fervor are found in the "real" Orthodox camp rather than among the more "moderate" segments, who are still enamored by modernity. That many *baalei teshuva* are attracted to the more extreme brands of Orthodoxy is considered as evidence that in our polarized society the demand is for an unadulterated version of Torah, not the wishy-washy compromises that are supposed to be the hallmark of centrist Orthodoxy.

The repeated attacks on its legitimacy damage the self-image of centrist Orthodoxy. The situation is aggravated because it cannot retaliate in kind. No responsible spokesman for centrist Orthodoxy can pretend that its approach enjoys a monopoly on Torah. Instead, centrist Orthodoxy must be content with the more modest claim that it, too, represents one of many valid and viable approaches to Torah.

While this relatively pluralistic stance engenders serious competitive disadvantages in an age of polarization, there are compensations in terms of long-range spiritual benefits. The need to take right-wing criticisms seriously prevents the development of self-righteous attitudes. The stinging rebukes serve as important correctives to what otherwise might turn into a one-sided reading of the imperatives of the Jewish tradition. The occasional lapses into a troublesome inferiority complex are the price paid for the willingness to grapple with the opposing views of admired charismatic leaders, even though they are frequently advanced in a tone of strident triumphalism. Because it cannot simply respond to right-wing criticism by polemics and apologetics, centrist Orthodoxy finds it necessary to subject its polemics to constant review and re-examination lest authentic Jewish values be compromised and confrontation with modernity degenerate into accommodation. To remain spiritually viable, centrist Orthodoxy must vindicate itself by demonstrating that its position reflects an authentic religious vision rather than a concession to expediency. It must offer convincing proof that spiritual excellence does not presuppose a retreat into an intellectual or spiritual ghetto. Centrist Orthodoxy can recapture its spiritual momentum only by producing models illustrating how participation in the culture, science, technology, commerce and industry of the world need not lead to lower religious standards but rather to heightened opportunities for the enhancement of Torah and its application to concrete realities.

Centrist Orthodoxy's relative openness to pluralism makes it impossible to treat it as a monolithic movement. While agreeing on the basic premise that uncompromising obedience to Halakhah is fully compatible with the encounter with modernity, profound ideological differences separate such seminal figures as Samson Raphael Hirsch, Rav Kook, or the Rav (Joseph B. Soloveitchik). Adapting Cardinal Newman's characterization of the university, one might describe centrist Orthodoxy not "as a school, or collection of schools, but an atmosphere."

Among the most divisive issues are Zionism and the State of Israel, cooperation with non-orthodox groups, non-vocational advanced secular studies, and the roles of contemporary values in determination of Orthodox policies. Yet for all the controversies within centrist Orthodoxy, it is still the case that, as a general rule, more positive attitudes on these issues are encountered in centrist rather than right-wing circles. Thus a high correlation exists between centrist ideology and Zionism. This seems eminently reasonable. After all, Zionism should appeal more to individuals who believe that religious faith calls for an encounter with the real world than to those who advocate an escape into insulated spiritual ghettos as a religious ideal. But we must avoid falling into the trap of oversimplification. It must be remembered that among the most uncompromising opponents of Zionism are the followers of Samson Raphael Hirsch, who rule out the legitimacy of a pre-Messianic Jewish state and therefore contend that any involvement with the culture of the world must be channeled through participation in the economic, political and cultural activities of the various host countries of the Jewish people.

Even more divisive are the controversies involving cooperation with non-Orthodox groups. Here again, the battle lines are cut across the various camps. As a matter of fact, Samson Raphael Hirsch, the pioneer of *Torah im Derekh Eretz*, was far more insistent on total separation from Reform than various halakhic authorities of Eastern Europe, who unequivocally opposed all attempts at acculturation. By now, however, the bulk of right-wing Orthodoxy frowns on any form of cooperation with non-Orthodox religious movements, lest such cooperation be misinterpreted as legitimization of ideologies or practices that violate halakhic norms. For all practical purposes, the issue is only alive within the circles of centrist Orthodoxy. One wing maintains that the precariousness of the Jewish condition in the modern world, the all-out effort required to halt the total disintegration of the Jewish community in the face of assimilationist pressures, as well as the constant need to show a united Jewish front in rallying support for the State of Israel and various Jewish communities threatened by anti-Semitism, make it imperative that Orthodox Jews cooperate with non-Orthodox individuals as well as organizations in the pursuit of common objectives. The other wing, however, contends that participation in umbrella organizations on the part of centrist Orthodoxy compromises its own authenticity and, in spite of all declarations to the contrary, is bound to be misrepresented as *de facto* recognition of the legitimacy of non-halakhic approaches to Judaism. But while there are some differences of opinion as to whether participation implies recognition, it must be emphasized that even the most "liberal" exponents of centrist Orthodoxy will categorically refuse to condone any deviation from Halakhah, which, as far as Orthodox Jews are concerned, constitutes the supreme standard of all normative questions.

Although the various segments comprising the Orthodox camp are united in their commitment to unconditional obedience of Halakhah, this by no means implies uniformity of opinion regarding specific issues. halakhic decision-making is not a mechanical process. Subjective factors play an important role in the selection and interpretation of the relevant halakhic data. This being the case, the ideological proclivities of a given halakhic authority are bound to intrude upon the formation of halakhic judgments. A telling illustration is provided by the wide range of opinions on the value of secular studies, which run the gamut from enthusiastic endorsement as a religious *desideratum* to outright prohibition (at least of the humanities), with reluctant acceptance for purely vocational purposes in the middle.

Of more recent vintage are halakhic controversies pertaining to the status and function assigned to women. The ideological question regarding whether and to what extent contemporary values should be taken into account in halakhic decisions determines to what extent, if any, efforts to update the position of women should be encouraged. Those who look askance at any concessions to modernity tend to oppose any kind of innovations designed to provide women a more prominent and active role. Even within centrist circles there are many staunch traditionalists who categorically reject any change in the *status quo*. Their conservatism makes them wary even of such innovations as providing opportunities for intense Talmud study for women even though such a program was launched at Yeshiva University with the explicit approval of the Rav.

Considerably more controversy has been provoked by the inauguration of women's public prayer groups and the proposal of legally binding measures to redress some of the disadvantages suffered by women in divorce proceedings. Rightist elements tend to reject any efforts to modify traditional practices or procedures, even if the changes satisfy the most stringent requirements of Halakhah. Accommodations to modernity are perceived as threats to Jewish authenticity. Unfortunately, amid the present climate of polarization, this leads to a situation that whenever centrist halakhic rulings are at variance with those of the right wing, they are branded as violations of "authentic" halakhic procedure.

However, the chasm between right-wing and centrist Orthodoxy extends far beyond the realm of specific halakhic issues. The whole is greater than the sum of its parts. The two camps are so far apart that much of the tension manifests itself in areas where halakhic disputes do not figure at all. Characteristically, right-wing Orthodoxy shies away from involvement with public-policy controversies, unless they directly affect the specific interests of the Orthodox community. Since there are no explicit halakhic rulings available to guide us on such issues as the promotion of civil rights, the protection of the environment, nuclear disarmament, etc., it would be, in their view, both irresponsible and presumptuous for Orthodox Jews to take sides solely on the basis of their own subjective moral intuitions. In their opinion, to advocate controversial policies on purely moral grounds, in addition to needlessly exposing the Jewish community to the risk of alienating important segments of public opinion betrays – so it is charged – a lack of Jewish authenticity because one allows oneself to be swayed by ideals and values derived not from distinctively Jewish teachings but from the prevailing cultural milieu.

To be sure, many exponents of centrist Orthodoxy would go along with the rightmost delineation of a proper Jewish agenda. But there is a fundamental difference. Right-wing circles object, as a matter of principle, to involvement with issues that are halachically neutral. For centrists, it is a matter not of principle but of pragmatism. They simply question the prudence of exposing a vulnerable minority such as the Jewish community to the risks associated with standing in the forefront of moral "progress," where there really is no assurance that what is perceived as morally desirable reflects Jewish categories of thought rather than merely the intellectual fads of the age.

Others in the centrist movement strenuously disagree. They maintain that the Jewish community has a religious obligation to bring its moral vision to bear on public policy. Piety does not exhaust itself in compliance with specific rules and regulations but also mandates the cultivation of moral sensitivity. It is rather revealing that the seminal thinkers of centrist Orthodoxy emphasize the religious significance of moral intuitions. Samson Raphael Hirsch referred to "inner revelation" (the progress of moral perceptions through the ages) as a source of religious truth. Rav Kook condemned the kind of piety that constructs itself to the narrow confines of mere obedience to explicit regulations as *"prosste frumkeit"* (vulgar piety). Time and again, Rav Soloveitchik dwells on the important role of moral intuitions both in the halakhic process itself and regarding ethical issues that cannot be resolved by recourse to purely halakhic reasoning.

In all fairness, however, it must be conceded that some Orthodox elements that are far removed from right-wing orientations frequently create the impression that halakhic Judaism is totally indifferent to moral issues. Meir Kahane unabashedly proclaimed utter disdain for democratic values because they are allegedly incompatible with halakhic norms. He stigmatized those who balked at his misrepresentation of the imperatives of the Jewish tradition as being so tainted by Western value systems that they were guilty of distorting Judaism. Similar charges have been made by apologists for the Jewish underground group uncovered in the mid-1980s in Judea and Samaria, and for that matter by spokesman for Gush Emunim, who castigate their opponents for attaching undue weight to modern secular values.

But for all the prominence given to these views, there is really no justification for the widely-circulated charge that Orthodoxy turns its back on the moral dimension because of its fundamentalist thrust. Even as Yeshayahu Leibowitz, who rejects all such notions that all of Judaism is completely reducible to purely halakhic norms, nevertheless grants that many ethical norms and values are actually mandated by Halakhah as *mitzvot bein adam le-havero* (commandments pertaining to human relations). In his scheme, what is expelled through the front door is re-admitted through the back door. Although moral values as such are dismissed as religiously irrelevant in Leibowitz's theocentric system, they nonetheless reappear – attired in halakhic garb – as an integral part of Jewish piety. It must be pointed out that the classic rabbinic sources already stress that the cultivation of a morally sensitive personality is part of the mitzvah "You shall walk in His ways." It therefore becomes to a certain extent merely a matter of terminology whether one advocates moral sensitivity as such or a broader definition of mitzvot as an integral part of the Orthodox platform.

However, there remains an important dispute regarding the question of whether one may legitimately draw on prevailing values to supplement halakhic formulations. To be sure, no one in the Orthodox camp, barring perhaps some totally unrepresentative leftist elements, would sanction a moral critique of a halakhic norm. Unconditional surrender to halakhic norms is *sine qua non* of an authentic Orthodox position. Since Halakhah is acknowledged as the revealed will of God, there can be no higher authority superseding it. Centrist and right-wing Orthodoxy agree that the property of "overridingness" must be assigned to Halakhah, not to the promptings of our conscience. But there is ample room for disagreement as to the extent, if any, to which moral intuitions can play a role in the halakhic process or in situations where there are no explicit halakhic rules available for guidance.

Because of its uncompromising adherence to Halakhah as the ultimate normative standard, centrist Orthodoxy is dismissed by some critics as obscurantism. They especially deplore the refusal of centrist Orthodoxy to resort to critical scholarship and scientific methodology to ascertain the meaning of Halakhah. Since for normative purposes centrist Orthodoxy deliberately confines itself to the traditional canons of interpretation, it is alleged that, for all its attempts to dress up in modern garb, it essentially adheres to the same "outmoded" value system as "fundamentalist" Orthodoxy.

There is no doubt that these critics are correct. Centrist Orthodoxy is committed to the eternal validity of the Torah. While it may look on modern scholarship as an important tool for the understanding of the Torah, its findings must be subordinated to the methods of procedure and canons of interpretation that from a halakhic perspective are acknowledged as divinely revealed and constitute the ultimate foundation of the faith commitment of the Jewish people.

RELIGIOUS ZIONISM: COMPROMISE OR IDEAL?[1]

RELIGIOUS ZIONISM HAS FALLEN on hard times. The dramatic decline of its fortunes in the face of an unprecedented resurgence of the more extreme right-wing Orthodoxy calls for *cheshbon ha-nefesh* – an agonizing reappraisal of our ideology as well as our strategy and tactics. But we cannot do justice to this task without taking account of the historic context of these developments.

The impressive gains made by the *Charedim* at the expense of the *datiim* are not isolated phenomena but reflect world-wide trends that can observed in various religious communities. A tidal wave of religious fanaticism has engulfed not only Iran and the Arab countries but, in many parts of the world, has unleashed a militant fundamentalism that rejects modernity with a vengeance. It skillfully exploits the malaise induced by profound disenchantment with the modern secular value system, which is blamed for the horrors of Auschwitz, Hiroshima and Chernobyl. The plea to return to a pre-modern approach to religious faith strikes a responsive chord within a generation that has lost its faith in human progress and that has counted and weighed science and technology and found them wanting as avenues to human fulfillment.

Jews have added grounds for disenchantment with the values of modernity. The trauma of the Holocaust, reinforced by the sordid spectacle

---

[1] From *Religious Zionism: After Forty Years of Statehood.* Edited by Shubert Spero and Yitzchak Pessin. Jerusalem: Mesilot, World Movement of Mizrachi-Hapoel Hamizrachi, 1989.

of Israel's isolation on the international scene and combined with renewed outbreaks of antisemitism in various countries, has left us with gnawing doubts about the worthwhileness of our much-vaunted Western civilization, which made possible the perpetration of crimes unequaled in human history. We have good reason to be turned off by such a culture and to turn inward. But the more we move in this direction, the more we are attracted to ideologies that categorically reject the blandishments of such a benighted civilization. Obviously, the greatest beneficiaries of this disillusionment with modern secular values are the champions of the most traditional approaches to Judaism, which claim to brook no accommodation with modernity and therefore enjoy the advantages of being perceived as the most authentic bearers of the Jewish religious tradition.

Amidst such a climate of opinion, the more moderate elements that seek some form of co-existence between Judaism and modernity face a serious handicap in the battle for the soul of the Jewish people. They are stigmatized as compromisers, guilty of distorting the Torah in order to accommodate the demands of the secular world. It is highly revealing that many people feel that *Torah im Derekh Eretz* was a *hora'at sha'ah* – an emergency measure that was legitimate only as a temporary expedient to forestall the total assimilation of German Jewry. But even many who continue to sanction exposure to modern culture do so solely for pragmatic reasons and insist that the religious ideal is represented by the "Torah world," which has managed to avoid contact with the corrosive acids of modernity.

Religious Zionism can hardly be expected to thrive in an atmosphere in which the rejection of modernity is hailed as the hallmark of religious authenticity, separating the high-grade "ultra Orthodox" from the low-grade plain Orthodox. After all, Religious Zionism can hardly claim to represent unbroken continuity with tradition.

It must be admitted that the Zionist revolution marked a radical break with the past. It is a matter of historic record that for many centuries Jewish life was completely under the spell of a quietistic pietism. It was taken for granted that the fate of the Jewish community hinged solely upon its spiritual merits and that human efforts expended in the sphere of political action were exercises in futility. Jewish suffering could come to an end only through divine intervention. The hardships and travails of the *Galut* were not caused by socio-economic or political factors but were rather punishment for sinful conduct. Hence, only spiritual regeneration (usually narrowly defined in terms of more intensive Torah study, more concentration in prayer and more meticulous performance of mitzvot) could lead to redemption. To take matters into our hands rather than to await passively the arrival of the Redeemer was denounced as heretical renunciation of faith in the Providential design of history.

When seen against this background, the advocacy of human efforts designed to bring about fundamental changes in the socio-political situation is tantamount to the adoption of a secular value system. Since the State of Israel reflects Zionist ideals that are totally incompatible with the quietistic stance that held sway in the Jewish community for many generations, anyone who attaches religious significance to such a state is viewed with suspicion. Their "sin" is compounded by the acceptance of the idols of modernity such as democracy, freedom of conscience, and so on. Because the *datiim* are accused of having made illicit concessions to modern secularism, they are branded as the spiritual inferiors of the *Charedim*, who are deemed to represent the ultimate in Orthodox commitment (witness the term ultra-Orthodox).

Even more detrimental to the self-image of modern Orthodoxy, which represents the ideological centerpiece of Religious Zionism, is the widespread belief that it does not merely permit the intrusion of non-halakhic values but that, apart from ideological differences, its adherents are much "cooler" in their religious commitment than their *Charedi* counterparts. Whether this perception is accurate, as Professors Charles S. Liebman and Eliezer Don-Yehiya contend, or not hardly matters. The mere fact that many modern Orthodox people believe it to be factually true gives rise to an inferiority complex that saps the vitality of Religious Zionism. Laxity in religious observance and lack of fervor hardly make for an attractive religious option.

To recapture its appeal to the religious imagination, Religious Zionism must shed its self-image as a movement championing compromise and moderation at the expense of passionate commitment. It can no longer afford to be perceived as a synthesis between two disparate elements, namely religion and nationalism. Instead, it must project itself as a genuinely religious movement and convincingly demonstrate that the nationalism it espouses is not of nineteenth-century vintage, but is rooted in the Torah idea of the Covenant.

In the brilliant formulation of the Rav (Rabbi Joseph B. Soloveitchik), the *Berit Avraham* (the Covenant with Abraham) mandates that we identify with every Jew and that we form a special attachment to Eretz Israel as the land of our destiny. Regardless of all differences of ideology and culture, Jews form a community of fate. Since the Torah is addressed to each and every Jew, we have no right to restrict our concern to the protection of the religious community's interests. We are charged with responsibility not merely for the preservation of isolated religious enclaves but for the creation of a society with will foster loyalty to the Torah on the part of the entire Jewish community. Our task is to transform the entire Jewish community from a community of fate into a community of faith. Hence our readiness to cooperate with non-observant Jews in the advancement of common goals such as *Yishuv ha-Aretz* and defense of the state stems not from relative indifference to religious values, but rather from the profound conviction that the advancement of the material welfare of *Kelal Yisrael* – as Rav Kook never tired of pointed out – represents not secular but truly religious concerns.

Even more vital for a healthy self image is the recognition that for all its discontinuity with some of the attitudes that predominated in the pre-Emancipation era, Religious Zionism is no less authentic than the quietism advocated by *Neturei Karta*. To be sure, during the height of Jewish powerlessness, especially in the wake of the Expulsion from Spain, Jews gravitated towards an extreme pietism. So deeply ingrained was this aversion to any form of political activism that large segments of Hungarian Orthodoxy went as far as to oppose any type of intervention or negotiation with governmental authorities for the purpose of securing more political and economic privileges for the Jewish community.

But there is little justification for the assumption that Judaism mandates total disparagement of human efforts. While containing a pietistic streak and exhorting the believer to leave some things to God, Judaism, contrary to Spinoza, Feuerbach and Marx, does not engender the kind of self-alienation which robs man of his dignity. Many Jewish authorities interpret the Torah in such a manner that religious faith leads to the responsible use of power rather than the evasion of responsibility in areas where human action could make a difference.

There is certainly no echo of the Promethean myth in the Jewish tradition. Far from representing an unwarranted intrusion into divine prerogatives, self-reliance and creativity constitute the fulfillment of the task entrusted to man. Man, who is created in the image of God, is summoned to become a co-creator with Him. In order to realize that there are Jewish authorities who place a premium upon activist involvement in the world rather than quietistic submission to harsh realities we need only remind ourselves of the enormous role assigned to *Yishuv ha-Olam* in the Maimonidean scheme or of Samson Raphael Hirsch's enthusiasm for the Emancipation on the grounds that it made possible the implementation of the *Torah im Derekh Eretz* ideal. Especially striking is the Rav's thesis that creativity in the area of science and technology is not a secular value but a religiously endorsed legitimate exercise of human dignity in keeping with the divine blessing of *ve-kivshuha*. It should also be noted that for Rav Kook, the improvement of the Jewish people's material conditions were not secular pursuits at all. They were considered an integral part of the spiritual regeneration that paved the way for the Redemption.

While Religious Zionists must overcome their debilitating religious inferiority complex and especially their readiness to settle for lower standards of religious observance, they must be wary of overreacting and claiming a monopoly on valid approaches to Torah. There is no need to delegitimize alternative perspectives. Within the framework of Torah there is ample room for pluralism. We may even see in right-wing extremism a much-needed corrective to the value structure of a basically secular culture. But we must resist attempts to discredit our religious philosophy as an accommodation or, as Professor Neusner put it in a recent book, as "selective piety." We have every right to insist that our openness to the values of modernity and our readiness to embrace some of the elements of its culture do not compromise our spiritual integrity. While the yeshiva world defines the "four cubits of Halakhah" in an extremely narrow fashion, we can invoke the Rambam's authority to justify a broader perspective and welcome whatever modern values can be harnessed in the service of our religious mandate. We have every right to maintain that we represent continuity with the tradition of Rambam, Ramban, Meiri, and so on, which can best be summed up, in the telling phrase of Samson Raphael Hirsch, as the "inner Revelation" that enhances our comprehension of the divine tasks assigned to us.

We are convinced that this kind of understanding of Torah as a *Torat Chayyim* – addressed not merely to a religious elite but to all segments of the Jewish people as a blueprint for life in the here and now – holds the greatest promise for reclaiming the loyalty of *Kelal Yisrael* to Torah. But to achieve this goal, we must pursue it not with cold detachment but with fiery commitment befitting the *esh dat*. It is up to us to demonstrate that our "moderation" reflects not lack of passion but our fervent commitment to our Torah ideals.

ON JEWISH LIFE

ALIENATION AND EXILE[1]

MUCH OF CURRENT THOUGHT revolves around the theme of alienation and estrangement, and for good reason. Modern man has been subjected to a relentless process of de-personalization in the pressure chambers of a technological society whose operations are geared to mass production and standardization. Moreover, to cope with the increasing complexities of an age of automation, ever more delicate methods of control have become necessary. Thus, paradoxically, the more control man is capable of exerting over his environment, the more he himself becomes enmeshed in a network of pressures and forces against which he feels too helpless to assert himself. Far from enhancing man's sense of importance, his spectacular technological triumphs have actually left him with a gnawing feeling of impotence. Diminished in stature, he has become a thing rather than a person, an object rather than a subject, an "it" rather than a "thou."

Small wonder, then, that in artistic, literary, and philosophical circles, one encounters steadily mounting anxiety over the fate of the individual. It has even been said that the entire existentialist movement basically represents a reaction to the sense of alienation that has gripped modern man.[2]

Concern over self-alienation is by no means a monopoly of the intellectual elite. Revolutionary mass movements such as socialism and communism derive much of their messianic fervor from the Marxian

---

[1] *Tradition* 6:2 (Spring 1964): 93–103.
[2] F.H. Heinemann, *Existentialism and the Modern Predicament*. New York: Harper Torchbooks, 1953.

ideology which held out to the disillusioned and frustrated the promise not only of a redistribution of worldly goods but of a society in which the light of a new social gospel would redeem mankind from the blight of alienation.

Other influential thinkers – both secular and religious – have indicated with varying effectiveness that our deep-rooted anxieties arise not merely out of social or economic dislocations, but also out of the spiritual condition of modern man. In this view, self-estrangement is but the final phase in the long process of disintegration that began with the erosion of the religious basis that once provided the foundation for our structure of values and ideals.

Yet not all thinkers share this aversion to alienation. Far from it! In many quarters a certain degree of alienation, instead of being viewed with apprehension as a major threat to man's humanity, is actually welcomed enthusiastically as a prerequisite to all genuine creativity. Considerable admiration is evoked by the alienated "outsider's" inability to feel at home in the universe, for this state of mind is credited with inducing the creative tensions that in turn lead to the quest for moral, spiritual, and intellectual advancement. It was perhaps on the basis of such an orientation that Matthew Arnold went so far as to define religion as a "criticism of life." What ultimately seems to matter in this view is not so much the possession of a positive, definite set of values or commitments, but rather the sense of estrangement and detachment which is engendered by a religious approach to life. Religion is singularly equipped to fulfill this function because it calls for the ability to participate in the affairs of the world with a certain sense of detachment, to immerse oneself in the currents of time while retaining the consciousness of an eternal destiny.

Any ideology that makes a virtue out of not belonging is likely to hold a special attraction for the modern Jew who even in an open and democratic society – with all its assimilationist pressures and blandishments – sooner or later experiences the frustrations of being a rejected outsider. But when one views the world from the perspective of the "outsider," the feeling of not belonging loses its sting of bitterness. An apparent curse is converted into a genuine blessing. Being Jewish – or, better, "not being a *goy*" – becomes equated with the ideal of an authentic human life: not to feel at home in the universe because one deliberately elects to remain a foreigner, refusing to become completely naturalized as a full-fledged citizen of the world.

Jewishness, in the phrase of Ben Halpern, becomes "a ticket of admission to the community of alienated intellectuals."[3]

Religiously non-observant Jewish intellectuals are especially prone to identify Judaism with such a negative stance. Intellectuals, in general, tend to be wary of specific, positive commitments. Because of their proclivity for detachment, they gravitate towards an orientation of alienation, which, as Daniel Bell put it, "guards one against being submerged in any cause, or accepting any particular embodiment of community as final."[4] It is to be expected that the Jewish intellectual will project this mentality onto his approach to Judaism. Understandably, his views on Judaism are bound to reflect the predilections of those who constitutionally seem to shy away from all positive commitments. Since the intellectual finds it so much easier to identify with a Judaism that is couched in negative terms, he is apt to define Jewishness as the negation of the pretensions of other cultures and religions.

For leading intellectuals such as Milton Konvitz,[5] Leslie Fiedler, Arthur Cohen[6] and Will Herberg,[7] it is the consciousness of living in *Galut* that emerges as the defining characteristic of being Jewish. To be a Jew is synonymous with being in exile – the experience of a sense of alienation. In the words of Leslie Fiedler, once Jews become "insiders, they cease to be Jews."[8]

There can be no doubt that the ever-present awareness of living in a state of *Galut* (both physically and metaphysically!) has etched itself deeply in the consciousness of the genuine Jewish personality. For that matter, the yearning for Messianic redemption constitutes a vital ingredient of our religious faith. We must not forget this even at the moment of gaiety and merriment. This is why at a wedding ceremony, a note of sadness is injected: a glass is broken to remind us that no joy can be complete until the dawn of the ultimate redemption. Since only "then shall our mouths be filled with laughter" (Psalms 126:2), it is not permissible nowadays to abandon oneself

---

[3] Ben Halpern, "A Theological Jew," *Jewish Frontier,* February 1964, p. 13.

[4] Daniel Bell, *The End of Ideology.* NY: Macmillan, 1962, 16, 17.

[5] Milton R. Konvitz. "Zionism: Homecoming or Homelessness?" *Judaism* (Summer 1956): 204–211.

[6] Arthur Cohen, *The Natural and The Supernatural Jew.* New York: McGraw-Hill Book Co. 1962.

[7] Will Herberg, *Judaism arid Modern Man,* New York: 1951, 275–281.

[8] *The New York Times,* June 9, 1963.

completely to unrestricted hilarity. When one is conscious of the intrinsic limitations of *Galut* existence, one cannot embrace a philosophy of "letting go" and lose oneself completely in momentary thrills. Those who yearn for ultimate redemption cannot help but maintain a certain degree of reserve and detachment – no matter how intense the satisfaction of the moment and however rewarding the immediate task at hand may be.[9]

However, one must not jump to the conclusion that Judaism basically represents a principle of negation. As Aharon Lichtenstein has already noted, purely negative definitions of Jewishness amount to distortions of the true character of the Jewish people.[10] Of course, it is true that since the days of Abraham it has been the historic destiny of the Jew to function as the *Ivri* – the one who stands in opposition to the rest of the world.[11] Indeed, a good case could be made that the Jew personified what Tillich has called the "Protestant Principle" – the refusal to absolutize the relative. Throughout history Jews have protested against the various idolatries that have held sway. Time and again they have refused to worship at the shrine of the false gods. Yet, notwithstanding some prominent theologians, there is more to Judaism than the struggle against mythology. The smashing of idols – and for that matter, the breaking of a glass – does not exhaust the meaning of Jewish existence. Judaism is not merely a classic exercise in cool, critical detachment; there is ample provision for the romance of whole-hearted "engagement" with the fiery ideals of Torah. Torah was never conceived purely as a criticism of life – it was life itself! Those who concentrate purely on the critical function of Judaism without considering adequately its positive commitments end up not with a picture, but a caricature.

One of the most interesting illustrations of the distortions that are bound to occur whenever Judaism is forced into a straitjacket of purely negative thinking is provided by Ahad ha-Am's famous description of the nature of Jewish ethics, which played such a decisive role in the making of the modern Jewish mind. It was largely due to the impact of this influential thinker that so many Jews were prepared to repeat uncritically the Christian cliché that Jewish ethics is one of justice and not of love. We should bear in mind that Ahad ha-Am adduces only very flimsy "evidence" in support of his sweeping

---

[9] BT *Berakhot* 31a; see *Tosafot ad loc.*
[10] Aharon Lichtenstein, "The Jewish Fraternity." *Judaism,* Summer 1963.
[11] *Bereshit Rabbah* 42:13.

thesis that Jewish ethics is based exclusively upon justice. His case rests on the fact that Hillel, in his classic formulation to a prospective convert, reduced the essence of Torah to the maxim: "What is hateful to you, do not do unto your neighbor." For Ahad ha-Am, it is of crucial importance that Hillel did not express the golden rule in positive terms. Why could Hillel simply not have quoted the biblical verse "Love thy neighbor as thyself" (Leviticus 19:18)? Ahad ha-Am concludes that Hillel was compelled to paraphrase the biblical verse in order to forestall misunderstanding on the part of the heathen. It had to be spelled out clearly that the Jewish interpretation of "Love thy neighbor as thyself" does not call for the cultivation of benevolence, kindness, or altruism. Love, so Ahad ha-Am contends, really does not figure in the Jewish scale of values. Insofar as Jewish ethical thinking is concerned, nothing but absolute justice truly matters.[12]

It can readily be seen that this doctrine roughly represents the equivalent of the Kantian categorical imperative. As Max Scheler[13] and others have pointed out, the Kantian scheme is essentially not a positive formulation of ethical precepts or maxims, but rather a principle of criticism, which can serve as a criterion for the *rejection* of certain attitudes or actions. The Kantian morality is not a system of *material* content, but a purely *format* principle that enables us to deny the propriety of certain types of motivation.

It could be maintained with a high degree of plausibility that Ahad ha-Am's formulation – and for that matter many other positions that reflect preoccupation with purely negative aspects of Judaism – arises out of the matrix of Kantian rather than genuinely Jewish categories of thought. Otherwise, how would it have been possible for him to gloss over such a pivotal concept as *chessed* (loving-kindness), which plays such a primary role in Jewish religious and ethical thought?[14] In view of the continued emphasis upon love in both biblical and rabbinic literature, there is not the slightest shred of evidence to support the contention that, because of its preoccupation with absolute justice, Judaism is completely indifferent to the cultivation of altruistic sentiments. What has happened to such concepts as

---

[12] Ahad ha-Am. *Essays, Letters, Memoirs.* Oxford: 1946, 130–137.

[13] Max Scheler, *Der Formalismus in der Ethik und die Materiale Wertelhik.* Halle: 1971.

[14] See David S. Shapiro, "The Concept of Chessed in Judaism." *Yavneh Studies* (Fall 1962): 27–45.

compassion and mercy, which rabbinic literature defines as the telltale mark of the few? Are we not supposed to balance justice with mercy?

It is, of course, true that without the restraint of justice, the blind application of love can lead to morally disastrous consequences. But this merely indicates that we cannot dispense with justice as a *regulative* principle, not that justice is superior to love. Notwithstanding Ahad ha-Am, who spoke of the preference of Judaism for abstract principles, there is ample room within the Jewish ethical and religious scheme for personal sympathetic involvement in the fate of one's fellow man. It is simply not correct to speak of Judaism as a cold, detached scheme that eliminates "subjective attitudes" because it is only concerned with the application of something "abstract and objective." Justice, to be sure, is essentially a negative concept; it rules out inequalities of treatment. But it is theoretically possible to devise rules of behavior which are equally bad for all parties concerned. Though satisfying the criterion of equality, they could hardly be termed just. Hence, even justice transcends considerations of equality: Moreover, it is highly questionable whether justice is the fundamental ethical concept. Kabbalistic doctrines (e.g., the primacy of *chessed* over *gevura* in the order of *sefirot*) could be cited to buttress Professor Tillich's contention that not justice, but love is primary and that justice must be defined in terms of the proper distribution of love.[15]

The claim that the essence of Judaism lies in the negation of all pretensions to finality[16] rather than in the affirmation of specific positive values may be buttressed by citing the *prima facie* kinship of this position with Maimonides's world view. After all, Maimonides did not merely formulate a "negative theology" in his "theory of attributes," but even his ethical ideal of the "middle road" appears to be primarily an attempt to negate any form of extremism. At first sight, Maimonides's advocacy of a middle course strikes one as a sort of caveat prescribed by a detached sage who views with skepticism any manifestation of unbridled radicalism. Such counsel of

---

[15] Paul Tillich, *Love, Power and Justice.* London: Oxford University Press, 1954.

[16] For a striking illustration of this position, see Leo Baeck's statement: "Absence of the supporting crutch of dogma is in the very nature of Judaism" *(The Essence of Judaism,* 16). Equally revealing is the following passage: "The price Judaism paid for the possession of a philosophy was the sacrifice of certainty, of a formula of creed" (*ibid.,* 12).

moderation may be expected from the classical philosopher who looks askance at the excesses of romanticism and warns us not to go overboard emotionally in the pursuit of any specific value.

Yet in reality, Maimonides is far from espousing a prudential morality of compromise. His views cannot be attributed to the outsider's reluctance to become completely engaged with any specific ideal or goal. Anyone who has read his moving account of love for God, which is couched in such passionate terms,[17] will be unable to label Maimonides a reserved, detached, or even disillusioned philosopher who, out of disenchantment, put the brakes on any genuine emotional involvement.[18] As a matter of fact, notwithstanding its obvious resemblance to the Aristotelian "golden mean," Maimonides's ideal of the "middle road" "does not reflect so much the classic aversion to any form of imbalance ('Nothing in excess') but a fundamental Jewish religious ideal of striving to 'walk in the ways of God.'"[19] In the Maimonidean scheme, choosing the middle road ceases to be an exercise in prudential morality; it becomes the fulfillment of a most positive religious imperative: "the imitation of God." It is to the extent that man succeeds in harmonizing polar values that he emulates his Creator; for, according to rabbinic theology, it was through the fusion of love and justice, mercy and righteousness, truth and peace, that God – both immanent and transcendent – created the universe. Thus the "middle of the road" approach as espoused by Maimonides does not at all amount to a negation of any specific value. What it does reflect is an awareness of the need for creative tension between polar values. Conceived in this fashion, the middle of the road is far from being a state of equilibrium. It is a road in the fullest sense of the term, calling for dynamic movement and engaging man's total moral and intellectual resources.

It must be noted that this creative tension, which is so indispensable to all genuine human progress, need not be induced – as so many modern

---

[17] *Hilkhot Teshuvah* 10:6.

[18] *Hilkhot Deot* 1:5.

[19] My interpretation of Maimonides's "middle road" can in some measure be attributed to my recollection of a lecture delivered by Rabbi Soloveitchik in Detroit at the 1954 convention of the Rabbinical Council of America. As I recall, Rabbi Soloveitchik demonstrated how the Kabbalistic doctrine of the *sefirot* with its emphasis upon the synthesis of *chessed* and *gevura,* or of *netzah* and *hod,* which result in the emergence of *tiferet* and *yesod* respectively, parallels Maimonides's notion that the middle road is the road of God.

intellectuals suggest – by a sense of alienation and estrangement. As Maimonides seems to imply, creative tension may have its source in the spiritual restlessness which grips those who experience a sense of genuine relatedness and commitment to God. Veering between polar values, at once drawn to God in love and recoiling from Him in fear, the righteous have ample cause for the restlessness which, as the Talmud asserts, is their eternal lot.[20]

For a proper appraisal of Maimonides's position, we must also bear in mind that, with all his emphasis upon the essentially negative character of all theology, the *Guide* concludes on an affirmative note. The ideal to which man is summoned calls not merely for purely intellectual endeavor to master the doctrine of negative attributes. The knowledge that God is Wholly Other – the very apex of the entire philosophical quest – must be counterbalanced by *imitatio Dei,* the attempt to emulate the ways of God in a relentless quest for loving-kindness, justice, and charity. Lest the consciousness of God's utter transcendence give rise to a sense of total alienation, man is bidden to pattern his conduct after the divine "attributes of action" that enable him to "walk in His ways."

It may, of course, be argued that the very ideal of holiness entails a sense of alienation from the world. The very concept of *kedushah* (holiness) denotes separation. In Talmudic language, holiness implies *geder ervah* (the limitation imposed upon the libido). The contrast between natural inclinations and holiness is stressed in Numbers 15:39, where we are admonished to submit ourselves to the discipline of the mitzvot instead of following the inclinations of our own "hearts and eyes."

Yet we are not justified in concluding that holiness stands in irreconcilable opposition to the natural. Within Judaism there is no antithesis between nature and spirit, for both are religiously neutral. It is for this reason that Judaism aims not at the suppression but the utilization of the natural in the service of the Creator, the Author of both nature and spirit. The network of the mitzvot provides a formula designed to enable man to fulfill a supernatural but not unnatural vocation. Through the performance of the mitzvot, the domain of the mundane can be hallowed and endowed with supernatural significance.

---

[20] BT *Berakhot* 64a.

The attainment of this goal is by no means an easy task. It unquestionably demands a good measure of self-control and discipline. But the further man advances in his spiritual quest, the less resistance he encounters. He may even reach the point where he can identify himself with the divine task because Torah ceases to be merely imposed from without. It is at this stage that Torah truly becomes his own – part and parcel of his very personality. At this ideal level, man becomes really free, for he is fully engaged in Torah. He is no longer merely an object manipulated by all sources of internal or external pressures. He is a subject in the fullest sense of the term, actively molding his existence in keeping with a divine purpose. Thus, in the Chabad scheme, the Tzaddik has overcome all struggle and is completely liberated from the sway of forces that restrict his inner freedom. Or, as Rabbi Kook put it, man is truly his own natural self to the extent that he is suffused with the love of God.

It should be noted that the emphasis upon estrangement, aloofness, and detachment from the world, which is so characteristic of modern Jewish thought, has largely been the result of thinkers who have emancipated themselves from the yoke of the mitzvot. Having stripped Judaism of all traditional practices and belief, they were left with only one facet of Jewish existence: the state of living in *Galut*. To be a Jew was to be different for the sake of being different. Accordingly, the *Galut* was no longer looked upon as a dismal blight. It became the highest type of Jewish existence, providing conditions where Judaism could shine in the brightest colors. It was felt that only the *Galut* could fully reveal the uniqueness of the Jewish people, a uniqueness which was defined in purely negative terms: a stance of critical non-conformity and alienation with respect to the "natural."[21] Thus, by a strange twist, the tragic necessity of the *Galut* was converted into a supreme religious virtue.

Obviously, this kind of orientation is incompatible with Halakhah-centered Jewish thought. How can the *Galut* be enthusiastically endorsed as the apex of Jewish spirituality when so many vital areas of Halakhah are inoperative in the Diaspora? *Galut* dealt a crippling blow to Jewish religious life. Gone is the opportunity to practice *mitzvot ha-teluyot ba-aretz* (mitzvot that

---

[21] Thus, for Leo Baeck, "The special task of Judaism is to express... the ethical principle of the minority... it stands for the enduring protest of those... who assert their right to be different..." (*op. cit.*, 273). See also David Riesman's "A Philosophy for 'Minority' Living." In *Individualism Reconsidered*. New York: 1955, 48–66.

can be observed only in the Land of Israel) and to fulfill the numerous laws that are applicable only under normal conditions, when the Jewish people settled in its natural habitat rallies around a central *Bet ha-Mikdash* (Temple) as the abode of the *Shekhinah*.

From the standpoint of Halakhah, the abnormal *Galut* existence is not a desideratum but a serious handicap. To be sure, Jewish piety has been able to flourish even under such adverse conditions. By the same token, even under normal conditions there loom certain dangers to the spiritual integrity of the Jew who may crave that "the house of Israel be like all the nations." The Jew possesses no natural immunity from the spiritual diseases that so frequently strike the body politic of all types of communities.

Twice in our history it became necessary for the Temple to be destroyed because the Jewish people was on the verge of completely perverting its religious ideals. But the resulting *Galut* was viewed as a punishment, not as the emergence of a higher or more rewarding form of spirituality. To overcome the alienation of the *Galut* (both in the physical and metaphysical sense) became the beckoning goal for the Jew. The plight of *Galut* was bearable only because in the Jewish heart there lived the hope for a more natural life, when to be a Jew will not mean to be an outsider but to be involved in temporal affairs, engaged with mundane matters in a society that bears witness to the Kingdom of God – in short, a world where the *Shekhinah* will no longer be in exile.

ORTHODOX JUDAISM AND HUMAN PURPOSE[1]

As a theocentric religion, Judaism regards the universe not as a self-sufficient cosmos, but as the creation of a transcendent God who is the source of all existence, value and meaning. Since the purpose of all creatures is grounded in the Creator, all questions concerning the purpose of any being must ultimately involve the Divine Plan for His creatures. But, as the Book of Job so dramatically shows, the purposes of a transcendent, infinite God are completely beyond the ken of our finite, limited intelligence.

To be sure, the Jewish liturgy asserts that "God created everything for His glory."[2] But, as Maimonides suggests, this statement does not really provide a teleological explanation. It does not really help us to determine why a particular being should possess the specific set of characteristics with which it is endowed. We have no way of knowing why a different set would not have served equally well to glorify God. Actually, following Maimonides's explanation, the statement is merely the equivalent of saying that we are incapable of fathoming the ultimate purpose of any creature and that we therefore cannot go beyond the assertion that a creature exists because God, for reasons totally unintelligible to us, willed its existence.[3]

Since there is no conceivable set of circumstances that would invalidate the proposition, "Whatever exists, exists for the glory of God," the

---

[1] From *Religion and Human Purpose,* edited by W. Horosz and T. Clemens, 105–122. Dortrecht: Martin Nijhoff Publishers, 1986.

[2] BT *Ketubbot* 8a. See also Mishnah *Avot (Kinyan Torah,* 6:11).

[3] Maimonides, *Guide of the Perplexed* III, 13 and 25.

proposition cannot be invoked as an explanation for the occurrence of any particular event or process. Yet, though devoid of explanatory value, the notion of an inexplicable Divine Purpose governing the universe has far reaching implications. Once the notion of a transcendent Divine Purpose[4] is accepted, it follows that the meaning of any particular event or process can no longer be completely expressible in terms of an immanent purpose manifesting itself in history or in nature.[5] At the very most, natural processes or historic events disclose fragmentary meanings. Their full meaning can be grasped only from a vantage point outside of both nature and history. Thus, in the final analysis, faith in Divine Purpose merely provides the believer with the assurance that the Author of nature and history has a purpose for His creation which is discernible only to the extent that He chooses to disclose it to His creatures.

The perspective of the believer is radically different from that of the atheistic existentialist who asserts the basic meaninglessness of all existence. To be sure, both despair of discovering within the universe itself a meaningful structure. But there remains this fundamental difference: whereas the atheistic existentialist is confronted with a world of absurdity in which all meaning and purpose amounts to nothing but the fabrications and projections of the individual, the believer finds himself in a universe that reflects the inexplicable purpose and the providential plan of a benevolent God. Even the manifest absurdities of existence are attributed to the limitations of the human perspective. How could reality be conceived as absurd if it represents Divine Creation and is governed by His Providence? This optimism comes to the fore in the Biblical account of Creation. The verdict "It was very good" was pronounced upon the completion of the entire process (Genesis 1:31).

---

[4] To be sure, Judaism does not merely operate with the notion of a transcendent God. God is at the same time immanent in His creation. But since Judaism insists upon divine transcendence, God's purposes can never be completely intelligible to those that are within the natural or historic order. See later in this chapter.

[5] Of course, rationalistic Jewish theologians have within their system room for an immanent teleology. Though Maimonides maintains that there is no rational explanation why God has created a world, he nevertheless affirms that the universe possesses a purposeful structure. It should also be noted that some rationalistic theologians (e.g., Bahyah ibn Pakuda and Saadia Gaon) go as far as to claim that the purpose of all of reality is the salvation of man, who is regarded as the highest creature.

The assertion of the goodness and meaningfulness of the world is not shaken by the existence of evil. Understandably, there was considerable reluctance on the part of the Rabbis to attribute the authorship of evil directly to God. Thus the Jewish liturgy finds it necessary to reformulate the passage from Isaiah which refers to God as the "one who creates evil" (Isaiah 45:7). Instead, there is substituted for this term, which might prove offensive to some religious sensibilities, the more neutral description of God as the "one who creates all things."[6] But subsuming evil under the category of "all things," while removing a shocking linguistic expression, does not really solve the problem. In view of Judaism's radical monotheism, one cannot dispose of the difficulty by ascribing evil to a force antithetical to or independent of God. Classic Jewish sources are most emphatic in their denunciation of any form of dualism that would eliminate the problem of evil by limiting the power of God.[7]

Some leading Jewish thinkers are inclined to explain away the problem of treating evil as a sheer illusion or privation of good. They dismiss evil as a mere appearance because they would view the existence of evil as incompatible with the goodness of God's creation. But this essentially idealistic approach does by no means reflect the preponderant Jewish attitude.

Despite the fact that Rabbi Akiva declared that "whatever God does is for the good,"[8] the distinction between good and evil is not abolished. While one blesses God for evil in the same manner as one does for good, there is a radical difference between the types of blessings recited on the respective occasions.[9] However, those who feel that a religion such as Judaism, which takes history and normative ideals so seriously, cannot dismiss evil as a mere appearance are left with a serious problem. Why should an omnipotent God choose to create evil in order to promote the goodness of the totality? Recourse to the Leibnitzian notion of the "best of all possible worlds" seems rather unsatisfactory, since it would set limits to God's omnipotence.[10]

---

[6] Daily morning prayer.

[7] See especially BT *Berakhot* 33b, *Megillah* 25a and *Berakhot* 54a.

[8] Cf. Maimonides' treatment of evil as a mere negation. *Guide* III, 10–12.

[9] BT *Berakhot* 60b.

[10] Any attempt to treat evil as necessary to the attainment to the greatest possible good subjects God to the domain of necessity. The Leibnitzian view is of no avail to

Ultimately, one would have to resort to the notion of the incomprehensibility of the divine plan to man, the solution which appears to be preferable to any of the alternatives presented so far.

An even more disturbing feature of the problem of evil arises from the fact that the divine, Providential plan seems to include even moral evil. The prophet Isaiah, for example, does not hesitate to describe the wickedness of Assyria as the "rod of Divine anger" (Isaiah 10:5).[11] There can be no doubt that sages of the Talmud are sensitive to the problem as to how benevolent God can will that human beings perform morally wrong actions to achieve His purposes in history. In their non-systematic fashion, they wrestle with the problem when they speak of God's silence in the face of the destruction of His sanctuary[12] and develop the paradoxical notion that God chooses to manifest His power and greatness by His apparent withdrawal from the historic scene.[13]

While the Rabbis were fully aware of the nature of the underlying paradox,[14] they made no attempt to offer a solution to it.[15] Similarly, they fail to come to grips with the difficulties inherent in the notion that an omnipotent God's purpose for history requires man's voluntary cooperation. There is no systematic effort made to reconcile God's omnipotence and omniscience (which entails His foreknowledge) with the existence of human

---

anyone who is unwilling to surrender the distinction between logical and factual truth.

[11] See also Jeremiah's attitude towards Nebuchadnezzar's role as an instrument of divine purpose (Jer. 25:9; 27:6; and 43:10).

[12] BT *Gittin* 56 b.

[13] BT *Yoma* 69b; JT *Berakhot* 6:3.

[14] Most of the discussions of the problem of evil in the Talmudic and Midrashic literature relate not to the question not of how a benevolent God can permit the existence of evil, but rather to an entirely different issue involving God's justice: How can a just God permit a situation where there is apparently no correlation between an individual's moral worth and his happiness?

[15] A most illuminating discussion of the entire problem as to how an omnipotent God can be involved in historic process as the Lord of history is contained in Emil L. Fackenheim's *God's Presence in History*. Although the bulk of this essay was completed before the appearance of the book, I wish to record my indebtedness to Prof. Fackenheim, whose views exerted a considerable influence on my own thinking on the subject.

freedom.[16] The Rabbis simply state, "All is in the hands of Heaven except the fear of Heaven."[17] Apparently, Jewish religious thought employs what Raphael Morris Cohen has called "scissorial concepts." The emphasis upon man's utter dependence upon an omnipotent God must be balanced by the insistence upon human responsibility. Notwithstanding all logical difficulties, Judaism must postulate both divine omnipotence and human freedom. Without either of these two components operating in dialectical tension, the entire Jewish concept of Jewish piety, which revolves upon man's responsibility to an omnipotent God, would be utterly impossible.

Committed as it is to absolute monotheism, Judaism cannot brook any limitations upon Divine Power. Yet according to the Jewish view, for mysterious reasons God has chosen to need man's *freely given* services. Creatures that lack freedom automatically contribute to God's glory, fulfilling their purpose because they are bound to act in accordance with His Will. But man is given freedom of choice as to whether to fulfill the role that Divine purpose has assigned to him. He can either glorify or desecrate God. Were man merely a helpless puppet in the hands of an absolute Deity, he could not possibly be regarded as the bearer of the Divine image.[18]

---

[16] It is often taken for granted that the problem of how one can reconcile the postulation of human freedom with Divine foreknowledge is already posed in the famous mishnah in *Avot* 3:15, which is usually translated as "Everything is foreseen, but permission is given to man." However, this translation follows the interpretation of Maimonides (Commentary to the Mishnah *ad loc.*). In his work, *Hazal, Emunot ve-Deot* (Jerusalem: 1968, 229), Prof. Ephraim E. Urbach has shown that Maimonides has actually read his own philosophical views into the ancient Mishnah. Prof. Urbach adduces linguistic proof that the intent of the Talmudic passage in question has nothing to do with the metaphysical issue that Maimonides raised. The Hebrew term *tzafui* does not at all suggest divine foreknowledge. It merely denotes that all is seen (by God) while permission is given to man. It may also be of interest to point out that Potesquière comments caustically on Maimonides's attempt *(Hilkhot Rabad on Teshuvah* 5:5) to resolve the paradox, saying that in view of the implausibility of Maimonides's solution, it would have been preferable had he refrained from raising the question altogether. See also Julius Guttmann, Philosophies of Judaism (Garden City, NY: 1964), 38.

[17] BT *Berakhot* 33b.

[18] That the two notions are closely related appears to follow from the sequence of Rabbi Akiva's statements as recorded in *Avot* 3. The first (*Avot* 3:14) develops the notion that man is beloved because he is created in the image of God. It is after this statement dealing with the unique position of man, that the next mishnah stresses man's freedom and responsibility.

We should also bear in mind that in the Jewish scheme, man does not fulfill the divine purpose by blind submission to the divine will. Human reason and conscience play an important role in determining the meaning of the divine imperatives addressed to man. To be sure, Orthodox Judaism maintains that man can carry out his purpose only by obedience to the divine commandments which were revealed to man. But this emphasis upon revelation does not – à la Tertullian – result in the condemnation of reason and the elevation of absurdity to the supreme religious value. Viewed from Jewish perspective, true commitment to God entails the utilization of one's rational resources and ethical convictions, which must operate in dialectical tension with the content of the Revelation, in order to ascertain the true meaning of God's demands upon man.[19] This is why the Jewish concept of Torah stresses man's creativity so much. Man, as it were, is a partner with God in creating the Torah. The very conception of an Oral Torah involves not merely blind submission to an authoritative body of revealed teachings, but also creative effort on the part of man, who employs his intelligence, reason and moral insights towards the shaping of a "Torah of life." This more earth-bound Torah is now entrusted to duly qualified human beings for its proper interpretation. Its true meaning becomes the product of interaction between the infinite God and finite man.

Since Jewish thought is compelled to harmonize human responsibility with the absoluteness of Divine power it is not surprising that it is marked by a rather ambivalent attitude towards the efficacy of human action. On the one hand, emphasis on divine omnipotence tends to make man's fate exclusively dependent upon Divine Providence. In the words of the liturgy, "Heal us and we shall be healed, save us and we shall be saved."[20] Saving power belongs only to God; His designs cannot be thwarted. "Except the Lord build the house, its builders labor in vain."[21] But it is significant that the Psalmist still emphasizes the need for man's toil. Without it, God will not build the house.[22] And for that matter the Bible places upon man responsibility for healing individuals, for man is charged with the

---

[19] Cf. A. Carlebach, "Autonomy and Theonomy," *Tradition* (Fall, 1963): 5–28.
[20] The daily liturgy.
[21] Psalms 127:1.
[22] Rabbi Joseph B. Soloveitchik, "The Lonely Man of Faith." *Tradition* (Summer 1965): 5–67. This essay contains a most relevant discussion of this issue.

responsibility of being a partner with God in the process of Creation.[23] While ultimately the result of human efforts may fall short of our expectations, "Although it is not incumbent on you to finish the work, still you are not free to desist from it."[24]

Of course, it is impossible to delimit the extent to which any human action can achieve its intended result, since the fate of the individual is governed by God's providential plan. We encounter within the Jewish tradition a wide spectrum of attitudes towards the relative weight to be assigned to human actions. In a famous passage, the medieval Biblical exegete, Ibn Ezra,[25] disparages all human efforts to improve one's material well-being, which according to him is completely determined by God's Providence. According to this view, only matters of spiritual welfare are influenced by man's performance. Since man's material conditions depend exclusively upon Divine Providence, there is no point in attempting to improve one's lot. This fatalistic and quietistic approach, which is adopted by some thinkers, clashes head-on with the position advocated by the proponents of a more activist approach, who categorically reject a policy of passive submission.[26] One might plausibly argue in accordance with this view that implicit in the notion of human dignity and responsibility[27] is the belief that man can shape his destiny at least to some extent and that he bears some responsibility for the state of his material condition.

Rabbi Soloveitchik attributes the ambivalence of the Jewish position with respect to the efficacy of human action to a dialectical tension inherent in man's ontological status.[28] That man is torn between feelings of self-importance and utter insignificance reflects not any malfunction of the human psyche, but a complex ontological status that condemns him to

---

[23] Exodus 21:19. See also BT *Bava Kama* 85a, Joseph B. Soloveitchik, *op. cit.*, 53 and BT *Shabbat* 119b. See also Rabbi Joseph B. Soloveitchik, "Ish ha-Halakhah." *Talpiot* (1944): 710–18.

[24] Mishnah *Avot* 2:16.

[25] See Ibn Ezra's Commentary to Exodus 20:14.

[26] See especially Rabbi Menachem Meiri, *Bet ha-behirah* to *Moed Katan* 28a and *Shabbat* 156a. Cf. also Ephraim E. Urbach, *op. cit.*, 251.

[27] Cf. Rabbi Joseph B. Soloveitchik, "The Lonely Man of Faith," *loc. cit.,* especially 14–16.

[28] Although this theme is developed primarily in his "The Lonely Man of Faith," his earlier essays, "Confrontation" (*Tradition* [Spring/Summer 1964]: 3–28) and especially his *Halakhic Man,* should not be overlooked.

perpetual restlessness. On the one hand, man is conceived as an exalted creature who, in partnership with God, is called upon to help perfect the world and to use his intelligence and energy to harness the forces of nature. On the other hand, confronted as he is by his inability to wrest ultimate meaning from the triumphs wrought in the conquest of nature, man realizes the utter insignificance of all his achievements as a finite creature. According to Rabbi Soloveitchik, it is only through a covenantal relationship with God that man can overcome a sense of absurdity and futility. In this encounter with God, man not only experiences God's care and concern for him, but becomes aware that God in turn, for mysterious reasons, has chosen to desire man's commitment to Him. But, significantly, this covenantal relationship, which provides human existence with transcendental meaning, does not allow man to escape from his existential responsibilities in the here and now. "The Torah was not given to the ministering angels" but to human beings,[29] and man's transcendental significance derives precisely from the fact that he is commanded by God to perform actions that can be carried out only by spatio-temporal creatures operating in an ever-changing, transient world. Man must not lose himself in the higher regions of being; he must carry out his divine tasks in a concrete, existential world that not in spite of, but precisely because of the limitations that stem from its finitude, constitutes the proper scene of man's operation. It is here that the finite and infinite meet and where man can perform the deeds that have significance in the realm of eternity even though they take place in time.

That God has revealed His Will to man is a cardinal tenet of Judaism. No attempt is made to explain the mystery of why an omnipotent God would have chosen to entrust a finite creature with tasks necessary for the fulfillment of a divine purpose. But it is regarded as the very hallmark of our humanity to be the addressees of Divine commandments. Some commandments (such as the seven Noahide laws) apply to all human beings.[30] According to Judaism, being human implies to be singled out for the service of God. It is precisely the fact that God demands the fulfillment of a certain task from finite man that provides the measure of our humanity and endows our existence with transcendent relevance.

---

[29] BT *Berakhot* 25b.
[30] BT *Sanhedrin* 29b.

Since God has chosen to enter into a special covenant with the people of Israel, he has placed upon it additional obligations designed to make it "a kingdom of Priests and a holy nation" (Exodus 19:6). The imposition of numerous commandments, which are contained in the Oral and the Written Torah, is looked upon as a sign of special love, "Because the Holy One, blessed be He, wanted to bestow a special privilege upon Israel he gave them so many provisions of the Torah and so many Commandments."[31] Human existence possesses value to the degree that it is related to a divine task which is commanded by God. It is also revealing that the Book of Ecclesiastes which grapples with the meaning of human existence, after struggling with a variety of contradictory formulations, finally gives up the attempt to find a rationally appealing solution and concludes on the note "The end of the matter: fear God, observe His commandments, because this is the whole man."[32] A well-known rabbinic comment notes that it is this verse which provides the ultimate rationale for all existence.[33]

The Jewish religious ideal with its emphasis upon obedience to God's revealed Will does not seek the dissolution of man's individuality through mystic union with God.[34] Were man to lose himself completely in God and cease to function as an individual, he would no longer be able to stand in a covenantal relationship with God. For this relationship can exist only if man *qua* man responds to God's love and commits himself to His service. In the benediction which is recited after the reading of the Torah, God is extolled as "having given us a Torah of Truth and thereby implanting within us a life of eternity." The very finiteness of human existence, with all its intrinsic limitations, does not represent an unmitigated metaphysical evil, but rather the condition in which man alone can execute the unique religious task which God has assigned to him.

A telling illustration of the Jewish attitude towards the transcendental meaning of our finite life is provided by the Kaddish prayer which is recited

---

[31] BT *Makkot* 23b.

[32] Ecclesiastes 12:13.

[33] BT *Shabbat* 30b.

[34] To be sure, Judaism has its share of thinkers who advocate the mystic ideal of union with God. But it must be borne in mind that essentially Judaism revolves around Halakhah, which presupposes man's standing in relationship to God, not merging with Him. See Rabbi Joseph B. Soloveitchik, *Halakhic Man,* and my essay on "Pluralism and Halakhah," *Tradition* 4/2 (Spring 1962): 221–240 (page 308 in this volume).

by the mourner who confronts the mystery of human existence. Although the Kaddish is a doxology which contains no reference whatsoever to the phenomenon of death, it indirectly serves as an expression of the Jewish response to the finitude of human existence. Confrontation with death does not lead to a declaration of futility or absurdity, because fragmentary individual human life is seen within the context of the ultimate eschatological goal of Judaism – the sanctification of the Divine Name. And even though an individual's life falls short of the realization of all its goals, it nonetheless possesses meaning because even its partial accomplishments may contribute to the realization of the Divine plan.[35]

Against this background it is easy to account for the worldly and life-affirming attitude of Judaism. One hour devoted to Torah and good deeds in this world is held to be superior to all the life in the hereafter even though, according to rabbinic belief, the satisfactions enjoyed in the hereafter are infinitely greater than those available in this world.[36]

In a philosophy of life that stresses man's total commitment to a God who is not merely the Author of life, but the Lord of history, there is no area that can be excluded from the claims of the all-demanding Sovereign of the Universe. The prescriptions of the Torah regulate the entire gamut of personal, interpersonal, social, economic and political concerns. The ultimate eschatological goal of all religious activity is the establishment of the kingdom of God where the Sovereignty of God will be acknowledged in all human affairs.[37] While the complete fulfillment of this ideal must await God's redemption of man in the Messianic age, it is the religious duty of the individual to devote his total existence towards this objective.

Contrary to widespread misconceptions, Judaism does not equate commitment to the service of God with mere compliance with formal rules of the law. Actually, observance of the law is regarded merely as a necessary, but not a sufficient, condition of piety. There is no basis for the charge of "legalism" which so often is raised by poorly informed critics, since the

---

[35] Jacob B. Agus, "The Meaning of Prayer." In Abraham Ezra Milgram (ed.), *Great Jewish Ideas*, 23.

[36] Mishnah *Avot* 4:17.

[37] See S. Schechter, *Some Aspects of Rabbinic Theology*, 80–96.

classical Jewish sources abound with maxims stressing the necessity of extending the domain of piety far beyond the area covered by legal requirements. Hillel, one of the foremost Jewish legal authorities, prescribes that "all one's actions should be performed for the sake of God." In keeping with this precept he was able to treat even such trivial tasks as tending to the needs of one's own body as acts of religious devotion. Similarly, another Talmudic sage, Bar Kappara, cites the verse "In all thy ways thou shalt acknowledge Him"[38] as the underlying religious principle of the entire Torah.[39] According to the medieval scholar Nahmanides,[40] one strives for holiness and piety through the practice of self-restraint even in activities that, from a purely legalistic point of view, are perfectly legitimate.

The social consciousness is imperative. Indifference to the plight of others is regarded as a grievous sin. Concern for the welfare of one's fellow human being must express itself in the attempt to improve both his spiritual and material condition.[41] While Judaism is fully cognizant of the fact that unsatisfied material wants may at times be helpful in inducing feelings of dependency upon God and thus may be instrumental in disposing individuals towards the demands of piety,[42] there is in no way any suggestion that suffering should be condoned because of its potential spiritual rewards. On the contrary, Judaism looks upon suffering (including poverty) as an evil to be eradicated. Individuals who do not contribute to *yishuv ha-olam* (the promotion of social well-being) are stigmatized as morally defective.[43] Conversely, considerable religious significance is attached to those activities that enhance human welfare. Talmudic legislation was replete with ordinances promulgated for the improvement of the world *(tikkun ha-olam)*.[44] Maimonides goes so far as to say that many of the laws of Torah are primarily designed to promote social well-being on earth.[45] To be sure, for

---

[38] Leviticus Rabbah 34:3; Proverbs 3:6.

[39] BT *Berakhot* 63a.

[40] *Commentary to the Torah,* Leviticus 19:2.

[41] Maimonides *Hilkhot Deot,* 6:7 *Hilkhot Avel* 1–6. See also Solomon Schechter, "Notes on Lectures in Jewish Philanthropy," in *Studies in Judaism,* Vol. 3, 239–276, and Isadore Twersky, "Some Aspects of Jewish Attitude toward the Welfare State," *Tradition* (Spring 1963): 137–158.

[42] BT *Hagigah* 9b, *Leviticus Rabbah* 13:4.

[43] BT *Sanhedrin,* 24b. See also Samuel Belkin, *op. cit.,* 90–92.

[44] *Mishnah Gittin* 5:3. *Hilkhot Yesodei ha-Torah* 4:13; *Hilkhot Deot* 7:8.

[45] *Guide of the Perplexed* III, 27, 33 and 35.

Maimonides, the socio-political objectives of the Torah were merely subsidiary to the ultimate end – man's intellectual and spiritual perfection.[46] But what matters for our purposes here is the fact that even for Maimonides, notwithstanding his stress upon intellectual rather than practical virtues, "the preservation of the population of the country and its stability"[47] is not merely a purely socio-utilitarian desideratum, but represents a fundamental religious imperative. In this connection it should be pointed out that according to Jewish belief, one is not only morally obligated to prevent the suffering of one's fellow man, but one must not remain indifferent even to one's own material plight. An individual is required to prevent his own pauperization.[48]

As a general rule, Judaism maintains: "Your own life takes precedence over that of your fellow man."[49] Judaism would not subscribe to Berdayev's epigrammatic formulation that "bread for oneself is a material matter; bread for one's neighbor is a spiritual matter." From a Jewish perspective, to secure bread for oneself and to avoid unnecessary suffering also constitutes a spiritual imperative. The endorsement of activities leading to the promotion of human welfare must not, however, be confused with a "success" or "work" ethics. There is no equivalent in Jewish sources to the Calvinistic emphasis on material success as an index of spiritual worth, nor is there an echo of the Lutheran notion of a "calling." While material wealth and success are regarded as blessings, there is no trace whatsoever of the suggestion that man as the steward of God's possessions has a moral obligation to augment them according to the best of his abilities. Judaism knows of no obligation to succeed. On the contrary, excessive preoccupation with material success is regarded as a severe handicap because it prevents the individual from devoting sufficient time and energy to the study of Torah and other spiritual pursuits.[50] While *yishuv ha-olam*

---

[46] *ibid.*

[47] *ibid.,* III, *p.* 27. For a thorough discussion of Maimonides's position with respect to the social utility of the commandments see Isadore Twersky, "Some Non-halakhic Aspects of the Mishneh Torah" in Alexander Altmann (ed.), *Jewish Medieval and Renaissance Studies,* 103–105.

[48] BT *Ketubbot* 50a and 67b; *Arakhin* 28a.

[49] BT *Bava Metzia* 42a.

[50] *Mishnah Avot* 3:5; 4:10. BT *Eruvin* 55a. See also Maimonides, *Hilkhot Talmud Torah,* Chapter 3.

(improvement of material conditions) and *derekh eretz*[51] (activities necessary for the civilization of the world) are regarded as desiderata, they do not occupy the highest rank within the hierarchy of values. To make possible the concentration upon the study of the Torah, the ideal religious personality, the *talmid chakham* (the Torah scholar) is urged to forego, if necessary, the satisfaction of many legitimate needs.[52] After all, in case of conflict, lower values must be sacrificed for higher ones. What ultimately matters from a religious perspective is not the degree to which human activity is productive of socially desirable consequences, but rather the extent to which an individual is faithful in fulfilling his covenantal obligations to God.

As opposed to religious systems that view human efforts to transform the environment with indifference if not hostility because they supposedly represent undue concern with matters that should be left to the Deity, Jewish writings never suggested that man's mastery over nature is cause for guilt. When man harnesses the forces of nature to promote human welfare, he does not usurp powers rightfully belonging to God, but carries out the provisions of Divine Mandate. When the Bible condemns the building of the Tower of Babel, it is not because the exercise of human creativity and the display of technological prowess represents an intrusion upon the domain of God. We vainly search the Jewish sources for parallels to the Promethean myth where human achievement is treated as a threat to Divine prerogatives. What provokes Divine wrath, according to rabbinic interpretations of the Tower of Babel story, is not man's success in the conquest of nature, but rather his idolatry – his arrogant rebellion against God through the assertion of his own independence and self-reliance.[53] A similar motif appears in the Biblical Tree of Knowledge episode where man defies God because he is deluded into thinking that he too, could play God. ("And you shall be as God, knowing between good and evil.")[54] Yet to denounce outright defiance

---

[51] For a discussion of the centrality of this concept on Jewish thought see Max Kadushin, *Worship and Ethics*. Binghamton: Global Publications, 1991, 39–62 and 244–250.

[52] BT *Berakhot* 43b. See also Maimonides, *Hilkhot Talmud Torah*, Chapter 3.

[53] See BT *Sanhedrin* 109a.

[54] Genesis 3:5.

of God's supremacy is a far cry from maintaining that intellectual or technological attainments as such involve man in the sin of hubris or, as some other-worldly religions suggest, reflect an undue interest in basically mundane concerns which divert man's attention from what ought to be the true focus of his goals.

Judaism's positive stance towards so-called secular concerns aiming at the improvement of human welfare rests on two basic premises.

1. Man's faith in God entails not an abdication of responsibility for the world, but rather a responsibility to God to "walk in His ways" and promote the welfare of His creatures.

2. The contingency, transience and finitude that characterize empirical reality do not deprive it of metaphysical worth. To exist in time rather than in eternity does not constitute a metaphysical evil. Conditions prevailing in a world of constant flux do not lose their significance simply because they lack the aspect of timelessness which is the hallmark of the transcendental realm. The here and now matters to God who, according to rabbinic tradition, seeks the in-dwelling of His Presence primarily in the lower regions of being.[55]

Thus, concern for the transcendent does not provide the believer with an escape from the harsh realities of our existential world. Suffering and want cannot be dismissed as inconsequential. On the contrary, the alleviation of misery assumes the dimension of a religiously meaningful act.

According to Jewish belief, Israel has been assigned a special role in the Divine Plan for the redemption of the world and the establishment of God's Kingdom. Torah, worship, and lovingkindness provide the spiritual foundations of the world and constitute the *raison d'être* of the Universe. In an unredeemed world it is Israel that must act as God's witness[56] attesting to His Sovereignty and serving as the light of the nations. Because he belongs to the people of Israel, a Jew cannot satisfy his religious obligations simply as a human being who confronts his God purely as an individual. Unless he also abides by the terms of the special covenant governing the singular relationship between the people of Israel and God, he is derelict in his

---

[55] Bereshit Rabbah, 19:13. Cf. also Rabbi Joseph B. Soloveitchik's Study "*Halakhic Man.*" Compare also note 32 above.
[56] Isaiah 43:10.

responsibility. God commands him to consider himself as a member of the Jewish people and to share in the unique religious vocation for which the people of Israel has been summoned.

Although the meaning of human existence is found not in self-realization or self-fulfillment, but in the total commitment to a divinely appointed task, Judaism nonetheless maintains that the *summum bonum* is attained as a *consequence* of a life dedicated to this ideal. Eternal beatitude is vouchsafed under those who align themselves with the divine purpose. To be sure, under ideal circumstances, the quest for personal salvation should not enter as a motive of piety. "Do not act like servants who serve the master for the sake of reward."[57] Those who truly love God do not have to be prodded towards religious behavior by the prospect of eternal bliss. As Maimonides put it, those who are influenced by expectations of reward serve God not out of love but out of fear.[58] But while, ideally, concern for personal salvation should not be a factor, Judaism possesses far too realistic a conception of human nature as to frown upon appeals to self-interest as an inducement to piety.[59] Following the Biblical precedent which links loyalty to the covenant with the enjoyment of divine blessings, rabbinic Judaism harps upon the great rewards awaiting the faithful in the World to Come. A well-known rabbinic dictum unabashedly recommends that one look upon this world as merely the ante-chamber to the next. "One should prepare one's self in the ante-chamber in order that one may enter the palace itself."[60]

This attitude also comes to the fore in the opening statement of one of the most popular pietistic treatises. In his *Mesilat Yesharim,* Rabbi Moses Chaim Luzzatto advises the believer to base all behavior upon the realization that "Man was created only for the purpose of finding bliss in God and enjoying the radiance of His presence in the World to Come."[61]

It is of special interest that many of the rationalistic Jewish thinkers look upon the beatitude granted the faithful in the hereafter not as an extraneous

---

[57] Mishnah *Avot* 1:3.
[58] *Hilkhot Teshuvah* 10:1–2.
[59] See especially Lipman Heller, *Tosafot Yom Tov on Avot* 1:3.
[60] Mishnah *Avot* 4:16.
[61] Moses Chaim Luzzatto, *Mesilat Yesharim,* Chapter I.

reward conferred by God as a gratuitous compensation for good deeds, but rather as a spiritual achievement wrought by pious conduct and the cultivation of a religious personality.[62] For the rationalist, a regimen aiming at spiritual perfection is bound to yield spiritual rewards.

Though proceeding from entirely different premises, Kabbalistic thought also harps upon the centrality of human initiative and effort in the realm of the spirit. It is revealing that for a leading eighteenth-century exponent of rabbinic Judaism who operates largely with Kabbalistic categories, the achievement of immortality emerges as an aspect of man's creativity.

According to Rabbi Hayyim of Volozhin,[63] "There is simply no ready-made hereafter for which a man can qualify by dint of his piety. It is man himself who must create through his own spiritual efforts the realm of spirituality that constitutes his portion of the World to Come."[64] Viewed from this perspective, immortality is no longer postulated simply as an inducement to religious piety or as a solution to a theological dilemma posed by God's creation of a world where apparently there is no correlation between moral worthiness and the enjoyment of happiness; it rather represents a manifestation of the unique capacity for creativity that is possessed by man by virtue of his singular ontological status as a member of both the natural and the spiritual realm. It is because in man the finite encounters the infinite that he plays such a dominant role in the redemptive process. According to the Kabbalistic scheme, human initiative is needed to start a cosmic chain reaction whose repercussions are felt in the highest regions of being. The process of *tikkun,* involving the redemption of Universe from evil and the ultimate reunification of God with His *Shekhinah* (Divine Presence), must originate with man's creative efforts.[65]

The anthropocentric orientation of the Kabbalah represents by no means a radical break with the rabbinic tradition. Numerous Talmudic statements can

---

[62] According to Maimonides, immortality of the soul is not something given, but it is gained by the human soul through moral and intellectual efforts which actualize a potentiality for immortality.

[63] Rabbi Hayyim of Volozhin, *Nefesh ha-Hayyim* I, 12, *Ruah Ha-Hayyim* I, 1. See also my essay on Rabbi Hayyim of Volozhin in Leo Jung (ed.) *Guardians of our Heritage,* 205 (page 105 in this volume).

[64] *ibid.*

[65] Cf. Gershom G. Scholem, *Major Trends in Jewish Mysticism,* 265–284.

be adduced in support of the thesis that man as the "crown of creation"[66] must provide the *raison d'être* for the entire Universe. This is one of the reasons why the destruction of human life is regarded as the equivalent of the destruction of the entire Universe.[67] Because of the sanctity and importance attached to each human life, every person should look upon himself as if the entire Universe was created for his sake.[68] Another Talmudic saying admonishes an individual to recognize that his actions may determine not only his own fate, but also that of the entire world.[69]

To be sure, one encounters considerable dissent from the notion that man holds a preeminent position within the order of creation. Among medieval philosophers it was especially Maimonides who emphasized that the Jewish tradition must not be read in an anthropocentric fashion.[70] Although in his legal works many of the maxims stressing man's personal responsibility for the world are incorporated, a metaphysics which reflects an excessive human parochialism is totally unacceptable to a Maimonides, who sees no need to accord man a preeminent metaphysical status in order to buttress his position as the bearer of the image of the Divine.

With man dethroned from his supremacy in the hierarchy of created beings, it is not surprising that Maimonides[71] accepts the opinion of those Talmudic Rabbis[72] who look upon the Messianic Redemption merely as the emergence of a new kind of social order, which, notwithstanding its great importance to man, is not really treated as an event of overriding cosmic significance. It is readily understandable that for rationalistic theologians it is difficult to ascribe more than merely human significance to the redemption of mankind through supernatural intervention. The situation, of course, is altogether different for those religious thinkers for whom history rather than natural philosophy provides the basic matrix of their thought. It has often been pointed out that Judaism is a historic religion which emphasizes God's concern and involvement with the historic process.[73] Significantly, as Rabbi

---

[66] For a thorough discussion of this topic consult Ephraim Urbach, *op. cit.*, 190–226.

[67] *Hilkhot Melachim* 12:1–2.

[68] BT *Sanhedrin* 91b.

[69] BT *Kiddushin* 40 b.

[70] *Hilkhot Melachim* 12:1–2.

[71] *ibid.*

[72] BT *Sanhedrin* 91b.

[73] See Emil L. Fackenheim, *op. cit.,* especially Chapter 1.

Yehuda Halevi[74] and Nahmanides[75] have stressed, the Decalogue invokes not the God of Creation, but the God of History. The exodus of Egypt constitutes the dominant religious motif of Judaism and a host of religious practices, observances and institutions are directly related to this central event which at the same time is also regarded as the paradigm of the ultimate redemption.

It is not merely an accident that representative Jewish thinkers take such divergent positions in their evaluation of the importance of the role which the historic process plays in the Divine scheme. There can be little doubt that the disagreement manifests the dialectical tension between the Immanence and the Transcendence of God which is built into the very foundations of Judaism. The more one stresses the absolute transcendence of the Creator, the more one recoils from involving God in the historic process. Conversely the more emphasis is placed upon God's Immanence, the more one is prone to accept doctrines which reach their most radical formulation in the daring mystic notion that God whose *Shekhinah* is in exile in some sense is redeemed together with the redemption of the world.[76] This dialectical tension which gives rise to a host of intellectually disturbing paradoxes provides much of the thrust and vitality of the Jewish religious experience. It prompts the Jew while recognizing that his righteousness is of no avail to God ("If he be righteous, what boon is this to Thee?"[77]) to consider himself responsible for the sanctification of the Divine Name and for discharging his religious obligations sustained by the faith that man's actions either strengthen or weaken the power of the Divine.[78]

It is to be expected that a religious system that views God both as a transcendent Creator as well as a God of History is bound to give rise to troublesome paradoxes that are beyond intellectual solution. But it should be borne in mind that the belief in a God of history in itself – apart from any problems posed by the concurrent postulation of a transcendent Creator – engenders its own polar tensions.

---

[74] *Kuzari*, Chapter 1.

[75] See *Commentary to the Torah*, Exodus 20:2.

[76] BT *Megillah* 29a, Jer. Talmud *Taanit* 1:1. *Mekhilta de-Rabbi Ishmael*, 1, 114.

[77] The Neilah prayer of the Day of Atonement liturgy.

[78] *Midrash Rabbah*, Lamentations 1:35. See also Rabbi Hayyim of Volozhin, *Nefesh ha-Hayyim*, I, 3–4. Cf. Abraham J. Heschel, *The Prophets*, especially 221–323.

Man is charged with responsibility for the state of the world and bidden to use his creative resources for the solution of the agonizing problems that beset mankind. Yet according to Jewish doctrine, the purpose of the historic processes cannot be realized without Divine direct intervention in the redemptive process. This, in a sense, is the gist of the Messianic idea which, according to Gershom Scholem, represents an "antiexistentialist idea"[79] inasmuch as it allegedly makes it impossible to attach any significance to actions that are performed by unredeemed individuals. If, ultimately, the meaning of history is completely in the hands of God, who alone through supernatural intervention brings about the Redemption, then – so this distinguished authority on Jewish mysticism argues – concrete acts that individuals perform within the historic process are deprived of true value. They cannot really matter with respect to the attainment of the supernatural objective which alone confers meaning upon historic acts. But it appears that Professor Scholem's characterization of the Jewish attitude as antiexistentialist is rather one-sided. The very fact that ultimately God finds it necessary to intervene in the historic process in order to fulfill it does not only underscore the intrinsic limitations of all human endeavors, but also points to their radical importance in the cosmic scheme. Human efforts to establish justice and to promote benevolence are not senseless gestures without any hope of success. However limited their relative import may be, there is a divine guarantee that ultimately, with the establishment of the Kingdom of God, these ideals will prevail.

In Judaism, the all-out resistance to the deification of man and the refusal to place upon his shoulders sole responsibility for the historic process does not lead to the kind of quietism that, in the history of religion, has so often stifled all human initiative and reduced man to a puppet manipulated by the omnipotent Deity. Judaism has never been characterized by "the abandonment of self-responsibility" which, for William James, constituted the hallmark of the religious attitude.[80] Instead, veering forever between antithetical poles, Judaism summons man (individually as well as collectively) to uphold his dignity and worth without risking the plunge into the abyss of self-idolization which has plagued modern secular man.

---

[79] Gershom Scholem, *Judaica*, 74.
[80] William James, *The Varieties of Religious Experience: A Study in Human Nature.* Charleston: 2007, 260.

A JEWISH THEOLOGY AND PHILOSOPHY OF THE SABBATH[1]

AN IMPORTANT CAVEAT must be heeded in any discussion of the philosophy or theology of the Sabbath. Judaism constitutes a way of life rather than the profession of a creed. Because it revolves around the observance of Halakhah (religious law) rather than the affirmation of articles of faith, precise dogmatic formulations are eschewed. No matter how far theological beliefs may diverge from the mainstream of Jewish thought, they qualify as perfectly legitimate expressions of Judaism as long as they are compatible with the acknowledgment of the binding authority of the Halakhah. As Abraham of Posquière put it in his strictures against Maimonides, one would not be excluded from the community of faith even if one were to veer so far from the dominant theological view as to ascribe corporeal attributes to God.[2]

Since Judaism sanctions such enormous latitude in matters of belief, it is impossible to develop a philosophy or theology of the Sabbath that can lay claim to objective validity. All I hope to achieve in this paper is to provide a conceptual framework for what the experience of the Sabbath means to me and to show how the philosophy and theology I read into the Sabbath contribute to the enhancement of my personal appreciation and love of the

---

[1] From *The Sabbath in Jewish and Christian Traditions.* Edited by Tamara C. Eskenazi, Daniel J. Harrington and William Shea. New York: Crossroad, 1991.

[2] Abraham of Posquière, *Hasagot ha-Ravad le-Mishneh Torah ad Hilkhot Teshuvah* 3:7 (Jerusalem: 1984).

Sabbath and enables me to treat it as the very focus of my existence. My formulations are merely offered as possible interpretations of the postulates underlying the normative teachings of Judaism, which are embodied in the Halakhah.

In this connection it might be useful to refer to the *Pesikta de-Rav Kahana,* which notes that the Sinaitic revelation addressed each individual in the voice appropriate for that person.[3] Similarly, the kabbalists point out that the divine revelation was heard by each individual in a different form. In keeping with this emphasis on the subjectivity that characterizes the realm of Aggadah as opposed to objectively binding halakhic norms regulating conduct, my objective is a very limited one: I merely want to develop *a* philosophy or theology of the Sabbath, for which I make no claims except that it satisfies the needs of my personal existential situation.

To be sure, in striking contrast to the many areas of religious practice where classical biblical and rabbinic sources hardly offer any clue to their theological or philosophical meaning, we suffer from an embarrassment of riches in the attempt to explore the spiritual meaning of Sabbath observance. The numerous scriptural references to the Sabbath allude to a variety of themes, ranging from creation to the Exodus from Egypt, from constituting a day of rest for the individual to a summons to a "holy convocation." The Sabbath is portrayed also as a sign of the covenant between God and Israel that God created heaven and earth in six days.[4]

Especially revealing is the difference between the two versions of the Decalogue as presented in Exodus and in Deuteronomy. The former concerns itself exclusively with the creation theme and focuses on the theocentric aspects of the Sabbath, reminding humans that the world does not belong to them but to God. Refraining from work on the Sabbath is interpreted primarily as the acknowledgment of God as the Creator of the universe. A person's right to engage in creative activity is limited to what is explicitly sanctioned by God and contributes to the fulfillment of God's purposes. To be legitimate, human activity must conform to the pattern established by God, who stopped the process of creation on the Sabbath. In sharp contrast to this exclusive emphasis on surrender to God, which seeks to guard humans against self-deification and the worship of their own

---

[3] *Pesikta de-Rav Kahana* 12:25.
[4] Exodus 31:17.

powers, the version of the Decalogue in Deuteronomy includes, in addition to the creation theme, a reference to the Exodus from Egypt and dwells upon the benefits accruing to man and woman from the Sabbath as a day of liberation and rest. This humanistic motif is further elaborated in prophetic writings, which mandate that the Sabbath be proclaimed as a day of delight and treated with the honor due such a sacred and joyous event. The Tannaim developed these ideas by stressing that the Sabbath should not merely be treated as a commandment but hailed as a special and unique gift that the Almighty bestowed upon Israel.[5]

Although with reference to the Sabbath, a relatively large number of themes are adumbrated in Scriptures and subsequently developed in rabbinic literature, it appears that, contrary to Hermann Cohen's opinion, acknowledgment of God as the Creator rather than the liberation of humanity constitutes the dominant motif of the Sabbath experience.[6] Despite the fact that the Torah enjoins the remembrance and the sanctification of the Sabbath as well as the cessation of whatever activity interferes with the observance of a day of rest, the drastic penalties that the biblical legal code provides for desecration of the Sabbath are reserved exclusively for violations of the prohibition against *melakhah* (work). Public desecration of the Sabbath through performance of *melakhah* is deemed the equivalent of the rejection of the entire Torah. According to talmudic law, any individual guilty of such conduct is deprived of many privileges associated with membership in the Jewish community and in some respects is treated as a non-Jew. Although according to many contemporary authorities the upheavals of the post-Emancipation era have for all practical purposes rendered this law inoperative, it is of the utmost importance to bear in mind that traditionally, observance of the prohibitions against *melakhah* was a *conditio sine qua non* of membership in the Jewish community. Since the Sabbath functions as sign between God and Israel that God is the Creator of heaven and earth, the desecration of the Sabbath amounts not merely to an act of disobedience but in effect to an outright denial of one of the most central tenets of Judaism: the affirmation of God as the Creator of the universe.

---

[5] BT *Shabbat* 10b.

[6] Hermann Cohen, *Religion der Vernunft* (trans. Ephraim Fischoff; Leipzig: G. Foch, 1919), 180–182.

According to the rabbinic interpretation, no matter how strenuous an activity may be, it does not fall under the category of biblically-prohibited work unless it constitutes *melekhet machshevet,* that is, an activity performed with design and purpose.[7] To do so, it must not only resemble the thirty-nine types of work that, according to Jewish tradition, were necessary for the construction of the mobile sanctuary that was built in the desert; it must also follow the normal procedures and customary objectives associated with the activity in question. If an activity is carried out in an abnormal fashion *(ke-le-achar yad),* it is only rabbinically prohibited but does not constitute an infringement of the biblical prohibition against *melekhet machshevet.*

That creative activity rather than toil represents the defining characteristic of work sheds considerable light on the reason why the Sabbath plays such a pivotal role in the Jewish scale of values. It clearly indicates that such "social hygiene" functions as rest or relief from drudgery represent merely secondary considerations. Performing an activity in an awkward manner or without a purposeful, constructive intent would hardly affect the amount of effort expended. Were the suspension of toil and labor the primary goal of the Sabbath as a day of rest, the elements of purposeful activity could not be invoked as criteria determining whether or not a particular activity constitutes *melakhah.*[8]

The halakhic definition of *melakhah* is not toil or labor but rather purposeful work that points to the specifically religious dimension of the Sabbath, which transcends considerations of social or psychological utility. If Isaiah[9] and Nehemiah[10] single out the Sabbath as the hallmark of faithfulness to the covenant, it was because they saw in the Sabbath the concretization of the most fundamental tenets regarding a person's relationship to God and to nature. Maimonides even declares that the original divine legislation issued at Marah provided only for the Sabbath and ethical laws; no other ritual laws were deemed necessary at that time.[11] Small wonder, then, that the Sabbath is regarded as the quintessence of Judaism. As Dayan I. Grunfeld phrased it so aptly, the "Sabbath epitomizes the whole

---

[7] BT *Betzah* 16a.

[8] See my article "Sabbath and Creation," in *Yavneh Shiron,* edited by Eugene Flink (New York: Yavneh Students Organization, 1968), 51–53.

[9] Isaiah 56:2,14.

[10] Nehemiah 9:13.

[11] *Guide of the Perplexed* 3:32.

of Judaism."[12] Viewed from this vantage point the prohibition against *melakhah* emerges as a much-needed reminder to humans that for all their powers of creativity, they too are merely creatures of God.

To be sure, human creativity and dominion over nature represent perfectly legitimate activities. Judaism does not subscribe to the Promethean myth that condemns human creativity as an act of defiance of the heavenly powers.[13] There is really no basis for Erich Fromm's suggestion that the prohibition against work on the Sabbath aims at the reconciliation of humanity with nature and the restoration of the peace that has been disturbed as the result of human efforts to assert dominion over nature.[14] However appealing this explanation may be in an age that is becoming increasingly sensitized to ecological issues, the Jewish religious tradition can hardly be invoked to justify such an anti-technological bias. According to an often-quoted Midrashic statement, even under the idyllic conditions that prevailed in the Garden of Eden it was necessary for man to engage in work and to tend and guard the earth.[15] It is also highly significant that the act of circumcision, which according to numerous commentators symbolizes man's task to become a partner with God in helping perfect the world,[16] takes precedence over the prohibitions against work on the Sabbath. There is therefore scant plausibility to Fromm's suggestion that the Sabbath is intended as a protest against interference with nature. There is really nothing in the Jewish tradition to support the thesis that reconciliation with nature as evidenced by the cessation of human constructive activities constitutes an integral part of the messianic ideal of perfect *shalom* – the ultimate peace of which the Sabbath is the forerunner.

It therefore seems much more likely that the prohibitions against work on the Sabbath are grounded not in anti-technological attitudes but in the realization of the debilitating spiritual hazards posed by human creativity. It

---

[12] Dayan I. Grunfeld, *The Sabbath: A Guide to its Understanding and Observance*. London: Sabbath League of Great Britain, 1956, 11. Dayan Grunfeld has pioneered in popularizing the ideas of Samson Rabbi Hirsch in the English-speaking world. Their influence can readily be perceived in my own treatment of the relationship between the Sabbath and the creation theme.

[13] See my article "Orthodox Judaism and Human Purpose," in *Religion and Human Purpose*, edited by W. Horosz and T. Clements (Dordrecht: Nijhoff, 1986) 106–122.

[14] Eric Fromm, *The Forgotten Language*. New York: Grove Press, 1985, 488–491.

[15] *Avot de-Rabbi Natan*, 11:1.

[16] See *Sefer ha-Chinukh*, chapter 2.

is one thing to endorse human creativity as the fulfillment of a God-given mandate to conquer the world and to harness the forces of nature for the satisfaction of human needs and is another to become oblivious to the enormous dangers to the image of God within humanity, which, as we have so painfully discovered in an age of secularization and desacralization, are likely to result from our technological triumphs. We are prone to become so intoxicated with our success in subduing nature that we may succumb to the danger of arrogant self-idolization and forget that the entire universe, including our own creative capacities, is not a self-contained cosmos but God's creation, which must recognize its dependence on him.

The regularity and order prevailing within the realm of nature tend to obscure the divine source of all existence. It is for this reason that precisely on the day when, according to the biblical account, the world began to function in accordance with the laws of nature, it is incumbent upon us to acknowledge God as the Owner and Master of the universe.

By abstaining from productive activity on the Sabbath in conscious imitation of the Creator, who "stopped" his work of creation on the Sabbath, we affirm that what appear to the secular mind as purely natural phenomena are in actuality manifestations of the divine. Thus the Sabbath reveals what nature conceals. It is interesting to recall in this context that, according to the *Zohar,* the letters of the term *Elohim* suggest that this name of God reflects the quest for the ultimate meaning of reality, which can be apprehended only when we raise the question *Mi eleh* (Who are these?).[17] In a similar vein, Rabbi Schneur Zalman of Liady noted that the numerical equivalent of the term *teva* (nature) is *Elohim.*[18] It is through the Sabbath experience that we are directed to penetrate beneath the surface to the core of reality and to become aware that the universe is not a self-sufficient cosmos but is created and sustained in its being by the divine Creator, the source of all reality.

Since the experience of the holiness of the Sabbath is the matrix of the formation of proper perspectives on the "secular" domain, it is readily understandable why the Jewish religious tradition looks upon the Sabbath as the very purpose of all of creation. Accordingly, the Sabbath was not primarily intended as a day of rest enabling a person to return refreshed to

---

[17] *Zohar* 1:1b.

[18] Rabbi Schneur Zalman of Liady. *Tanya: Sha'ar ha-yihud ve-ha-emunah.* Brooklyn: Kehot Publication Society, 1953, chapter 6.

worldly tasks with renewed vigor and zest. Instead, the liturgy in the Friday evening service extols the Sabbath as "the very goal of the making of the heaven and earth." Jewish life is supposed to be Sabbath-centered. The Jew does not rest on the Sabbath to prepare himself or herself for the tasks awaiting in the following week. Instead, the Jew literally lives for the Sabbath. He or she works six days in preparation for the goal of life – to enter the sacred precincts of the sanctuary in time that the Sabbath represents.

Nahmanides pointed out that the biblical commandment "Remember the Sabbath day to sanctify it" implies that the Sabbath is the only day of the week worthy of being designated by a name.[19] The rest of the days are defined solely in terms of their relation to the Sabbath. In Hebrew there is no word for Sunday or Monday, and so on; they are simply the first or the second day of the week. It is noteworthy that the Midrash interprets the biblical phrase "God finished the work He had made on the seventh day"[20] as implying not merely that the work was concluded on the seventh day but that it became perfect only on the seventh day.[21] As Rashi interpreted it, until the Sabbath was created, the world was without *menuchah* (tranquility).[22]

Although the exclusively theocentric formulation of the fourth commandment in the book of Exodus in describing the "Sabbath unto God" does not mention the social and psychological benefits accruing to one from its observance, the version of the Decalogue as presented in the book of Deuteronomy adds the themes of liberation and rest to be enjoyed by all creatures. Both Hermann Cohen and Erich Fromm write from a basically humanistic perspective, which frowns on obedience to heteronomous norms as being devoid of all ethical worth.[23] They concentrate on what they regard as the ethical implications of the Sabbath as set forth in Deuteronomy, which are contrasted with what they describe as the mythological features contained in the creation story, which form the core of the fourth commandment in Exodus 19. It appears to me that this approach reflects a dogmatic insistence on forcing Judaism into a

---

[19] *Commentary to the Torah*, Exodus 20:8.
[20] Genesis 2:2.
[21] Genesis Rabbah 10:10.
[22] Rashi on Genesis 2:2.
[23] Hermann Cohen, *Religion der Vernunft*, 180–182; Fromm, *Ye Shall Be As Gods* (New York: Holt, Rinehart & Winston, 1966) 193–199.

Procrustean bed of humanistic categories. The additional references in Deuteronomy to anthropocentric themes do not in any way detract from the theocentric aspects mandating total surrender to God as the Creator and master of the universe. Significantly, it is precisely in the version in which the humanistic benefits are introduced that the Torah stresses that the observance of the Sabbath is in conformity to a divine imperative ("as God has commanded thee").

This being the case, it would be far more appropriate to treat the anthropocentric and the theocentric dimensions of the Sabbath experience as reflections of the dialectical tension between these two components rather than as irreconcilable positions. Contrary to E. Feuerbach and K. Marx, a person's unconditional submission to the Creator does not devalue human existence but adds an extra dimension of meaning and significance, which enables him or her to experience true dignity and freedom. The Sabbath experience makes us aware of the fact that our ontological status is based not on what we make but on what we are. As bearers of the divine image, people must not be "thingified" – reduced to self-alienated commodities or tools – but must be accorded the dignity due creatures endowed with infinite, intrinsic spiritual value. Through the observance and experience of the Sabbath, Jews learn that in the divine economy, a person's worth depends not upon social utility as an agent of production but derives from the intrinsic sanctity of the human personality.

At first blush it may strike us as strange that the observance of the Sabbath, which cuts a person down to size by mandating that his or her creative powers may be exercised only within the parameters approved by God, simultaneously elevates a person's dignity by providing us with it day of universal rest and liberation, which engenders the experience of *oneg Shabbat* – the enjoyment of delight, peace, and harmony. But we should remember that classical Jewish thought has always proceeded from the premise that it is only through submission to the authority of a transcendent God that humans achieve true dignity and inner freedom. In the often-cited formulation of the rabbinic sages, "one attains freedom only when one is engaged in Torah."[24]

The dialectical nature of the Sabbath experience is suggested also in a well-known Midrash that states that "every thing pertaining to the Sabbath is

---

[24] *Avot* 6:2.

double... a double portion (of manna)... double sacrifices... double penalties... double rewards... double admonitions... and the Sabbath Psalm is double."[25] The two loaves of bread that are *de rigueur* for Sabbath meals[26] reflect this emphasis on the duality characterizing Sabbath observance. Significantly, the Talmud points out that the two versions of the fourth commandment were simultaneously commanded by God to Israel in one single pronouncement.[27] The emphasis on the twofold nature of the Sabbath also comes to the fore in the rabbinic doctrine that with the arrival of the Sabbath the Jew is endowed with a *neshamah yeterah* (an additional soul), which departs at the conclusion of the Sabbath.[28]

Since the Sabbath represents in a sense the bridge between the natural and the transcendent realms, the Talmud took it for granted that the Sinaitic revelation occurred on the Sabbath.[29] It seemed obvious to the rabbinic mind that the day which, according to the Bible, symbolized the incursion of the divine upon the world of nature, represented the ideal time for his revelation to Israel.

Another theme that is associated with the Sabbath is that of redemption. Although in the Torah the connection between the Sabbath and liberation is made only with reference to the Exodus from Egypt, rabbinic thought expands the concept by treating the Exodus as the prototype of the divine redemption – a process that will be completed only in the messianic redemption, when the kingdom of God will be acknowledged by all of humanity. The proper observance of the Sabbath, therefore, is regarded not merely as a reminder of the past liberation but also as a promise of the future realization of our eschatological hopes. It is for this reason that, in the opinion of the sages, the meticulous observance of the Sabbath on the part of the entire Jewish people would ensure the arrival of the Messiah.[30] Because of the close association between the Sabbath and the redemption, the liturgy for welcoming the Sabbath includes a number of psalms that give

---

25 *Midrash Tehillim* on Psalm 92:1.
26 BT *Shabbat* 117b.
27 BT *Rosh Hashanah* 27a.
28 BT *Betzah* 16a.
29 BT *Shabbat* 86b.
30 BT *Shabbat* 118b.

vent to the feeling of exhilaration and jubilation that will be precipitated by the establishment of the kingdom of God.[31]

The Sabbath does not merely point to the redemption of the world from moral evil. Since the Sabbath atmosphere is supposed to make us oblivious to unfulfilled wants and unfinished tasks, it provides a foretaste of the World to Come. This is why when the prayer of grace is recited after the Sabbath meal, the phrase "May the All-Merciful One cause us to inherit the day that is completely a Sabbath of rest and eternal life" is added to the weekday version.

It is interesting that the Talmud records two distinct modes of preparation that are appropriate for the proper encounter with the Sabbath. One amora (a talmudic sage) is reported to have urged his disciples to welcome the Sabbath as a queen, while another taught that the Sabbath should be greeted as a bride.[32] In other words, one opinion emphasized the majesty, awe, and reverence with which the Shabbat should be approached, whereas the other stressed the intimacy with the divine that should be engendered by the encounter with what the liturgy describes as "the most desirable of days." Since the two approaches need not contradict each other, they should be synthesized in the ideal Shabbat experience. Rabbinic authorities until this very day are divided over the question of whether there is a requirement to experience real *simchah* (joy) on Shabbat or whether one is merely obligated to engage in activities that can be described as *oneg* (pleasant) but do not necessarily lead to the higher level of *simchah* which is mandated for holidays. Be that as it may, there is universal agreement that the Sabbath must be respected not only by refraining from work in the technical sense but by staying away from any activity, that interferes with the atmosphere of holiness which ought to prevail on the Sabbath. The dignity of the Sabbath demands that one not only dress and eat differently from the rest of the week, but that one's entire demeanor and conduct reflect the sanctity of the Sabbath. Subjects that disturb the spiritual atmosphere of the Sabbath are to be avoided in conversation.[33]

For a proper appreciation of the sanctity of the Sabbath it should be borne in mind that the Sabbath, God's sanctuary in time, commands the

---

[31] See Yechiel Michel Epstein, *Arukh ha-Shulchan, Orach Chayim* (New York: Halakhah Publishing, 1950) 277:2.

[32] BT *Shabbat* 119a.

[33] BT *Shabbat* 69a.

kind of reverence that must be accorded to God's sanctuary in space. It is highly significant that the Torah juxtaposes the two types of sanctuary in the twice-repeated verse "Ye shall keep My Sabbath and revere My sanctuary."[34] Moreover, the Torah harps repeatedly on the overriding importance of the observance of the Sabbath in connection with the demand to build a sanctuary for God. It is precisely this close linkage between the two types of sanctuaries that prompted the sages to define *melakhah* in terms of the categories of work that were needed for the construction of the sanctuary in the days of Moses.

Because the Sabbath is treated as a sanctuary of God, it is readily understandable that Jewish mystics employ spatial metaphors to describe the unique holiness that envelops the world with the arrival of the Sabbath. According to the *Zohar,* "On Friday evening a tabernacle of peace descends from heaven…. When Israel invites this tabernacle of peace to their homes as a holy guest, a divine sanctity comes down and spreads its wings over Israel like a mother encompassing her children."[35]

It must be realized, however, that the holiness of the Sabbath mandates not merely the cessation of certain types of "secular" activity but also the fulfillment of a number of specific positive obligations. Both the arrival and the departure of the Sabbath must be marked by special ceremonies *(Kiddush* and *Havdalah)*. Moreover, according to Nahmanides's interpretation, the inclusion of the Sabbath among the days of "holy convocations" implies that Jews are not merely required to sanctify the Sabbath individually but are supposed to assemble for the purpose of divine worship and the reading of the Torah. In other words, the Sabbath experience is designed not only to impact upon the Jew individually but also to stimulate the formation of a unique sense of religious community. As a Midrash puts it, Israel's loneliness can be overcome only by the realization that it is mated with the Sabbath, the symbol of its unique spiritual destiny.[36]

Thus it can be seen that, properly observed, the Sabbath is not just a day of rest and total inactivity. Although the Sabbath was maligned by antisemitic writers in the ancient world as evidence of the Jewish predilection to lassitude, which exacts a heavy price in terms of loss of productivity and usefulness, the Sabbath represents a day of spiritual

[34] Leviticus 19:30 and 26:2.
[35] *Zohar* Genesis 48a–b.
[36] Genesis Rabbah 11:8.

creativity[37] which, in the words of Ahad ha-Am, has made possible the very survival of the Jewish people. That the Sabbath is to be regarded as a day of positive achievement rather than of lack of activity can be seen from the fact that the Torah employs the term *la'asot* (to make) in conjunction with the admonition to keep the Sabbath.[38] As Rabbi Kook expressed it so aptly, the Sabbath figures not only as a day of rest but also as a day of holiness.[39] Abstention from activities aiming at the conquest of nature do not exhaust the meaning of the Sabbath. Physical rest must be used for all-out spiritual efforts to respond to the challenge posed by the dynamic ideal of holiness that constantly beckons us toward ever greater heights of religious and moral perfection in the never-ending quest of *imitatio Dei*. This is perhaps what was supposed to be conveyed by the daring Kabbalistic doctrine that the Sabbath symbolizes the union between the male (active) and the female (passive) metaphysical principles which, according to Jewish mysticism, provide the foundation of the universe.[40]

---

[37] See Norman Lamm, "Ethics of Leisure," in *Faith and Doubt*. New York: Ktav, 1971, 197–198. I have also learned a great deal from Abraham J. Heschel's *The Sabbath: Its Meaning for Modern Man* (New York: Farrar, Straus and Giroux, 1951) as well as from the profound insights of Yitzchak Hutner in his *Sefer Pachad Yltzchak* (Brooklyn: Gur Aryeh Institute, 1982).

[38] Exodus 31:16 and Deuteronomy 5:16.

[39] Abraham Isaac Kook, *Olat ha-Reiyah* (Jerusalem: Mossad Harav Kook, 1949) 2:146.

[40] See *Zohar* Exodus 135a–b; *Zohar* Genesis 48a–b; and Nahmanides, *Commentary to the Torah*, Exodus 20:8.

META-HALAKHIC PROPOSITIONS[1]

IT IS COMMONLY ASSUMED that halakhic Judaism pursues a policy of non-intervention in all purely theoretical, philosophical, or theological issues. The rigid objective standards which the Halakhah provides for the regulation of conduct are contrasted with the enormous latitude accorded to the individual in the formulation of a philosophy of life. That Orthodox Judaism has been able to accommodate within its ranks mystics and rationalists, empiricists and pragmatists, idealists and existentialists is often cited as conclusive evidence of the impeccable neutrality that the Halakhah maintains in all matters of theory. Claiming sovereignty only in the realm of practice, the Halakhah is supposedly content to leave the domain of ideology entirely to the subjective whim and personal preference of the individual.

Uncritical acceptance of this dichotomy between theory and practice is fraught with serious dangers for the exponents of halakhic Judaism. Carried to its logical conclusion, it reduces the Halakhah to a "religious behaviorism," completely stripped of any relevance to the ethical, spiritual and intellectual dilemmas besetting man. We end up with a brand of "Halakhic Positivism" that rules out from the Jewish universe of discourse all questions pertaining to the meaning of human existence and relationships.

There are, of course, some extremists who will go along with the radical position of Professor Yeshayahu Leibowitz who places even the quest for social justice and the search for ethical values beyond the pale of halakhic

[1] From *The Leo Jung Jubilee Volume,* edited by Menachem M. Kasher, Norman Lamm, and Leonard Rosenfeld, 211–221. New York: Jewish Center, 1962.

Judaism. According to Professor Leibowitz, the Halakhah represents a purely formal legal structure, completely indifferent to intellectual, ethical, or aesthetic values. Its only concern is to "organize the rules of human life against a background of law, the aim of which is the service of God."[2]

But most religiously sensitive individuals will object to such radical surgery that amputates from the body of Judaism all meaningful human aspirations and ideals. They will feel constrained to join Professor Heschel's rebellion against a narrowly conceived "Pan-Halakhism" that shrinks the fabric of Judaism from a multi-faceted, all-embracing commitment of the total personality to a specialized field of "sacred physics." Because it is assumed in these circles that the Halakhah as such has no concern with the realm of ideas, attitudes, or ideological commitments, the burden of supplying the Jew with a philosophy of life is assigned to the non-halakhic components of Judaism. We therefore encounter a tendency to shift the center of gravity from the "four cubits of the Halakhah" and place major emphasis upon such non-halakhic elements as aggadah, philosophy, mussar, or mysticism.

This solution is bound to be very unpalatable to those who regard the Halakhah as the most authentic and genuine manifestation of the spirit of Judaism. If the Halakhah is to occupy the supreme position in the Jewish hierarchy of values, we should be able to expect from it at least some measure of guidance towards the development of a philosophy of life that renders human existence meaningful. We shall, therefore, do well to investigate whether the Halakhah is actually devoid of all theological and philosophical presuppositions or whether it may be feasible to construct a philosophy of halakhic Judaism out of the halakhic data available to us.

The more closely one examines the question, the more one wonders how serious thinkers could ever have suggested that the impact of the Halakhah is confined to the realm of practice. There can be no doubt that the Halakhah sets definite limits to our freedom of thought. Obviously atheism, agnosticism, and various forms of naturalism are incompatible with the Halakhah which renders mandatory the belief in one God. By the same token, the Halakhah postulates the acceptance of such notions as divine providence, revelation, reward and punishment and therefore commits us to a number of specific metaphysical propositions.

---

[2] Yeshayahu Leibowitz, "The World and the Jews." In *Forum*, vol. 4, 85.

These obvious facts will suffice to refute the claim of Spinoza and Mendelssohn[3] that Judaism is devoid of any cognitive significance because, allegedly, it is the business of religion to regulate conduct, not concepts.

Yet there remains a kernel of truth that has been distorted in the radical version adopted by the above-mentioned philosophers. The Halakhah certainly does not provide an explicitly formulated theological or philosophical system of thought. Moreover, the theoretical propositions which are either stated or presupposed by the Halakhah are characterized by a high degree of vagueness and elasticity. A striking illustration is furnished by the often quoted dictum of Rabbi Abraham ibn David, who stated boldly that even the attribution of corporeality to God does not exclude one from the fold of halakhic Judaism.

Yet for all its lack of precision in matters purely theoretical, in the final analysis the Halakhah still circumscribes the area in which all authentic Jewish thought must move. At the very minimum, it establishes standards for the rejection of philosophies incompatible with halakhic attitudes.

However, it still remains to be seen whether the cognitive significance of the Halakhah is exhausted by this essentially negative function. It is the purpose of this paper to show that there is a class of propositions to be called "meta-halakhic propositions" which contain the Halakhah's ontological and axiological presuppositions. These meta-halakhic propositions represent the metaphysical and ethical propositions that can be extracted from halakhic data and which, unlike general aggadic concepts, form an integral part of the halakhic system. Without in any way belittling the value of aggadic material, it is our contention that we must turn to these propositions – as Dr. Belkin did so admirably with some of the basic halakhic concepts that he develops in his brilliant study *In His Image*[4] – for the formulation of a philosophy of life that will reflect the spirit of halakhic Judaism.

---

[3] We should bear in mind that for Mendelssohn, Judaism presupposes metaphysical propositions and that form the core of the universally valid religion. In Mendelssohn's scheme, Judaism is merely revealed law and not revealed religion because the theoretical assumptions such as the existence of God, immorality, etc., form part of the overall religion of reason. Cf. I. Heinemann, "Unity in Moses Mendelssohn's Philosophy of Religion." *Metzudah* (1954): 197–219.

[4] Samuel Belkin, *In His Image*. New York: Aberland-Schuman, 1960.

In order to appreciate our point of view more fully, it is advisable to contrast it with that of Heschel, who defines the Halakhah in purely behavioristic terms. In his scheme, there is an unbridgeable chasm between the personal world of the Aggadah and the objective world of the Halakhah, because, allegedly, the Halakhah does not concern itself with matters of belief, faith, or attitude. As Heschel put it:

> The statement "Moses received the Torah from Sinai" does not express a halakhic idea. For Halakhah deals with what man ought to do, with what man can translate into action, with things that are definite and concrete. The event at Sinai, the mystery of revelation, belongs to the sphere of the Aggadah.[5]

Heschel seems to be unaware that a statement such as "Moses received the Torah from Sinai" cannot be classified as ordinary aggadic material. The denial of the statement renders an individual a *min* (apostate) with all the halakhic implications that this status entails. Heschel fails to recognize that the statement in question is presupposed by the Halakhah and must therefore be regarded as a meta-halakhic proposition.

Heschel's failure to distinguish between ordinary aggadic material and meta-halakhic propositions comes to the fore in the following quotations:

> Halakhah thinks in the category of quantity; Aggadah is the category of quality: Aggadah maintains that he who saves one life is as if he had saved all mankind. In the eyes of him whose first category is the category of quantity, one man is less than two men, but in the eyes of God, one life is worth as much as all of life.[6]

What strikes us is Heschel's blindness to halakhic values, which causes him to overlook the fact that the Halakhah refuses to apply quantitative standards to human beings. For is it not a halakhic dictum that a group of people must not surrender one innocent to a band of gangsters even though the sacrifice of one individual will allow a large number of people to be saved? Does this not prove that far from maintaining that "one man is less than two men," the Halakhah recognizes the infinite value of the individual human being? If Heschel feels that only the Aggadah is conscious of the

---

[5] A. J. Heschel, *God in Search of Man*, 328.
[6] *ibid.*, 337.

value of quality, then this is not the fault of the Halakhah but rather is due to Heschel's failure to recognize meta-halakhic propositions.

Now, the objection will probably be raised that what divides us from Heschel is merely a question of terminology, because what we have termed meta-halakhic propositions will find accommodation in Heschel's system under the label of Aggadah. But it would not be correct to treat this as a purely verbal issue. For what is actually involved is a disagreement over the crucial question of whether the Halakhah entails a definite set of ontological and axiological propositions.

If the thesis to be developed in this paper is correct, then there are a number of ethical and metaphysical propositions which do not merely happen to be held by halakhic scholars who at the same time are also masters of the Aggadah, but which form an integral part of the Halakhah itself. These meta-halakhic propositions are by no means merely epiphenomena without causal relationship to the halakhic process. Far from being merely the superstructure, they represent the axiological and ontological structure of the Halakhah.

Unlike Bialik,[7] who regarded the entire realm of the Aggadah as organically related to the Halakhah, treating the latter as the concretization of the former, we object to the blurring of the line of demarcation separating the two spheres. Halakhah and Aggadah do not form a continuum. We categorically reject any view that regards the Halakhah as the harvest of the seeds that blossomed forth from the Aggadah. But we do maintain that there exists a special class of philosophical and theological propositions that contribute to the warp and woof of halakhic thought.

However, there is an *a priori* objection that is frequently raised against any attempt to construct a philosophy of Halakhah. The fact that such a number of conflicting philosophies have been espoused by leading halakhic scholars is invoked as proof of the Halakhah's strict neutrality on all questions relating not to concrete practice but to abstract ideology. This argument, however, rests upon a glaring fallacy. It is conveniently overlooked that even in the domain of pure Halakhah the clash of conflicting opinions is far from rare. And if we are prepared to reconcile the objective validity of the Halakhah with the prevalence of differences of opinion on concrete questions of law, we cannot rule out *a priori* the

---

[7] Hayyim Nahman Bialik. *Kol Kitvei Hayyim Nahman Bialik*. Tel Aviv: 1955. 207–213.

feasibility of a philosophy of Halakhah on the ground that serious differences of opinion are encountered among leading Jewish thinkers.

It must be borne in mind that whatever degree of uniformity exists on questions of actual practice is largely due to the existence of a mechanism that makes for the acceptance of the majority view. Nevertheless, it must not be forgotten that even in the realm of Halakhah itself there exists a basic distinction between theory and practice. A member of the Sanhedrin had every right to advocate his own views on any question of law, however strongly they may have differed from those of his colleagues on this august body. Yet when it came to the realm of practice, once the question was settled by the Sanhedrin, he could not abide by his own personal ruling, but had to conform to the majority position, though he was still free to defend and advocate his personal views in the hope that ultimately the Sanhedrin would be persuaded to reverse its decision.

Obviously, questions of truth cannot be settled by majority vote, even of a Sanhedrin. Yet unless there is to be complete anarchy, some method must be found for the resolution of conflict as it affects religious practice. Nowadays, as every student of the Halakhah knows, the literature abounds with suggestions offered *le-halakhah ve-lo le-ma'aseh* – merely as halakhic theory, but not intended as concrete proposals for action until such time as the majority of responsible scholars concurs with them.

It need not be emphasized that the sphere of meta-Halakhah does not lend itself to the kind of uniformity that can be attained in the field of practical Halakhah. But the fact that differences of opinion are unavoidable does not at all imply that meta-halakhic propositions are purely subjective. No matter how decisive a role the subjective factors play in molding the philosophical outlook that any given halakhic scholar may extract from the halakhic sources, there remains an objective core.

Similarly, in the final analysis opinions in matters pertaining to the objective Halakhah also reflect the personality of the individual scholar. Of course, it is true that subjective factors will come to the fore more drastically in matters pertaining to abstract theory than in the more concrete problems relating to the regulation of conduct. But this is a difference of degree rather than kind. Hence, we are not justified in making any absolute distinctions between a fundamentally objective Halakhah and a supposedly purely subjective philosophy of Halakhah.

275

Instead of artificially erecting a wall of separation between the two domains, we should candidly acknowledge the considerable extent of the interaction between them. As we shall demonstrate later on, differences of opinion on halakhic questions frequently reflect divergent philosophies of life. Of course, this does not imply that the halakhic scholar reads his own independent value judgments into the halakhic sources. Nothing would be further from the truth than the assumption that the halakhic scholar starts out with preconceived notions that he subsequently justifies through ingenious interpretations and skillful selection of texts. Texts do not merely serve as pretexts. But, at the same time, texts must be interpreted and applied to concrete situations. And it is in this area that the halakhic scholar is guided by his own subjective value judgments, which, in turn, are largely influenced by his understanding of the Halakhah. "The Torah is not in Heaven"; it must be interpreted by human beings who are forever confined within the limits of their own subjectivity.

That the halakhic process involves the continuous interaction between subjective and objective components becomes evident to anyone who takes the pains to familiarize himself with the history of halakhic thought. Countless examples could be adduced to show that the ideology of a given halakhic scholar cannot be dismissed as a causally inconsequential epiphenomenon. We need but recall the Vilna Gaon's famous stricture against Maimonides, in which he charges the latter with having been misled in a specific ruling by his proclivity for general philosophy.[8] Nor can there be any doubt that when Maimonides explicates the commandment "Thou shalt walk in His ways" in a manner so closely akin to the Aristotelian ideal of the "Golden Mean," the entire ideological background of a Maimonides went into the making of this daring interpretation. By the same token, it is quite obvious that Maimonides's entire philosophy of life is reflected in his decision to regard the study of natural science as implied in the commandment of "loving God."

To turn to some more recent but equally convincing examples, we may note the fundamental difference of opinion concerning *Torah li-shma* that divided Rabbi Schneur Zalman of Liady and Rabbi Hayyim of Volozhin. Will anyone question that their radical disagreement on this issue reflects ultimately the wide chasm separating their respective world views?

---

[8] Baer ha-Gra, *Yoreh Deah*, 179, 13.

In a recent study, Dr. Aharon Wertheim[9] compiled massive evidence to show that Hassidism developed certain unique attitudes towards halakhic questions. To cite an especially interesting illustration, Dr. Wertheim points to the eagerness with which Hassidim press for the establishment of *eruvin* as an indication of their penchant for unification. For the Hassid, the divisiveness engendered by separate domains between which transportation is prohibited must be overcome and transcended through an *eruv*. Because the *eruv* is such a desideratum in the Hassidic scale of values, their halakhic authorities are consistently inclined to be more lenient in rulings affecting the permissibility of an *eruv*. Similarly, the Hassidic tendency to be extremely lax in complying with the talmudic specifications governing the timing of prayers has been associated by Dr. Wertheim with the mystic tendency to overcome all limitations of time and space in the quest for the "higher unity."

There is no need to multiply examples to demonstrate what is so obvious: halakhic decisions both influence and, in turn, are influenced by a given scholar's meta-halakhic position. Therefore, it should not surprise us that there is no one philosophy of Halakhah to which all halakhic authorities can subscribe. However, the intrusion of subjective factors, which makes it impossible to speak of *the* philosophy of Halakhah, does in no way interfere with our contention that some meta-halakhic propositions explicate the ontological and axiological presuppositions underlying various specific halakhic approaches. For it is their relationship to halakhic data – not their specific content – that determines whether or not a given set of axiological and ontological statements can qualify as *a* philosophy of Halakhah.

It must be borne in mind that the halakhic datum, too, is never a pure given. Just as scientific data are not mere sensations but become scientifically relevant (i.e., data) only through activities of the human mind (selection, interpretation, construction, and so on), so does the halakhic datum presuppose an act of interpretation on the part of an individual thinker. This is why, however tinged with subjectivity a halakhic opinion may be, it nevertheless represents a legitimate datum for the meta-Halakhah as long as it has been evolved by bona fide halakhic procedures. If the canons governing halakhic reasoning have been observed, then, no matter what the ultimate conclusion might be, we can invoke the rabbinic dictum, "Both

---

[9] Aharon Wertheim, *Halakhah ve-Halikhot ba-Hasidut.*

these and these are the words of the living God." In other words, the status of "halakhic datum" is conferred upon an opinion solely by virtue of it having evolved in conformity with the halakhic process.

These considerations will clarify how it is possible for philosophers of Halakhah to run such a wide gamut of mutually incompatible attitudes. For if the data itself are tainted by subjectivity – due to the organic interaction between halakhic "raw material" and the subjective construction of the individual halakhic thinker – then, obviously, the theories and interpretations of the meta-Halakhah that are based upon the halakhic data will bring the divergent attitudes into even sharper focus.

The postulation of various philosophies of Halakhah thus disposes of the *a priori* argument that is so frequently advanced against the very possibility of formulating meta-halakhic propositions. Nevertheless, we must come to grips with another type of objection. Thus, Dr. Agus[10] contends that a critical examination of the classical formulations of halakhic Judaism proves the futility of any attempt to develop a self-sufficient, independent philosophy of Halakhah. Pointing to the published works of such champions of halakhic Judaism as Rabbi Hayyim of Volozhin and Rabbi Joseph B. Soloveitchik, Dr. Agus charges that for the validation of halakhic thinking, these giants of Halakhah also had to fall back upon non-halakhic sources such as the Kabbalah or medieval philosophy. This supposedly shows that there is no such discipline as a self-enclosed philosophy of Halakhah.

However, upon closer analysis, we can detect that this *a posteriori* argument is based upon a serious fallacy. It implies that the mere employment of categories of thought that are suggested by non-halakhic sources automatically makes one liable to expulsion from the domain of unadulterated halakhic thinking. This mistaken notion shows a total misconception of the meaning and function of a philosophy of Halakhah.

The source from which a given proposition was first suggested is completely irrelevant to the question whether or not it is acceptable within the framework of the meta-Halakhah. To employ an analogy from general philosophy, a proposition may belong to the category of *a priori* propositions, although it was formed only on the basis of a variety of empirical experiences. Similarly, although the source of a particular meta-halakhic proposition may interest us from a psychological point of view, logically,

---

[10] Jacob B. Agus, *Guideposts in Modern Judaism,* 41–43.

there is only one criterion determining the status of a meta-halakhic proposition. Whether or not a specific proposition can qualify as a meta-halakhic proposition depends not upon its content, let alone its genetic origin, but solely upon its relationship to the halakhic data. Just as the validity of a scientific hypothesis hinges upon its success in correlating a certain set of scientific data, so the validity of a meta-halakhic proposition must be evaluated solely in terms of its ability to formulate the presuppositions of the Halakhah. As long as this function is performed satisfactorily, we have every right to brush aside a question pertaining to the origin of meta-halakhic ideas.

From this it follows that champions of halakhic thinking are perfectly free to draw upon extra-halakhic sources as mental aids in the formulation of meta-halakhic propositions, provided that they restrict themselves to ideas which can be harmonized with genuine halakhic thinking. Thus, Rabbi Soloveitchik is perfectly justified in using kabbalistic notions as long as they do not entail a predilection for escaping from existential reality into the higher regions of being, which alone can satisfy the mystic's craving for undifferentiated oneness. As a matter of fact, a careful reading of his *Ish ha-Halakhah*[11] shows that he is extremely selective in the admission of non-halakhic material and employs only such kabbalistic or philosophical notions as can be assimilated unquestionably as meta-halakhic propositions into the framework of an authentic halakhic approach.

Another serious error is inherent in Dr. Agus's strictures. It has never been suggested that the halakhic man, as a concrete individual and not merely as an abstract philosophical prototype, must disavow all additional spiritual interests. Thus, Rabbi Hayyim of Volozhin was not merely a man of Halakhah; at the same time, he was also an eminent kabbalistic of great stature. Rabbi Hayyim himself, aware of a clash between these two worlds, stated in a famous passage, "In truth, from His side, all existence is equally filled by His Being without any separations, distinctions, or divisions, as if creation had not taken place at all. We are neither capable of nor permitted to contemplate this fact at all, but seek to do His mitzvot in the world that is revealed to understanding."[12] Rabbi Hayyim realized that the world of Halakhah as such rested upon the assumption of a "radical pluralism" which

---

[11] Rabbi Joseph B. Soloveitchik, *Halakhic Man*.
[12] Rabbi Hayyim of Volozhin, *Nefesh ha-Hayyim*, 3:6.

could not be harmonized with the goal of the *yihuda ila'a* (highest unity) formulated by the Kabbalist.

But the fact that at times Rabbi Hayyim ventured forth from the solid domain of the halakhic man and became enthralled with the heavenly mysteries does not in any manner imply that he did not enunciate a number of extremely important meta-halakhic propositions. Thus he showed in a most convincing manner that insofar as halakhic thinking is concerned we must operate with the assumption that the immanent God has completely concealed Himself in order to make possible the appearance of an independent world. The Halakhah simply cannot function on the premise that God's actual presence permeates all of reality alike. Typical of Rabbi Hayyim is the climax of his critique of the Hassidic position. He pointedly asks how the study of the Torah could be prohibited in unclean places if each place must be regarded as being equally filled with God's presence. This leads to the conclusion that halakhic thinking cannot dispense with the postulation of individual finite entities existing in time and space. We must therefore reconcile ourselves to the fact that while, metaphysically speaking, God may be immanent in the world, meta-halakhically speaking, His presence is a mystery transcending the bounds of human cognition. The halakhic approach to life is closed not upon ultimate metaphysical reality but upon the *appearance* of the world to the finite human mind, which sees not an undifferentiated whole but the separate, distinct spatio-temporal entities that compromise the radical pluralism of the Halakhah.

A thorough study of *Nefesh ha-Hayyim* would bring to light many other meta-halakhic propositions even though Rabbi Hayyim's treatment is far from systematic, let alone exhaustive. Yet for our present purposes there is no need to pursue the subject in greater detail since we are only interested in showing the feasibility of meta-halakhic propositions.

The systematic formulation of meta-halakhic propositions is a formidable task that probably transcends the energies of any one scholar. The harnessing of the collective resources of halakhic scholars may be the only way in which the ontological and axiological foundation of halakhic Judaism can be made explicit to the modern Jew who is searching for an authentically Jewish ideology.

TRADITION AS A WAY TO THE FUTURE: A JEWISH PERSPECTIVE[1]

THE THREE COMPONENTS of our overall theme – family, community and tradition – form not merely a closely-connected triad but actually constitute a single theme in variations. In a sense, community and tradition may be regarded as horizontal and vertical extensions of family.

The anomie, the alienation, the rootlessness, the disintegration of the family, and the erosion of a sense of community, which we are witnessing in our depersonalized society, are not isolated phenomena but parts of a syndrome. They are all symptoms of the underlying malaise of our age: the excessive individualism which has so catastrophically affected modern attitudes towards family, community and tradition. The ecological crisis that threatens the very survival of humanity has its roots in what I call the "egological crisis" – the one-sided focus on the isolated and insulated individual. As Robert Bellah declared in his *Habits of the Heart,* "Modern individualism seems to be producing a way of life that is neither individually nor socially viable."[2]

The epitome of secular modernity is best summed up in the formulations of the atheist philosopher Sartre, who declared, "Hell is others" and "Freedom is nothingness." This tragic finale is the logical conclusion of philosophies of life, which reject all attempts to secure a transcendental

---

[1] *Trinity Journal of Church and Theology.*
[2] Robert Bellah, *Habits of the Heart: Individualism and Commitment in American Life.* Perennial Library: 1986, 144.

foundation for human values. When ethical values merely represent purely arbitrary subjective commitments of individuals, any attempt to escape from the absurdity of the human condition is not merely an exercise in futility but an act of self-deception or bad faith.

The sense of meaninglessness is exacerbated under the conditions of our atomized mass societies in which individuals are reduced to mere ciphers. Lacking a sense of meaning and purpose, members of the "now generation" are condemned to a life of emptiness, revolving around the endless pursuit of instant gratification. It is therefore hardly surprising that we are witnessing a growing disenchantment with modernity.

This is one of the major reasons why liberalism has lost so much of its popularity in the face of a rising tide of communitarian philosophies. The chaotic conditions of most urban centers, the high incidence of crime, the disintegration of the fabric of society have bred disillusionment and have intensified a nostalgic quest for the good old days. The formerly widely-held assumption that reason and science are capable of solving or at least ameliorating our problems has been found wanting. Contrary to the predictions both of Marxists and liberals that humanity will gravitate more and more towards the acceptance of universal values, we observe, even in the face of a global economy, the resurgence of participation in the astounding impact of ethnicity and nationalism, especially after the Cold War. What is especially relevant to this conference is that the reversal of the fortunes of universalism and the revival of particularism have resulted in totally unexpected setbacks for the ecumenical movement.

While the yearning for the imagined tranquility and serenity of more traditional societies is fully understandable, we must entertain an important *caveat* that, in the words of Thomas Wolfe, "We cannot go home again." We must somehow find a way between the Scylla of extreme conservatism agitating for a return to an irretrievable past and the Charybdis of dismissing all traditions as an albatross around our necks. Such a third way should enable us to reconcile the revolutionary thrust of prophetic ideals with healthy respect for traditional structures and institutions.

This can be accomplished only if we recognize that the underlying cause of the disintegration of the very fabric of our society is modern individualism's failure to take seriously the insight of biblical anthropology that "It is not good for man to be alone." With its focus on autonomy as the matrix of all values, it was taken for granted that, in the final analysis, individuals should be treated as self-enclosed entities. Biblical anthropology, on the other hand, stresses the human need for community. According to Genesis 2, woman was formed from man's side. Man is incomplete until he is reunited with the missing dimension of his existence. The primary goal of marriage is not reproduction, but the establishment of a true union with one's partner, without whom one cannot be a complete person.

This conception of love and marriage sharply conflicts with modern notions. Whereas Freud wanted to reduce love to sexuality and Eros to libido, the biblical view, as Paul Tillich has shown, relates love to the existential need for union with another self. Accordingly, the sexual impulse is no longer the foundation of love, but merely the instrument for bringing about the total union of husband and wife.

The ideal of biblical religions is *devekut* (attachment) rather than self-sufficiency or autonomy. Significantly, the first time this term appears in the Bible is in Genesis 2:24, concerning the proper relationship to one's spouse. But the same term is also employed in Deuteronomy regarding the ideal relationship with God that we ought to cultivate. The late Rabbi Soloveitchik brilliantly portrayed the human need for the establishment of a "covenantal community" with God in order to overcome existential loneliness.

The biblical conception of freedom also reflects concern for family and community rather than self-centered autonomy and independence. It may be symbolic that the Liberty Bell in Philadelphia contains only one part of the verse in Leviticus (25:19). "Thou shalt proclaim liberty to the land and all the inhabitants thereof." Completely ignored, however, is the sequel of the verse, which spells out the real purpose of liberty: "It shall be a jubilee unto you; and ye shall return every man unto his family."

The sense of community that Judaism advocates is by no means limited to linkage with one's contemporaries, but extends to past and future as well. This is why on Yom Kippur we seek atonement not only for our own sins but also for those of our ancestors. The term *Knesset Yisrael* denotes a transcendent community. The Jewish liturgy pointedly refers to God not merely as our personal God but also as the "God of our fathers." Time and again Jews are admonished to remember, be it the Sabbath as a sign attesting to the divine creation of the universe, the exodus from Egypt, the theophany at Sinai, the battle against the Amalekites, or various other specific historic events.

The emphasis upon the relevance of the past and the weight assigned to the authority of tradition is even more pronounced in the Torah's basic norm, "Ask your father and he will declare unto thee, thine elders and they will tell thee" (Deuteronomy 32:7). In keeping with this orientation, the Talmud interprets the exhortation of the book of Proverbs (1:8), "Hear, my son, the instruction of thy father, and forsake not the teaching of thy mother," as implying the demand for reverence for established traditions of the community. In this spirit, Jewish religious law mandates adherence to *minhag* (established customs and procedures).

This approach goes completely against the ethos of many Western societies which, under the influence of utilitarianism or pragmatism, worship progress and scoff at respect for traditional values. As Margaret Mead put it so tellingly, "The 'Now Generation' has its roots in the future, not the past." Or in the words of a well-known American poet, Robert Frost, "The past is a bucket of ashes." This is perhaps why an American witticism recommends, "Treat each day as if it were your first."

Whereas for modern man only the moment seems to be of significance, all biblical religions underscore the importance of the historic dimension. For all their fundamental differences, they focus on particular, contingent events such as Creation, Revelation and the establishment of covenants. Small wonder, then, that early Christians recognized that their theological affirmations which were grounded in history were bound to constitute a "scandalon" to the Greek mind, which could take seriously only what was validated by universally valid principles rather than by appeals to historically significant events. As Pascal pointed out, those who profess biblical religions worship not the God of the philosophers, but the God of Abraham, Isaac and Jacob.

In contrast with the historic thrust of biblical religions, the Greek mentality preferred the realm of immutable laws of nature or reason over the merely contingent. Plato, for example, refused to bestow the honorific term "knowledge" on what was only grounded in sense experience. Even for Aristotle, there could be no knowledge of the particular or the individual since knowledge was made possible only by the assimilation of the "forms" of the entities encountered.

Hand in hand with this predilection for the universal and eternal goes the devaluation of time in Greek thought. For Aristotle, neither the past nor the future were real. Time merely is the aggregate of now – the intervals between what is no longer and what is not yet.

As a religion based upon a variety of historic covenants (from those established with the Patriarchs to those entered into with the people collectively at Sinai and subsequently in the land of Moab prior to their entry into the land of Israel, and to the ultimate Davidic Covenant), Judaism was totally out of tune with the ethos of the Enlightenment, which tended to identify revealed religion with superstition and clamored for emancipation from what they regarded as the sole criterion of truth and value prompted the leading thinkers of the Enlightenment to reject any attempt to accord any weight to Revelation or tradition. This is why Kant went as far as to deny any religious significance to Judaism which, in his opinion, was nothing more than a mere legal code sanctioned by the tradition of a community.

So deeply ingrained was the aversion of the Enlightenment to religious traditions that the French Revolution, unlike most other revolutionary movements, never invoked the Exodus from Egypt as justification for its own struggle for liberation. No historic precedent could be of value to those who insisted that all institutions and structures must always be justified *de novo* by purely rational criteria and not by an appeal to tradition or established practice.

That even nowadays it is widely assumed that a return to traditional values is not a live option is evidenced by Robert Bellah's assertion that even those who are completely disenchanted with modernity would view "a return to traditional forms… as a return to intolerable discrimination and oppression."

This identification of tradition with enslavement to the past represents the very antithesis of the tradition-directed approach advocated by religions that are based upon the belief in historic revelations. Thus the Decalogue begins with "I am the Lord thy God, who brought thee out of the land of Egypt, out of the house of bondage." Many commentators took pains to point out that the historic experience of the Exodus rather than the belief in divine creation of the universe provides the foundation of the Jewish religion. For that matter, the observance of various holidays is primarily linked with the commemoration of historic events. In the Jewish liturgy reference to the Exodus from Egypt is made twice daily in fulfillment of the obligation to "acknowledge the yoke of the Kingdom of God."

The Exodus is also considered a precursor of the ultimate Messianic Redemption. Israel Ba'al Shem Tov, the founder of the Hassidic movement, went as far as to declare, "Remembrance is the beginning of Redemption."

In a similar vein, Rabbi Abraham Isaac Kook declared that the Exodus from Egypt will only be completed with the dawn of the Messianic era.

In his *Exodus and Revolution,* Michael Walzer adduces compelling evidence that throughout history, the remembrance of the Exodus, far from fostering passive acceptance of the status quo, has actually inspired numerous progressive and revolutionary movements. It was precisely the memory of the past that captured the imagination of those who refused to reconcile themselves to the inevitability of oppression and injustice and prompted them to strive and struggle for a better future. The Exodus was viewed not as the culmination but as the beginning of a process leading to the attainment of perfect justice and dignity.

The Jewish tradition does not idealize the past, but regards its study as the source of guidance for the future. The events recorded in Genesis were treated as prototypes of future events. "What happened to the Patriarchs is a sign of what will happen in the future." Although the Torah is not a metaphysical or cosmological treatise, the account of Creation, according to the Midrash, was included because we can derive important normative lessons from it. Jewish thinkers stress that humans are given the task of finishing the work that God began with the creation of the universe.

It should be pointed out that the Jewish tradition does not look upon Revelation merely as a historic event that transpired in the past. Human beings bear an ongoing responsibility for the interpretation of the meaning of the divine Revelation for *their* time. There is a delightful rabbinic story about Moses's inability to understand Rabbi Akiva's hermeneutics of the text of the Torah. The very conception of the Oral Torah, for all its dependence upon Mesorah (the authority of the tradition that is invoked to certify its authenticity), assigns a creative role to human beings in the elucidation of the meaning of Torah for their generation. It was this capacity for creative interpretation that enabled the Tannanim to declare several Biblical laws inoperative because they were intended for a totally different set of social conditions. Similarly, later authorities frequently stated that some of the provisions of Talmudic law were no longer binding on account of changed circumstances. This clearly shows that the belief in the immutability of a divinely revealed law by no means amounts to a tyranny of the past. The proper use of tradition involves not mere mechanical adoption, but the kind of appropriation which is sensitive to the requirements of modifications, necessitated by the vicissitudes of the historic process. As T.S. Eliot put it,

"Tradition cannot be had except by great labor." Recognition of the need for the dialectical tension between the heritage of the past and the demands of autonomy makes it possible to employ the insights of the past towards the building of a future in which human beings will be adequate to the task of serving as partners with God in completing His Creation, Revelation and Redemption.

It is of the utmost importance for us to realize that a sense of historic continuity is indispensable to a meaningful life. As Samuel Pisar has expressed it, "We don't live in the past, but the past lives within us." To repress traditional values for the sake of an illusory emancipation from the bondage of the past represents an act of dehumanization. Without memory or anticipation, without a relationship to the time continuum that includes the past as well as the future, we lose our very humanity. We cannot exist merely as members of humanity in general. Our humanity must be manifested in its very particularity. The Mishnah emphasizes that although each individual is endowed with the image of God, no two human beings are alike. Therefore, every person bears the image of God in a unique manner. The Bible does not mandate love of humanity as an abstraction. Instead, we are commanded, "to love thy neighbor" in his/her particularity.

Modern history abounds with tragic examples of how the sacrifice of various national or ethnic traditions in the quest for universal religious, political or social visions has wrought havoc with numerous societies. As a Jew I deplore that in exchange for the Emancipation, it was expected that we surrender our distinctiveness. We were granted equal rights with the tacit understanding that we totally assimilate into the mainstream of European society. Similarly, many of the social problems plaguing the United States can be attributed to the "melting pot" philosophy that did not take into account the need for individuals as well as groups to maintain their respective tradition: Regrettably, many missionaries, too, failed to take seriously the specific traditions of native populations. They expected converts to break with their past completely and swallow the entire Western culture hook, line and sinker. This attitude gave rise to many totally unnecessary conflicts that devastated many native societies.

It goes without saying that committed as I am to transcendental, universally valid values, I am not advocating a historicist position. But since the past lives in us, we must accept ourselves for what we are and realize that we form links in a historic tradition. It therefore behooves us to let our timeless ideals be filtered through the contingencies of our particularity. It is only through linkage with our families, communities and traditions that we can embark on a journey that may lead to the acme of *devekut* (attachment), which can be reached by "those who are attached to God [and therefore] are fully alive" (Deuteronomy 4:4).

THE FAITH OF THE JEWISH PEOPLE[1]

THE "LANGUAGE BARRIER" constitutes a formidable obstacle to conveying to Catholics as insight into how Jews perceive the nature of their religious identity. Terms such as "faith," "religion," "salvation" and "messiah" have entirely different connotations for Jews and Christians. The two religious communities do not merely differ on matters of theological belief but reflect divergent approaches towards the very scope and function of religion.

There can be no meaningful communication unless it is realized that Judaism is not really a religious denomination in the ordinary sense of the term, but the faith of a particular ethnic group – the Jewish people. Just as water is not simply an aggregate of oxygen and hydrogen but an entirely new substance formed out of the combination of its two constituent elements, so Judaism is not just a mixture of religion and ethnicism but a unique compound. The interaction between religion and ethnicism produces a whole that cannot be reduced to its constituent parts.

Judaism is a monotheistic faith that proclaims numerous teachings of universal applicability and import. But it does not seek converts. It claims no monopoly on salvation. Non-Jews need not accept the particular commandments addressed to the Jewish people, which was elected by God for a special role in history – to serve as witness of God and as a light to the nations. In order to qualify for a share in the World to Come, non-Jews are required only to reject idolatry and accept the Seven Noahide Laws (the basic principles of monotheistic morality). It is for this reason that as early as

[1] *New Catholic World* (September/October, 1985): 216–219.

the Middle Ages, a host of Jewish thinkers hailed Christianity's pioneering contribution in disseminating to the pagan world the belief in monotheism, thus paving the way for the ultimate establishment of the Kingdom of God, when all of humanity will submit itself to His rule.

But the universal teachings of ethical monotheism by no means exhaust the meaning of Judaism as the faith of the Jewish people. There is an irreducible particularistic dimension. It is the people of Israel which is bound by a special Covenant to God and singled out for a unique role in the divine economy. Therefore, one cannot convert to Judaism simply by accepting the tenets of the Torah. Another equally important requirement must be satisfied. One must also be prepared to identify with the Jewish people and experience a sense of solidarity and kinship with fellow Jews. Jewish conversion procedures are patterned after biblical formula as expressed in the Book of Ruth. "Your people is my people and your God is my God."

Professor Alfred Whitehead's well known characterization of religion as "what man does with his solitariness" is totally inappropriate for Judaism. Jews are related to God not simply as individuals but as members of a natural and historic community – the people of Israel. The patriarch Abraham was promised that his seed would become a "great *people*" through which "all the nations of the world will be blessed." The Sinaitic Covenant mandates that the community of fate of the Jewish people become also a community of faith – "a Kingdom of Priests and a holy nation."

With the exception of converts, one's Jewish identity hinges upon a biological basis. No rite of initiation is needed to qualify for membership. One does not have to opt for Judaism. Anyone born of a Jewish mother is automatically accorded the status of Jew. A person's Jewish identity is irrevocable, just as God's covenant with Israel is irrevocable. Even if a Jew accepts a different faith, he cannot evade his covenantal responsibilities. He remains a member of the Jewish people. Moreover, there is no escape from the burdens of the Jewish condition. During the Hitler era, having a single Jewish grandparent sufficed to suffer the degradation and tortures that the Nazis reserved for the members of the Jewish people.

Because Christians perceive themselves primarily as a spiritual community, they find it difficult to appreciate the enormous religious significance that Jews attach to the preservation of their ethnic identity and to the bonds connecting them to the Land of Israel. In the Jewish view, the holiness of the land of Israel is not primarily the function of sacred sites, be it the Temple Mount, the Cave of Machpelah, the Tomb of Rachel, and so on. The land itself is sacred not because of any natural characteristics but because, in the words of God to Abraham, it is "the land I will show you." It is the arena where the ultimate fulfillment of Israel's divine mission must take place. Significantly, the return of the exiles to the land of Israel is an indispensable feature of the messianic redemption. Only after the people of Israel are reunited with the Land of Israel will "the earth be full of knowledge of the Lord even as the waters cover the sea."

Characteristically, for Jews the messianic redemption is not couched in purely spiritual terms but possesses a distinctive earthly flavor. The establishment of the Kingdom of God goes hand in hand with the end of all war and oppression, the termination of all exploitation and violence and the abolition of all injustice and degradation. That Jews associate redemption with such temporal concerns as the establishment of a truly just society attests to the fact that in the Jewish scheme the material and spiritual, the natural and the transcendent, are intertwined. Concern for material well-being is not dismissed as a purely secular objective but rather acknowledged as part of our religious vocation. Jews do not seek an escape from the limitations and absurdities of their finite existence in the "here and now" through a flight into otherworldly realms of being. Instead, their religious goal is the sanctification of life in a quest for the kind of transcendence that links the finite with the infinite, the temporal with the eternal and material with the spiritual.

But the this-worldly thrust of Judaism must not be misconstrued as indifference to other-worldly concerns. According to classical Jewish belief, this world, in point of fact, is the ante-chamber of the World to Come. No earthly satisfaction can compare with heavenly bliss. "One hour of satisfaction in the World to Come outweighs all the pleasures of this world" (*Ethics of the Fathers*). But our world must not be dismissed as a vale of tears through which we must pass in order to merit future delights. Service to God in this world is an end in itself, not merely a means to qualify for salvation. It is precisely in the "here and now" that we carry out our religious mandate. According to the Rabbis, "One hour of repentance and good deeds in this world outweighs all of the life of the World to Come." Life is sacred because it enables us to fulfill our religious task. "The Torah was not given to the ministering angels, but to human beings who, in spite of their intrinsic limitations, are summoned to act as co-workers with God in the process of Creation."

As opposed to many other religions, Judaism places relatively little importance on precision in dogmatic formulation. Instead, it stresses obedience to the commandments. The Sinaitic Covenant described in the Pentateuch and interpreted by the Talmud revolves around observance of Divine law, the Halakhah. Halakhah (literally, walking in the ways of God) encompasses the totality of life. In every conceivable situation, man is mandated to live in accordance with the will of God. Nothing is too trivial to be brought under this "frame of reverence." Halakhah regulates conduct in the kitchen, the bedroom, the office, the factory, the hospital, the classroom as well as the synagogue.

Although emphasis upon the minutiae of the law may strike outsiders as a spiritually insensitive "legalism," Jews regard meticulous adherence to the letter of the law merely as the foundation of piety. The ultimate goal is the transformation of the human personality through the exposure to the spirit of the law. Halakhah serves as the point of departure for an all-inclusive quest to commit every fiber of one's being to the service of God. Those who take religion seriously can never become complacent. The religious task is "to acknowledge God in all the ways" – not merely in the relatively few areas where conduct is explicitly regulated by formal law. Ideally, all our actions should be performed for the "sake of God."

Such a conception of piety engenders not smugness but restlessness. "The righteous enjoy no rest either in this world or the next." The hallmark of genuine piety is not self-centered complacency but the ongoing quest to reduce the gap between what we are and what we ought to be.

It should hardly be surprising that in our secular age in which hedonism and materialism are rampant, these lofty ideals are more honored in the breach than in practice. Only a relatively small proportion of the Jewish people takes its faith so seriously as to be prepared to make the sacrifices necessary to observe the stringent discipline imposed by Jewish law. In response to the pressures of modernity, a variety of religious movements have arisen that seek to reinterpret classical Judaism in such a manner as to make it less demanding and less incompatible with the contemporary ethos.

Because of the irreconcilable theological differences between the various movements, we can no longer speak of an underlying religious unity of the Jewish community. Under prevailing conditions, there exists only one common theological denominator – the religious significance of the existence of the Jewish people are completely alienated from the synagogue and from all forms of religious practice. Assimilation and intermarriage have exacted a heavy toll. The erosion of Jewish religious commitment has adversely affected the Jewish will to survive as a distinctive community. According to some dire predictions, the Jewish population in the United States is likely to shrink to less than one million within the next few decades.

These developments confronts the Jewish community with the challenge of survival. It is highly revealing that even many avowedly secular Jews are deeply worried about the disintegration of the Jewish community. Non-Jews may be puzzled by what might strike them as an almost obsessive concern with survival of the ethnic community. They may view it as a manifestation of ethno-centrism, a "tribalism" devoid of all religious significance.

To appreciate Jewish attitudes, Christians must understand that for Jews, Jewish self-identification, attachment to the people of Israel and expression of solidarity with its fate constitute overriding religious imperatives. By the same token, the Jewish concern for the security and welfare of the State of Israel – widely regarded as the foremost instrument of the preservation of the Jewish people in the post-Holocaust era – must be seen not merely as an expression of secular nationalism but rather as the manifestation of a residual subconscious awareness of the religious vocation of the Jewish people.

Having endured the trauma of the Holocaust, Jews have good reason to perceive themselves as an endangered species. They are apprehensive over the resurgence of antisemitism, climaxed by the notorious "Zionism is Racism" resolution passed by the United Nations. At the same time, they have ample ground to worry about a "spiritual Holocaust" wrought by the blandishments of the "open society," which places a premium upon individualism and frowns upon the sense of tradition and the cultivation of group loyalties, without which Judaism cannot thrive.

Although it is widely recognized that Jewish survival is jeopardized in a completely secular environment, it must also be realized that as a beleaguered minority Jews are bound to feel threatened by the renewed emphasis upon the Christianization of America. They look askance at the introduction of denominational prayers because of the fear that young children will be subjected to subtle pressure to conform to the religious expression of the majority. It is precisely because so many Jewish children are raised in a spiritual vacuum that they may be lured to the majority faith and become totally lost to the Jewish people.

But while Jews seek to preserve the separation of church and state, they also have become increasingly aware that the greatest threat to their spiritual survival is posed not by competing faith-communities but by the materialistic ethos of our culture, which not only clashes with our religious value system but undermines the very foundations of all Jewish existence. It is for this reason that ever wider circles of religious, sensitive Jews welcome opportunities to cooperate with Christians of all denominations to inject a religious dimension into the public arena – through a common effort to resist exploration and manipulation, to overcome misery and suffering, and to devise social policies that reflect the belief in the sanctity of human life as the bearer of the image of God.

It is in this struggle for the unequivocal affirmation of the dignity and sanctity of the human personality that Jews and Catholics must see themselves as partners. In a fragmented world, where value-free science produces a technology that becomes the master rather than the servant of man, where means are divorced from ends and knowledge replaces wisdom, there is a desperate need to help recover a conception of life that stresses love rather than power, communion rather than division, integration rather than discrimination. Without diluting the integrity of their respective individual faith commitments, Jews and Christians must welcome each other as partners in the process of "mending the world," in the common quest to overcome the brutality, injustice, oppression and suffering that ensue when, instead of accepting our humanity, we either play God or reduce ourselves to dehumanized animals.

ON THE AUTHORITY IN THE HALAKHAH[1]

THE TORAH, which is revered as our most sacred text, is treasured as the very foundation of our national existence. Yet only if the Torah is interpreted in accordance with the teachings of the Oral Torah as transmitted and developed by *Chakhmei Yisrael* (the Sages of Israel) can it function properly as an authentic guide to practice. As Hillel pointed out to a prospective convert, no text is ever completely self-explanatory. Without additional oral explanations, we would not even be in a position to pronounce it properly.

Just as the variations in the pronunciation of a text reflect the speaker's background, the meaning of a given text – as evidenced by the many disagreements among literary critics or constitutional lawyers – depends in large measure upon the state of mind of the reader. It is therefore not surprising that the same text should hold such divergent meanings for different individuals. As a matter of fact, in literary and legal circles we often encounter the opinion that even if we could establish the author's original intent, this would not necessarily determine a text's actual meaning since the author may not have succeeded in conveying his meaning in the text.

Obviously, in the case of a text which is attributed to divine authorship, God's intent, if it could be definitively ascertained, would unquestionably be the final arbiter of its meaning. But there still remains the possibility that the divine author intended more than one particular meaning. Significantly, the Jewish tradition speaks of the "seventy faces of the Torah." In the words of

---

[1] Unpublished.

a well-known midrash, when God revealed Himself on Mt. Sinai, He spoke to each individual in his own voice.

No individual can presume to grasp the full meaning of a divinely revealed truth. How can finite man, who is beset by the intrinsic limitations arising from the human condition, pretend to be capable of deciphering the will of an infinite God through the study of texts which by necessity must pass through the filter of a limited and fallible human mind?

However, it must be realized that if all interpretations of divine texts were to be accepted as equally valid, it would be impossible for the Torah to function as the supreme authority in Jewish life. We would be totally bereft of any form of objective guidance on normative issues.

Everything would have to be left to the discretion of individuals, who would respond to the Torah in accordance with their own subjective preferences. But in the absence of shared values and norms it is hardly feasible to establish a religious community. If Israel were to emerge as "a kingdom of priests and a holy nation," in keeping with its covenantal obligations, it was imperative that a human agency be recognized as the source of authority on normative issues. This accounts for the Jewish tradition's insistence that for normative purposes the meaning of the Torah depends upon what the authorities of a given generation declare it to be.

To be sure, no human being can claim to possess the absolute truth. The Rabbis never suggested that they were privy to the secrets of the mystery of mysteries, the Will of God. After all, they were teachers, not prophets. Their confidence in their ability to determine the meaning of the Torah rested upon an entirely different basis. It was their firm conviction that, according to the terms of the Covenant, Israel was not merely a passive recipient but an active participant in the creation of the Oral Torah, which was supposed to complement and supplement the Written Torah. Whatever teachings were developed in accordance with the appropriate methodology for the exposition of Torah, notwithstanding their originality and novelty, were viewed not as accretions but as integral parts of the Revelation vouchsafed to Moses.

The Sages' contention that the meaning of the Torah was what they declared it to be had nothing to do with pretensions to infallibility. They never advanced the claim that their particular hermeneutics yielded absolutely certain insights into the Will of God as disclosed in His Torah. It is highly significant that they did not dismiss opinions conflicting with their own as worthless. On the contrary, the Mishnah and Gemara record numerous minority opinions. Regardless of the nature of its content, as long as an opinion had evolved in accordance with the methodology of the Oral Torah, it deserved to be endowed with the status of representing "the words of the Living God." Moreover, the Sages did not rule out that at some future time a different consensus might develop and rabbinic authorities would eventually adopt what was currently a minority opinion. After all, the reason why the majority opinion was accepted was not because it was necessarily closer to the ultimate "truth," but because the Torah mandated that legal disputes must be resolved by majority rule.

So deeply ingrained was the belief that only the properly constituted authorities using the methods of the Oral Torah can legitimately interpret the meaning of the Torah in matters affecting practice that even heavenly voices or other miracles could not be invoked to support a halakhic position. Citing the Biblical phrase that Torah "is not in Heaven," as a well-known rabbinic story informs us, the Sages, refusing to be swayed by the evidence of supernatural phenomena, insisted that legal disputes can be resolved only by recourse to the rational inferences and hermeneutical rules sanctioned by the Oral Torah.

Obviously, the principle that the majority determines the authoritative meaning of the Torah governs only the resolution of differences that immediately affect human conduct, but is totally inapplicable to the determination of purely theoretical issues. This explains why some of the classic commentators, such as Ibn Ezra and Rashbam, did not hesitate to explain Biblical passages at variance with the legal meaning that the Talmud assigned to the respective passages. Obviously, truth cannot be ascertained by majority vote. But lest we end up with complete religious anarchy, majority opinion must decide the parameters of acceptable conduct as determined by the authorities of any given time.

The upheavals in Jewish life wrought by the Roman intervention and subsequent conquest gradually eroded the religious authority of the Sages. In the absence of a Sanhedrin or other central religious authority and especially with the cessation of the traditional *semikhah*, *Chakmei Yisrael* increasingly felt bound by the precedents that their predecessors established. This trend was reinforced by the fact that the Sages, apprehensive that the turbulent conditions prevailing in their time might make it impossible to preserve and transmit the Oral Torah without written records, invoked their emergency powers and lifted the prohibition against writing down the teachings of what was supposed to be a purely Oral Torah. The availability of written documents, which recorded the rulings of earlier authorities, is an important factor in discouraging later authorities from making revisions in the interpretation of the law.

In deference to the authority of previous generations the Amoraim operated by the rule that they would not differ with the opinion of a Tanna unless some other tannaitic opinion could be found in support of their view. Similarly, after the final redaction of the Babylonian Talmud, the Gaonim felt bound by the precedents set by the Amoraim even though, unlike the Sages of the Tannaitic era, the latter no longer possessed the credentials of full-fledged *semikhah*. Although there was no difference in their formal qualifications, a broad consensus developed that the Savora'im and the Gaonim had to acknowledge the authority of the earlier Amoraim.

To be sure, this arrangement did not involve total surrender to past authority. On the contrary, one of the standard rules governing Jewish jurisprudence stated that the law follows the later authorities. It was the basis of this procedural rule that whenever the Babylonian Talmud is in conflict with the Palestinian Talmud, the former enjoys precedence even though the Palestinian Talmud was completed much earlier. It was assumed that since the later authorities cited in the Babylonian Talmud were familiar with the Palestinian Talmud but disregarded its findings nonetheless, we too should abide by their decision, for in the final analysis, it is the consensus of recognized teachers of Torah that constitutes the ultimate authority for the Jewish people, which acts in partnership with God in determining the meaning of the Torah.

In similar fashion the Acharonim (commentators and deciders of the modern era) feel bound to acknowledge the authority of the Rishonim such as Alfasi, Rashi, Maimonides, Rabbenu Tam, Nahmanides etc. It was also the acceptance by the people that has lent special weight to the opinion of Rabbi Joseph Karo as expressed in the *Shulchan Arukh* and those of Rabbi Moses Isserles in his notes to that work. But it must be realized that in these instances, it was not the authority of the codes that commanded such deference, but rather the fact that their acceptance by the Jewish people over the centuries has endowed these works with special status. In the final analysis, the very authority of the *Chakhmei Yisrael* is not so much a function of their personal intellectual and spiritual qualifications, but rather derives from their being recognized as the legitimate representatives of the people of Israel in determining the meaning of the terms of the Covenant which involves a partnership between God and Israel.

HALAKHAH: THE TENSIONS BETWEEN THE CLAIMS OF TRADITION AND THE CLAIMS OF THE SELF[1]

THE TRADITIONAL APPROACH to Halakhah appears to be so heavily weighted in favor of the authority of the past as to give the impression that the halakhic system is totally indifferent to the claims of the autonomous human self. It is generally assumed that the halakhic process involves merely the mechanical application of pre-existing rules and procedures, rendering irrelevant the promptings of the human conscience. The purpose of this paper is to examine whether the Halakhah truly constitutes a completely closed system that is hermetically sealed off against the intrusions of autonomous value judgments.

At the outset, it must be emphasized that a theocentric system such as Judaism leaves no room for autonomous obligations in the strict sense of the term. In the final analysis, man is responsible to God rather than to himself. Far from constituting the source of obligation, the human self merely apprehends what are perceived to be transcendent norms issued by a divine Commander. As Saadiah Gaon[2] defines "rational commandments," they are not self-imposed duties, but rather divine commandments that may be apprehended by our cognitive faculties and do not require for their validation any reference to a supernatural act of Revelation. Similarly, when

---

[1] Unpublished.

[2] *Emunot ve-deot*, Part 3.

Bahya ibn Pakuda[3] refers to "duties of the heart," what he has in mind are not simply dictates of the human conscience but rather divine imperatives that are apprehended by our human conscience. As Meiri would put it,[4] the commandments perceived by the human heart are like the letters of the Torah scroll. To adopt Paul Tillich's terminology, rational commandments are theonomous rather than autonomous. But while undoubtedly theonomy rather than heteronomy represents a religious ideal,[5] the authority of halakhic norms derives exclusively from their transcendent source. The very reason why Halakhah is accorded pre-eminent status as the supreme normative standard is that it is acknowledged as the will of God as mediated through the Oral Torah. It would be the height of arrogance to challenge the authority of the divine imperative. Hence, in the event of conflict with halakhic requirements, all ethical, aesthetic, intellectual or prudential considerations must be set aside.

The Talmud[6] attaches special significance to the formula employed by the Bible for the description of Israel's acceptance of the Sinaitic Covenant. The phrase "we shall do and we shall listen"[7] is construed as evidence of the unconditional and unqualified character of the submission due to divine authority. Covenantal obligations are absolute. They are obeyed not because of their intrinsic reasonableness but because of the authority vested in their Commander. It is for this reason that reservations expressed concerning even a single provision of Jewish Law would totally invalidate a conversion. Unless the yoke of the commandments is accepted *in toto*, the entire procedure is devoid of all significance.[8] Because the Halakhah is acknowledged as the Will of God, all other concerns must be subordinated to it. Even such a basic religious value as concern for the dignity of individuals cannot be invoked to justify violation of a law of the Torah. To permit humanistic considerations to override divine commandments would

---

[3] *Chovot ha-Levavot*, Introduction.

[4] Meiri, *ad Shabbat* 105b.

[5] See the famous Midrashic statement (*Avodah Zarah* 19a) that what at first is experienced as the heteronomous Torah of God may subsequently as the result of the appropriation of the Torah's value system on the part of the *talmid chakham* be converted into his very own Torah.

[6] BT *Sabbath* 88a.

[7] Exodus 24:7.

[8] BT *Bekhorot* 30b. See also Maimonides, *Hilkhot Issurei Biah* 14:5.

be tantamount to the desecration of the divine name.[9] In support of this thesis, the Talmudic sages refer to Proverbs: "There is no wisdom, no understanding nor counsel against God."[10]

At this point it is imperative to guard against possible misunderstanding. Unconditional surrender to divine authority must not be confused with acceptance of the Kiergegaardian doctrine of the "suspension of the ethical." On the contrary, since God constitutes the perfectly moral being, obedience to divine commands is a moral (not merely religious) requirement. Thomas Aquinas has conclusively shown that a teleological ethics, which is founded upon the premise that it is the function of ethical norms to yield the best possible consequences, has no difficulty, whatsoever with obedience to any divine command. No matter how unethical or immoral a divine imperative may appear to us, God's superior wisdom and benevolence guarantees that obedience to His commands is bound to result in the greatest possible good. But even deontological ethics need not find it difficult to accommodate obedience to divine commandments as an ethical requirement even in situations where the obedience to these norms clashes with other *prima facie* moral obligations. After all, God is worshipped not merely as the supreme power, but as the omni-benevolent being. Since commandments issued by an absolutely moral being cannot possibly be immoral, conflicts between moral duties and divine commandments must be treated as cases of conflict between different types of moral obligation (i.e., between a *prima facie* duty and an overriding moral duty).[11] That Kierkegaard[12] felt constrained to divorce the ethical from the religious and to treat the sacrifice of Isaac on the part of Abraham as the ultimate triumph of religious faith over ethics is largely due to his inability to extricate himself from the stranglehold of a rigid Kantian deontological ethics. Otherwise, he could have found it relatively easy to treat Abraham's compliance with the apparently "absurd" commandment as the fulfillment of the ethical duty to obey the instructions of the highest moral authority.

---

[9] BT *Berakhot* 19b; *Eruvin* 63a; *Sanhedrin* 82a; *Shavuot* 30b.

[10] Proverbs 21:30.

[11] See Philip L. Quinn, *Divine Commands and Moral Requirements*. For a recent discussion, see Steven L. Ross, "Another Look at God and Morality," *Ethics* 94 (1983): 87–98.

[12] Søren Kierkegaard, *Fear and Trembling*.

But it is one thing to assert that obedience to divine commands is an overriding ethical principle and another to adopt a theological definition of the terms "good" or "right." Nothing we have said implies that the property "being commanded or willed by God" represents the defining characteristic of "good" or "right." Our position is fully compatible with the view that the meaning of terms such as "right" or "good" is totally independent of any reference to divine approval. Following Plato's *Euthrypho*, we can continue to assert that God approves actions because they are good, not the reverse; that they are good because God approves them. All that we maintain is that for the believer in an absolutely moral God; it is axiomatic that everything ordained by God must also possess the property of being good.

There is a cogent reason why we object so vigorously to defining "good" in terms of divine command. We are not ready to surrender the by now classical distinction between (A) purely revelational commandments and (B) those for which autonomous human reasons can be adduced. If the attribute of "being willed or commanded" were both a necessary and sufficient condition of goodness, we would no longer be able to make a distinction between these two types of commandments since, in the final analysis, even commandments in category B would derive their significance exclusively from the property of being commanded by God. Nevertheless, the distinction between purely revelational and rational commandments[13] plays an enormous role in the system of many Jewish thinkers. Maimonides goes so far as to claim that an entirely different set of motives is required for the two types of commandments. Commandments in category B involve more than mere submission to divine authority. Instead, it is essential that the value system of these ethical laws be appropriated. Thus, for example, the duty of giving to charity is not fulfilled properly unless the act of giving results from a charitable disposition. Because of the importance attached to the motive, the giving of charity is viewed not merely as an intrinsically significant act but also as a means towards the cultivation of a morally "desirable" disposition. Maimonides operates with the Aristotelian notion that virtuous dispositions result from the performance of moral actions which, although not virtuous themselves, are performed in keeping with the requirements of virtue. Hence, with respect to commandments in category B, heteronomy can never be adequate. It becomes the religious goal to

---

[13] *Commentary to Mishnah*, Eight Chapters.

convert the heteronymous imperative into an autonomous norm. As long as the performance of our moral action involves a struggle with other inclinations, the ideal has not been attained. It is our task to walk "in the ways of God," which for Maimonides implies the mandate to cultivate ethical traits of character. But the situation is completely different with respect to commandments in category A where appropriation of the norms is not included in the religious requirement. On the contrary, the greater the effort needed to overcome opposing inclinations, the higher the religious value of such acts, since the "reward is proportionate to the pain."[14]

But it is not only within the sphere of agent-morality that autonomous considerations play a role. Upon closer examination, it becomes evident that the entire halakhic process reflects an extraordinary sensitivity to ethical considerations. Although halakhic jurisprudence ultimately rests upon norms and procedures attributed to divine revelation, ethical categories are included among the numerous factors that must be taken into account in the process of halakhic decision-making. The Talmudic sages took it for granted that whenever a Biblical text was fraught with ambiguity, the morally most appealing interpretation should be accepted. Whenever there is doubt concerning the meaning of an ambiguous Biblical text, the rabbinic tradition invokes the hermeneutic rule that the Torah must be interpreted in keeping with the principle, "Its ways are ways of pleasantness and all its paths are peace."[15] This in no way represents an attempt to subject the word of God to the scrutiny of the human conscience. What is involved is something entirely different. It is assumed that whenever a question arises as to the meaning of the ordinance of a divine legislator, the morally more attractive alternative is bound to reflect the real intent of the law.

Principles such as "the ways of pleasantness" and "the ways of peace" serve not merely as hermeneutical principles for the purpose of eliciting the "true" meaning of texts. They constitute a mandate to enact legislation designed to promote human welfare and to extend the range of social responsibility. Talmudic literature abounds with references to ordinances and acted out of concern for *tikkun ha-olam* (the mending of the world), *darkhei shalom* (the ways of peace), *mi-penei evah* (to reduce enmity).[16] As the author of

---

[14] BT *Succah* 32a; BT *Yevamot* 87b.

[15] Proverbs 3:17.

[16] See *Encyclopedia Talmudit*, "*Darkhei Shalom*," vol: 7, 716–724.

Maggid Mishneh points out,[17] that the Torah does not merely contain explicitly formulated specific norms and also a generally moral prescription "to do whatever is right and proper."[18] Hence, changes in socio-economic conditions necessitate the development of the appropriate institutions and procedures, enabling us to implement our moral imperatives in the light of newly emerging situations. In addition, there is an overriding religious imperative which is irreconcilable with Yeshayahu Leibowitz's cavalier dismissal of ethical considerations as halakhically irrelevant. Jewish law mandates *kiddush ha-shem* (the sanctification of the divine name). Conversely, conduct resulting in *chillul ha-shem* (the desecration of the divine name) must be avoided.

The Jewish people can hardly carry its role as a "holy people" and serve as "witnesses of God" if lack of sensitivity to moral standards evokes a negative image of it. Hence, adherence to commonly accepted standards of moral propriety is a halakhic requirement. We need but recall Rabbenu Gershom's revolutionary ban against polygamy and divorcing one's wife without her consent to realize the extent to which the evolution of halakhic practices is conditioned by modifications of our moral perceptions.

The awareness that the Halakhah responds to changes in a society's cultural milieu by no means interferes with the belief in the immutability of the Torah. After all, it is the very hallmark of the Oral Torah to apply the Torah's teachings to ever-changing realities. The complexion of a society is no less changed by transformations of its cultural ethos than by modifications of socio-economic conditions. Just as the secular methods prevailing in our modern era prompted authorities of the stature of Rabbi Yaakov Ettlinger and the Chazon Ish to declare that the Talmudic rulings governing the treatment of Sabbath desecrations or of heretics are not applicable under prevailing conditions, it should be possible to invoke contemporary moral perceptions as factors in determining to what extent a variety of other Talmudic prescriptions may be affected by the novel conditions of a modern, democratic society.

In this connection, it is important to emphasize that contrary to widespread misconceptions, the formation of halakhic opinion goes far beyond the mechanical exercise of applying ready-made rules and

---

[17] *Hilkhot Shechenim* 14:5.
[18] Deuteronomy 7:18.

procedures. A halakhic scholar does not operate like a computer reacting automatically in terms of information stored in its memory. Genuine halakhic creativity involves the operation of subjective elements, which exert an influence upon the selection and interpretation of what are deemed relevant texts and precedents upon which a particular legal decision is to be based. The mere fact that we encounter so many conflicting halakhic opinions on a variety of issues indicates that the process of halakhic decision-making cannot be insulated from intuitive factors. This being the case, even when not consciously invoked, autonomous value perceptions of a given halakhic scholar inevitably play a decisive role in the formation of his halakhic opinion.[19] To be sure, we do not wish to imply that the halakhic scholar simply relies on his own independent value judgments and then skillfully manipulates halakhic data to yield the desired conclusion. What we maintain is something entirely different. It is our contention that a specific halakhic opinion results from the interaction between the subjective and objective components of the halakhic process. However, it must be noted that even the subjective elements of a halakhic opinion do not represent independently obtained moral perceptions but rather reflect the intuitive perceptions emerging from exposure to halakhic data.

But while intuitive value judgments play only a relatively limited role in the formation of halakhic opinions, there are other areas of normative decision-making where autonomous value judgments play a dominant role. It must be borne in mind that there are many agonizing moral dilemmas where one cannot obtain guidance from halakhic rulings because the issue simply is not covered by halakhic legislation. In such situations even the halakhist has no choice but to fill the void by recourse to purely subjective value judgments. That there are areas where even the renowned halakhic experts are unable to provide normative guidance on the basis of purely legal considerations and have no alternative but to resort to intuitive elements is attested by the notion of *daat Torah,* which has come into vogue. This term denotes policy recommendations that, while they cannot be buttressed by explicit halakhic norms, nevertheless command the authority due to opinions that arise from the thorough conditioning of cognitive faculties through exposure to Torah study and observance. In other words, it is assumed that

---

[19] For a more extensive treatment, see my essay, "Meta-halakhic Propositions," in *Leo Jung Jubilee Volume,* edited by Kashev, Lamm and Rosenfeld. New York: 1962, 211–221 (page 270 in this volume).

as a result of his immersion in Torah, the *talmid chakham* will develop a value system and ethos that will affect his purely subjective opinions in matters that go beyond the area governed by halakhic norms. Thus, Judaism transcends the relatively narrow limits of an "ethics of obedience" to encompass an "ethics of responsibility" as well.[20]

Viewed from this perspective, Halakhah not only provides a set of rules and regulations to be obeyed, but serves also as the matrix for the development of a religious conscience. In all likelihood, moral intuitions of such a conscience will significantly diverge from those that are molded primarily by the encounter with a secular utilitarian or hedonistic ethos.[21]

In the final analysis, it is the function of the Halakhah to serve, true to its name, as the avenue towards the development of a Jewish "ethics of responsibility" that mandates the ongoing cultivation of the kind of autonomous moral perceptions that emerge from the engagement of the human self with the ethos of the tradition.

---

[20] See my article, "Covenantal Imperatives." In *Samuel K. Mirsky Memorial Volume*, edited by Gersion Appel, 3–12. Jerusalem: 1970 (page 46 in this volume).

[21] See my essay, "Law as the Basis of a Moral Society." *Tradition* (Spring 1981): 42–53 (page 61 in this volume).

PLURALISM AND THE HALAKHAH[1]

OF LATE IT HAS BECOME FASHIONABLE to view atomic fission as the symbol of a disintegrating civilization. Our atomic misery makes for strange bedfellows. Spokesmen for science and religion vie with each other in decrying the ills of atomization and fragmentation – the villains blamed for the weird array of psychological, social, and political ailments that plague modern man.

Amidst such a climate of opinion, we are prone to ignore the intellectual and psychological hazards that can result from preoccupation with the other extreme – the craving for absolute unity – that is so often regarded as the hallmark of religious orientation.[2] We tend to forget that without division, separation, and specialization, all significant human thought must come to a standstill. Moreover, it must be borne in mind that the Platonic emphasis upon the *essential* unity that underlies all *existential* diversity has given rise to various political systems that swallow up the individual in the ocean of collectivity. Similarly, the grandiose attempt of Hegel to reduce Reality to the One Absolute unfolding itself in a logic of history has led (via its Marxian adaptation) to the emergence of modern communism with its utter

---

[1] *Tradition* 4 (Spring 1962): 221–240.

[2] Of course, it is true that the religious personality gravitates towards the ultimate Unity that lies beyond all empirical diversity. Abraham, the Jewish "knight of faith," is described in the Midrash as the religious genius who, through his discovery of God, restored the original unity of the world "in the same manner as a tailor sews together a garment that has been ripped apart" (*Bereshit Rabbah*, 39:3).

contempt for the rights of the individual. By the same token, Higher Criticism – the fantastic attempt to undermine the authority of the Bible, especially of the Pentateuch, by stigmatizing the canonical writings as clumsy hodgepodges of assorted passages from numerous authors – does not at all reflect the influence of atomization or fragmentization. On the contrary, the methods of Higher Criticism, as Professor Kaufmann[3] has shown, were inspired either by Hegelian notions concerning the unfolding of the Absolute in history or by the totally unwarranted extension to the domain of religious thought of Darwinian notions concerning the evolution of the species. In either case, the fragmentization of the Pentateuch can be traced back to the overzealous search for unity – manifesting itself in the obsession to find a single master formula for the understanding of all of reality.

It may be contended that these arguments discredit only certain brands of monistic philosophies but do not affect the validity of the so called "unity theme."[4] It will therefore be the purpose of this paper to show that for cogent reasons, Judaism held in check its monistic trends and assigned priority to the pluralism inherent in the halakhic approach.

Although Kabbalistic thinking is composed of a variety of strands, it is marked by a strong bent towards radical monism. Drawing upon this conceptual framework, Rabbi Lamm portrayed a masterful picture of a worldview that regards all forms of separation as a cosmic tragedy relieved only by the comforting realization that with the fulfillment of our eschatological hopes, all divisiveness is destined to be overcome.

This standpoint is akin to the orientation of the mystic to whom any form of separation from the ultimate One is intolerable. Hence, escape from the illusory world of appearance and union with the ultimately Real become the only worthwhile goals of life.

Significantly, many of the foremost halakhic thinkers displayed a proclivity for this mystic approach. Even such a staunch advocate of a rigorous Halakhah-centered orientation as Rabbi Hayyim of Volozhin could not completely suppress his monistic longings. They come to the fore in a passage that unabashedly admits the illusory character of all existential

---

[3] Walter Kaufman, *Critique of Religion and Philosophy.* New York: Doubleday and Company, 1961, 379 ff.

[4] Norman Lamm, "The Unity Theme and Its Implications for Moderns." *Tradition* (Fall 1961): 44–64.

diversity. Taking the kabbalistic notion of the "Higher Unity" to its logical conclusion, Rabbi Hayyim acknowledges that, metaphysically speaking, Absolute Reality is constituted of undifferentiated oneness. "In truth, from His side, all of existence is filled with His being without any separations, distinctions, or divisions, as if creation had not taken place at all."[5] Of course, Rabbi Hayyim is quick to recognize that such an attitude is completely incompatible with any form of normative Judaism. This is why he immediately proceeds with the important proviso: "We are neither capable of contemplating nor permitted to contemplate this fact at all, but must seek to perform His mitzvot in the world that is revealed to our understanding."[6]

Obviously, the very foundation of the Halakhah would collapse if all distinctions were merely of an illusory character. Large segments of Jewish law presuppose the reality of spatial and temporal distinctions. Even more disastrous would be another corollary of viewing the world from the perspective of the "Higher Unity." If God's presence permeates all reality equally, then the very difference between sacred and profane, pure and impure, between good and evil itself, ought to be completely obliterated. The implications of this position would lead to such a radical anti-nomianism that even the excesses of the Sabbatean heresy would pale into insignificance by comparison.

Rabbi Hayyim could not brook any world view that would assign only relative importance to halakhic norms. In a manner characteristic of the essentially pluralistic approach of halakhic Judaism, he does not even attempt to resolve the tension between his mystic, monistic leanings and his halakhic, pluralistic orientation. Instead, he pragmatically postulates the existence of finite, individual entities as indispensable to the functioning of the halakhic process.[7]

In marked contrast to this position, Rabbi Lamm, in his quest for unification, invades the very stronghold of pluralism: the Halakhah. While he concedes the essentially pluralistic outlook of the Halakhah as a whole, he nonetheless contends that Judaism's penchant for absolute unity comes to the fore in one of the most pivotal areas of the Halakhah: the laws of the Sabbath.

---

[5] *Nefesh ha-Hayyim*, by Rabbi Hayyim of Volozhin, Part III.
[6] *ibid.*
[7] *ibid.*

From Rabbi Lamm's brilliant presentation, the various halakhic injunctions and regulations concerning the Sabbath emerge as an eloquent protest against man's involvement in the world of nature. Since all creativity in the world of nature depends upon processes that use atomization and fragmentization, the abstention from creative work on the Sabbath is designed to remove man from the "World of Disunity" and lead him towards a higher plane of existence where all separation and division are surmounted.

This poetic description of the higher symbolic function of the Sabbath – as a manifestation of the "Higher Unity" towards which Judaism aspires – has a deeply moving quality. But it cannot be adduced as evidence for the unity thesis. For nowhere can it be shown that this interpretation reflects halakhic categories of thought. In point of fact, the argument has employed purely Kabbalistic notions to provide a rationale for Sabbath observance. As a matter of fact, it could easily be shown that this essentially mystic explanation clashes with numerous other halakhic norms which look upon creativity in the world of nature not as a necessary evil but as the realization of the religious duty to become a partner with the Holy One, Blessed be He, in the process of creation."[8] Those who are not privileged enough to share the same proclivity for mystic thinking are free to adopt an entirely different rationale for Sabbath observance. Admirers of Samson Raphael Hirsch, for example, would find in the Sabbath not a protest against man's involvement with the mundane but rather an enthusiastic endorsement of human creativity. Accordingly, we link ourselves with the divine scheme of creation when, in conscious imitation of the Creator, we too, interrupt our own creative efforts on the Sabbath.

As a general rule, halakhic thinking is marked by a far more affirmative attitude towards uniqueness and individuality than is suggested by the broad espousal of monism. Judaism does not strive for Nirvana – the dissolution of all individuality and particularity in the ocean of undifferentiated oneness. The Book of Genesis (1:31) informs us that the verdict "It was good" was pronounced by God not before but after the process of separation had been initiated and distinctions had made their appearance in the world of creation. The Psalmist certainly was not embarrassed by the manifold and made no attempt to discover any underlying unity. On the contrary, he exclaimed:

[8] BT *Sabbath* 119b; cf. also Rabbi Joseph B. Soloveitchik, "Halakhic Man."

"How manifold are thy works, O God!" (Psalms 104:24). The absolute Unity of the Creator does not imply the oneness of the creation at all. Moreover, according to a well-known midrash, it is precisely in the lower world of creation, not in the higher regions of Being, that the Divine Presence has its abode.[9]

Of course, Judaism has its share of mystic thinkers who yearn passionately for redemption from the world of disunity and disintegration. Thus Maimonides extols *mitat neshikah* (death by Divine kiss) which enables the soul to become reunited with God.[10] A contemporary mystic, Professor Heschel, sums up his philosophy of life with the statement, "For the pious man it is a privilege to die."[11]

But it must be borne in mind that such attitudes do not arise out of the matrix of halakhic thinking. Instead, they reflect points of view that relegate the Halakhah to a peripheral position. In the case of Maimonides, we should note that his glorification of *milat neshikah* as the liberation of the soul from the prison of finite limitation goes hand in hand with other non-halakhic trends such as the downgrading of the role of the mitzvah,[12] a stringent asceticism, and the advocacy of philosophical reflection as a means to mystical union with God. Obviously, these views do not express halakhic categories of thought, but attest to the powerful influence which Neo-Platonism exerted on Maimonides. Insofar as Professor Heschel's position is concerned, it is hardly necessary to point out that he represents a school of thought in which the Halakhah plays only a very subordinate role.

As opposed to these flights from earthly realities, the halakhist's attachment to the world of existential diversity is typified by Rabbi Hayyim's trenchant observations concerning the proper motivation for Torah study.

---

[9] The fundamental differences between the halakhic and the Kabbalistic attitudes are clearly formulated in Rabbi Joseph B. Soloveitchik's classic study, "*Ish ha-Halakhah*," 651–735. This pioneering work is indispensable to an understanding of the philosophy of Halakhah.

[10] *Guide of the Perplexed*, III:51.

[11] A.J. Heschel, *Man Is Not Alone: A Philosophy of Religion*. Philadelphia: Jewish Publication Society, 1951, 296.

[12] See *Guide of the Perplexed*, III:51, where Maimonides compares the religiously observant but philosophically naive individual to one who, while anxious to enter the palace of a king, has not even seen it. However, in fairness to Maimonides we should remember that the concluding chapter of the *Guide* implies a far more positive attitude towards religious practice.

In the Hassidic scheme, the study of Torah was looked upon as a means to communion with God. This view is rejected by Rabbi Hayyim, who insisted that *Torah li-shmah* was to be taken literally as the study of the Torah for its own sake.[13] Superficially, the argument rests on solid, practical ground. Of course, it is impossible to concentrate upon involved and intricate Talmudic problems if concern for mystical union with God diverts one's attention from the legal question at hand.

In reality, however, the issue goes far deeper than the requirements of the psychology of learning, which call for a maximum of undivided attention for the attainment of optimum results. The very ideal of losing oneself in the all-embracing One clashes with the spirit of the Halakhah, which emphasizes serving the One in and through a pluralistic world. Hence, we should study Torah in order to comprehend the divine will as it relates to man's task on earth, not to reach the mystic goal of *bittul ha-yesh* (the obliteration of individuality in the union with God).[14]

Because halakhic thinking veers away from the ultimate implications of any system that revolves around the absolute Unity of Reality as a whole, it represents the very antithesis of what William James described as the typical religious attitude. To quote a particularly revealing passage in *The Varieties of Religious Experience*, "The abandonment of self-responsibility seems to be the fundamental act in the specifically religious, as distinguished from moral, practice."[15] That religion lends itself to this kind of interpretation was demonstrated by Dr. Robert Servatius, Adolf Eichmann's defense attorney, in an especially shocking manner during the Eichmann trial. In a ridiculous attempt to shift the onus of guilt from his client to Divine Providence, Servatius implied that the extermination of six million Jews formed an integral part of a divine design for human history. The absurdity of such an obnoxious defense maneuver should not blind us to the fact that the so-called, religious attitude, unless counter-balanced by halakhic components,

---

[13] Rabbi Hayyim of Volozhin, *op. cit.,* Part IV.

[14] For similar reasons, Rabbi Hayyim objected to excessive emphasis upon Mussar (pietistic literature) at the expense of halakhic literature. Our main objective in life is not simply to seek communion with God, but to understand His will as it relates to our specific tasks in all sorts of situations (see *Nefesh ha-Hayyim,* Part IV).

[15] William James. *The Varieties of Religious Experience.* New York: New American Library, 1958, 229.

may in fact lead to an evasion of moral responsibility. If evil and suffering are parts of a cosmic scheme that "as a whole" is good, why not resign oneself to the prevalence of tragedy in the comforting faith that the calamities of our fellow man contribute to the ultimate goodness of the universe?[16] Why struggle against moral lapses if seemingly discordant notes constitute part of the higher harmony of an orchestra directed by a Divine Conductor?

Such attitudes of resignation and passivity are completely foreign to halakhic Judaism. In its scheme, man is not merely a creature but also co-creator, "God's partner in the creative process."[17] Jewish tradition pins upon every individual the responsibility for the very survival of the cosmos. We must act as if our action were to decide the very existence of the universe.[18] Thus religion leads not to the evasion but the accentuation of personal responsibility.

Unlike the Stoic philosopher, the religious Jew cannot be indifferent to the suffering of his fellow man. Judaism advocates a philosophy of involvement – not detachment. It may be granted that from the standpoint of "reality as a whole" or, as Spinoza put it, "under the aspect of eternity," the suffering of the individual may vanish in the total good. The Midrash[19] goes so far as to credit death and suffering with winning for the universe the stamp of divine approval contained in the phrase, "God saw everything that He had made, and, behold, it was very good."[20] Yet this does not entitle any individual to adopt a philosophical attitude towards *preventable* suffering, especially that of his fellow man.

As human beings, we must come to grips with individual situations and specific problems. We cannot act with reference to "reality as a whole." All significant human action would come to a standstill if we were to proceed upon the assumption that all our distinctions are meaningless because they are transcended in the infinite. Our ethical behavior and social action must be predicated upon the admittedly limited perspective of finite, mortal

---

[16] Cf. the grotesque distortion of the religious attitude contained in Daniel Bell's "Reflections on Jewish Identity." *Commentary* (June 1961): 472: "Orthodoxy leads to quietism, suffering is the badge, one accepts it as the mark of fate."

[17] BT *Sabbath* 119b.

[18] BT *Kiddushin* 40b.

[19] *Bereshit Rabbah* 9:9–13.

[20] Genesis 1:31.

creatures who catch only a partial (and probably even distorted) glimpse of the truth. But any attempt to rise above such a limited standpoint will only end up with a vicious relativism (even moral solipsism) where all distinctions between good and evil, right and wrong, become completely blurred.

With this proviso, we can wholeheartedly accept many spiritual benefits that spring from the "religious" attitude. When personal tragedies are accepted as necessary to the good of the whole, the burden of sorrow can be borne with a measure of equanimity. By stepping beyond our self-enclosed frame of reference, we can remove the sting of bitterness from much of our pain. A Hassidic sage expressed this in a striking comment on the Biblical verse, "God blessed Abraham with all."[21] It was Abraham's ability to regard each isolated event as part of an overall scheme that made his life the blessing it was.[22] In a similar vein, the same Hassidic leader read a profound insight into the Talmudic dictum, "All that God does is for the good."[23] If we look upon events not as isolated units but as parts of an all-embracing Whole we shall discern that, all appearances to the contrary, they are really for the good.[24] It was this kind of faith that came to the fore in the moving statement of Israel Baal Shem Tov: "Because I am conscious of God, all things are of equal value to me."[25]

As one among the many strands that form the fabric of a pious life, such an attitude is highly commendable. But the situation is altogether different when absorption in the Whole becomes the dominant, let alone exclusive, feature of religiosity. Judaism is far too concerned with the fate of the individual to invite cavalier solutions to the problem of evil. The suffering of the individual remains a problem (witness the Book of Job!) in spite of the most idealistic systems that human fancy can construct. The goodness of the system as such does not answer the needs of the individual in the throes of anguish and sorrow. Religion should deepen our sense of compassion, not provide a glib metaphysical pseudo-solution that explains away the very problem of evil.

---

[21] Genesis 24:1.

[22] Rabbi Zusha of Hanipol, quoted in *Al ha-Torah* by Rabbi Mordecai HaKohen. Jerusalem: Orot, 1956, vol. 1, 63.

[23] BT *Berakhot* 60b.

[24] *ibid.*

[25] Quoted in *Keter Shem Tov* by Aaron of Apta.

Characteristically, the Halakhah is too realistic to recommend the adoption of an ultimate metaphysical perspective as a solution of the problem. True, we are required to bless God both for good and evil.[26] But the content of the respective blessings is altogether different in both cases. Good news we receive by hailing God as the dispenser of goodness; sad news prompts us to acknowledge Him as the "true Judge." Significantly, even when there is reason to expect that in the long run the present calamity may turn out to be a blessing in disguise, we still are not permitted to gloss over the immediate tragedy. Even momentary anguish cannot be dismissed lightly as something utterly inconsequential. This is why the Halakhah stipulates that no matter what the ultimate consequences of a given event may be, we must judge it in terms of the present and pronounce whatever benediction is warranted in the light of immediate circumstances.[27]

Refusal to draw a sharp line of demarcation between metaphysical good and evils (viewing the latter as something apparent rather than real) can easily result in confusion in the moral sphere as well. In all fairness, it must be pointed out that this is not a necessary corollary of metaphysical monism. It is quite possible to uphold the distinction in the moral sphere while rejecting it in the realm of metaphysics. But there can be no doubt that metaphysical monism tends to spill over into the ethical domain. This need not take such extreme formulations as the Sabbatean and Frankist heresies. There are many Hassidic doctrines that tend to blur the absolute distinction between right and wrong. The justification of *averah li-shmah* (the sin that is committed with the express purpose of serving God), especially on the part of the *tzaddik,* represents a particularly telling example. The views of the late Rabbi Kook also gravitate in this direction at times. As Pinchas Rosenbluth pointed out in a recent essay, if the lights of holiness shine forth from the most secular and even atheistic manifestations of culture, if all of reality is "holy and divine" and all evil purely illusory, then we are deprived of all significant criteria for moral evaluation.[28] Indeed, an element of goodness (a spark of holiness) may possibly be found even in an immoral act, even as the most moral human act may be tainted with some evil (due to the intrinsic limitations imposed upon everything finite). But unwillingness to make any

---

[26] BT *Berakhot* 54a.

[27] *ibid.,* 60a.

[28] Pinchas Rosenbluth, "*Ha-mashber ha-ruchani shel ha-yahadut ha-modernit le-or tefisato shel ha-Rav Kook u-teguvato.*" *Deot* (Tishri 5721): 13–21.

distinction at all will undermine the very structure of all morality. No crime can be justified on the ground that in the long run it has proved a boon to mankind. Pharaoh's brutalities against the Jewish people cannot be defended on the grounds that they were necessary as background for the exodus from Egypt, which forms such a keystone of Judaism. To revert to the criticisms leveled by Pinchas Rosenbluth,[29] Rabbi Kook's thought seems at times to confuse the ideal with the real, the ultimate Messianic perspective with the requirements of the harsh present-day realities in all their ugliness and baseness.

The same kind of confusion comes to the fore in Rabbi Lamm's powerful plea for the reevaluation of our attitude towards secular studies. His view aspires to a synthesis that knows no essential gulf between time sacred and the secular, because "all knowledge is… ultimately integrated in the great *yichud* of the Holy One and his *Shekhinah.*"[30]

Here again we must fall back upon the vital distinction between the temporal and eternal, the immediate and the ultimate. The categories of normative Judaism are geared to the requirements, not of a Messianic area in which all differences are transcended, but of our present world that abounds in existential diversity. The fact that secular knowledge can also serve a religious purpose by no means detracts from the singular and unique importance of Torah in the narrower sense of the term.

At this point it will be of special importance to remember that Judaism attaches a great deal of weight to distinctions even within the domain of the sacred itself. Considerable attention is paid to different forms and degrees of holiness. Within halakhic thought, particular emphasis is placed upon the lines of demarcation between the various branches and aspects of Torah. Legal principles governing ritual questions need not necessarily apply to civil law and, conversely, the standards of civil law cannot be automatically extended to the ritual law.[31]

Far more fundamental is the distinction between Halakhah and Aggadah. Methods and processes appropriate to the one are completely irrelevant to the other. To fuse the two, in accordance with Bialik's recommendation,[32]

---

[29] *ibid.*

[30] Norman Lamm, *op. cit.,* 63.

[31] Cf. *Kiddushin* 3b, *Ketubbot* 4b, et al.

[32] Cf. Hayyim Nahman Bialik's essay, "Halakhah ve-aggadah," in *Kol Kitvei Bialik.* Tel Aviv: Dvir, 5715, 207–213.

would only result in a confusion of languages. We would end up in a Babel of confusion, similar to the one that would arise from the mixing of the language of poetry with that of science.

In keeping with this emphasis upon the autonomy of the various areas of religious thought, the Halakhah is hermetically sealed against intrusion of all elements that interfere with the canons and procedures of strictly halakhic reasoning. According to a well known talmudic episode, the rabbis, in the midst of a heated debate, not only refused to be swayed by the evidence of miracles, but categorically objected to heeding a heavenly voice that seemed to substantiate a minority opinion. Rabbi Eliezer was overruled – in spite of the supernatural support he was able to marshal for his point of view, for "Torah is no longer in Heaven."[33] Rabbi Joseph Karo fared no better when he sought acceptance for some of his rulings on the ground that they were vouchsafed to him by his heavenly mentor (the *maggid*). For that matter, only the Pentateuch, and no other part of the Bible, can serve as the basis for the derivation of laws.[34] When it comes to question of laws, "The scholar is superior to the prophet."[35] The notion of "progressive revelation," which plays such a dominant role in Conservative and Reform theology, is completely alien to traditional Judaism. For interpretations of the law we rely exclusively on the following two sources: (1) The content of the Sinaitic revelation as recorded in the Pentateuch and (2) the principles of interpretation of time Oral Torah. It must be borne in mind that subsequent prophetic revelations are completely devoid of authority in matters affecting the proper elucidation of the intent of the Law.[36]

Respect for the autonomy of the diverse fields of religious knowledge represents not merely an indispensable methodological principle, violation of which would result in intellectual chaos or disastrous confusion of languages. Within the Halakhah itself, there is noticeable a marked accent upon diversity and a deeply ingrained aversion to all types of *reductionism*. In sharp

---

[33] BT *Bava Metzia* 59a.

[34] BT *Chagigah* 10b; BT *Bava Kamma* 2b; BT *Niddah* 23a.

[35] BT *Bava Batra* 12a.

[36] We refer here only to authoritative interpretations of the Law, not to temporary suspensions or other measures dictated by *hora'at sha'ah* (emergency regulations necessitated by the exigencies of the moment were within the scope of prophetic competence).

contrast to many other religious systems, there is no single mood, emotion, or attitude, be it love, faith, or self-surrender, that can claim a monopoly in the Jewish religious economy. Variety is the order of the day. According to the Talmud, the biblical verse "In *all* thy ways thou shalt acknowledge Him"[37] (author's italics) best sums up the sweeping range over which Jewish piety holds sway.[38] There are innumerable avenues of service to God; every psychological drive can be harnessed in the process.

Of course, we are bidden to love God. But for that matter, we are also supposed to fear Him. We are neither in love with love, nor in fear of fear. Both sentiments represent solid pillars supporting the arch of Jewish piety. The daily liturgy reflects this all-embracing attitude in the prayer, "Unify our hearts to love and fear Thy name."[39] Notwithstanding all the scathing theological attacks directed against us on this score, during the "Days of Awe" we unabashedly continue to turn to God with the request, "Place Thy *fear* upon us."[40] We seek not the conquest of fear but its proper use.

It has become fashionable to ridicule what Walter Lippmann has branded "lower forms of religion" in which appeals to self-interest are sanctioned.[41] But Judaism maintains that every attitude can be hallowed (not merely sublimated) in the service of God. In this scheme, there is room for self-regarding as well as altruistic motives, for the Freudian *libido* as well as the "death-instinct," for self-realization as well as self-surrender. All the components of our complex psychological make up can be channeled into the service of God.

To cite a typical example, the Talmud approves of charity even if it is inspired by such a strictly prudential mentality as expressed in the proverb "Charity is the salt (preservative) of money."[42] Now it may be argued that the Talmudic sages were so preoccupied with the communal benefits accruing from the practice of charity that they were completely uninterested in the giver's motive. But it would hardly be proper to impute to the sages of old the kind of mentality associated with a certain type of professional fundraiser to whom nothing matters but the campaign's success. There is

---

[37] Proverbs 3:6.

[38] BT *Berakhot* 63a.

[39] From the Ahavah Rabbah prayer: "*Ve-yached levavenu le-ahavah u-le-yirah et shmekha.*"

[40] "*U-vekhen ten pachdekha…*"

[41] *A Preface to Morals* by Walter Lippmann. Boston: Beacon Press, 1960.

[42] BT *Ketubbot* 66b.

clear-cut evidence that the rabbis were most definitely concerned with the propriety of the motive. They went so far as to negate altogether the value of any donation that was motivated by any form of haughtiness.[43] Nietzsche was by no means original in his discovery that at times, charity springs from resentment rather than from love.[44] The Talmudic sages were astute enough psychologists to recognize how frequently base emotions are concealed behind the veneer of charity. They might even concur with many of Nietzsche's biting denunciations of certain types of charity. Yet – and here an unbridgeable chasm separates the two points of view – insofar as the rabbinic position is concerned, only what transpires at the conscious level need be taken into consideration in the evaluation of the worthwhileness of a philanthropic act.

Charitable giving is condemned only when it serves as a vehicle for the expression of haughtiness or similar attitudes – e.g., when a "philanthropist" relishes the feelings of superiority over his "inferior" fellow man who must depend upon him for sustenance. In cases like these, when philanthropy represents a deliberate act of self-aggrandizement rather than an expression of lovingkindness, it must be regarded as a spiritual liability. But the rabbis could not go along with Nietzsche in cases where charity arises out of a *sublimated* sense of resentment. What takes place on the subconscious level cannot detract from the spiritual merits of an act. On the contrary, the transformation of an undesirable psychological trait into a wholesome quality would be regarded as a spiritual triumph of the highest order. Man fulfills his task to the extent that he succeeds in the sublimation of immoral drives by harnessing them into the service of his Creator.[45] Approaching the subject from a Christian perspective, Scheler discounts the value of any form of charity that is grounded on any other emotion but love. In Scheler's scheme, charity, as opposed to mere philanthropy, cannot have its ultimate root in any undesirable psychological trait. The Jewish standpoint is altogether different. However pre-eminent a position we assign to altruistic

---

[43] BT *Bava Batra* 10b.

[44] Cf. *The Genealogy of Morals* by Friedrich Nietzsche. New York: Doubleday, 1956, esp. 3:18; cf. also *Also Sprach Zarathustra*. Leipzig: Kroner, 1918), 88–90 and 127–130.

[45] This point of view differs sharply from that expressed by Max Scheler in his celebrated "Das Ressentment im Aufbau der Moralctt." In *Vom Umsturz der Werte*. Bern: A. Francke, 1945, 33–131.

love in our scale of values, we must reckon with other psychological factors. Given sufficient self-discipline and self-control, other psychological drives and urges can be sublimated and eventually channeled into religiously approved outlets. To illustrate our point concretely, Scheler disparages the moral worth inherent in the selfless actions of a nurse who chose her profession out of a subconscious delight in watching suffering at close range. Instead of harboring disdain for this nurse, Judaism would credit her with a colossal spiritual victory. One who sublimates an ugly urge to the extent that it becomes the driving force behind a life of selfless service is deserving not of sneering derision, but of wholehearted admiration.

Owing to the intrinsic limitations besetting human nature, this ideal can never be fully realized. Therefore, the rabbis encouraged the performance of good deeds, even if prompted by ulterior motives. This realistic approach was justified on the ground that eventually, the habit of performing good deeds may gradually transform our mentality and ennoble our character to such an extent that we may reach a level of religiosity where the good deed is inspired only by the sublime desire to serve God. Although many scholars maintain that such completely disinterested service is within the reach of man, Rabbi Hayyim of Volozhin, in espousing a rigorous halakhic approach, tones down what he considers to be extravagant claims for the efficacy of this approach. What emerges is a far less idyllic picture of man's capacity for selfless service. Rabbi Hayyim anticipates no miracle cure for selfishness and ego-centeredness. All he expects is that, as the result of the repeated performance of good deeds, our character may become sufficiently refined so that at least *some* of the motives prompting our good deeds will stem from the desire to serve God.[46] Yet this ideal motive can actually co-exist with numerous other purely selfish and even base drives and urges. Reinhold Niehbuhr and other neo-orthodox Christian theologians may be completely right in their analysis of the selfishness that mars so much of what parades as selfless love. But Judaism suffers from no perfectionist pretensions. Granted that even our noblest sentiments and finest actions are tainted by residual traces of selfishness, resentment, and even outright hostility, we still are not justified in repudiating altogether the worthwhileness of moral effort. In the Jewish scheme, the recognition of our imperfections leads not to a Pauline obsession with "original sin" but to a design for the "ultimate sanctification"

---

[46] Hayyim of Volozhin, *op. cit.,* appendix to Part 3; Chapter 3.

of all the elements comprising our psychological and biological makeup. We end up not with a vicious perfectionism where the damned and doomed individual will depend for his redemption upon a gratuitous act of "grace" to be bestowed upon those who possess "faith" – but with a wholesome stress upon moral responsibility, manifesting itself in a never-ending quest towards self-perfection.

The ultimate objective of such incessant striving obviously will mirror the peculiar structure of Jewish piety with its accent upon ethical and psychological pluralism. We do not seek the exclusive cultivation of any one or even a select set of "ideal" attitudes, accompanied by the repression of other "lower" drives. Our pattern for man's unification is woven out of a variety of strands. It is through integration rather than reduction of psychological capacities that we aim for unity. We are by no means embarrassed by the staggering psychological riches with which we are endowed – even though they cannot be neatly listed in an inventory and categorized in a ready-made system of classification.

The highways and byways of thought are strewn with the wreckage of all sorts of grandiose attempts to arrive at comprehensive ethical systems based upon over-simplified versions of human motivation. Thus the hedonists deluded themselves that with the discovery of the pleasure principle they had found the magic key to the complexities of life. Although the utilitarians rightly diagnosed the limitations of hedonism, they did not escape similar pitfalls when it came to the formulation of their own criteria for moral evaluation. For Spencer and other evolutionists, ethics was to be based upon sheer "survivalism," while Nietzsche espoused – with such tragic consequences for the twentieth century – the "will to power." Freud, at least in his early period, suffered from a "pan-sexualist" approach to human behavior, and to this day the younger Huxley has not overcome his fascination with an unadulterated evolutionist ethics.

Some of the most obnoxious features of the Kantian morality provide especially telling illustrations of the inevitable pitfalls besetting systems of morality that are committed to the universal applicability of any one absolute principle. Thus, for Kant, a lie cannot be sanctioned even to save a human life! Similarly, suicide would be condoned for a woman who was violated. For a rigid formalist like Kant, the sanctity of life cannot be preserved in a person in whom immorality has become objectified. Kant is so enamored of consistency that in the formulation of the categorical imperative all other considerations are brushed aside. The outcome of such one-sidedness is not a system of love, but the love of a system. If necessary, Kant would echo the sentiments of the gruesome Roman proverb: "Let justice be done though the world perish!"

Judaism shies away from all attempts to do violence to the complexities of ethical issues. Working through any category *ad nauseam* – be it in the realm of normative ethics or descriptive psychology – will produce only dizziness and confusion. Moral balance can be achieved only through the careful weighing of the various factors that enter into our ethical dilemmas. This is why the Jewish formula for spiritual and moral equilibrium prescribes that justice be tempered with mercy, the quest for truth be reconciled with that for peace, and the sense of duty be supplemented with such sentiments as compassion, love, and so on.

Christian theologians, especially Niebuhr and Tillich, have introduced into modern thought the awareness of the self-contradictions and absurdities that arise when the implications of ethical principles are taken to their ultimate conclusions. But the fact that moral and ethical intuitions lead to antinomies does not warrant the adoption of a purely anti-nomian attitude. There is no need to resort to a purely "situational" ethics, let alone to a renunciation of the intrinsic worth of all moral endeavor. As Rabbi Rackman demonstrated so convincingly in his incisive essay "The Dialectic of the Halakhah,"[47] the halakhic structure manages to incorporate divergent and even antithetical values within a system of law. The attainment of this objective is due to the ingenious use of a system of checks and balances, preventing any one principle from completely dominating the sphere of morality. Thus the Halakhah succeeds in combining a stress upon moral laws with awareness that all moral principles must be handled with care lest their rigorous application, without counter-balancing safeguards, yield a harvest of moral paradoxes and absurdities.

Perhaps an analogy from the history of philosophy might be helpful at this point. Although Kant has compiled an impressive list of antinomies which arise from the employment of our rational faculties in the realm of metaphysics, the logical consequences to be drawn from this premise is that we must proceed with extreme caution and restraint in the exercise of reason

---

[47] Emanuel Rackman, "The Dialectic of the Halakhah." *Tradition* (Spring 1961).

– not to throw it to the winds altogether. By the same token, our awareness of the limitations assailing ethical norms does not warrant utter despair over the moral enterprise. The road of morality may be fraught with grave perils – the abyss of ethical absurdity gaping on both sides. But instead of frantically searching for "salvation through faith" and "grace," the Jew traverses the narrow ridge over the abyss, holding on to the guiding rail provided by the checks and balances embedded in the halakhic system.

Proceeding under halakhic guidance, we can safely uphold the infinite worth and dignity of the human individual without risking a plunge into the abyss of self-idolization. Since the Halakhah protects us from confusing freedom with autonomy, there is no danger that we may become so intoxicated with the idea of self-emancipation as to reject, with Kant, any law that is grounded upon divine authority (i.e., revelation) as unworthy of a free moral creature. For the Halakhah, the road to freedom does not lead over the repudiation of all heteronymous ethics. On the contrary, true freedom in the halakhic scheme is born out of the union of self-surrender with self-emancipation. There can be no freedom, the rabbis assert, "unless man is engaged in Torah."[48]

Yet this engagement does not simply imply withdrawal from reason. However spacious the intellectual mansion of Judaism may be, it simply has no room for the debunking of reason and the denigration of all humanistic aspirations that is so characteristic of much of modern existentialism. Professor Leibowitz ignores many vital areas when he describes the Halakhah as being completely indifferent to humanistic values such as the search for justice, truth, peace, and so on.[49] Actually, the halakhic approach is by no means so one-sided, narrow, and formalistic as to banish from its domain everything but blind submission to the rules of the Law. After all, man is bidden "to walk in His ways" and to strive for moral perfection. Judaism demands far more than merely a set of specific observances. As Nahmanides pointed out, a commandment such as "You shall be holy"[50] goes far beyond the sum total of individual precepts.[51] In quest of such a beckoning ideal, man must develop his admittedly very limited moral and intellectual capacities, not blunt them as an expression of "ontological

---

[48] *Avot (Kinyan Torah)* 6:2.
[49] Yeshayahu Leibowitz, "The World and the Jews." *Forum* 4 (Spring 1959): 83–90.
[50] Leviticus 19:2.
[51] Nahmanides, *Commentary to the Torah,* Leviticus 19:2.